Caro-Kann Defence:
Panov Attack

Anatoly Karpov, Mikhail Podgaets

Translated by Jimmy Adams

First published in the United Kingdom in 2006 by

Batsford
151 Freston Road
London
W10 6TH

An imprint of Anova Books Company Ltd

The text is printed under edition Russian Chess House, Moscow 2006

ISBN-10: 07134 9011X
ISBN-13: 9780713490114

A CIP catalogue record for this book is available from the British Library.

10 9 8 7 6 5 4 3 2 1

Printed and bound by MPG Books Ltd, Bodmin, Cornwall

This book can be ordered direct from the publisher at the website: www.anovabooks.com, or try your local bookshop

Distributed in the United States and Canada by Sterling Publishing Co., 387 Park Avenue South, New York, NY 10016, USA

Contents

	Page
Foreword	5
Chapter One	
1 e4 c6 2 d4 d5 3 ed cd 4 c4 ♘f6 5 ♘c3 ♘c6 6 ♘f3	7
Index to Chapter One	35
Chapter Two	
1 e4 c6 2 d4 d5 3 ed cd 4 c4 ♘f6 5 ♘c3 ♘c6 6 ♗g5	36
Index to Chapter Two	61
Chapter Three	
1 e4 c6 2 d4 d5 3 ed cd 4 c4 ♘f6 5 ♘c3 g6!?	62
Index to Chapter Three	91
Chapter Four	
1 e4 c6 2 d4 d5 3 ed cd 4 c4 ♘f6 5 ♘c3 e6 6 ♘f3 ♘c6	92
Index to Chapter Four	102
Chapter Five	
1 e4 c6 2 d4 d5 3 ed cd 4 c4 ♘f6 5 ♘c3 e6 6 ♘f3 ♗b4	103
Index to Chapter Five	139
Chapter Six	
1 e4 c6 2 d4 d5 3 ed cd 4 c4 ♘f6 5 ♘c3 e6 6 ♘f3 ♗e7	141
Index to Chapter Six	224
Appendix: Steiner System	
1 e4 c6 2 c4	226
Index to Steiner System	256
Illustrative Games	257
Index to Illustrative Games	276

Foreword

The opening system, characterised by the moves **1 e4 c6 2 d4 d5 3 ed cd 4 c4!?**

is so called in honour of the Soviet master and theoretician Vasily Panov, who published his analysis in 1930. For the sake of accuracy we mention that as far back as 1925 the idea of exchanging on d5 followed by the dash of the c-pawn was tried by A.Alekhine (in a game against Tartakower) but without success. In 1931 was played the famous game Nimzowitsch - Alekhine, in which the 4th world champion was successful in his fight against the Panov Attack, but, starting the following year, he included it in his own opening repertoire with stunning successes. Eight wins in ten games –

such a score is the envy of every opening variation!

In 1933 the variation was tested by M.Botvinnik in a match against S.Flohr – with variable success (one out of two), but in the following years the Panov Attack served Mikhail Moiseevich faithfully. Spectacular and convincing victories over H.Kmoch (Leningrad 1934), R.Spielmann (Moscow 1935), A.Budo (Leningrad 1938), A.Konstantinopolsky (Sverdlovsk 1943), H.Golombek (Moscow 1956) – are proof of this.

In our day the Panov Attack has rather receded into the background, but in no way has it become a second class opening system. It is enough to say that it is employed by elite grandmasters – M.Adams, J.Polgar, A.Morozevich and V.Ivanchuk.

The fortune of the Panov Attack in matches is likewise remarkable. We recall the world championship matches Chiburdanidze – Ioseliani (Telavi 1988) and Karpov – Kamsky (Elista 1996); in both contests there was a dispute over the Panov Attack, and only with great difficulty did Black contain the opponent's attack.

The material presented in this book is laid out in the following way.

In the first half the authors deal with those defences in which Black refrains from the move e7-e6. Thus, Chapter One is devoted to the variation **1 e4 c6 2 d4 d5 3 ed cd 4 c4 ♘f6 5 ♘c3 ♘c6 6 ♘f3**; Chapter Two – the variation **1 e4 c6 2 d4 d5 3 ed cd 4 c4 ♘f6 5 ♘c3 ♘c6 6 ♗g5**. In Chapter Three is given an analysis of the continuation **1 e4 c6 2 d4 d5 3 ed cd 4 c4 ♘f6 5 ♘c3 g6**.

In the second half we deal with the main line: **1 e4 c6 2 d4 d5 3 ed cd 4 c4 ♘f6 5 ♘c3 e6** The positions arising after the exchange on d5 (or c4), with the isolation of the d4 pawn, are analogous to several schemes in the Queen's Gambit Accepted, Nimzo-Indian Defence, or completely transpose into them. Consequently readers who study the given formations have at their disposal a universal scheme, suitable for immediate application in a number of openings which at first sight look completely different.

The material in the second half is divided into three: after **6 ♘f3** Black can choose between **6...♘c6** (Chapter Four), **6...♗b4** (Chapter Five) and **6...♗e7** (Chapter Six).

In the **Appendix** we analyse the individual Steiner System: **1 e4 c6 2 c4!?**

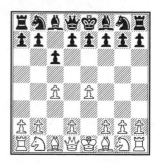

In certain cases this system inevitably transposes into the Panov Attack, but in others its branches resemble Indian or Slav opening schemes. It is important to mention that by examining the Panov Attack together with the Steiner Attack, the reader obtains exhaustive information both on the attacking potential of the c2-c4 idea in the Caro Kann Defence and also on Black's possibilities of neutralising the attack.

The **Illustrative Games** section includes fresh practical material to supplement the theory of the Panov Attack.

Chapter One

1 e4 c6 2 d4 d5 3 ed cd 4 c4 ♘f6
5 ♘c3 ♘c6 6 ♘f3

And so, we return to the plan where Black rejects the immediate advance e7-e6. Obviously, he intends to resolve the problem of the centre in another way.

There are two main paths: 5...♘c6 and 5...g6, but first we deal with **5...♗e6!?** (after 1 e4 c6 2 d4 d5 3 ed cd 4 c4 ♘f6 5 ♘c3)

The idea looks artificial, but with improvements, above all by the English grandmaster Anthony Miles, the thrust of the bishop gained a reputation of being an interesting and in any case useful move for the continuation of the struggle.

6 ♘ge2 Considered the most dangerous – the knight heads for f4, from where it will 'exert itself' over the d5 and e6 squares. No advantage

comes out of 6 cd ♗xd5 7 ♘xd5 ♕xd5 8 ♗e2 ♘c6 9 ♗f3 ♕c4 10 ♘e2 in view of 10...e5! 11 b3 ♕a6 12 ♗xc6+ ♕xc6 13 0-0 ♖d8 (Kosten – Miles, Edinburgh 1985), while 6 c5 will be examined later under a different order of moves – 5...♘c6 6 ♘f3 ♗e6 7 c5.

6...dc 7 ♘f4 ♗g4 A necessary intermediate move. Weaker is 7...♗c8 8 ♗xc4 e6 because of 9 d5! e5 10 0-0! He cannot accept the piece sacrifice – 10...ef? 11 ♖e1+ ♗e7 12 d6, while 10...♗d6 led to an undoubted advantage for White in the game Hebden – Martin (Edinburgh 1985): 11 ♘h5 ♘xh5 12 ♕xh5 0-0 13 ♘e4 ♕e7 14 ♗d2 ♘d7 15 ♗c3 f5 16 ♘xd6 ♕xd6 17 ♕e2 etc.

In reply to 7...♗g4 White usually goes into the variation 8 f3 ♗d7 9 ♗xc4 e6 10 d5 e5 (but not 10...ed?! in view of 11 ♕e2+ ♗e7 12 ♘fxd5 ♘xd5 13 ♘xd5 ♗e6 14 ♗f4! ♗xd5 15 0-0-0 0-0 16 ♗xd5 with an enormous advantage, Yurtaev – Fette, Lungby 1990) 11 ♘d3, but after 11...♗d6 things do not turn out badly for Black, for example: 12 ♗g5 ♗f5

7

13 ♘f2 ♘bd7 14 ♗d3 ♗xd3 15 ♕xd3 (Dzhandzhava – Komarov, Novosibirsk 1989), and here, in the opinion of L.Dzhandzhava, 15...♕b6! secures full equality.

A new (and very successful) fight for the advantage was undertaken by the English grandmaster A.Kosten: **8 ♕a4+!?** (instead of 8 f3) **8...♗d7 9 ♕xc4 e6 10 ♗e2 ♘c6 11 0-0 ♖c8 12 ♖d1 ♗d6 13 d5!**

To exploit the opponent's backward development, White has every right to deliver a blow in the centre. Taking the pawn is too dangerous; the knight must retreat. If 13...♘b4?! 14 ♕b3 ed, then 15 a3 ♘c6 16 ♘fxd5 with advantage. He could win a pawn: 13...♘e7 14 ♕b3 ♗xf4 15 ♗xf4 ♘fxd5, but after 16 ♘xd5 ♘xd5 17 ♗d6 ♗c6 18 ♕g3 the weakness of the dark squares is deeply felt.

In the game Kosten – Komarov (France 1994) Black preferred **13...♘a5 14 ♕d3 e5**, not noticing **15 ♘e6!** A beautiful tactical blow secures White slight, but stoic pressure in the endgame (he has the two bishops to his credit): **15...fe 16 de ♗xe6 17 ♕xd6 ♕xd6 18 ♖xd6 ♔e7 19 ♖d1 ♖hd8 20 ♗e3** etc.

We will return to the idea ♗c8-e6, when going into the position after 5...♘c6 6 ♘f3.

5...♘c6 The idea of the move in comparison with 5...e6 is clear: Black immediately attacks the d4 pawn, leaving the light-squared bishop with more room for action on the c8-h3 diagonal.

White has two possibilities of fighting for the initiative. The first is linked to Botvinnik's idea 6 ♗g5 (the whole of Chapter Two is devoted to this), but here we deal with **6 ♘f3**. Because of the deployment of the knights against one another this system is still called the Four Knights.

Of course, 6...♗g4 looks the most natural, but we will also deal with other bishop moves.

6...♗f5?! An almost completely forgotten continuation. According to an analysis by Nenarokov White has a slight positional advantage after 7 c5! e6 8 ♗b5! ♘d7 9 ♗f4 ♗e7 10 h3 0-0 11 0-0.

6...♗e6!? is already known to us, although with the inclusion of the moves 5...♘c6 6 ♘f3 things are changed somewhat (White has neither a check on a4, nor the manoeuvre ♘g1-e2-f4, but play appears on the pin of the knight c6). After 7 c5 (on 7 ♕b3 simplest is 7...dc! 8 ♗xc4 ♗xc4 9 ♕xc4 e6 – the recommendation of E.Vladimirov) Black is faced with a not very easy choice.

7...g6 is insufficient for equality in view of 8 ♗b5! ♗g7 9 ♘e5! In the old game Dake – Alekhine (Pasadena 1932) Black got a bad position without any hint of counterplay: 9...♕c8 10 ♕a4 ♗d7 11 0-0 0-0 12 ♗f4 a6 13 ♗xc6 bc? 14 ♖fe1 ♘h5 15 ♗d2 ♖a7 16 ♖e2 ♗e8 17 ♖ae1.

Of course, 13...bc? is a serious positional mistake; in general Botvinnik considered that after the correct 13...♗xc6 Black should not experience difficulties: 14 ♘xc6 bc 15 ♖fe1 ♘h5 16 ♗g5 ♕g4!, and dangerous is 17 ♗xe7 because of 17...♘f4! with an attack.

But a desire to test Botvinnik's analysis in practice is something we do not see. For example, the game Anand – Miles (Wijk aan Zee 1989) developed not 'à la Botvinnik' but just 'à la Alekhine': 9...♗d7 10 ♗xc6 bc?! (why not still 10...♗xc6!?), and White again obtains the sought for advantage: 11 0-0 0-0 12 ♖e1 ♗e8 13 h3 ♔h8 14 ♗f4 ♘g8 15 b4 f6 16 ♘f3 ♕d7 17 a4 a6 18 ♗h2 g5 19 ♕e2 h5 20 ♕e6!

Not leading to equality is 7...♗g4!? (instead of 7...g6) 8 ♗b5 ♗xf3 9 ♕xf3 e6. Black has secured himself against the threat ♘f3-e5, but at the

cost of the loss of the important light-squared bishop. The further continuation of the game Brunner – Miles (Bad Worishofen 1989) was 10 0-0 ♗e7 11 ♗f4 0-0 12 ♗xc6 bc 13 b4 ♘d7 14 b5 ♖c8 15 ♖ab1 ♗f6 16 bc ♖xc6 17 ♘b5 ♕a5 18 ♖fc1 ♖a8, and White agreed to a draw. Too early! The plan to improve the position lies on the surface: 19 a3! ♘f8 (not possible is 19...a6 20 ♘d6 ♗xd4? because of 21 ♘b7! ♕a4 22 ♖b4) 20 ♖b4 ♘g6 21 ♗g3 ♗e7 22 ♖cb1. The only open file is in White's hands, his pieces are also very active. One cannot talk about equality.

Perhaps grandmaster Dreev has penetrated the position the deepest: 7...a6!?

Sympathetic prophylaxis. Now White's play to pin the knight c6 is rendered harmless, and the bishop e6 need not be given up. In the game Brunner – Dreev (Biel 1995) followed 8 h3 ♗f5 9 ♗e2 g6 10 0-0 ♗g7 11 ♗f4 0-0 12 ♘e5 ♘d7! 13 ♘xd5 ♘dxe5 and the opponents concluded peace.

6...♗g4 is the main continuation.

The threat to the d4 pawn assumes an all the more tangible outline.

7 cd We are convinced that other moves are noticeably weaker than the capture on d5.

There is no point in playing 7 c5? – after 7...♗xf3 8 gf g6 Black's position is better.

There is less benefit in 7 ♗e3 e6 8 ♗e2 ♗e7 9 0-0 0-0 10 ♘e5 ♗xe2 11 ♕xe2 dc! (a well-known device: the weakness of the c6 pawn after the exchange of knights is balanced out by the play against the the isolated d4 pawn) 12 ♘xc6 bc 13 ♕xc4 ♕d7 (De Firmian – Christiansen, Key West 1994).

7 ♗e2 – A trappy move. If Black is tempted by the bait – 7...dc?!, then after 8 d5 ♗xf3 9 ♗xf3 ♘e5 10 0-0 he risks, as they say, not getting out of the opening. How serious it all is was shown if only by the game Mikenas – Flohr (Folkestone 1933): 10...♕d7 11 ♕e2 ♘xf3+ 12 ♕xf3 0-0-0 13 b3! e6 14 bc ed 15 ♗f4 d4 16 ♘b5 ♗c5 17 ♖ab1 ♕c6 18 ♕h3+ ♕d7? The second, and this time decisive mistake. On 18...♖d7 the result of the game is quite unclear, whereas now...

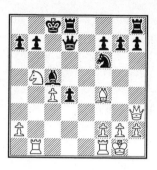

19 ♘xa7+! ♔xa7 20 ♕a3!, and Black had to resign.

It is best for Black not to accept the Greek Gift, but calmly play 7...e6. There are no pawn weaknesses, also no problems with development – where is White's advantage coming from?

7...♘xd5 8 ♕b3 Yet again unfashionable is 8 ♗e2 e6 9 0-0 ♗e7 10 h3 ♗h5. The only problem for Black is that he lags behind his opponent in development by one or two tempi. White can possibly try to exploit this by 11 ♕b3!, but Black has sufficient defensive resources:

11...♘b6!? 12 ♗e3 0-0 13 ♖fd1 ♘b4!? 14 d5!? ♘4xd5 15 ♗xb6 ♕xb6 16 ♘xd5 ed 17 ♖xd5 ♕xb3 18 ab ♗xf3 19 ♗xf3 ♗d8! 20 ♖d7 ♗b6, and the extra pawn plays no role at all;

11...♗xf3!? 12 ♗xf3 ♕d7!? (the most concrete way to equality) 13 ♗xd5 ed 14 ♕xd5 ♕xd5 15 ♘xd5 ♖d8 16 ♘xe7 ♔xe7 17 ♗e3 ♘xd4 18 ♖fe1 ♔f6 19 ♖ac1 ♘c6.

In the famous game Nimzowitsch – Alekhine (Bled 1931) was played 8 ♗b5 ♕a5 9 ♕b3 ♗xf3 10 gf ♘xc3. In this position the great chess inventor Aron Nimzowitsch got confused:

11 ♗xc6+?! bc 12 ♕b7? ♘d5+! 13 ♗d2 ♕b6! 14 ♕xa8+ ♔d7 15 0-0 ♘c7. The queen can still be saved (16 ♗a5), but the game – already not.

A year later the 4th world champion himself showed the right way for White: 11 bc! e6 12 d5!, and after 12...ed?! he obtained a very strong initiative: 13 0-0 0-0-0 14 ♗xc6 bc 15 ♖b1 (Alekhine – Winter, London 1932). However the point in this theoretical debate, like the given game Keene – Roth (Aarhus 1976), is 12...a6! (instead of 12...ed?!) 13 dc ab 14 cb ♖b8 15 ♖b1 ♖xb7 16 a4 b4 17 ♗d2 ♕e5+ 18 ♔f1 ♕d6 with equality.

However, is it the point?... Many chessplayers do not trust forcing variations, where it all hangs 'on one nail'. Then in reply to 8 ♗b5 they should play 8...♖c8!? This solid continuation allows Black to achieve equality without unnecessary worry. This is how events develop: 9 h3 ♗h5 10 0-0 e6 11 ♖e1 ♗e7 12 ♖e5 ♘xc3 13 bc ♗g6 14 ♗xc6+ ♖xc6 15 d5 ♖xc3 16 ♕e1 ♗c7 (worth considering is 16...♖d3!? 17 ♗b2 ♖xd5 18 ♖xd5 ed 19 ♗xg7 ♖g8, and if 20 ♗f6, then

20...♔f8!) 17 de 0-0 18 ef+ ♗xf7 19 ♗g5 ♗xg5 20 ♘xg5 h6 21 ♘xf7 Draw (Hasin – Bagirov, Baku 1961).

8...♗xf3 9 gf (once again 9 ♕xb7? is not possible because of 9...♘db4! 10 gf ♖b8 trapping the queen). On the board is the tabiya of the Four Knights system.

Black has two acceptable continuations: 9...♘b6 (I), leading to immense complications, and 9...e6 (II), after which the game is simplified and transfers to an endgame. The remaining possibilities are clearly weaker.

Thus, losing is 9...♘xd4? 10 ♗b5+! ♘xb5 11 ♕xb5+ ♕d7 12 ♕xd7+ ♔xd7 13 ♘xd5 (Rantanen – Baljon, Valetta 1980).

Also poor is 9...♘db4? 10 ♗e3 – the same knight cannot untie itself and there is no one to come to its aid. In the game Geller – Orev (Kislovodsk 1968) there followed 10...a5 11 d5 a4 12 ♕d1 ♘b8 13 a3 ♘4a6 14 ♗b5+ ♘d7 15 0-0 ♘c7 16 ♗xa4, and White's advantage grew to decisive proportions.

Dubious is 9...♘xc3?! True, White (though it is now time!) had better forget about the b7 square – in the variation 10 ♕xb7?! ♘xd4 11 bc

11

♘c2+ 12 ♔e2 ♖b8 13 ♕c6+ ♕d7 14 ♕xd7+ ♔xd7 15 ♗h3+ ♔c6 he does not win the knight, for example: 16 ♗f4 e5! 17 ♖ac1 ef 18 ♖xc2 ♗c5 with equality (analysis by Moiseev and Ravinsky). However simpler is 10 bc ♕b6 11 d5 underlining White's positional advantage.

I
9...♘b6

White is at a crossroads: 10 ♗e3 (A) or 10 d5 (B).

A

10 ♗e3 Let us say at once: not the strongest move. Although even in this case, as shown by practice, Black finds it quite difficult to refute it upon accurate play.

10...e6 As we see, Black has everything in order with his pawn structure. But here the lag in development can assume threatening proportions. Very much depends on White's following move. Thus after 11 ♖d1?! ♗b4! 12 a3 ♗a5 Black easily shakes off any fear – White will not succeed in carrying out d4-d5 in the near future. In the game Marin

– Magem (Berga 1995) play continued 13 ♗d3 ♖c8 14 ♖g1 0-0!? 15 ♔f1 (the idea of castling is shown in the variation 15 ♗h6 g6 16 ♗xf8 ♘xd4!) 15...♗xc3 16 bc g6 17 ♗h6 ♖e8 18 ♖g5 ♘d5 19 c4 ♘a5!, and White's attack is finally extinguished.

The break in the centre leads to unclear consequences: 11 d5 ed 12 ♖g1 g6. For example, the game Plaskett – Wells (London 1991) led immediately to such complications that it is practically impossible to commentate on them: 13 0-0-0 ♗d6!? 14 ♖g5 d4! 15 ♘e4 0-0 16 ♔b1 ♗e7 17 ♖b5 ♕d7 18 ♗h6 ♖fd8 19 a4 d3!? 20 ♖xd3 ♘d4 21 ♕d1 ♘xb5 22 ♖xd7 ♖xd7 23 ♕e1 ♘d4 etc.

Most often White chooses between 11 ♖g1 and 11 0-0-0.

1) **11 ♖g1** At first glance, the move does not require any particular explanation. With the attack on the g7 pawn White slows down the development of the bishop f8 and thereby gains some time to organise the break d4-d5.

None the less, as we see later, this is not all so simple...

a) First of all we mention that it is dubious to win a pawn – **11...♘xd4?! 12 ♗xd4 ♕xd4** in view of **13 ♗b5+ ♔e7 14 ♖d1 ♕e5+ 15 ♔f1 g6 16 ♘e4 f6 17 ♔g2 ♔f7 18 ♖ge1** with a very strong attack.

For that reason we deal with the most logical and possibly the strongest continuation, but...not the most interesting!

b) **11...g6**

12 0-0-0 In the game Zaichik – Dolmatov (Kutaisi 1978) White decided in general to do without the break d4-d5. The experiment ended unsuccessfully: 12 ♖d1?! ♗d6 13 h4 0-0 14 h5 ♘b4! 15 a3 ♘4d5 16 ♘e4 ♗f4 17 hg hg 18 ♗h3 ♔g7, and Black stands to win.

12...♗e7 Rejecting 12...♗g7?, and not without reason: after 13 d5! ♘xd5 14 ♘xd5 ed 15 ♗c5! it becomes clear that the dark-squared bishop should guard the a3-f8 diagonal. In the game Sveshnikov – A.Ivanov (Leningrad 1976) this happened and Black did not succeed in rectifying the situation: 15...♕c7 16 ♖e1+ ♗e5 17 f4 ♘e7 18 ♕b5+ ♔f8 19 ♖xe5 ♖c8 20 b4 b6 21 ♗h3!

13 d5! The attempt to put off the pawn break 'till later' and play in a

more refined way does not work, since after 13 ♗h6 ♕c7 14 ♗h3 Black succeeds in hiding away his king: 14...0-0-0! There is a draw (and a very beautiful one) for White, but no more than that: 15 d5 (15 ♘b5? ♘xd4+) 15...♘xd5 16 ♖xd5! (not possible is 16 ♘xd5? ♖xd5, and on 17 ♖xd5 or 17 ♕xd5 follows 17...♘d4+!) 16...♕xh2 17 ♖g3 ♗h4 18 ♗f4! ♗xg3 19 ♖xd8+ ♖xd8 20 ♗xe6+! fe 21 ♕xe6+ ♖d7 22 ♕g8+! with perpetual check.

After 13 d5 you get the feeling that White is about to embark on a 'squeeze' to hold the opponent's king in the centre, but in actual fact everything turns to quite everyday equality. **13...ed 14 ♘xd5 ♘xd5 15 ♖xd5 ♕c7,** and then:

16 ♕c3 ♗f6! 17 ♕c5 (alas, the bishop is untouchable: 17 ♕xf6? ♘d4+ 18 ♔d2 ♕c2+ etc.) 17...♗e7 18 ♕c3 ♗f6 with repetition of position (Sveshnikov – Hodgson, Sochi 1986) or

16 ♔b1 0-0 17 f4 ♖ad8 18 ♗g2 ♗f6 19 ♖c1 ♖xd5 20 ♕xd5 ♖d8 21 ♕b5 a6 22 ♕a4 ♖d6. Two bishops – this is a plus, but how will it be with a defective pawn formation on the

king's flank? Most likely, White will not manage to win (Lautier – Illescas, Ubeda 1997).

c) **11...♗b4!?** Here it is! It seems that the g7 pawn can also be disregarded. This sacrifice was first made by Kasparov in a game against Ehlvest (Moscow 1977). We mention that playing 11...♗e7?!, with the same aim, is noticeably weaker in view of the forcing variation 12 ♖xg7 ♘xd4?! 13 ♗b5+ ♔f8 14 ♗h6 ♘f5 15 ♖xh7+ ♔g8 16 ♖xh8+ ♔xh8 17 ♗f4 ♘d4 18 ♕d1 ♘xb5 19 ♘xb5 etc. (Illescas – van der Doel, Escacdes 1998).

After 11...♗b4 arises the most interesting moment in the whole variation with 11 ♖g1.

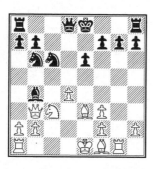

If 12 ♖xg7, then of course Black does not go for the win of the d4 pawn but concentrates his forces on the c-file: 12...♘d5 13 0-0-0 ♖c8 14 ♔b1 ♗xc3 15 bc a6 16 ♖c1 ♘a5 17 ♕a3 ♕b6+ 18 ♔a1 ♘c4 with a menacing initiative.

Possible is 12 0-0-0, but then, by exchanging the knight c3, Black renders harmless the break d4-d5: 12...♗xc3! 13 bc ♕f6!? This position

was twice defended by Ukrainian master Peter Marusenko, and both times successfully:

14 ♖g3 h6 15 ♗d3 0-0-0 16 ♗e4 ♖d7 17 ♖g4 ♖hd8 followed by ♘c6-a5-c4 (Nieminen – Marusenko, Port Erin 1999);

14 f4 0-0 15 f5!? ♕xf5 16 ♗h6 g6 17 ♗xf8 ♕xf2 18 ♗d3 ♖xf8 with obvious compensation for the exchange (Spanton – Marusenko, Port Erin 2000).

In the above mentioned game, Ehlvest – Kasparov, White preferred to wait a while with castling and play **12 ♗b5!? ♘d5 13 ♖xg7** But even here after **13...♕b6!?** Black found counterplay: **14 ♔f1 ♘xc3 15 ♗xc6+ ♕xc6 16 bc ♗f8 17 ♖g5 ♗e7 18 ♖b5 ♕xf3 19 ♖xb7 0-0 20 ♖b1 ♗f6 21 ♕d1 ♕h3+ 22 ♔e2 ♔h8**

As before, he is a pawn down, but there is no coordination in White's ranks. Perhaps in practical play his game is even more difficult than Black's. Incidentally, in the further struggle Kasparov succeeded in gaining the upper hand.

There is nothing surprising in the fact that the idea 11 ♖g1 has left the scene. If the threat to the g7 pawn does not trouble Black in the least, is it worth spending time on the rook move?

2) **11 0-0-0** White leaves the rook h1 alone and on the whole concentrates on preparation for the break d4-d5.

11...♗e7 It is difficult to say definitely if there is any benefit in the inclusion of the moves 11...♕c7 12 ♔b1. One thing is clear: Black cannot now play 12...0-0-0 in view of 13 ♘b5 ♕b8 14 d5! ♘xd5 15 ♗h3! a6 16 ♖xd5 ♖xd5 17 ♕xd5 ab 18 ♗xe6+! winning.

12 d5 After the development of the bishop f8, the move 12 ♖g1 looks particularly insignificant. But White played exactly this in the grandmaster games Nunn – Chandler (Bristol 1981) and Ehlvest – Oll (Riga 1995). This is how things continued: 13...0-0 13 d5 ♘xd5 14 ♘xd5 ed 15 ♖xd5 ♕c7, and now after either 16 ♔b1 ♕xh2 (Chandler's move), or 16 ♕c3 ♗f6! (as Oll played) White, it goes without saying, cannot get organised.

After **12...ed** arises a critical position for the 11 0-0-0 variation.

a) **13 ♗xb6** brings no advantage but only if Black takes on b6 with the queen. However after 13...ab 14 ♘xd5 0-0 15 ♖g1 ♗f6 16 ♖g4! White remains with some chances, for example:

16...♖a5 17 ♔b1 ♖c5 18 ♘xb6 ♘d4 19 ♕b4 ♖c6 20 ♘c4 (Short – Miles, Brighton 1984);

16...♕d6 17 ♘xb6 (it is worth waiting a while with this capture; 17 ♔b1!?) 17...♘d4 18 ♖gxd4 ♗xd4 19 ♘xa8 ♖xa8 20 ♗c4 ♖f8 21 ♕xb7 ♗xb2+! (Hebden – Nunn, Marbella 1982).

Meanwhile here the endgame after **13...♕xb6 14 ♕xb6 ab 15 ♘xd5** is completely harmless for Black, which has been repeatedly confirmed in practice:

15...♖xa2 (possibly even stronger is 15...♗d8!? 16 ♔b1 0-0 17 f4 ♖e8 18 ♗c4 ♗f8 19 ♖he1 ♖xe1 20 ♖xe1 ♖c8 21 ♗b5 ♘e7 22 ♘e3 ♗c7, and Black's position is even somewhat preferable, Zahariev – Kir.Georgiev, Corfu 1991) **16 ♔b1 ♖a5 17 ♗b5 ♔f8!** Here it is already too late for 17...♗d8?!: 18 ♖he1+ ♔d7 19 b4! ♖a3 20 ♗d3 g6 21 ♖e3 ♖a7 22 b5 ♘d4 23 ♗f1. The position of the king on d7 seems inconvenient for Black (Morovic – Campora, Dubai 1986).

18 ♘xe7 ♔xe7 19 ♖he1+ ♔f6 20 ♖d6+ ♔g5!? 21 ♖g1+ ♔f4 White has got the most out of the position but there is no hiding the pawn weaknesses on the king's flank. Black's counterplay should be enough for a draw. (Potkin – Kazakov, Moscow 1998).

b) Black's task is more complicated after **13 ♗b5!? 0-0 14 ♘xd5 ♘xd5 15 ♕xd5**

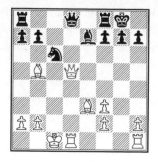

In the game Onischuk – Kutsin (Nikolaev 1995) Black did not choose the best order of moves to transpose to the endgame: 15...♕c7?! 16 ♕d7! ♖fc8 17 ♔b1 ♗f6 18 ♕xc7 ♖xc7 19 ♗xc6! Both 19...bc 20 b3, and 19...♖xc6 20 ♖d7 b6 21 ♖c1 leave no doubt: the endgame is highly unpleasant. Probably upon best defence Black is capable of defending this position, but he would not want to reach it again.

Therefore worth considering is **15...♘b4!?** Here the transfer to an endgame does not give White the advantage: 16 ♕xd8 ♖fxd8 17 ♖xd8+ ♖xd8 18 a3 a6! etc. Winning the b7 pawn leads to a draw by perpetual check: 16 ♕xb7 ♕a5 17 a4 ♖ac8+ 18 ♔b1 ♖c7 19 ♕e4 a6 20 ♗d7 ♖xd7! 21 ♖xd7 ♕xa4 22 ♕xe7 (not possible is 22 ♖xe7? ♖c8) 22...♕c2+.

This leaves **16 ♕e4**, but then **16...♕a5 17 ♗c4 ♗f6**. The struggle is somehow imperceptibly concentrated around the white king. Possibly it is nothing serious but in any event Black directs the play.

18 a3 (also interesting is 18 ♔b1 ♖ae8! 19 ♕g4 h5 20 ♕f4 ♖d8) **18...♕c7! 19 ♗f4** (a double-edged

move, but otherwise Black simply has a good game, for example, 19 ab?! b5 20 ♗c5 ♖fe8 or 19 ♔b1 ♘c6) **19...♘a2+** (the knight is in a very dangerous position but how can he concretely trap it?) **20 ♔c2** (20 ♔b1 ♕b6 21 ♗e5 ♖ae8) **20...♕b6 21 ♗e5** (21 ♖b1 ♖ac8 22 ♗e3 ♕b5 23 b3 ♘c3) **21...♗xe5 22 ♕xe5 ♖ac8 23 b3 ♕xf2+ 24 ♔b1 b5,** and Black is close to victory.

If these variations are correct, then 15...♘b4 removes all questions about the variations arising from 13 ♗b5!? 0-0 14 ♘xd5 ♘xd5 15 ♕xd5.

c) **13 ♘xd5 ♘xd5 14 ♖xd5 ♕c7 15 ♔b1 0-0**

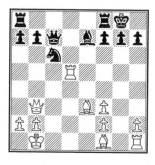

Starting with 10 ♗e3, both sides have made perhaps the most natural and logical moves. A position has been reached which is most important for the evaluation of the whole variation. The initiative is undoubtedly on White's side but how great is it? In his favour he has the advantage of the two bishops plus chances of developing an attack on the g-file. For his part, Black is able for the present to defend his king against serious trouble, and if nothing comes of White's attack, the weakness of the f3, f2, h2 pawns can outweigh all other nuances.

Meanwhile White has in prospect to solve a local problem: where to develop the light-squared bishop?

16 f4 Apparently the best. White intends to install the bishop on the h1-a8 diagonal. Other continuations promise less:

16 ♗e2 ♖ad8 17 ♖hd1 ♖xd5 18 ♖xd5 ♗d6 19 h4 ♗f4 20 a3 (on 20 ♗xf4 ♕xf4 21 ♕xb7 unpleasant is 21...♘d4) 20...♗xe3 21 fe ♖e8. White's attack is done with (Korneev – Izeta, Alcobendas 1994);

16 ♗d3 ♘b4 17 ♖h5 ♘xd3 18 ♕xd3 g6 19 ♖c1 ♕b8 20 ♗h6 ♖d8 21 ♕c3 ♗f8 22 ♗xf8 ♖xf8, and Black again defends (Kharlov – Evseev, Kazan 2001).

16...♘b4 It is unclear how to improve White's play in the variation 16...♖ad8 17 ♗g2 ♖xd5 18 ♗xd5 ♗f6 19 ♖d1 g6 20 h4 ♖d8 21 h5 gh!? 22 ♖g1+ ♔h8 (Narciso – Matulovic, Belgrade 2001), but the jump of the knight for some reason is more popular.

17 ♖d4 A critical position for the variation.

Of course, it is possible to simply go back with the knight, thereby

tacitly offering a draw: 17...♘c6. In the games below White rejected the draw, but we see nothing of substance to show there is a winning plan:

18 ♖d1 ♖ad8 (or 18...♗f6 19 ♗g2 ♖fd8 20 ♗e4 ♖xd1+ 21 ♖xd1 ♖d8, Anand – Karolyi, Frunze 1987) 19 ♗g2 ♗f6 20 ♕a4 ♕c8 21 ♖c1 ♕g4 22 ♗xc6 bc 23 ♖xc6 ♖b8. The extra pawn is on hand, but the weak king b1 is really sick, and the pawn islands on the king's flank are going nowhere (Shchekachev – Iruzubieta, San Sebastian 1996).

However the main thing is that the tempting idea **17...♕c6?!** does not work. After **18 ♖g1** whichever rook is placed on d8 – White, exploiting the poor position of the enemy king, will quickly aim his forces in the direction of the king g8:

18...♖ad8 19 ♗g2 ♕g6+ 20 f5! ♕xf5+ 21 ♗e4 ♕a5 22 a3 ♘c6 23 ♖xd8 ♘xd8 24 ♗d4 ♗g5 (Acs – Ruck, Paks 1996), and here it was possible to obtain a great advantage by force: 25 ♗c3 ♕c5 26 ♗b4 ♕e5 27 ♖e1!

Also having its minuses is **18...♖fd8 19 ♗g2 ♕g6+ 20 f5! ♕xf5+ 21 ♗e4 ♕a5 22 ♗h6 g6** (22...♗f8 23 ♗xg7! ♗xg7 24 ♖xb4 with a win).

**23 ♗xg6! hg 24 ♖xg6+ ♔h8
25 ♗g7+ ♔g8 26 ♗f6+ ♔f8
27 ♗xe7+ ♔xe7 28 ♕e3+ ♔f8
29 ♕h6+ ♔e7 30 ♖e4+ ♔d7
31 ♖d6+ ♔c8** (also losing is 31...♔c7
32 ♖e7+ ♔c8 33 ♕c1+ ♔b8 because
of the quiet 34 ♕f4! ♕xa2+ 35 ♔c1
♕a1+ 36 ♔d2 ♕xb2+ 37 ♔e1)
**32 ♖xb4 ♕f5+ 33 ♔a1 ♖xd6
34 ♕xd6 ♕e6 35 ♕c5+ ♔b8 36 ♖c4**
The heavy piece ending is completely
hopeless for Black.

However success in a single
analytical variation cannot hide the
fact that on the whole Black is close
to equality in the 10 ♗e3 system. In
the overwhelming majority of cases
White does not succeed in developing
an attack; it will all come down to an
endgame in which White has purely
academic chances of victory.

Parallel with the theory of 10 ♗e3
our knowledge of 10 d5 has been
increased. Here too it gradually
becomes clear that quite frankly
things are bad for Black...

B
10 d5 After **10...♘d4** White has a
choice between two continuations.

The move 11 ♕d1 leads to
boundless complications (in which it

is Black who will rather have the
chance to confuse the opponent);
11 ♗b5+, which suggests itself,
allows a weighty advantage without
any 'ifs and buts'.

1) **11 ♕d1 e5!** The move 11...♘f5
is both illogical (why move away
such a splendid knight?) and simply
weak: after 12 ♗b5+ ♘d7 13 0-0 g6
14 ♖e1 ♗g7 15 ♗g5 f6 16 d6!
finishes things off. The bishop cannot
be taken – 16...fg 17 de ♘xe7 (or
17...♕c8 18 ♖c1 with irresistible
threats) 18 ♘d5, while on 16...e5
follows 17 ♖xe5+!

12 de On the other hand he cannot
take the support away from the knight
– 12 f4?! ♗d6 13 fe ♗xe5 14 ♗e3
leads to a position in which it is only
Black who has chances: 14...♘f5
15 ♗xb6 ♕xb6 16 ♕a4+ ♔d8
17 ♗h3 ♗xc3+ 18 bc ♖e8+ 19 ♔f1
♕f6 20 ♕f4 ♖e5 (Worley –
Marusenko, Newport 2001).

After 12 de on the board we have
the most critical position of the whole
variation with 11 ♕d1. If Black wants
to 'get to grips' with the struggle, he
needs to have a thorough think about
the position reached.

We now have a choice of four
continuations. It is possible to take

the pawn (12...♘xe6 or 12...fe), or play a gambit: 12...♕f6 or 12...♗c5.

In fact the choice is between two moves. The rest are not very suitable:

a) **12...♘xe6 13 ♗b5+ ♘d7 14 ♗e3 ♗b4 15 f4 ♘c7 16 ♗xd7+ ♕xd7 17 ♕xd7+ ♔xd7 18 0-0-0+ ♔c6 19 ♖d4 ♗xc3 20 ♖c4+ ♔d5** (Balashov – Sveshnikov, Lvov 1973) **21 ♖xc7**. White's advantage is measured by pawns, and this is only the start.

b) **12...♕f6?! 13 ef+ ♔xf7 14 ♗g2 ♗b4** (or 14...♖e8+ 15 ♘e4 ♗b4+ 16 ♔f1 ♕e5 17 ♕d3, Titz – Vizer, Graz 2001) **15 0-0 ♗xc3 16 bc ♘e6 17 f4 ♖ac8 18 ♗e3 ♖hf8 19 ♖e1** with the advantage (Ekstrom – Krizsany, Basel 1999). Of course, Black can improve his play but all the same 12...♕f6 looks suspect.

c) While here **12...♗c5!?** might prove just the ticket! Let us see how harmoniously Black is ready to develop his pieces. The rooks will occupy the central d- and e-files, the queen jumps over to h4. The compensation may be worth more than the sacrificed pawn.

13 ef+ Refraining from an immediate capture does not solve the problem: 13 ♗b5+ ♘xb5 (also interesting is 13...♔f8!? 14 ♗e3 ♘xe6 with the better game, Eising – Kuijf, Amsterdam 1984) 14 ef+ ♔f8 15 ♕xd8+ ♖xd8 16 ♘xb5 ♔xf7 17 0-0 ♘c4 18 ♘c3 ♖d3 19 ♘e4 ♗d4. It is obvious that Black will not be struggling for equality (van Wely – Lautier, Monaco 1998).

13...♔xf7 14 ♗e3 ♖e8 15 ♗d3!? Shirov's recommendation – 15 ♗e2

♕h4 16 ♘e4 – cannot spoil Black's mood. Incidentally, Shirov himself pointed out that Black has at least a draw in hand: 16...♖xe4!? 17 fe ♕xe4 18 0-0 ♘xe2+ 19 ♕xe2 ♕g6+ 20 ♔h1 ♕e4+.

15...♕h4! 16 ♘e4 ♖ad8!

The gambit has given up on glory! In the game Grinfeld – Shirov (Budapest 1996) White tried to curb the opponent's initiative: **17 ♗xd4** (or 17 0-0 ♗d6 18 ♘xd6+ ♖xd6) **17...♖xd4 18 0-0 ♗d6 19 ♕b3+ ♔f8 20 ♘xd6 ♖xd6,** which only partially succeeded. Shirov won this fascinating game, indeed the move 12...♗c5 is possibly the main weapon against the variation 11 ♕d1 as a whole.

d) **12...fe** Not as thrilling, but a more popular continuation.

13 ♗e3 The neutral 13 ♗g2 has been repeatedly tried. Now the thrust (along the lines of the game Grinfeld – Shirov) 13...♕h4?! does not achieve its objective in view of 14 f4! ♖d8 15 0-0 ♖d7 16 ♗e3 ♘f5 17 ♕b3 ♕g4 18 ♔h1 ♗d6 19 ♖g1 ♘xe3 20 fe with an obvious advantage (Grinfeld – Kuijf, Munich 1992). But the simple 13...♗e7!? 14 0-0 0-0 15 f4 ♕d7 16 ♕d3 ♖ad8 seems fully satisfactory. After 17 ♕e4 ♗b4! 18 ♔h1 ♕c6! the position is completely equal. (Al-Modiahki – Dzhumaev, Malaysia 1994).

13...♗c5 Now White has a choice: to continue his development with the move 14 ♗g2 or to take the position to the edge by 14 b4.

d1) **14 b4!?** Leading to forced play in which Black's chances of equalising the game are higher than White's chances of obtaining the advantage.

In short, even 14...♗xb4!?, apparently, cannot be refuted: 15 ♗xd4 ♘d5 16 ♕b3 ♖c8 or 15 ♕xd4 ♕xd4 16 ♗xd4 ♘d5 17 ♖c1 ♖c8 18 ♔d2 0-0, and it is not clear how all this will end.

The natural choice after 14 b4 is between 14...0-0 and 14...♕f6.

d11) **14...0-0 15 bc ♘xf3+ 16 ♔e2 ♕h4!?** More often played is 16...♕f6, but then by transposition of moves we get into into d12.

17 cb It is clear that in positions of this kind the cost of a move increases again and again; correspondingly also the cost of a mistake increases. Thus, in the game Eilertsen – Henriksen

(Norway 1990) it was enough to 'miss' just one thing – 17 ♗g2?, and in an instant the position becomes difficult: 17...♖ad8 18 ♕b3 ♖d2+! 19 ♗xd2 ♘d4+ etc.

17...♖ad8 18 ♕a4 Fainthearted is 18 ♕xd8? ♕xd8 19 ♖d1 ♕h4! 20 ba ♕c4+ 21 ♖d3 ♘e5 with a decisive advantage (Arytunov – Marusenko, Kiev 1998).

In this very sharp position from the game Pisk – Pingitzer (Stockerau 1992), Black rushed to give check with the knight on d4. The attack was ruined. Meanwhile worth considering is **18...♕h5!?** with the sample variation: **19 ♗g2 ♘h4+ 20 ♔f1** (not possible is 20 f3 ♖xf3!) **20...♘xg2 21 ♕e4** (on 21 ♔xg2 strong is 21...♕g6+ 22 ♔f1 ♕d3+ 23 ♘e2 ♕xe3 24 ♕h4 ♖d2 25 ♖e1 ♕xb6, and White's pieces are virtually stalemated) **21...♕h3 22 ♔e2** (it is difficult to evaluate the position after 22 ♕xg2 ♕xe3 23 ♘e4 ♕xb6!?) **22...♘f4+.** Alas, no good is 22...♖f4?! (hoping for 23 ♗xf4? ♘xf4+ 24 ♕xf4 ♕d3+ 25 ♔e1 ♕xc3+ 26 ♔e2 ♕d3+ with perpetual check) in view of 23 ♖ad1! ♖xd1 24 ♗xf4 ♖xh1 25 ba ♘xf4+ 26 ♔d2. The pawn, which has in a surprising way reached a7, is one step away from a complete triumph.

23 ♗xf4 ♖xf4 24 ♕e3 ♕f5!? 25 ♖ac1 Also in the event of 25 f3 it is difficult for White to avoid perpetual check: 25...♖xf3!? 26 ♕xf3 ♖d2+ 27 ♔xd2 ♕xf3 28 ba ♕f4+ etc.

25...♖d3!? How beautiful, also so forced. After this move White, in order to avoid perpetual check, has to give up two pawns (on f2 and b6).

The tempting 25...♖f8 does not work in view of 26 ♖hf1 (only not 26 ba? ♖xf2+ 27 ♔e1 ♖f3 28 ♕e2 ♕f4 or 28 ♕e4 ♖xc3!) 26...♖f3 27 ♕d4 ♖f4 28 ♕d6!? ♖xf2+ 29 ♖xf2 ♕xf2+ 30 ♔d1 ♕e3 31 ♔c2 ab 32 ♖d1, and White's chances are to be preferred.

26 ♕xf4 ♕xf4 27 ♔xd3 ♕f3+ 28 ♔d2 ♕xf2+ 29 ♘e2 ♕xb6 30 ♖hf1 h6 The material correlation is far from standard but we do not think there is any risk of Black losing this position with reasonable play.

d12) **14...♕f6** (more popular than the queen sortie to h4) **15 bc ♘xf3+ 16 ♔e2 0-0**

In the game S.Polgar – Skembris (Corfu 1990) White played 17 ♗g2?!, on which, in the opinion of grandmaster Skembris, 17...♘c4! was very strong. Obviously there are no alternatives to **17 cb**.

17...♖ad8 It is necessary to add that bad is 17...♕xc3? 18 ♗g2 ♕c4+ 19 ♕d3 with a great advantage (Zhuravlev – Gutman, USSR 1972).

18 ♕c2 The time has still not come to give up the queen: 18 ♗g2 ♖xd1 19 ♖axd1 ♕xc3 20 ♗xf3 ♕c4+ 21 ♖d3 ♖xf3!, and a draw is not far off (Kuijf – Bersma, Hilversum 1987).

18...♘d4+ 19 ♗xd4 ♕xd4 20 ♘e4 Not possible is 20 f3?? ♖xf3 with a mating attack (Mayro – Ngyen, correspondence, 1983).

20...♕xa1 21 ♗g2 ♕e5 22 ba After 22 ♖b1? ♕xh2 23 ♔f1 ab Black has more material and his king is better (L.B. Hansen – Kuijf, Grestel 1990).

Now however Black's main problem is how to cope with the a7 pawn?

22...♕b5+ 23 ♔e3

23...♕a6! The only move! Giving check on b6 was no use – White covers with the queen on c5. Now however everything ends pleasantly for Black. Thus, in the game Rozentalis – Lalic (Moscow 1994) after 24 ♖b1 ♕xa7+ 25 ♔e2 ♖c8 26 ♕b3 ♕a6+ the opponents agreed a draw. The French analysts Prie and Tirard propose as strongest **24 ♖c1**, but also here after **24...♕xa7+ 25 ♔e2 ♖a8!?** Black's chances are in no way worse.

It is clear that in the variation 14 b4, White, though he will obtain one, and then even two extra pieces, is risking slightly less than the opponent. This is why many prefer not to get involved in an exchange of blows, but quietly continue development – 14 ♗g2. However there is simply no quiet life.

d2) **14 ♗g2 ♕h4** Black played the opening superficially in the game Romero – Bersma (Amsterdam 1987): 14...0-0 15 0-0 e5 16 ♘e4 ♘d7 17 ♘xc5 ♘xc5, and after 18 f4! the white bishops dominated.

15 0-0 ♗d6 16 h3 ♘f5 17 ♘e4!? A move that calls 'for a fight'. The game Malaniuk – Yudasin (Moscow

1991) ended peacefully: 17 ♕b3 0-0 18 ♕xe6+ ♔h8 19 ♕e4! ♕f6 20 ♕g4 ♕f7! 21 f4 ♘c4 22 ♗c1 ♘h6 23 ♕f3 ♗xf4, while the idea 17 ♘b5?! ♖d8 18 ♘xd6+ ♖xd6 in general is not worth considering: after 19 ♕e2 ♔f7! Black is already playing for a win (Winants – Adams, Wijk aan Zee 1995).

On 17 ♘e4 there are four replies. We examine them, from the weakest to the strongest.

Unsatisfactory is 17... ♘xe3?! 18 fe ♖d8, as was played in the game T.Horvath – Hamdouchi (Hungary 1995). After 19 ♕b3 ♕e7 20 f4 ♘d5 21 f5! White's advantage had grown noticeably.

On 17...♘d5 White is forced... to exchange all the pieces, apart from the rooks! Let's look at it: 18 ♗g5 ♕h5 19 f4! ♕xd1 20 ♘xd6+ ♘xd6 21 ♖axd1 h6 22 ♖fe1 ♔f7 23 ♗xd5 ed 24 ♖xd5 hg 25 ♖xd6 gf 26 ♔g2. In this endgame, unpleasant and truly 'black' work awaits the second player.

White can reckon on a minimal advantage after 17...♕e7. He will need to count on the light-squared bishop: 18 f4 0-0 19 ♘xd6 ♘xd6 (things are not essentially changed by

19...♘xe3 20 fe ♖ad8 21 ♕b3 ♖xd6 22 ♖ad1 ♖fd8 23 ♖xd6 ♖xd6 24 ♖c1) 20 ♗xb6! ab 21 ♖e1. There is not full equality; though it may be slight, everywhere White has a plus.

17...♗e7!? – this is the strongest move! The bishop must be retained for the attack. Black should not think about material losses, the main thing is to defend the e6 pawn and bring the king's rook into the battle. Further events could swing about in the following way:

18 ♗xb6 ab 19 ♕b3 ♔f7 20 ♕xb6 ♖hd8 21 ♖fc1 (21 ♖fe1 ♘d4) **21...♖d7 22 ♖c7 ♖ad8 23 ♖xb7** He could also take the pawn with the queen – Black's attack is no weaker against this: 23 ♕xb7 ♖d1+ 24 ♖xd1 ♖xd1+ 25 ♗f1 ♕h6 26 ♕a6 ♕g6+ 27 ♔h2 ♕h6 and it is not apparent how White can consolidate his position.

23...♖d1+ 24 ♖xd1 ♖xd1+ 25 ♔h2 ♔f8! 26 ♖b8+ ♔f7 The most sensible thing is to agree to a draw after a repetition of moves: 27 ♖b7. A few sharp moves – **27 ♕c7?! ♔g6 28 ♕e5** (the threat was 28...♗d6+! 29 ♘xd6 ♕f4 mating) **28...♗f6** – and already it is Black who is playing for a win!

For example: **29 ♕xe6** (or 29 ♕c7 ♗g5! 30 ♘xg5 ♕xf2 31 h4 ♖d2) **29...♕f4+ 30 ♘g3 ♘xg3 31 ♕e8+ ♔h6 32 fg ♗e5!!**

Theory knows a great deal about the variation 11 ♕d1, but it does not know the main thing: where is the clear advantage for White? In the variation 11...e5 12 de fe he has extra material, but not a quiet life; in the variation 11...e5 12 de ♗:c5!? White can do little more than think about how not to lose.

The problem is that practice cannot wait until the theoreticians decide among themselves. It happens that to find a desired advantage in an individual variation – practical players there and then have switched to something else. And it turns out that the abandoned variation, as it were, is hanging in the air. This does not mean at all that it will always be bad – simply that at the present moment slightly better ideas are to be found elsewhere.

Today the variation 11 ♗b5+ looks stronger than 11 ♕d1, but who knows what tomorrow will bring?

2) **11 ♗b5+!**

11...♘d7 A forced choice. After 11...♘xb5 12 ♘xb5 a6 (the threat was 13 ♗f4 ♖c8 14 ♘xa7) 13 ♘c3 Black has many such possibilities, but an acceptable one among them is not to be found:

13...♕c7 14 ♗e3 ♘d7 15 ♖c1 ♘e5 16 ♕a4+ ♕d7 17 ♕e4 ♘g6 18 0-0 f5 19 ♕e6!, and Black cannot save himself (Bashkov – Magomedov, Chelyabinsk 1990);

13...♖c8 14 0-0 ♘d7 15 ♕xb7 g6 16 ♖e1 ♖b8 17 ♕xa6 ♗g7 18 ♗g5 with an easy win;

13...♘d7 (relatively best) 14 ♕xb7 g6 15 0-0 ♗g7 16 ♖e1 0-0 with some chances of continuing the struggle. However, after 17 ♗g5! White's advantage is still very great (Rozentalis – Adams, Hastings 1997).

12 ♕a4 ♘xb5 Also this move is forced – let's investigate why.

The f3 pawn cannot be taken: 12...♘xf3+? 13 ♔f1 ♘e5 14 ♗f4 a6 15 ♗xd7+ ♘xd7 16 d6 b5 17 ♕d4 ♘f6 18 ♖e1 ♕d7 19 ♖g1 ♖c8 20 ♖xg7! (Bashkov – Marusenko, Polica 1992).

The main boost to the variation is the fact that Black is deprived of the defence 12...e5? 13 de ♘xe6 in view of

...14 ♗g5! This surprising blow finishes off the game: 14...♘xg5

15 0-0-0, and Black resigned (Bologan – Borges, Linares 1999).

13 ♕xb5 g6 As shown by the game Alburt – Dorfman (Erevan 1975), weak is 13...e5? 14 de fe. White achieves an advantage in the most natural way: 15 ♗e3 ♕c7 16 ♖c1 etc.

14 0-0 A healthy move. White does not need to provoke complications and, even more so, look for them. Thus, there is no need to take the pawn at once – 14 ♕xb7?!, as after 14...♗g7 15 0-0 0-0 Black has sufficient compensation. The immediate 14 ♗g5 looks more interesting, though White will hardly manage to save a tempo on short castling.

14...♗g7 15 ♖e1! Feeling for the right idea: the e7 pawn ought to be attacked by the rook e1 instead of the bishop g5.

In the present position the move 15 ♗g5 is trappy: 15...h6? is not possible in view of 16 ♗xe7! ♔xe7 17 ♕b4+ ♔e8 18 ♖ae1+ ♗e5 19 f4 ♕h4 20 ♕e4 winning (Von Gleich – Fette, Hamburg 1987). But after 15...0-0 15 ♖e1 it all returns to the channels of the main variation.

15...0-0 16 ♗g5 The tabiya of the variation 11 ♗b5+.

It seems that all Black's attempts to avoid trouble have been no help. Here are just a few paths of fruitless endeavour:

16...♘e5?! 17 ♖e3 ♖e8 18 ♗f4 ♘d7 19 ♕xb7 – White has an extra pawn and the opponent has no compensation (Dvoretsky – Izeta, Terrasa 1996);

16...♘f6 17 ♕xb7 (it is not clear how to react to 17 ♖ad1!?) 17...♖b8 18 ♕xe7 ♖xb2 19 ♕xd8 ♖xd8 20 ♖ad1, once again with a healthy extra pawn (anlysis by V. Chekhov);

16...f6 17 ♗f4 ♘e5 18 ♖e3 ♕c8 19 ♗g3 g5 20 ♗xe5 fe 21 ♕b4 ♗f7 22 ♖d1 a5 23 ♕g4, and it remains only to complain about the fate of the bishop g7 (Korneev – Moreda, Malaga 2001);

16...♖e8?! 17 d6 f6 18 ♘d5! (it is obvious that Black has no available resources) 18...ed (no help are either 18...fg 19 de ♕c8 20 ♖ac1, or 18...e6 19 ♘c7 a6 20 ♕b3 fg 21 ♖xe6!) 19 ♖xe8+ ♕xe8 20 ♘c7 ♕e5 21 ♕xd7 ♕xg5+ 22 ♔h1 with the unstoppable 23 ♘e6 (Stripunsky – Gershov, New York 2000).

16...♗f6 Even quite recently this move was considered relatively promising and in any case – acceptable. But now it is hopelessly out of date.

17 ♗xf6 ef Now he does not have to defend the weakness on e7. True, in return Black presents the opponent with a passed d-pawn, hoping subsequently to blockade it. The alternative is 17...♘xf6, but after 18 ♕xb7 ♖e8 19 ♖ad1 ♕d6 20 ♘e4 ♘xe4 21 ♖xe4 it is difficult to persuade oneself that there is real compensation for the material (Sanchez – Pablo, Barbera 1997).

After 17...ef, it seems that a convenient moment has arrived to finally gobble up the b7 pawn...

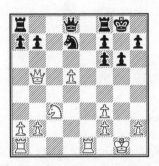

On the theme **18 ♕xb7!?** only one game is known: Cohen – Marusenko (Tel Aviv 2003). But one is soon convinced that it is still too early to take the pawn! This is how events developed: **18...♘e5 19 ♖e3 ♘c4!? 20 ♖e2 ♘e5 21 ♕b4!?** It is more natural to look at 21 f4, but after 21...♖b8 22 ♕xa7 ♘f3+ 23 ♔g2 Black has available a complicated combination: 23...♕c8! 24 h3 ♖xb2! Things are not bad for White, but also not brilliant: 25 ♖xb2 ♕xc3 26 ♕b7 ♘h4+ 27 ♔h2 ♘f3+ 28 ♔h1 ♘d2! or 25 ♕e3 ♘h4+ 26 ♔h2 ♖xe2 27 ♘xe2 ♕c4.

21...♘xf3+ 22 ♔g2 ♕d7 Here White cannot maintain the tension – 23 ♖e7?, after 23...♘h4+! he would be forced to part with material and lose.

The right defence lies in **23 ♕f4!?** ♘e5 (or 23...♘g5 24 ♖e3 ♖fe8 25 ♖ae1, and White consolidates his forces) **24 ♖d1 ♖fe8 25 ♘e4** Black's threats have run dry, while it is not easy to defend the f6 pawn.

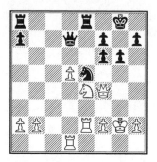

Here is a sample variation of the unfolding events:

25...♘g4 (or 25...♕g4+ 26 ♕xg4 ♘xg4 27 d6 f5 28 d7) **26 h3 f5 27 ♘c5 ♕b5 28 ♖xe8+ ♖xe8 29 hg ♕xc5 30 gf ♕b5 31 d6 ♕xb2 32 d7 ♖d8 33 ♕c7 ♕b6 34 ♕xb6 ab 35 f6**, and the white king heads for c7.

One cannot recommend this path for White – there are too many twists and turns. At any moment one could stumble. Far clearer is 18 ♖ad1, counting on the d-pawn and the weakness of the f6 square.

18 ♖ad1! ♘e5 There is no solution to the problem in 18...♖e8 19 ♖xe8+ ♕xe8 20 ♕xb7 ♖b8 21 ♕xa7 ♖xb2 22 ♕a3 ♖b6 23 ♕a4 ♕c8 24 ♕d4, and by now White has two passed pawns (Shchekachev – Bergez, San Quentin 2001).

19 ♖e3 ♕c8 20 d6 ♖d8 It is a miserable endgame after 20...♕c6 21 ♕xc6 ♘xc6 22 d7 ♖fd8 23 ♘e4 ♔g7 24 ♘d6 (Gallagher – Krizsan, Lugano 1999). He has to give up the knight for the pawn or else the rook.

But how to break up the opponent's defence after 20...♖d8 ? It is

premature to play 21 ♕d5 ♕f5 and Black still holds on (Dolmatov – Dyachkov, Elista 1996).

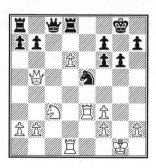

21 ♘d5! An excellent discovery by Romanian grandmaster Mihai Marin which effectively refutes Black's whole system of defence. In the game Marin – Fressinet (Sitges 1999) there followed **21...♘xf3+ 22 ♔f1! ♘xh2+ 23 ♔e1 ♔g7 24 ♘xf6!** The very moment to lower the curtain.

Indeed, talking about the variation 9...♘b6, the ending has turned out sadly for Black. Nothing can be done about it – the variation is difficult. White needs only to refrain from trifles (10 ♗e3) and firmly tread the smooth path – 10 d5! ♘d4 11 ♗b5+!

Sometimes it is useful to play dull, correct chess. With the black pieces go over to the endgame and make a laborious draw there.

II
9...e6

Reliable, solid, correct.

10 ♕xb7 ♘xd4 (but no way 10...♘db4?! 11 ♗b5 ♖c8 12 ♗e3

♗e7 in view of 13 d5! ed 14 ♘xd5 0-0 15 ♗xc6 ♘xc6 16 ♘xe7+ ♕xe7 17 ♖d1 ♕a5+ 18 b4, and Black's prospects are bleak, Peng Zhaoqin – Stefanova, Wijk aan Zee 2002) **11 ♗b5+ ♘xb5**

12 ♕c6+! An important intermediate move, forcing the black king to occupy an uncomfortable position. Of course White can also play at once 12 ♕xb5+, but without particular success: 12...♕d7 13 ♕xd7+ ♔xd7 14 ♘xd5 ed 15 ♗e3 ♗b4+ 16 ♔e2 ♖hc8 17 ♖ac1. The game Rozentalis – Bologan (Philadelphia 1994) continued 17...a6 18 ♔d3 g6 19 ♗d4 ♔e6 20 h3 ♔f5 with approximate equality, but possibly the most accurate was 17...♗d6!?, keeping in his sights the h2 pawn and intending to place the bishop on e5.

12...♔e7 13 ♕xb5 Interesting but not too convincing is 13 ♘xb5!? However there are more than enough ways for Black to go wrong.

Thus the game Vasyukov – A.Zaitsev (Berlin 1968) ended literally two moves later: 13...a6!? 14 ♘d4 ♘b4?? (14...♕c8, and White

has nothing in particular) 15 ♗g5+!

To put it mildly, Black's play was dubious in the game Gulko – Ignatiev (Moscow 1969): 13...♔f6?! 14 ♖g1 ♗b4+ 15 ♔f1 h6

16 b3! The best place for the bishop is the b2 square. It is essential that the a1-h8 diagonal is not covered over: on 16...♖c8 17 ♗b2+ ♗c3 there is the decisive queen sacrifice 18 ♘xc3! ♖xc6 19 ♘xd5+ ♔f5 20 ♘e3+ ♔f4 21 ♖d1! White is going for a real hunt: 21...♖d6 22 ♖c1! or 21...g6 22 ♖xd8 ♖xd8 23 ♔e2 h5 24 ♗f6 winning.

Ignatiev played 16...♕c8 17 ♗b2+ ♔e7, but after 18 ♘d4 g6 19 ♕b5 ♗c3 20 ♘c6+ ♔d6 21 ♗xc3 ♘xc3 22 ♕e5+ ♔xc6 23 ♕xc3+ ♔b6 24 ♕b4+ ♔a6 25 ♖g4! Black can save himself from mate only at too high a price.

In reply to 13 ♘xb5 we can recommend 13...♖b8!?, for example: 14 ♘d4 ♕d7 15 0-0 ♖c8 16 ♕a6 ♔e8 (interesting is 16...♔f6!? 17 b3 ♘c3!?) 17 ♗e3 ♘b4 18 ♕e2 ♗d6 19 ♖fd1 ♘d5 20 ♘b5 a6, and Black has nearly beaten back the opponent (Vorisek – Hollman, Czech Republic 1995).

After 13 ♕xb5, on the board is the tabiya of the variation.

In the famous game Fischer – Euwe (Leipzig 1960) was encountered 13...♘xc3?! 14 bc. It seems that White has a small cartload of weak pawns, but Fischer showed his opponent that the weakest is the isolated pawn on a7: 14...♕d7 15 ♖b1 ♖d8 (or 15...♕xb5 16 ♖xb5 ♔d6 17 ♖b7 f6 18 ♔e2 ♔c6 19 ♖f7 a5 20 ♗e3 with the advantage – analysis by Fischer) 16 ♗e3 ♕xb5 17 ♖xb5 ♖d7. Strongest here was an immediate 18 ♖a5; however Fischer won the game also with the simple 18 ♔e2.

Black also failed to equalise in the game Balashov – Hort (Buenos Aires 1980): 14...♕d5 15 ♖b1!? ♖d8 16 ♗e3 ♔f6 17 ♖g1!?

Later an attempt was made to improve Black's play by – 14...f6!? But, as shown by practice, this defence does not eliminate the problem: 15 ♗a3+ ♔f7 16 ♖d1!? ♕c8 17 ♖d7+ ♔g8 18 ♗xf8 ♕xc3+ 19 ♔e2 ♖xf8 20 ♖hd1 h5 21 ♖d8 ♕a3

22 ♖1d6! An extremely unpleasant move for Black. Until here 22 ♖1d7 ♖h6 23 ♖xf8+ ♕xf8 was played (Christiansen – Shamkovich, South Bend 1981), and the black queen succeeded in closely covering its king. Now however after 22...♕xa2+ 23 ♔f1 ♕a1+ 24 ♔g2 the king g8 has to rely on its own agility: 24...♔f7 25 ♖8d7+ ♔g8 26 ♖xe6 ♖h6 27 ♕f5! (Rantanen – Burger, Gausdal 1982).

13...♕d7 Essentially, here was White's last chance to avoid the endgame. Whether it was necessary to avoid it is another question, but a second such chance will not present itself.

If he does not exchange queens, then it is necessary to choose between 14 ♕a5 and 14 ♕e2.

There is no advantage to be had in 14 ♕a5?! ♘xc3 (the modern treatment is – 14...f6!? 15 0-0 ♘xc3 16 bc ♔f7 17 ♕a6 ♗c5 18 ♗f4 ♖hc8, and in any event it is not Black who is fighting for equality, Onischuk – Dreev, Yalta 1995) 15 ♕xc3 (or 15 bc f6 16 ♖b1 ♔f7 17 ♕a6 ♗e7 18 ♖b7 ♕d5 19 ♗a3 ♖he8 20 0-0 ♕xf3, Gaprindashvili – Chiburdanidze, Pizunda 1978) 15...f6 16 ♗e3 ♔f7 17 0-0 ♗e7 (M.Tseitlin – Kasparov, Daugavpils 1978). With queens, the weakness of the a7 pawn is an insignificant factor; it is his free development and prospects of attacking the f3 pawn that are more important.

More interesting is 14 ♕e2!? – White prefers a direct attack on the king to positional niceties. The recipe for defence is already well known to us: the king should hide on f7: 14...f6! 15 ♘xd5+ ♕xd5 16 0-0 ♔f7 17 ♖d1. On principle, it is difficult to establish in this position that Black is threatened with real danger. But accuracy must never be relaxed. Thus, in the game Taeger – Rogozenko (Bad Weissee 1997) the Romanian grandmaster for some reason or other did not take under control the d7 square and after 17...♕f5?! 18 ♖d7+ ♗e7 19 ♗e3 was forced to part with the a7 pawn. Instead of 17...♕f5?!, 17...♕b7 18 ♕e4 ♖b8 19 ♕xb7+ ♖xb7 20 ♖b1 ♗e7 21 ♗e3 ♖c8 looks more healthy. All Black's problems are behind him (Nirosh – Bageri, Teheran 1998).

14 ♘xd5+ ♕xd5 For Black (with the king on e7) there is absolutely no reason to avoid the exchange of queens. And that is why 14...ed?! is foolish: 15 ♕e2+ (Fischer recommends 15 ♕b4+ ♔e8 16 ♕d4) 15...♕e6 16 ♗e3, and the black king is again threatened with an attack.

After 14...♕xd5 arises the first serious fork in the variation 9...e6. White can choose between the immediate 15 ♕xd5 (A) and the intermediate 15 ♗g5+ (B).

A

15 ♕xd5 ed

In this position there are three completely different plans of play for White: 16 ♗e3, 16 ♗f4 and 16 0-0.

1) **16 ♗e3 ♔e6 17 0-0-0** Appropriate, as it was for this reason that White played 16 ♗e3. The attempt to switch ideas (refraining from castling queenside) brings no advantage:

17 ♖c1 ♗b4+ 18 ♔e2 ♖hc8 19 ♔d3 a5 20 ♖xc8 ♖xc8. The bishop endgame is not winning for White, but otherwise Black is left with the only open c-file (Pigusov – Dreev, Tallinn 1986);

17 ♖g1 ♗d6! 18 ♖xg7 ♗e5 19 ♖g4 ♗xb2, once again with equal chances (Rogers – Adams, London 1988).

17...♗b4 This is how the great specialist in the system – grandmaster Alexei Dreev, likes to play. However also in the event of 17...♖c8+ 18 ♔b1 ♗c5 White has no advantage: 19 ♖hg1 g6 20 ♖g4 ♖hd8 21 ♖a4 ♗b6 (Gdanski – Adorjan, Polanica Zdroj 1992) or 19 ♖he1 ♔d6 20 ♖d3 ♖hd8 (Kavalek – Rogoff, Berlin 1975) with obvious drawing tendencies.

After 17...♗b4 the statistics of results of games are somewhere around the 50% mark. It is rare that one of the opponents manages to extract a full point:

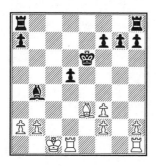

Unpromising is 18 ♗d4 f6 19 ♖hg1 ♔f7 and the bishop has to go back: 20 ♗e3 ♖hd8 21 ♖g4 a5 22 ♖d3 ♖d7. White's position is not worse (Garcia – Becerra, Matanzas 1995);

18 ♖d3 ♖hd8 19 a3 ♖ac8+ 20 ♔b1 ♗c5 21 ♖e1 ♗xe3 22 ♖exe3+ ♔f6 23 ♖d4 ♖c4. White has achieved nothing (Franco – Dominguez, Mondariz 2002);

18 ♔b1 ♖hc8!? 19 ♖d3 ♗c5 20 ♖e1 ♗xe3 21 ♖dxe3+ ♔f6 22 ♖e7 ♖c4. The f2, f3 and h2 pawns feel the draught (Stripunsky – Dreev, Internet 2001).

18 a3 ♖hc8+ 19 ♔b1 ♗c5! The defensive strategy is the same in any case: to force a bishop exchange, since it is well-known that nobody can win the rook endgame.

20 ♖he1 ♗xe3 21 ♖xe3+ ♔d6 22 f4 ♖ab8 23 ♖d4 with a draw (Vaganian – Dreev, Odessa 1989).

2) **16 ♗f4** Far more interesting than 16 ♗e3. Now forcing an exchange of bishops is considerably more difficult; Black can no longer allow himself to play 'on general principles.'

16...♔f6!? The other choice is 16...♔d7!? 17 0-0-0 ♔c6, and he is all ready for ♗f8-d6.

17 0-0-0 ♖d8 18 ♖hg1 ♖d7 19 ♗e3! h6 In the game Kindermann – Lobron (Berne 1990) Black did not properly appreciate the bishop transfer and played 19...♖g8?! There followed 20 ♖g4! and without delay the rook was swept over to a4 – White had an obvious advantage.

20 ♗d4+ (also here it is perhaps worth thinking about the manoeuvre ♖g1-g4-a4!?) **20...♔f5 21 ♗xg7 ♖xg7 22 ♖xg7 ♖c8+ 23 ♔d2 ♔f4 24 ♔d3 ♖xf3 25 ♖e1 ♔f4 26 h3 ♖c4 27 ♖e3 ♔f5 28 ♖f3+ ♔e6 29 ♖g4 ♖xg4 30 hg ♖b7** Though 'more pleasant' for White, the game did not leave the drawing zone (Onischuk – Dreev, Moscow 2002).

3) **16 0-0** On principle, the most logical move. The rooks combine for an attack on the a7 and d5 pawns (likewise they would not mind seizing the open c-file), while the king is brought over for defence of its own pawn weaknesses on the f and h-files.

Black ought to be able to defend the most vulnerable points in his position – besides a7 and d5, such should be considered all the squares on the 7th rank. From there comes the first link in the plan – the manoeuvre ♖a(h)8-d8-d7! Then, by developing the bishop on f6, he is ready to blackmail the opponent with an advance of the d-pawn. On d5 this is a weakness, but if it gets as far as d3...

Moreover it is useful to fix the enemy pawns on the king's flank by means of g7-g5.

16...♔e6 17 ♖e1+ ♔f5 White is at a crossroads: 18 ♗e3 or 18 ♖d1. The first move is idealistic, the second – popular.

a) **18 ♗e3 ♗e7 19 ♖ac1!?** Only this move, encountered in the game Sermek – Golubovic (Bled 1994),

sets Black some problems. Upon other continuations it is easy to equalise the game:

19 ♖ad1 ♖hd8 20 ♖d4 g5 21 ♖ed1 ♔e6 (A.Ivanov – Seirawan, Durango 1992);

19 ♖ed1 ♖hd8 20 ♖ac1 ♖d7 21 ♖d4 ♗f6 22 ♖f4+ ♔g6 23 ♖c6 ♖e8 (Klinger – Ivanchuk, Baguio 1987).

19...♖hc8!? What is the principal fine point in this position? In the fact that White is ready to meet the natural 19...♗f6 with the move 20 ♖c5! Earlier this nuance carried no significance. Thus, in the game Smejkal – Filip (Luhacovice 1968) followed 20...♖hd8 21 b4 ♔g6 22 b5 d4 23 ♗d2 d3 24 a4 ♖ac8 25 ♖ec1 ♖xc5 26 ♖xc5 ♖d4 27 a5 ♖a4, and the opponents agreed a draw.

The improvement lies on the surface: instead of 21 b4?! (the prematurely advanced pawn will become a target of attack) he should play 21 b3! Precisely this was seen in the game Sermek – Golubovic. After 21 b3 White can torment the opponent for a long time. Probably, upon accurate defence, he will not break through Black's position, however it is not worth consciously going in for this type of position.

19...♖hc8 denies the rook the c5 square, while Black compensates for his pawn deficit by the activity of his pieces, supporting the passed d-pawn:

20 ♖xc8 ♖xc8 21 ♗xa7 ♗f6 22 ♖d1 ♔e6 23 ♗d4 ♗xd4 24 ♖xd4 ♔e5!? 25 ♖d2 ♖c1+ 26 ♔g2 g5

We have reached a complicated rook ending which Black should not lose:

27 f4+!? (or 27 a4 d4 28 a5 ♖a1 29 b4 ♔d5 30 b5 ♖xa5 31 ♖b2 ♖a7 32 f4 g4!) **27...gf 28 ♔f3 ♖h1 29 ♖e2+** (29 b4 ♖b1) **29...♔d6 30 ♔xf4 ♖xh2** with a probable draw.

b) **18 ♖d1 ♖d8 19 ♗e3 ♖d7 20 ♖ac1** The alternative is 20 ♖d4!?, and after 20...♗c5 21 ♖f4+ ♔e5 White needs to decide whether to exchange bishops or leave them on the board:

22 ♖c1 ♗xe3 23 fe ♖b8 24 b3 ♖bb7 and Black is a little worse (Adams – Morovic, Leon 1995);

22 ♗d2!? ♖c8 23 ♖c1 ♖dc7 24 ♖e1+ ♔d6 25 ♖g4 ♖e7 26 ♖xe7 (or 26 ♖xg7 ♖xe1+ 27 ♗xe1 ♗d4 28 ♖xf7 ♖c2 with obvious compensation for the material) 26...♔xe7 27 ♖xg7 ♗d4 28 ♖xh7 ♖c2 Black should not have any particular problems in achieving a draw.

20...♗e7 21 ♖d4 Also seen is 21 ♖c4 ♗f6 22 ♖c5 ♖hd8 23 b3 ♗e5 24 ♖a5 ♗c3!, and the d5 pawn becomes dangerous (Wahls – Adorjan, Germany 1989).

21...g5!? The most idealistic, although 21...♗f6!? 22 ♖f4+ ♔g6! 23 b3 h6! 24 ♖c6 ♔h7 is also not bad. In the game Belyavsky – Ivanchuk (Truskavetz 1987) White fell into a disguised trap: 25 ♗d4? ♗g5! 26 ♖f5 f6! The rook f5 is left only in a state of anxiety.

22 ♖a4 ♗f6 23 b4 It is possible to recommend 23 b3!? (only not 23 ♖xa7?! ♖xa7 24 ♗xa7 ♗xb2 25 ♖c7 ♔e6), though in the game Reinderman – Henkin (Antwerp 1993) White did not achieve too much: 23...d4 24 ♖c5+ ♔g6 25 ♗d2 ♖e8.

23...d4 24 ♖a5+ ♔g6 25 ♗d2 ♖e8 26 ♔f1 d3 This position was reached in the game Arkipov – Filipenko (Belgorod 1989) and Adams – Dreev (Wijk aan Zee 2002). A draw is not far off.

B

15 ♗g5+!?

This looks rather fresher than 15 ♕xd5 ed. White tries to weaken the e6 square, where (after doubling) White's rooks can penetrate.

15...f6 16 ♕xd5 ed 17 ♗e3 ♔e6 18 0-0-0 Very interesting is **18 ♖g1!?** with the idea of getting at the g-pawn. But in the game A.Sokolov – Vogt (Lenk 2000) Black was able to 'unravel' by 18...g6 19 0-0-0 ♗b4 20 a3 ♖ac8+ 21 ♔b1 ♗c5 22 ♖ge1 ♗xe3 23 ♖xe3+ ♔d6 24 ♖de1 d4! With such a passed pawn (and, what is of no little importance, cutting off of the white king along the c-file) Black is not under much risk.

18...♗b4 The last fork in the whole system.

1) **19 ♖hg1** does not give Black any trouble: **19...g5! 20 a3 ♗d6 21 ♖ge1 ♗e5** (Gavrikov – Dreev, Biel 1995).

2) In a series of grandmaster games was tried the idea **19 ♖d3!? ♖hd8 20 ♔b1!?** (20 a3 ♖ac8+ 21 ♔b1 ♗c5 22 ♖e1 ♔d6! with equal chances, Karpov – Kramnik, Linares 1993)

20...♖d7 21 ♖c1 a5 22 ♖c6+ ♔f5 23 ♖b6 ♗e7 24 ♖b5 ♔e6 25 a4 ♗b4 with a very complicated struggle (Bologan – Velicka, Berne 1999).

3) Insufficient for a serious advantage is **19 ♔b1**, and then:

19...♖hc8 20 ♖d3 ♖c4 21 ♖hd1 ♖h4 22 ♖xd5 ♖xh2 23 ♖d7 ♗f8 24 ♖xa7 ♖xa7 25 ♗xa7 h5 26 a4. The edge pawn hurries to queen. We bet on White! (Pilgaard – Flambort, Budapest 2003);

19...♖hd8!? 20 ♖d3 a5!? 21 a3 ♗f8! 22 ♖e1 ♔f5 23 ♖c1 ♖d7 Still not a draw, but already close (Nielsen – Dominguez, Esbjerg 2002).

4) **19 a3** In the variation 15 ♕xd5 ed 16 ♗e3 ♔e6 17 0-0-0 ♗b4, 18 a3 is considered a main move; the insertion 15 ♗g5+ f6 changes little. True, the e6 square is weakened a little. But how to exploit this?

19...♖hc8+!? 20 ♔b1 ♗c5 21 ♖he1 ♗xe3 22 ♖xe3+ ♔d6 23 ♖de1 It seems that White has achieved something – he threatens a check on e6. But...

23...♖c4! And it becomes clear that the apparently terrible threat of invasion on e6 in fact doesn't worry

Black: 24 ♖e6+ ♔c5 25 ♖c1 ♖xc1+ 26 ♔xc1 ♔d4 27 ♖e7 ♖c8+ 28 ♔d2 ♖b8 29 b4 a5! with a draw (Gulko – Harikrishna, Bled 2002).

He can get to the 7th rank, but this changes little to the assessment of the position: **24 ♖e7 ♖h4 25 ♖1e6+** (25 b4 d4) **25...♔c5 26 ♖xg7** (26 ♔c2 ♖xh2 27 ♔d3 ♖xf2) **26...♖xh2 27 ♖xf6 ♖xf2 28 ♖xh7** (28 ♖f4 h5) **28...♖b8** The variations are simple, the assessment transparent: draw (Belikov – Dreev, Moscow 1992).

The paradox of the Four Knights system 1 e4 c6 2 d4 d5 3 ed cd 4 c4 ♘f6 5 ♘c3 ♘c6 6 ♘f3 lies in the fact that the 'rate of movement' in it is determined by Black, but 'the rudder' is invariably directed by White!

It all depends on Black whether the game develops at a mad tempo (6...♗g4 7 cd ♘xd5 8 ♕b3 ♗xf3 9 gf ♘b6) or it proceeds softly, softly (9...e6). But in the first case (after 9...♘b6?!) theory leads Black to a painfully narrow corridor for manoeuvre (10 d5! ♘d4 11 ♗b5+!), while in the second (9...e6 10 ♕xb7 ♘xd4 11 ♗b5+ ♘xb5 12 ♕c6+! ♔e7 13 ♕xb5 ♕d7 14 ♘xd5+ ♕xd5) he has to switch, as it were, to a... tricycle! Attacking with such an outmoded vehicle is complicated – how to outrun the opponent? No matter how much he pedals, the speed is almost zero.

White too has nothing special to be happy about. No adherents play 9...♘b6?!, and it is only possible to reckon seriously on an endgame victory after 9...e6 if the opponent is significantly lower rated. Conclusion? If a win is needed at all costs, then it is hardly appropriate to go for the Four Knights system as White. After 6 ♗g5 the play is richer, indeed the theory less. But about this – in Chapter Four.

Index to Chapter One

1 e4 c6 2 d4 d5 3 ed cd 4 c4 ♞f6
5 ♞c3   7
5...♞c6 6 ♞f3 ♗g4 7 cd ♞xd5
8 ♕b3 ♗xf3 9 gf
I. 9...♞b6   12
 A. 10 ♗e3   12
 10...e6
  1) 11 ♖g1   12
   a) 11...♞xd4   13
   b) 11...g6   13
   c) 11...♗b4   14
  2) 11 0-0-0   15
  11...♗e7 12 d5 ed
   a) 13 ♗xb6   15
   b) 13 ♗b5   15
   c) 13 ♞xd5   16
 B. 10 d5   18
 10...♞d4
  1) 11 ♕d1   18
  11...e5 12 de
   a) 12...♞xe6   19
   b) 12...♕f6   19
   c) 12...♗c5   19
   d) 12...fe   20

13 ♗e3 ♗c5
 d1) 14 b4   20
  d11) 14...0-0   20
  d12) 14...♕f6   21
 d2) 14 ♗g2   22
 2) 11 ♗b5+   23
II. 9...e6   26
10 ♕xb7 ♞xd4 11 ♗b5+ ♞xb5
12 ♕c6+ ♔e7 13 ♕xb5 ♕d7
14 ♞xd5+ ♕xd5
 A. 15 ♕xd5 ed   29
  1) 16 ♗e3   29
  2) 16 ♗f4   30
  3) 16 0-0   31
 16...♔e6 17 ♖e1+ ♔f5
   a) 18 ♗e3   31
   b) 18 ♖d1   32
 B. 15 ♗g5+   32
 15...f6 16 ♕xd5 ed 17 ♗e3 ♔e6
 18 0-0-0 ♗b4
  1) 19 ♖hg1   33
  2) 19 ♖d3   33
  3) 19 ♔b1   33
  4) 19 a3   33

Chapter Two

1 e4 c6 2 d4 d5 3 ed cd 4 c4 ♘f6
5 ♘c3 ♘c6 6 ♗g5

Before going over to an examination of 6 ♗g5, we pause for a little while to look at other moves of the dark-squared bishop.

6 ♗e3 does not claim to obtain an opening advantage. On the contrary, the minus of developing the bishop on e3 should be exploited, as was successfully achieved in masterful fashion by Black in the game Paglilla – Sorokin (Buenos Aires 1993): 6...e6 7 ♘f3 ♗e7 8 a3 0-0 9 c5 ♘e4 10 ♕c2 f5! 11 ♗b5 f4! After 12 ♗c1 ♘g5 13 ♘xg5 ♗xg5 14 ♕d3 ♕f6 15 ♘e2 e5! Maxim Sorokin was in full possession of the initiative.

The other thing that Black should know is – how to react to 6 ♗f4 g6 7 ♘b5!?

Analysis shows that the complications after 7...e5! 8 de ♗b4+ favour Black:

9 ♔e2 (more careful is 9 ♗d2 ♗xd2+ 10 ♕xd2 ♘xe5 11 cd, though even here the compensation, as they say, can be seen with the naked eye: 11...0-0 12 ♖d1 ♗f5 13 ♘c3 ♖e8 14 ♗e2 ♘c4 15 ♕c1 ♕b6) 9...♘h5 10 ♗e3 d4! 11 ♗xd4 (11 ♘xd4 is bad because of 11...♘f4+! 12 ♗xf4 ♘xd4+ 13 ♔e3 ♕b6 with a decisive attack) 11...♘f4+ 12 ♔e3 ♘e6 13 ♘f3 ♘exd4 14 ♘bxd4 ♗c5. The torment of the white king is obviously not worth the extra material.

6 ♗g5 The original source of this plan should apparently be considered the game A.Rabinovich – Tartakower (Carlsbad 1911), although we also habitually date its 'chronology' from the match Botvinnik – Flohr (Moscow/Leningrad 1933). In his commentary to one of the match games, Mikhail Moiseevich himself acknowledged that a weighty contribution to the elaboration of the system was made by the analysts A.Model and V.Ragozin.

White attacks the d5 square; correspondingly, from now on Black ought to decide how to deal with this. The centre can be given up – 6...dc (A), but, perhaps, on the other hand, consolidated – 6...♗e6 (B). If however you are accustomed to playing aggressively, irrespective of which colour you are, then it is possible to go over at once to a counterattack: 6...♗g4 (C), 6...♕b6 (D) or 6...♕a5 (E). The position after 6...e6 by transposition of moves will be looked at in the second part of the book.

A

6...dc At once we have a division: 7 ♗xc4 and 7 d5.

1) **7 ♗xc4!?** White offers the opponent a real gambit and, it seems, Black has every right to accept the gambit. Only this must be done intelligently.

a) Weak is 7...♘xd4?! 8 ♘f3 ♘xf3+ 9 ♕xf3 ♕c7 10 ♗b5+ ♗d7 11 0-0. The advantage in development assumes threatening proportions, for example, 11...♗xb5 12 ♘xb5 ♕b6 13 a4 a6 14 ♗e3 ♕d8 15 ♖fd1 ♘d7 16 ♕xb7! ab 17 ♖xd7! (Gipslis – Schultze, Biel 1995).

But proving that the initiative is worth a pawn will be considerably more difficult after an exchange of queens. Therefore **7...♕xd4!? 8 ♕xd4 ♘xd4 9 0-0-0 e5!**

What luxury for the black knight on d4! It covers the dangerous d-file, defends against attacks on b5. It must be driven away, but how?

On 10 f4 there is 10...♗g4!? 11 ♘f3 ♗xf3! (the knight d4 is the way to any material blessings: 11...♘xf3?! 12 gf ♗xf3 13 fe! ♗xh1 14 ef or 13...♗xd1 14 ♖xd1 – analysis by B. Kantzler) 12 gf ♖c8! (do you notice how often in this variation Black succeeds in making counterattacking moves with tempo) 13 fe ♖xc4 14 ef g6 (also possible is 14...♘e6 15 ♖he1 ♖c8 16 ♔b1 h6 17 ♗e3 gf, though after 18 ♘d5 White's position is still better, P.-H. Neilsen – Dominguez, Esbjerg 2003) 15 ♖he1+ ♘e6 16 ♔b1 (if White decides that he will play his own 'Evergreen Game', then disappointment awaits him: after 16 ♖xe6+?! fe 17 f7+ ♔xf7 18 ♖d7+ ♔g8 19 ♗f6 b5 20 ♔d1 ♖f4 it is only Black who can aspire to victory, Vrenegor – van Wely, Holland 1993) 16...♖c6 17 ♘d5 ♗d6 18 ♗h6 ♔d7

19 ♖e2 ♖d8 20 ♗e3 ♗c5 21 ♗xc5 ♖xc5 22 ♖xe6 fe 23 ♘f4+ ♔d5! White's initiative is neutralised (S.-B. Hansen – P.-H. Nielsen, Copenhagen 1996).

There remains **10 ♘f3 ♘xf3 11 gf**, but then Black succeeds in hiding away his king.

11...♗e7 The alternative is 11...♗e6 12 ♗b5+ ♘d7, and in the event of 13 f4 f6 14 ♗h4 all problems are solved by 14...0-0-0! 15 fe ♘xe5 16 ♖xd8+ ♔xd8 17 ♖e1 ♗d6 (Lanka – Preissmann, Geneva 1993). Promising for White is another plan – doubling rooks on the d-file: 13 ♖d2!? f6 14 ♖hd1 ♖d8 15 ♗e3 a6 16 ♗a4 b5 17 ♗c2 ♗b4 18 a3 (Broberg – Heppner, Grunheide 1996) 18...♗xc3 19 bc ♔e7 20 ♖d6 etc.

12 ♖he1 0-0 13 ♖xe5 ♗d8 14 ♘e4 ♘d7 15 ♖f5 ♗c7!? Black played poorly in the game Sveshnikov – Oll (Moscow 1992): 15...♘f6?! 16 ♖f4 ♗e6?! After the exchange of all the minor pieces the rook invades on d7 with great effect.

16 ♘d6

This position was reached in the game Poluljahov – Maiorov

(Krasnodar 1995). Black played 16...♗xd6?! 17 ♖xd6 g6 18 ♖f4 ♘e5 19 ♗b3 ♗f5, but did not achieve full equality. The two powerful white bishops outweigh both the defective pawn structure and rather uneasy position of the king c1.

However grandmaster Poluljahov himself also suggested a better solution in this position: **16...♘b6! 17 ♖c5 ♗xd6 18 ♖xd6 ♘xc4 19 ♖xc4 ♗e6** Now the ending is absolutely equal.

Of course, Black has the right to decline the gambit on the 7th move. All the same, as we see, he risks more than his opponent, and upon mutually accurate play will be fighting only for equality. So is it possible that this is a rather simpler way?

b) **7...e6 8 ♘f3 ♗e7 9 0-0 0-0** – a solid, 'compact' way to achieve his objective (equality). This variation has a close affinity to the Queen's Gambit Accepted: 1 d4 d5 2 c4 dc 3 ♘f3 ♘f6 4 e3 e6 5 ♗xc4 c5 6 0-0 cd 7 ed ♗e7 8 ♘c3 0-0 9 ♗g5 ♘c6 (it being understood that in this variation the idea 9 ♗g5 is in no way considered to be the main line).

In practice more often than not White does not realise his ambition:

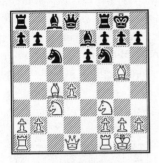

10 ♕d2 a6 (also possible is 10...b6, as the break in the centre leads only to equality and a speedy draw: 11 d5!? ♘a5 12 ♗d3 ed 13 ♖fe1 ♘c6 14 ♖ad1 ♗g4 15 ♗xf6 ♗xf6 16 ♘xd5 ♗xf3, Anand – Dreev, Hyderabad 2002; on this theme the same opponents played yet another game – see 10 ♖e1) 11 ♖ad1 ♘b4 12 ♗b3 b6 13 ♕e2 ♗b7 14 ♖fe1 ♘bd5 15 ♘e5 ♘xc3 16 bc ♘d5 17 ♗d2 b5 18 ♕d3 ♗g5. The game is equal (Pelletier – Dreev, Biel 2002);

10 ♖c1 a6 11 ♗d3 ♗d7 12 ♖e1 ♖c8 13 a3 ♘d5 14 h4!? (though this looks very strong, Black reacts in a cool way) 14...♘xc3! 15 bc h6 16 ♗xe7 ♘xe7 17 c4 b5! 18 c5 ♘d5 19 ♘e5 ♗c6 20 a4 ♕xh4 21 ♘xc6 ♖xc6 22 ab ab 23 ♗xb5 ♖c7 (Ivanchuk – Dreev, Moscow 2002). An interesting game – and again a draw.

10 ♖e1 a6 11 a4 ♗d7 12 ♕e2 (12 ♕d2 ♖c8 13 ♖ad1 ♘b4 14 d5 ed 15 ♗xd5 ♗c6 16 ♗b3 ♗xf3 17 gf ♕xd2 18 ♖xd2 ♘c6 19 ♔g2 ♖fd8

20 ♖xd8+ ♖xd8 21 ♖d1 ♖xd1 22 ♗xd1 ♘d5! with a draw, Anand – Dreev, Hyderabad 2002) 12...♘d5 13 ♗xe7 ♘cxe7 14 ♗xd5 ♘xd5 15 ♘xd5 ed 16 ♘e5 f6 17 ♘d3 ♖e8 18 ♕d2 and once again a draw (Gelfand – Dreev, Wijk aan Zee 2002);

10 a3!? Perhaps the most flexible way. Even the impregnable Dreev stumbles every now and then, as in these variations:

10...a6 11 ♕d3 b5 12 ♗a2 b4?! 13 ♘a4 e5?! 14 ♗xf6 ♗xf6 15 ♕e4! (Tkachiev – Dreev, Cap d'Agde 2000). Though White lost the game, this has nothing to do with the assessment of the position.

10...b6 11 ♕d3 ♗b7 12 ♖ad1 ♘d5 13 ♗c1!? ♘xc3 14 bc ♘a5 15 ♗a2 ♗xf3?! 16 ♕xf3 ♕c7 17 ♖d3 ♘c4 18 ♕h5 g6 19 ♕h6. Again Dreev stood worse, and... again he won (Bologan – Dreev, Cap d'Agde 2002);

10...h6 11 ♗h4 ♘h5! 12 ♗xe7 ♘xe7! (classical genre) 13 ♖e1 ♘f6 14 ♕d3 b6 15 ♖ad1 ♗b7, and Black can boldly look to the future (Kron – Tregubov, Tomsk 2003).

2) **7 d5!?** This idea of M.Botvinnik and his helpers was specially prepared for the match against Flohr.

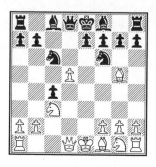

White gains time, but what is even more important – he also gains the d4 square for his queen. The knight c6 must move away. But to where: the centre or sideways?

a) **7...♘e5?!** In chess, surprisingly, not infrequently there are situations where natural, logical, healthy moves are not the strongest!

8 ♕d4 ♘d3+?! The second 'natural' move in a row – and saving the position is already difficult (if generally speaking possible). Also unsatisfactory is 8...♘fd7?! 9 ♗f4 ♘g6 10 ♗g3 (Beim – Zak, Graz 1996) – on moves with the knight Black has already spent 5 tempi, and as a result the knight looks so ridiculous! But 8...h6!? allows a continuation of the struggle (moreover we shall still be returning to this move).

9 ♗xd3 cd 10 ♘f3! In the 1st game of the Botvinnik – Flohr match was played 10 ♗xf6?!, and after 10...ef 11 ♕xd3 ♗d6 12 ♘ge2 0-0 13 0-0 ♖e8 Black fortunately avoided

danger. But only up to the 9th game of this same match...

By playing 10 ♘f3!, White is not distracted by trifles, but calmly completes the mobilisation of his forces. It is important that he retains the possibility of castling both on the short and the long sides – White can vary his plan depending on the situation.

Whichever pawn – h, g or e – makes a move, it looks like there will be trouble from which there is no escape:

10...h6 11 ♗f4 g5 12 ♗e5 ♗g7 13 ♕xd3 with advantage (analysis by Botvinnik);

10...g6 11 ♗xf6 ef 12 0-0 ♕b6 13 ♖fe1+ ♔d8 14 ♕h4! (the last difficult move in the game) 14...g5 15 ♕h5 ♗d6 16 ♕xf7 ♖f8 17 ♕xh7 g4 18 ♘d2 with an overwhelming position (Botvinnik – Flohr, Leningrad 1933, – the very same 9th game of the match!);

10...e6? 11 0-0-0! ♗e7 12 ♖he1 0-0 13 ♖xd3 ed, and 14 ♖xe7! ♕xe7 15 ♘xd5! is decisive (Furman – Naglis, Moscow 1970).

We return to the position before the 8th move and try out **8...h6!?**

The position is tenable by word of honour. But none the less – nobody has yet proved a win for White.

9 ♗f4 Also upon 9 ♕xe5 hg 10 ♗xc4 Black's life, as they say, is teetering on the edge of a precipice. Thus, in the game J. Polgar – Seirawan (Monaco 1993) Black could not withstand the pressure and after 10...a6 11 0-0-0 ♕d6 12 ♘f3 g4 13 ♖he1!? ♕xe5 14 ♘xe5 ♖xh2 15 d6! e6 16 ♘e4 ♘xe4 17 ♖xe4 he lost by a one-move blunder: 17...f6? (17...♗d7!) 18 d7+.

Apparently, after 9 ♕xe5 hg 10 ♗xc4 the most accurate defence lies in 10...♗d7!? The pawn sacrifice is temporary – 11 ♕xg5?! ♕c7! 12 ♗b3 ♖xh2 13 ♖xh2 ♕xh2 14 0-0-0 g6! (Kindermann – Balogh, Baden 1999), while 11 ♘f3!? allows a surprising pin of the white pieces: 11...g4 12 ♘g5 ♖h5! The continuation of the game Hernandez – Gonzalez (Reyes 2000) is interesting: 13 0-0 ♖c8 14 ♘b5 ♕b6 15 ♖ac1 a6 16 d6! ♖xg5! 17 ♕xg5 ab 18 ♗xb5! ♖xc1 19 ♗xd7+ ♔xd7 20 ♖xc1 e6 21 ♖c7+. Here Black missed the chance to equalise the game: 21...♔d8! 22 ♖xf7 ♕xd6 etc.

9...♘g6 10 ♗xc4 Tempting, but weak is 10 ♗g3 e6 11 d6

...in view of 11...♘e7! In the game Anand – Seirawan (Amsterdam 1992) White could not immediately recover from this blow: 12 ♖d1 ♘ed5 13 ♕e5 ♘d7 14 ♕e2?! (later Anand admitted that it was time to repeat moves: 14 ♕d4 ♘7f6 15 ♕e5) 14...♘xc3 15 bc g6 16 ♗e5 ♘xe5 17 ♕xe5 ♖g8 18 ♗xc4 ♗g7 19 ♗b5+ ♗d7 20 ♗xd7+ ♕xd7 21 ♕e3 ♕c6 and Seirawan's bishop is noticeably stronger than the white knight, although later on Anand's class told – and he won.

10...♘xf4 11 ♕xf4 a6 Wild positions need corresponding methods. For example, such as: 11...g5!? 12 ♕d2 ♗g7 13 ♘ge2 a6 14 0-0 ♕c7, and Black is only a little worse (Lalic – Almagro, Madrid 2003).

12 ♘f3 g6 13 0-0 Black also holds up after 13 ♘e5 ♕d6 14 0-0, albeit with help from the same resource: 14...g5!? 15 ♕e3 ♗g7 16 f4 0-0 17 ♖ae1 g4 18 ♗b3 ♗f5 19 ♖d1 ♖ac8 (Timofeev – Galliamova, Kazan 2001).

13...♗g7 14 d6

Thus went the encounter Vaganian – Ehlvest (Riga 1995). Grandmaster Jaan Ehlvest was afraid to take the pawn. And, possibly, for no reason: the variation 14...♕xd6!? 15 ♕xd6 ed 16 ♖fe1+ ♔f8 17 ♖ad1 ♘e8 does not convince us that White has the means to finish 'squeezing' this position.

However, if we talk as a whole, then, without any doubt, the move 7...♘e5?! leads to a difficult game for Black.

b) **7...♘a5!?** It is hard to believe, but this move – is the strongest!

8 b4 The most principled – White wants to trap the knight, stranded on the edge of the board. And perhaps he has no other way of playing:

8 ♘f3 hands back the lost tempo: 8...a6! 9 b4 (he must; if Black manages to carry out b7-b5, then he

will simply be left with an extra pawn) 9...cb 10 ab e6 11 ♗e2 ♗b4 12 ♖c1 ♕xd5, and Black has won the opening battle (Ravinsky – Tolush, Moscow 1944).

Rejecting the idea of winning the knight – 8 ♗xc4?! ♘xc4 9 ♕a4+ ♗d7 10 ♕xc4 – is likewise ineffective. If we believe the old analysis of A.Konstantinopolsky, Black has not bad play after 10...b5!? 11 ♕e2 (or 11 ♘xb5 ♖c8) 11...♕b6 12 ♗xf6 gf. Meanwhile in the game Rother – Schultze (Germany 1988) Black chose 10...g6 11 ♗xf6 ef and also did not miscalculate: 12 ♘f3 ♗g7 13 0-0 0-0 14 ♖fe1 ♕b6 etc.

8...cb 9 ab ♗d7! The point of the whole plan. By freeing the c8 square for the rook, Black is ready to meet the blow b3-b4 fully armed.

White's problem is that he has a crisis of ideas:

10 ♗xf6 gf 11 b4 ♖c8! 12 ♘e4 ♘c4 13 ♕b3 ♕c7 14 ♘f3 ♗g7 15 ♘c5 ♘d6 16 ♖xa7 f5 17 ♗d3 0-0 18 0-0 ♖a8 (Sveshnikov – Vuruna, Belgrade 1988);

10 ♗d3 e6 11 de ♗xe6 12 ♗b5+ ♘c6 13 ♕xd8+ ♖xd8 14 ♖xa7 ♗b4 15 ♗xf6 gf 16 ♘e2 0-0 17 ♖xb7 ♘a5 (Hector – P.-H. Nielsen, Copenhagen 1996). In both cases White cannot aspire to an advantage. So, all the same, he must advance the pawn:

10 b4 ♖c8! 11 ♘b5 ♘c4 12 ♘xa7 (on 12 ♗xf6 he has an effective blockade 12...♗xb5 13 ♗c3 ♘d6!) **12...e6! 13 ♕b3** Taking the rook was not possible in view of the check on b4 – but Black has two pieces under fire at the same time!?

13...♕c7! Everything is hanging by a thread, but will not fall! The queen defends c4, while the rook as before is untouchable – this time because of a check on e5. Moreover, also 13...♕b6!?, which occurred in the game Sveshnikov – Rupert (Budapest 1988), might equally prove sufficient to maintain the intrigue: 14 ♘xc8 ♗xb4+ 15 ♔e2 ♕c5!

14 ♗xf6 (14 ♘f3 ♘e5!? 15 ♗xf6 ♘xf3+ 16 ♔d1 gf 17 gf ♕e5!) **14...gf 15 ♘f3 ♘e5!** From the 12th move the rook was under fire, but... 'the grapes are sour' 16 ♘xc8 ♘xf3+ 17 gf ♕e5+ 18 ♔d2 ♕xa1 19 ♘c2 ♕d4 winning.

16 ♖d1

In the game Pukhyala – Kallio (Lakhti 1997) followed 16...♘xf3+ 17 gf ♕f4!? Worth considering was the simpler **16...♖a8!? 17 de** (17 ♘b5 ♘xf3+ 18 gf ♕e5+ 19 ♔d2 ♖c8, and

how to defend against the check on h6?) **17...fe 18 ♗b5 ♘xf3+ 19 ♕xf3 ♕e5+ 20 ♕e2 ♗xb5 21 ♘xb5 ♗xb4+ 22 ♔f1 ♖a1** winning.

B

6...♗e6!? A move well known from the time of the game Levenfish – Belavenets (Leningrad 1934). 70 years have passed and a refutation still not found.

In striving to prove that the development of the bishop on e6 in itself is artificial, **7 c5** suggests itself. But in the game Gelfand – Dreev (Munich 1994) Black 'unravelled' in five moves: 7...♘e4! 8 ♗h4 ♘xc3 9 bc ♕a5 10 ♕d2 ♗f5 11 a4 e5! Already it is time for White to think about equalisation.

7 ♘ge2 dc 8 ♘f4 looks ideal, and it seems that Black will have problems with countering d4-d5. However, though dangerous, Black seems to get away with taking the d4 pawn: 8...♘xd4 (or 8...♕xd4 9 ♘xe6 ♕e5+! – a recommendation of E.Mortensen) 9 ♘xe6 ♘xe6 10 ♗xc4 ♕xd1+ 11 ♖xd1 a6 12 ♗xe6 fe 13 0-0 h6 14 ♗e3 g6 15 ♘a4 ♗g7 with approximate equality (Kunin – Cherniaev, Port Erin 2000). We mention that after 7 ♘ge2 dc it is naive to count on 8 ♗xf6?! ef 9 d5? in view of 9...♘b4! 10 ♘f4 ♗f5 (Boudre – Miles, Ostend 1986).

White does not manage to pose any problems by 7 ♕d2 g6 8 ♗xf6?! ef 9 c5. After 9...h5! it becomes clear that the position of the white queen is poor: 10 ♗b5 ♗h6! 11 f4 0-0 12 ♗xc6 bc 13 ♘ge2 ♖b8 14 0-0 ♖e8 15 ♖ae1 ♗c8 16 ♘g3 ♗a6 with a comfortable game (Sveshnikov – Oll, Podolsk 1993).

The main continuations are considered to be 7 ♘f3, 7 ♗e2, 7 a3 and 7 ♗xf6.

1) **7 ♘f3 ♘e4!**

It can be shown that 8 ♘xe4 de 9 d5 does not cause Black any trouble: 9...ef 10 de ♕a5+ 11 ♗d2 ♕e5+ 12 ♗e3 ♕xe6 13 ♕xf3 0-0-0 14 ♗e2 g6 15 0-0 ♗g7 16 ♖ab1 ♗d4 (Estrin – Flohr, Vilnius 1960).

Another direct plan – 8 cd ♗xd5 9 ♘xe4 ♗xe4 10 ♗c4 – is also harmless: 10...♕a5+ 11 ♗d2 ♕f5 12 ♘g5 ♗d5 13 ♕b3 ♘xd4 14 ♕a4+ b5! 15 ♗xb5+ ♘xb5 16 ♕xb5+ ♕d7 (A.Minasian – Shurigin, Decin 1996).

Igor Zaitsev suggested **8 ♗d3!? ♘xc3 9 bc dc 10 ♗e4 ♗d5 11 ♕b1!?**

Completing his development is really not so simple, but all the same White's attack should not be underestimated.

Thus, in the game Al. Sokolov – Turov (Nijni Novgorod 1999) Black stood his ground by **11...b6 12 0-0 f6!? 13 ♗f4 g6 14 ♖e1 e6 15 ♕b5 ♔f7 16 ♖ab1 ♗xe4 17 ♖xe4 ♕d5**

2) Therefore **7 ♗e2!?** is more cunning – White 'deceives' with the development of his minor pieces. Which one will go to f3? Most likely the knight, but in certain variations – the bishop, when it will attack the d5 square.

However, after **7...♕a5!?** none of White's pretentious novelties can secure him an advantage.

The idea 8 ♗xf6 ef 9 cd ♗xd5 10 ♗f3 is too simple to seem right. Black equalises: 10...♖d8!? 11 ♗xd5 ♖xd5 12 ♘f3 ♗b4 13 ♕e2+ ♔d8! (Gulko – Rogers, Oropesa 1996).

Practice is concentrated around two ideas: 8 ♘f3 and 8 c5.

a) **8 ♘f3 dc 9 0-0 ♖d8 10 ♖e1!?** For the present the experimental sacrifice of a pawn 10 ♕c1?! does not justify itself:

10...h6 11 ♗d2 ♘xd4!? 12 ♘xd4 ♖xd4 13 b4 ♕d8 14 ♗e3 ♖d7

15 ♗d1 a6! 16 b5 ab 17 ♖b1 g5! (Rogers – Dreev, Biel 1993) or

10...♘xd4!? 11 ♘xd4 ♖xd4 12 b4 ♕d8 13 ♗e3 ♖d7 14 ♗xa7 g6 15 ♘b5 ♗g7 16 ♗xc4 ♗f5 17 ♘d4 0-0 18 ♘xf5 gf 19 ♗e3 ♘e4! 20 ♖b1 ♖c7 (Ramesh – Adianto, Madras 1996).

10...b5 11 ♕c1!? b4 12 ♗xf6 bc

13 d5!? ♗xd5 14 ♗xc3 ♕c5 15 ♕f4 e6 16 ♖ad1 For the sacrificed pawn White has somehow managed to develop a fair degree of initiative (Stocek – Zurek, Czech Republic 2003), however there can hardly be any doubt that the theory of this sub-variation will be rewritten in a very short time.

b) **8 c5 ♘e4 9 ♗d2!?** The creation of Alexander Morozevich. The more standard 9 ♘f3 ♗g4 (accepting the pawn sacrifice comes to no good: 9...♘xc3?! 10 bc ♕xc3+ 11 ♗d2 ♕a3 12 ♖b1 with a dangerous initiative for White) 10 ♗d2 ♘xd2 11 ♘xd2 ♗xe2 12 ♘xe2 g6 13 0-0 ♗g7 14 ♘f3 0-0 15 a3 ♕c7 leads to equality (Fedorowicz – Brenninkmeier, Amsterdam 1990).

9...♕c7 10 ♘f3 0-0-0 11 ♘ge2 g5 12 ♗xe4 de 13 ♕a4 ♗g7 14 ♘b5 How can he refuse such a thrust? The more so that the other natural move – 14 ♗xg5 – is far weaker: 14...♘xd4 15 ♘xd4 ♗xd4 16 ♕xa7 ♗xc5 17 ♕a8+ ♕b8 18 ♕a5 b6 19 ♕a4 ♖hg8 etc.

And yet analysis shows that it is worth waiting with the thrust to d5, and firstly defend d4: 14 ♗e3! If 14...h6, then 15 0-0-0, while 14...f5 allows a favourable return to the main idea: 15 ♗xg5 ♘xd4 16 ♘xd4 ♗xd4 17 ♘b5 ♕e5 18 ♖d1 with a strong initiative.

14...♕b8 15 ♗xg5 a6 16 ♘bc3 ♘xd4 Even more dangerous looks the capture on d4 with the bishop, however a direct refutation is something we do not see.

After 16...♘xd4 arises a position, key to the evaluation of the whole plan with 9 ♗d2!?

In the game Morozevich – Anand (Moscow 2002) White started peace negotiations: 17 ♗f4 ♗d7 18 ♕a5 ♘c6 19 ♕a4. A surprising decision, considering Morozevich's fighting qualities. But analysis proves its correctness: if the struggle continues then White risks losing everything; whereas his chances of victory are negligible. Here are some sample variations:

17 ♗xe7 ♗d7 18 ♕d1 ♗g4 19 ♗xd8 (also upon 19 ♗d6 ♖xd6 20 cd ♕xd6 the compensation for the material is most probably sufficient for a draw) **19...♖xd8 20 ♕c1 ♘xe2 21 ♘xe2 ♗xe2 22 ♕g5** (a necessary intermediate move; weaker is 22 ♔xe2 ♕e5) **22...♗b5 23 ♕xg7 ♕f4** (White is the exchange ahead, but the difference in the activity of the pieces might be felt deeply) **24 ♖d1 ♖xd1+ 25 ♔xd1 ♕xf2 26 ♕g4+ f5** (there is also nothing clear after 26...♔d8) **27 ♕g8+ ♔d7 28 ♕xh7+ ♔c6 29 ♕h8 ♔xc5 30 ♕c3+ ♔b6 31 ♕d2 e3!** Both the exchanges and the whimsical dance of the white queen have proved incapable of eradicating the opponent's initiative.

3) **7 a3!?** A non-standard idea, and the man who thought it up was also absolutely non-standard – Kazan master Rashid Nezhmetdinov.

Black's counterplay, associated with ♕d8-a5 and ♘f6-e4, is nipped in the bud: on 7...♕a5? follows 8 b4. This is welcome. The question is this – is it worth spending a whole tempo on such prophylaxis?

It is interesting that in the game Kasparov – Dreev (Moscow 1996)

Black immediately returned the tempo: 7...♗g4?! 8 f3 ♗e6. After 9 c5 g6 10 ♗b5 ♗g7 11 ♘ge2 0-0 12 0-0 ♗f5 13 b4 a6 14 ♗a4 h6 15 ♗e3 began a great struggle (with some advantage to White).

More often seen: 7...g6 or 7...♕d7.

a) Leading to a tough game, devoid of sudden changes, is **7...g6 8 ♗xf6 ef**, and then:

9 ♗e2 ♗h6 10 ♗f3 ♘e7 11 cd ♘xd5 12 ♘ge2 0-0 with approximate equality (Nezhmetdinov – Flohr, Moscow 1961); to combat the impending manoeuvre ♘g1-e2-g3 Black tries to restrict the knight by the advance h5-h4; at an opportune moment the pawn is also ready to go on to h3) 10 ♗b5 ♗h6 11 ♘ge2 0-0 12 0-0 ♖e8 13 b4 h4! 14 f4 ♕d7 15 ♕d2 ♗f5 16 ♖ae1 ♖e7 17 ♘c1 ♖ae8 18 ♖xe7 ♖xe7 (Hebden – Anic, France 2001). In this position White should bring the h4 pawn to a halt, so that he can then deal with it in earnest: 19 h3! But even then Black has chances of maintaining the tension, for example, 19...♗e4 20 ♕f2 g5!

9 **g3!?** (the most ideal) **9...♗h6 10 ♗g2 ♘e7 11 c5 0-0 12 ♘ge2 f5 13 ♕d3 ♕d7 14 0-0 ♔g7 15 ♖fe1 ♘g8 16 ♕b5!** Black has not managed to fully equalise the game (Chabanon – Eliet, France 2001).

b) **7...♕d7!?** A flexible move, as distinct from 7...g6. Black shows the opponent that he is not at all bothered by his undeveloped king's flank. He intends first to castle queenside, and then strike out at the centre; the bishop f8 will somehow get into play.

Most often White reacts with an exchange on f6, but other continuations are also possible:

8 b4 (8 c5 ♘e4!) 8...dc!? (not fearing the pawn fork) 9 ♗xf6 gf 10 d5 0-0-0! 11 ♗xc4 ♘e5 12 ♗b5 ♕c7 13 ♘ge2 (Lanka – Adianto, Adelaide 1990) 13...♔b8!? with counterplay (a recommendation of Z.Lanka);

8 ♗e2 0-0-0! 9 ♗xf6 (leading to a very sharp game is 9 c5 ♘e4! 10 ♘f3 ♗f5 11 ♗f4 f6!? 12 0-0 g5 13 ♗e3 e5! 14 de d4 15 e6! Kobalija – Khalifman, Maikop 1998) 9...gf 10 c5 (or 10 ♗f3 dc!? 11 d5 ♘e5 12 de ♕xe6 13 ♕e2 ♗h6 with an attack for the sacrificed piece, Kharlov – Alvarez, Kanete 1994) 10...♖g8 11 ♔f1 ♗f5 12 ♗b5 e5! (Sveshnikov – Tkachiev, Vienna 1996).

These examples, together with the previous ones, direct one's thoughts to the fact that Black has a certain plan: development of the queen, then castling long, taking on f6 with the g-pawn, and at some moment – e7-e5!

Subsequent events only reinforce this impression. It turns out that Black's play in the variation 6...♗e6 is not at all as chaotic as might appear at first glance.

8 ♗xf6 gf 9 c5 There is a standard reaction to 9 ♗e2: 9...0-0-0 10 c5 ♗f5 (after 10...♖g8 the position on the board is one that we have already examined in the game Sveshnikov – Tkachiev) 11 ♘f3 e5! 12 b4 ♖g8. The reply to 13 0-0 should not be 13...♗h3?! 14 g3 ♗xf1 15 ♗xf1, as occurred in the game C.Hansen – Hector (Malmo 1998), but 13...♗e4!? 14 g3 ♕h3 15 de fe 16 ♖e1 f5! In such positions the extra exchange is worth far less than the possibility of continuing the attack.

In the game Topalov – Leko (Vienna 1996) the move 9 g3 was seen. And once again Black achieved a comfortable game by just repeating the basic idea of the variation: 9...0-0-0 10 ♗g2 ♗g4! 11 f3 ♗e6 12 c5 (on 12 f4 ♗g4 13 ♕a4 Leko had prepared 13...e5! 14 cd ♘xd4 with the initiative) 12...♗f5! 13 b4 e5 14 ♘ge2 ♕e6!

9...♗g4 10 f3 ♗f5 11 ♗b5 On the board we have a critical position of the variation.

A recommendation of the well-known Latvian theoretician Zigurds Lanka – 11...h5 12 ♘ge2 ♗h6 13 0-0 ♖g8 – passed the test in the

European junior championship (Patras 1999). The game Edrichka – Berescu continued 14 ♔h1 ♖d8 15 ♕e1 ♔f8 16 ♕h4 a6 17 ♗a4 ♗g5 18 ♕f2 ♗d3 19 ♖ad1 ♕f5. Black has an acceptable game, but no more.

Interesting is 11...♖g8!?, immediately engaging in play along the g-file. Black thereby provokes a weakening of the opponent's kingside pawn structure: 12 g4 ♗g6 13 ♘ge2 h5 14 gh ♗xh5 15 ♘g3 ♖h8 16 ♕e2 ♗g6 17 f4 ♖h4 18 0-0 ♗h6 19 ♖ae1 ♔f8 20 f5 ♗h7. Black's position certainly looks wild but there is undoubted counterplay (Sveshnikov – Soln, Bled 1998).

But it is best not to split hairs and play, as we have already repeatedly observed: **11...e5! 12 ♘ge2 0-0-0!** After **13 0-0** Black, in the game Lanka – Leko (Budapest 1996), preferred 13...♕e6 14 ♔h1 ♗h6, and here, in Lanka's opinion, 15 b4!? followed by ♗xc6 and b4-b5 allows White to count on an attack. More accurate is **13...♗h6!? 14 ♔h1 ♖hg8 15 ♕a4** (Izoria – Mastrovasilis, Athens 2003). Here the opponents agreed a draw, though from Black's side this decision looks premature. Possible, even if there is nothing else, is **15...a6 16 ♗xc6 ♕xc6 17 ♕b3 ♔b8 18 ♖ad1 ♗e6,** and White still has a struggle for equality in prospect.

4) **7 ♗xf6** (the most principled) **7...gf!?** First played in the game Miles – Yusupov (Tunis 1985). Black easily won this game! The idea 7...gf made such an indelible impression on the Englishman that subsequently he himself began to capture with the g-pawn.

The other capture – 7...ef has now completely gone out of fashion, though it is also possible: 8 c5 a6!? 9 ♘ge2 b6 10 b4 ♗e7 11 ♕a4 b5 12 ♕b3 a5! 13 ♘xb5 ab 14 ♘f4 ♕a5 15 ♗d3 ♖b8 16 ♘xd5 0-0 17 0-0 ♖xb5 18 ♗xb5 ♕xb5 19 ♖fe1. Here, in the game Yurtaev – Dreev (Frunze 1988), Black replied with bishop to d8, whereas worth considering was 19...♖d8!? 20 ♘xe7+ (no good is 20 ♖xe6!? fe 21 ♘c7 in view of 21...♘xd4! 22 ♘xb5 ♘xb3 23 ab ♗xc5) 20...♘xe7 with the better chances.

The position after 7...gf!? is rather 'one-sided'. Black's play is simple and understandable – long castling, play on the g-file, preparation for e7-e5 etc. But what will White do? It is necessary to say that the majority of players will not be up to the task and will very quickly be forced to fight not for the advantage but already for a draw.

Thus in the original game was played 8 ♕d2 ♕a5 9 c5 0-0-0 10 ♗b5 ♖g8 11 f4 ♗h6 12 ♕f2? ♘b4 13 ♖d1

♗f5 14 a3 ♘c2+ 15 ♔d2 ♗e4, and after a few moves Miles resigned. Actually it is difficult to point out exactly where the decisive mistake was made – rather White's whole plan was wrong.

There are two main ideas: 8 ♘f3 or 8 c5.

a) **8 ♘f3** For the time being not resolving the pawn tension in the centre – first of all White wants to complete his development. Reasonable, but the opponent, seeing that in the near future he is not threatened with anything, also develops his pieces to their best squares. If nobody threatens anything then equality is reached. Or an immediate draw.

Thus, in the game Adams – Leko (Frankfurt 1999) the opponents completed their development almost without coming into contact with one another: 8...♗g7 9 ♗e2 0-0 10 0-0 ♕d7 11 ♖c1 ♖fd8 12 cd ♗xd5 13 ♘xd5 ♕xd5 14 ♗c4 ♕d7 15 ♕e2 e6 16 ♖fd1 ♘e7 and Black has a simple, comfortable game.

Also quite popular is **8...♕d7**, for example, 9 c5?! ♗g4 10 ♗e2 ♗xf3 11 ♗xf3 e6 12 0-0 ♗g7 13 ♗e2 a6 14 ♕a4 0-0 15 ♖fd1 f5! (Sax – Miles, Wijk aan Zee 1989) or

9 ♗e2 ♖d8 10 cd ♗xd5 11 ♘xd5 ♕xd5 12 0-0 ♗h6 13 ♕c2 0-0 14 ♗d3 ♘xd4 15 ♘xd4 ♕xd4 16 ♖ad1 ♔h8 17 ♖fe1 e6 18 ♗xh7 ♕b6 19 ♗d3 f5 (Fedorowicz – Miles, USA 1988). In all previous examples Black did not experience the slightest

problem in achieving equality.

b) **8 c5** Continuing the principal line, beginning with the move 7 ♗xf6. The problem is – that 'principal' still does not mean 'good'.

8...♕d7!? 9 ♗b5 ♖g8 10 g3 0-0-0! In the game Mainka – Miles (Bad Worishofen 1989) Black carried out a multi-move combination with a rook sacrifice: **11 ♕h5 ♗g4 12 ♕xh7 ♕e6+ 13 ♔f1**

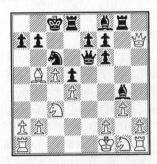

13...♘xd4! 14 ♕xg8 ♗h6 15 ♗e8 ♗h3+ 16 ♘xh3 ♕xh3+ 17 ♔e1 ♘c2+ 18 ♔e2 ♕h5+ 19 g4 ♕e5+ 20 ♔f3 ♘xa1 21 ♖xa1 d4! 22 ♘e2 d3 23 ♘c3 ♕xh2, and after a few moves he won. An impressive rout!

In the variation 6...♗e6!? the analysts still have a wealth of work to do.

C

6...♗g4?! (a sharp and, in our view, rightly forgotten move) **7 ♗e2** Also 7 ♕a4!? e6 8 cd ed 9 ♗b5 ♕d6 looks very sympathetic (Waitzkin – Blankenay, Chicago 1997) 10 ♗xf6 gf 11 ♔f1!

7...♗xe2 8 ♘gxe2 dc 9 d5 ♘e5 10 0-0 Let's assume that he succeeds in stirring up Black's position – to whose benefit will this be?

1 e4 c6 2 d4 d5 3 ed cd 4 c4 ♘f6 5 ♘c3 ♘c6 6 ♗g5

The game Mortensen – Birnboim (Haifa 1976) continued: 10...e6 11 ♕d4 h6 12 ♕xe5 hg 13 de ♗d6 14 ♕b5+ ♔f8 15 ♘g3 ♕b6. By transposing to the endgame – 16 ♕xb6 ab 17 ♖fe1, White retained the advantage.

Black acted more aggressively in the game Tal – Bronstein (Leningrad 1971): **10...h6 11 ♗f4 ♘g6 12 ♕a4+ ♕d7 13 ♕xc4 ♖c8 14 ♕b3 e5 15 de ♕xe6 16 ♕xb7** He lacks a single tempo to complete his development. **16...♗c5 17 ♘d4! ♗xd4 18 ♖ae1** winning.

D

6...♕b6?! A move combined with an idea devised and tested (in 1934 in a game against Spielmann) by the Czech Josef Reijfir. The first time everything turned out well – Spielmann played 7 c5? and after 7...♕xb2 8 ♘ge2 ♗f5 he did not obtain compensation for the pawn. After losing the game, Spielmann added the move 6...♕b6 to his own armoury. But he didn't have much luck: the first person he played queen to b6 against was Botvinnik.

7 cd!

In the game Botvinnik – Spielmann (Moscow 1935) Black lost his head and quickly succumbed: 7...♕xb2? 8 ♖c1 ♘b4 9 ♘a4 ♕xa2 10 ♗c4 ♗g4 11 ♘f3 ♗xf3 12 gf. A piece is lost – game over.

Unsatisfactory is 7...♘xd5?! 8 ♘xd5 ♕a5+ 9 ♘c3 ♕xg5. Black has developed only two pieces – and both are continually falling under attack. For example, 10 ♘f3 ♕f4 11 ♗b5 ♗d7 12 0-0 0-0-0 13 ♖c1 ♔b8 14 ♘e5! ♘xe5 15 de ♕xe5 16 ♕d3 ♕d6 17 ♖fd1 with a win (L.Guliev – Grigantis, St.Petersburg 1997).

Only by finding the one defence **7...♘xd4!**, can Black once again get interested in Rejfir's variation. The search first gathers pace around the moves 8 ♘ge2 and 8 ♗e3.

8 ♘ge2!? ♘f5 9 ♕d2 h6 10 ♗xf6 ef 11 ♘g3 ♗d6 12 ♗b5+ ♔f8 13 ♘ge4 ♗e5 14 0-0 g6 15 a4 a6. In this complicated position the opponents concluded a peace. (Polugaevsky – Bagirov, Alma Ata 1969).

8 ♗e3 e5 9 de ♗c5!? 10 ef+ ♔e7! (a real gambit!) 11 ♗c4 ♗g4!? (worse is 11...♖d8 12 ♘f3 ♕xb2 because of the surprising knight

50

sacrifice: 13 0-0! ♕xc3 14 ♖c1 ♕b2 15 ♖e1 ♔f8 16 ♘xd4 ♗xd4 17 ♕d3!, Romanov – Flerov, correspondence game, 1976) 12 ♕c1 ♗f5 13 ♗xd4 ♗xd4 14 ♕d2 ♖hc8 15 ♕e2+ ♔f8

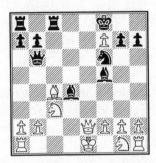

The position is extremely confusing, and it is not absolutely certain that White can extricate himself from his situation without loss. Thus, in the game Shardtner – Szallai (Budapest 1969) after 16 ♘f3 Black delivered the next sacrifice – 16...♖xc4!? 17 ♕xc4 ♗xf2+ 18 ♔f1 ♕xb2 19 ♖d1 ♗b6 – retaining the initiative.

But as soon as the move **8 ♘f3!** was discovered, Black once again (and this time finally) lost any interest in Rejfir's variation.

8...♕xb2 (he is prepared to suffer just for a pawn) **9 ♖c1 ♘xf3+ 10 ♕xf3 h6 11 ♗d2 a6 12 ♗c4 g6**

White has practically finished his development, whereas Black is lined up on the first rank. There is nothing surprising in the fact that White combines easily with a great supply of solidity.

13 d6! ♕a3 14 0-0 ♕xd6 15 ♘e4 ♕b6 16 ♗a5! ♕xa5 17 ♘xf6+ ef 18 ♖fe1+ ♗e7 19 ♕xf6 0-0 20 ♕xg6+ ♔h8 21 ♕xh6+ ♔g8 22 ♖xe7 winning (Rausis – Berges, Yvres 2002).

E

6...♕a5!? First encountered in the game Keres – Czerniak (Buenos Aires 1939). With this queen sortie the game turns out no less sharp than upon 6...♕b6?!, but Black's ambitions this time have far more basis. In the first instance he threatens ♘f6-e4, but even if he fails to achieve this, his claim for free development with visions of counterattack might still bring him quite a few dividends.

White can simply capture on f6; he can counter the jump of the knight to e4 directly (7 ♗d2, 7 ♕d2) or indirectly (7 a3), and can take the view that this is of no concern (7 ♘f3).

1) **7 ♗xf6 ef** Taking with the e-pawn is useful not only on general considerations; now on 8 c5?! there is the counter-blow 8...♗xc5! 9 dc d4, and Black's chances are at least no worse: 10 ♕a4 dc 11 ♕xa5 ♘xa5 12 ♗b5+ ♗d7 13 ♗xd7+ ♔xd7 14 0-0-0+ ♔c6 15 b4 ♘c4 16 ♘e2 (J.Polgar – Aguirre, Oviedo 1992). Here he should play 16...a5!, and White is forced to repeat moves: 17 ♘d4+ ♔c7 18 ♘b5+ etc.

8 cd Worth considering is 8 a3!? This idea was worked out in the 30s of the last century by the Soviet master Sergei Belavenets. White's threatened pressure on the queen's flank (c4-c5, b2-b4) forces the opponent to give up the centre:

8...dc 9 ♗xc4 ♗d6 (possible is 9...♗e7 10 d5 ♘e5 11 ♗b5+ ♗d7 12 ♗xd7+ ♘xd7 13 ♘f3 ♕a6!? 14 ♕e2 ♕xe2+ 15 ♔xe2 ♘e5 with an approximately level endgame, Kobalija – S.Guliev, Yalta 1996) 10 ♕e2+ ♔f8 11 ♕d2.

White seems to have prevented the manoeuvre g7-g6 followed by ♔f8-g7. In the game Ljubojevic – Adams (Belgrade 1995) Black took the opponent at his word and after 11...♗e6 12 ♗xe6 fe 13 ♘f3 ♔f7

14 0-0 ♖ad8 15 d5! he was forced to reconcile himself to a somewhat worse position.

But we think that the move 11...g6!? is still possible and, more than that, it is best. For example, 12 ♕h6+ ♔g8 13 ♘ge2 ♘e7 14 ♘g3 ♘f5 15 ♘xf5 ♕xf5, and the queen will not hang around very long on h6.

8...♗b4! Black's plan begins to manifest itself. It turns out that the win of a piece leads to a forced draw by perpetual check: 9 dc ♗xc3+ 10 bc ♕xc3+ 11 ♔e2 0-0 (also possible is an immediate 11...♕b2+ 12 ♔e1 ♕c3+) 12 f3 ♖e8+ 13 ♔f2 ♕e3+ 14 ♔g3 ♕g5+ (Zilberstein – Podgaets, Belzy 1997). The knight must be defended, but how?

9 ♕d2 ♗xc3 Events turn to an extremely confusing scenario after 9...♘e7?!

Before it was considered that White obtained the advantage by 10 ♗b5+ ♔d8 11 ♘ge2:

11...♘xd5 12 ♗c4 ♗e6 13 ♗xd5 ♗xd5 14 0-0 ♗c4 15 ♖fe1 ♖e8 16 a3 ♗d6 17 ♘g3 (Jansa – Vukic, Belgrade 1977) or

11...♗xc3 12 ♘xc3 ♘xd5 13 a4! ♗e6 14 0-0 ♖c8 15 ♖fc1 ♘xc3

16 d5! ♗d7 17 bc (Vaisser – Sveshnikov, Sochi 1983).

But in the game Sveshnikov – S.Guliev (Vladivostok 1994) Black made an important correction: the endgame after 10...♕xb5! 11 ♘xb5 ♗xd2+ 12 ♔xd2 ♘xd5 was harmless for him.

And yet the last word in this variation for the present remains with White: instead of 10 ♗b5+ more refined is 10 d6!? ♘d5, and only now 11 ♗b5+ ♗d7 12 ♗xd7+ ♔xd7 13 ♘ge2 ♖ac8 14 0-0 ♖c6 15 ♕d3 ♘xc3 16 bc ♗xd6 17 c4 with the advantage (Hamdouchi – Gonzalez, Malaga 1998).

10 bc ♕xd5 11 ♘e2 With the aim of ejecting the queen from its central position. The more natural 11 ♘f3 0-0 12 ♗e2 does not offer a tangible advantage in view of 12...♗g4! 13 0-0 ♘e5!

This exchanging combination leads the position to a draw: 14 ♘xe5 ♗xe2 15 ♕xe2 fe 16 de ♖fe8 17 ♖fe1 ♖ac8 18 ♖ad1 ♕a5 19 c4 ♕c3 20 ♖d7 b5!, and the b-pawn is untouchable because of 21...♖xe5! (Dueball – Libo, Germany 1988).

11...0-0 12 ♘f4 ♕a5 Hardly worth considering is 12... ♖e8+?! 13 ♗e2

♕d6. After 14 0-0 ♗f5 15 ♖fe1 ♖ac8 16 ♗f3 it is impossible to understand what Black has achieved with his intermediate check (Gulko – Gonzalez, Las Palmas 1996).

An immediate 12...♕d6 looks stronger, for example, 13 ♗e2 ♗f5 14 0-0 ♖ac8 15 ♖ac1, and the saved tempo can be spent on 15...♖fd8!? (Ornstein – Shamkovich, Gausdal 1984).

13 ♗e2 ♖d8 (in passing – a little trap: 14 0-0? ♖xd4!) **14 ♖d1**

Can Black restrain the pawn pair c3+d4? Can he get his own counterplay going, and if so, then where, in which part of the board? On this complex question perhaps depends the assessment of the whole variation 7 ♗xf6.

In the game Sveshnikov – Bagirov (Tbilisi 1978), right up to the end Black was not able to cope with solving the problems and after 14...♗f5 15 0-0 ♖ac8 16 ♕b2 ♕c7 17 g3 b6 18 ♗f3 he stood worse.

Bagirov showed more confidence in the same USSR championship (Tbilisi 1978) against Belyavsky: 14...♗e6!? 15 d5 ♘e5 16 c4 ♕c5 17 ♘d3 ♘xd3+ 18 ♕xd3 ♗d7 19 0-0 ♖ac8 etc.

Possibly the most important information about this position – is the recommendation of Evgeny Sveshnikov: **14...b6!? 15 0-0 ♗a6 16 ♖fe1 ♗xe2 17 ♖xe2 ♘e5! 18 ♕e1 ♘g6 19 ♘xg6 hg** The minor pieces are exchanged, and White's hanging pawns in the centre are rather weak.

2) **7 ♗d2** Not aspiring to much, as after **7...dc 8 ♗xc4 e6** it is not easy for White to justify the manoeuvre ♗c1-g5-d2. Three wasted moves have led only to the dark squared bishop running back in fear to its own pieces:

9 d5!? An attempt to force the game. In a quiet struggle – **9 ♘f3 ♗e7 10 ♘d5 ♕d8 11 ♘xe7 ♘xe7!** **12 0-0 ♗d7 13 ♗g5 ♗c6 14 ♖e1 h6 15 ♗h4** (Tal – Marovic, Malaga 1981) **15...♘f5** – White's chances are also not great.

9...ed 10 ♘xd5 ♕d8 11 ♕e2+ ♗e6 12 ♘f4 ♘d4 13 ♘xe6 fe 14 ♕d3 ♕b6!

White has managed to spoil the opponent's pawn structure and at the same time obtain the advantage of the two bishops. However this has left him still further behind in development. Therefore Black is counting on long castling, so as to develop immediate counterplay with support of the rook d8:

15 ♘e2 0-0-0 16 0-0 e5 17 ♘xd4 ♕xd4 18 ♕h3+ ♔b8 19 ♗a5 b6 20 ♕b3 ♗c5 21 ♗c3 ♕f4 22 g3 ♕g5 23 ♖ae1 e4!? (forced, but a promising sacrifice of a pawn) **24 ♗xf6 ♕xf6 25 ♖xe4 g5 26 ♕c2 h5!** With opposite coloured bishops the extra pawn has no significance. Moreover the menacing open h-file is unpleasant for White. He hurriedly offered a draw, which was accepted (Bronstein – Bagirov, Tallinn 1981).

3) **7 ♕d2!?** A move which upon a superficial glance looks dry. In fact White is urging the opponent to continue his over-aggressive play, as well as looking for a defence that will lead to an advantage for himself.

For example, **7...♗f5**, with the idea of a knight jump to b4, is parried by **8 ♘f3!** (but not **8 ♗xf6?!** ef **9 cd** precisely because of **9...♘b4!** **10 ♗b5+ ♔d8 11 ♔f1 ♘xd5** with unclear play, Gavrikov – Matulovic, Vrsac 1985) **8...♘b4 9 ♖c1 dc 10 ♗xc4 ♖c8 11 ♘e5!**

Black's raid has almost been beaten off and already White threatens the f7 square. On **11...e6** there is **12 ♗b5+ ♘c6 13 d5!** with decisive threats. In the game Vescovi – Moreda (San Vincent 2001) a combination occurred to Black: 11...♖xc4? 12 ♘xc4 ♕a6. He actually wins back the material but by now the game cannot be saved: 13 0-0! ♕xc4 14 ♕f4! ♕c8 15 ♘b5 ♘c6 16 ♗xf6 gf 17 d5 etc.

Well known to theory is also the sharp variation 7...dc?! 8 ♗xc4 e5 9 d5 ♘d4. It seems that Black's idea is irreproachable: he has established his knight in the centre and controls all the important squares. But the knight is unstable and White can exploit this: 10 f4! ♗d6 (according to an analysis by Keres, 10...♗f5 is no good because of 11 fe! ♘c2+ 12 ♔f1 ♘xa1 13 ef with an attack) 11 ♘ge2 ♘f5 12 ♗b5+ ♗d7 13 ♗xf6 gf 14 ♗xd7+ ♔xd7 15 0-0 ♘e3 16 ♖f3 ♘g4.

In the game Keres – Czerniak (from which, we recall, started the theory of the variation 6...♕a5) White, with a few accurate moves, brought clarity to what seems at first sight a confusing position:

17 ♕d3! ♖ag8 (the win of the exchange – 17...♕b6+ 18 ♔h1 ♘f2+ 19 ♖xf2 ♕xf2 – echoes badly after

20 ♕b5+ ♔d8 21 ♘e4!) 18 ♔h1 ♕b6 19 ♖af1 ♗c8 20 h3 h5 21 ♘e4 ♔b8 22 ♕b3! with a great advantage.

7...♗e6 8 ♗xf6!? Played according to the proverb 'better a bird in the hand than two in the bush'. There is more scope in 8 c5, but in the endgame after 8...♘e4!? 9 ♘xe4 de 10 ♕xa5 ♘xa5, for the present White cannot boast of any tangible achievements:

11 ♗b5+ ♘c6 12 ♘e2 0-0-0 13 ♗e3 ♘b4! (Lerner – Sveshnikov, Leningrad 1976) or

11 ♗d2 ♘c6 12 ♗c3 0-0-0 13 ♘e2 ♗c4! (Ribli – Torre, Alicante 1983).

8...ef 9 c5 a6!? In the game T.Ivanov – Timofeev (St.Petersburg 2001) Black did not want to prevent the bishop going to b5, and, perhaps, rightly so: after 9...g6 10 ♗b5 ♗g7 11 ♘ge2 0-0 White has the greater possibilities for active play.

10 ♘f3 b6!? 11 cb ♖b8 12 ♗d3 ♗e7 13 0-0 0-0 14 a3 ♕xb6 15 b4 g6 16 ♗b1 ♖fd8 17 ♗a2 White's advantage is either extremely small or nothing at all. (Seils – Dizdarevic, Soln 1996).

4) **7 a3** This is frequently (and successfully) played by the Latvian theoretician Zigurds Lanka.

We have already come across the prophylactic idea of the move a2-a3 – White tries to generate counterplay, connected with ♕d8-a5 and ♘f6-e4. But in the present situation prophylaxis is too late: if 7...♘e4 is met by 8 b4?!, then after 8...♘xc3 9 ♕c1 ♕d8 10 ♕xc3 dc White stands worse. Then why does he play 7 a3!? Obviously to provoke the knight jump to e4!

a) **7...♘e4?!** White has a choice: 8 cd or 8 ♗d2

a1) **8 cd ♘xc3 9 bc ♕xd5 10 ♘f3 ♗g4** In this position we must consider 11 ♗e3 e6 12 ♗e2 ♗e7 13 0-0 0-0 14 c4 ♕a5 with a complicated struggle, for example: 15 ♖b1 ♕c7 16 d5 ed 17 cd ♗xf3 18 ♗xf3 ♘e5 19 ♗e2 (Ribli – Kuczynski, Polanica Zdroj 1993) 19...♖xa3! 20 ♕b3 ♗d6 21 ♖fc1 ♕d7 22 ♕xb7 ♕xb7 23 ♖xb7 a5, and such an endgame most frequently ends in a draw.

But in the game Voitsekhovsky – Timofeev (St.Petersburg 2002) like a bolt from the blue came **11 ♗e2!?** White sacrifices a piece even though it is unclear when it will be regained. Nevertheless Black's defence is not very easy:

11...♗xf3 12 ♗xf3 ♕xg5 13 ♕a4 ♖c8 14 0-0 e6 Losing is 14...♕f5 15 d5 b5!? 16 ♕xb5 ♔d8 (not possible is 16...e6 17 ♕a4 ed? 18 ♗g4) because of 17 ♗g4! ♕xg4 18 dc ♔e8 19 ♖ad1 f6 20 ♖d4 ♕e6 21 c7+ ♔f7 22 ♖d8!

15 ♖fb1 Precisely this rook! On 15 ♖ab1? ♕e7 16 d5 ♕xa3 the whole of White's game goes to pot.

15...♕d2!? At the board Artem Timofeev did not decide on this move, but analysis shows that only in this way is it possible to continue the struggle:

16 ♖xb7 ♕xc3 17 ♖ab1 ♗d6 18 ♖7b3 ♕c2 19 d5 ♗c5 20 dc, and he needs to choose between two captures on f2. Whatever, Black will hold on.

This idea of Voitsekhovsky does not inspire us, but there is one more interesting path in store:

a2) **8 ♗d2!? ♘xd2 9 b4!?**

Here too the move a2-a3 is appropriate! Incidentally, the law-giver of fashion in this variation, Zigurds Lanka, has played exactly this move 9 b4, but also suggested completing White's development first – 9 ♕xd2 dc 10 ♗xc4 e6 11 ♘f3 ♗e7

12 0-0 0-0, and only now 13 b4!? In the game Lanka – S.Guliev (Cappelle la Grande 1997) Black reacted poorly: 13...♕h5?! (more solid is 13...♕c7), and White began a queen hunt: 14 ♘e4 ♖d8 15 ♖fe1 b6 16 ♘g3 ♕g4 17 ♖e4 ♕g6 18 ♖ae1 ♗f6 19 h3!

But all the same an immediate 9 b4!? is more interesting, the more so that White risks nothing. This is how further events might develop:

9...♕d8 10 ♕xd2 dc 11 d5 ♘e5 12 ♕d4 ♘g6 13 ♘f3 e5!? (a forced sacrifice of a pawn, otherwise Black will not manage to complete his development) **14 ♘xe5 ♕e7?!** Transferring to an endgame looks more reliable: 14...♘xe5!? 15 ♕xe5+ ♕e7 16 ♕xe7+ ♗xe7 17 ♗xc4 ♗f5 18 0-0 ♖c8 19 ♗b5+ ♔d8 (Palac – Dizdarevic, Skopje 2002). The pawn will probably be recovered, and Black will be able to moor to a drawing haven.

15 ♔d2! Obviously Black is counting on the pin along the e-file, but the game is up: 15...♘xe5? 16 ♖e1 f6 17 f4 with a quick win (Blehm – Yakupovic, Hallsberg 1999).

15...♕g5+ 16 f4 ♘xf4 17 ♘f3 ♕h6 18 ♖e1+ ♔d8 19 ♖e3! Leaving no doubt as to the assessment of the position. There could still follow 19...♗d6 20 g3 ♘g6 21 ♘e4 ♘e7 22 ♘xd6 ♕xd6 23 ♕xg7 ♕xd5+ 24 ♔c1 ♖g8 25 ♕f6 ♗e6 26 ♗h3!, and Black is in for it.

Disappointed in the results of the move 7...♘e4?! Black switched to another continuation:

b) **7...dc!? 8 d5 ♘e4!?** As shown by the Lanka game, weak is 8...♘e5?! 9 ♕d4!, and then:

9...♘d3+ 10 ♗xd3 cd 11 ♘f3! (in White's play there is something of the famous Botvinnik – Flohr game examined above, did you notice?) 11...♗f5 12 0-0 ♖d8 13 ♘h4! ♗d7 14 ♖fe1 ♕b6 15 ♕xd3 (Lanka – Fridman, Vilnius 1993) or

9...h6 10 ♗d2 ♘d3+ 11 ♗xd3 cd 12 ♘f3 e6 13 0-0 ♘xd5 14 ♖fe1! ♘xc3 15 ♗xc3 (Lanka – Pingintzer, Oberwart 1998), in both cases with a menacing initiative.

The position after 8...♘e4 deserves a diagram.

In the game Kovacevic – Dizdarevic (Istanbul 2000) the opponents, alike, frightened of getting their hands dirty, rushed headlong for a draw: 9 ♗d2 ♘xd2 10 ♕xd2 ♘e5 11 ♕d4 ♕c7 12 ♘b5 ♕a5+ 13 ♘c3 ♕c7. However we are interested in a forcing continuation of play:

9 dc!? ♘xg5 10 cb ♗xb7 11 ♗xc4 ♗c6 (on 11...♖c8 unpleasant is 12 ♗b5+ ♗c6 13 ♗xc6+ ♖xc6 14 b4!) **12 b4 ♕e5+ 13 ♘ge2 ♖d8 14 ♕b3** Leaving behind the opening, it is not easy to evaluate the chances of the two sides. Probably, they are still slightly superior for White.

5) **7 ♘f3!?** White takes the view that the opponent's idea (♕d8-a5 and ♘f6-e4) is none of his business!

The fact of the matter is that after 7... ♘e4?! 8 cd! ♘xc3 9 bc ♕xd5 10 ♗e2 a position is reached, more characteristic of the Grunfeld defence, but with an extra tempo for White. Which means that he has nothing to fear from 7...♘e4.

Also insufficient for equality is 7...♗e6 8 c5 ♘e4 9 ♗d2! ♘xd2 10 ♕xd2. In the game M.Tseitlin – Dizdarevic (Belgrade 1999) there followed 10...g6 11 ♗b5 ♗g7 12 0-0 0-0 13 ♗xc6 bc 14 ♖fe1 ♖fe8 15 a3 ♕c7 16 b4 ♗d7 17 b5! ♖ab8 18 a4. It is possible that White's advantage is not as great as it seems, but the fact that he has all the play – is beyond question.

7...♗g4! Black feels that there is something a bit better than the knight jump to e4. White's pieces are again pinned down and when the rook arrives on d8 Black's position will start to look particularly attractive.

White needs to do something quickly. But what? Weak is 8 ♗e2? dc 9 d5 because of 9...0-0-0! After

10 ♗xc4 e6 11 ♗xf6 gf 12 0-0 ♖g8! 13 ♗e2 ed! The way it is all coming together for Black couldn't be better (Uusi – Bagirov, Tallinn 1981).

Also not dangerous for Black is 8 cd ♘xd5 9 ♗d2 (suggested by Grigory Ravinsky).

Ravinsky's idea lies in a temporary queen sacrifice: 9...♘xd4? 10 ♘xd4! ♗xd1 11 ♗b5+ ♔d8 12 ♘xd5 etc. But the simpler 9...e6 10 ♗c4 ♗b4 dashes White's fantasy: 11 ♗xd5 ed 12 0-0 0-0 13 a3 ♗e7 14 h3 ♗h5 15 ♖e1 ♗f6 16 ♘e4 ♕d8 with equality (Klundt – Fette, Germany 1983).

The complications after 8 ♗xf6 ef 9 cd ♗b4! also turned in Black's favour: 10 ♕b3 (losing is 10 dc? ♗xc3+ 11 bc ♕xc3+ 12 ♔e2 0-0!) 10...♗xf3 11 dc ♗xc6 12 a3 (or 12 ♗c4 ♗a4! 13 ♗xf7+ ♔f8 14 ♕c4 ♗b5 15 ♕b3 ♖d8!, Alburt – Ruderfer, Dneprpetrovsk 1970) 12...♗xc3+ 13 ♕xc3 ♕d5 14 f3 ♕g5 15 ♔f2 0-0-0 16 ♖d1 ♔b8 17 ♗c4 ♖d7 18 ♖d2 ♖c8, and the winner can only be Black (van den Doel – van der Sterren, Rotterdam 2000).

Here it also turns out that the right move can only be found by the process of elimination. If everything else is bad, there remains...

8 ♕b3! What, for all that, makes the variation 7 ♘f3!? interesting? The two sides exchange surprises and one cannot say that these surprises will be pleasant for the opponent.

8...0-0-0 9 ♗xf6 Letting Black decide what is more important to him: reliability with his sights on a draw or playing va banque. Players who value reliability above all else will prefer 9...ef!? 10 cd (or 10 0-0-0 dc 11 ♕xc4 ♗xf3 12 gf ♔b8) 10...♗xf3 (leading to unclear consequences is 10...♖e8+ 11 ♗e2 ♖xe2+! 12 ♔f1!) 11 dc ♗xc6 12 0-0-0 ♗d6 with an acceptable game.

9...gf!? And, all the same, risk – it's a matter of honour!

A move far from being new, but here is the assessment... Many respected commentators clearly overestimated the strength of this move. In fact Black is taking a risk, and a high one!

10 cd ♘b4 11 ♗c4 (Botvinnik suggested not clinging on to the pawn, but playing simply 11 ♘d2) **11...♔b8 12 a3 e6 13 de fe 14 0-0 ♗xf3 15 ab ♖g8 16 g3 ♕h5**

17 ♖fc1?! (stronger is an immediate 17 ♗xe6) **17...♖xd4** This is how the game Martin – Baljon (Las Palmas 1977) continued. Two weak moves – 18 ♘b5? ♖d2 19 ♕e3?, and after 19...♖xg3+! there was no stopping Black.

He should play **18 ♗xe6!**, after which it is not clear how Black pursues the attack.

No good are either 18...♖xg3+!? 19 fg ♗c5!? 20 bc ♖d2 21 ♘e2! ♖xe2 22 h4!, or 18...♗h6 19 ♘e2! ♗xe2 20 ♖c5! (the same move also follows upon 19...♖h4). Finally, on **18...♗d6** again decides **19 ♘e2! ♖h4 20 ♖a5 ♗e5 21 ♖ac5**, and White wins.

The idea of Abram Rabinovich 1 e4 c6 2 d4 d5 3 ed cd 4 c4 ♘f6 5 ♘c3 ♘c6 6 ♗g5!? will soon be more than 100 years old, but questions not only do not diminish but, on the contrary, increase and multiply.

Is it possible to play 6...dc!? And if so, then what must White do: offer a gambit with the move 7 ♗xc4!? Or play in the centre: 7 d5!? And if in the centre, then how to react to 7...♘a5!? And how to win after 7...♘e5 8 ♕d4 h6!?

How can Black be punished for 6...♗e6!? You see, he cannot delay his own development in such an artificial way and remain unpunished. And how to obtain the advantage after 6...♛a5!?

Old theory reinvents itself – this is natural, but the new does not rush to occupy some free place. Does this mean that a variation is bad? Nothing of the sort. It means that its time has not yet come.

Index to Chapter Two

1 e4 c6 2 d4 d5 3 ed cd 4 c4 ♘f6		**b)** 7...♕d7	46
5 ♘c3 ♘c6 6 ♗g5	36	**4)** 7 ♗xf6	48
A. 6...dc	37	7...gf	
1) 7 ♗xc4	37	**a)** 8 ♘f3	49
a) 7...♕xd4	37	**b)** 8 c5	49
b) 7...e6	38	**C.** 6...♗g4	49
2) 7 d5	40	**D.** 6...♕b6	50
a) 7...♘e5	40	**E.** 6...♕a5	51
b) 7...♘a5	42	**1)** 7 ♗xf6	52
B. 6...♗e6	43	**2)** 7 ♗d2	54
1) 7 ♘f3	44	**3)** 7 ♕d2	54
2) 7 ♗e2	44	**4)** 7 a3	55
7...♕a5		**a)** 7...♘e4	56
a) 8 ♘f3	44	**a1)** 8 cd	56
b) 8 c5	45	**a2)** 8 ♗d2	56
3) 7 a3	46	**b)** 7...dc	57
a) 7...g6	46	**5)** 7 ♘f3	58

Chapter Three

1 e4 c6 2 d4 d5 3 ed cd 4 c4 ♘f6
5 ♘c3 g6!?

After this move the game enters a completely different scenario from the previous chapters. Combinational storms give way to a strict positional struggle; and first and foremost comes the ability to play complex endgames.

In fianchettoing his bishop, Black must be prepared to sacrifice the d5 pawn which, however, he hopes to recover after ♘b8-d7-b6 (or ♘b8-a6-c7). In order to defend the pawn, White will have to lose several tempi. As a result Black will outstrip the opponent in development and hope to obtain compensation (and also organise pressure on the d4 square) in return for his outlay.

There are two continuations which allow White to fight for the advantage: 6 cd (I) and 6 ♕b3 (II).

I
6 cd

Black has a choice between an immediate recovery of the pawn by 6...♘xd5 (A) and the move 6...♗g7 (B), after which he will remain behind in material for a short while.

A

6...♘xd5 Another branch: 7 ♗c4 or 7 ♕b3.

1) **7 ♗c4** Nothing is offered by play along the a4-e8 diagonal – 7 ♗b5+ ♘c6 8 ♕a4 ♘xc3! and it is dangerous to win the pawn: 9 ♗xc6+ bc 10 ♕xc6+?! ♗d7 11 ♕xc3 ♖c8 (analysis by M.Filip). In the game Karpov – Miles (Amsterdam 1981) White preferred the sensible 9 bc ♗g7 10 ♘f3 0-0 11 0-0, but after 11...♘a5! Black fully equalised the position.

7...♘b6 8 ♗b3 ♗g7 The main thing in this position is the development of the knight on f3. But first we look at some examples in which White preferred the development of the knight to e2.

9 d5!? 0-0 10 ♘ge2 ♘a6 11 ♗e3 ♗g4 12 f3 ♗d7 13 ♗d4 ♗xd4 14 ♕xd4 ♘c8 15 0-0 ♕b6 16 ♘e4 ♗b5 17 ♖fe1 ♘b4 18 ♘4c3 ♗xe2 19 ♕xb6 ab 20 ♖xe2 ♖d8 21 ♖d1 ♔f8 22 ♖d4 and the positional niceties which imbued the game did not cease even in the ending (Sermek – Zelcic, Split 2002);

9 ♗e3!? (Black needs to play very accurately if he is not to fall into a difficult position) 9...♘c6 10 d5 ♘e5 (10...♘a5!?) 11 ♘ge2 0-0 12 ♗d4 ♗g4 13 f3!? (upon 13 0-0 Black rightly carried out an exchanging operation – 13...♗xe2 14 ♕xe2 ♘f3+!? 15 ♕xf3 ♗xd4 16 ♖ad1 ♗xc3 17 ♕xc3 ♕d6, Skachkov – Evseev, Nefteugansk 2002) 13...♗d7 14 0-0 ♖c8 15 ♖f2 ♘ec4! 16 ♗xg7 ♔xg7 17 ♕d4+ ♔g8 18 ♘e4 ♗f5 (Sveshnikov – Hubner, Munich 1992).

As we see, every time the struggle continues on one and the same scheme: White hammers in a pawn nail on d5, then, after eliminating the pin on the knight e2 by f2-f3, exploits the vacant d4 square as a base for transfer of his minor pieces. Black has less space; a weak pawn on e7 (in certain variations – also a pawn on a7).

And all the same the above-mentioned factors are insufficient to assess the present type of position as obviously better for White. We have a complicated struggle in which White has a moral rather than a palpable advantage.

9 ♘f3 ♘c6 This move, provoking White into d4-d5, also need not be hurried. 9...0-0 10 0-0 ♗g4! 11 d5 ♘8d7 12 h3 ♗xf3 13 ♕xf3 ♖c8 14 ♗g5 ♘f6 looks fully worthwhile. Pursuing the 'advantage of the two bishops' here can hardly be realised since the bishops are up against a barrier; apart from this, all Black's pieces are well developed. A possible continuation is 15 ♖ad1 h6 16 ♗h4 ♘c4 17 ♗xc4 ♖xc4 18 ♗g3 ♘e8 19 ♖fe1 ♘d6 with unquestionable equality (Pogosian – Evseev, Moscow 1996).

10 0-0 0-0 11 d5 ♘a5 The opening is almost over; time to think about future plans.

There is no time for the prophylactic 12 h3: after exchanges on b3 and c3 Black gobbles up the d5 pawn with impunity. Therefore it is worthwhile for White to occupy himself in earnest with the e7 pawn.

With this objective in view, 12 ♖e1 has been tried but after 12...♘xb3 (it is not excluded that even more accurate is 12...♗g4!? 13 h3 ♗xf3 14 ♕xf3 ♖e8 15 ♗g5 ♘xb3 16 ab ♗xc3 17 bc ♕xd5 18 ♕xd5 ♘xd5 19 c4 f6 20 cd fg – when play clearly inclines towards a draw, Lein – Seirawan, Seattle 2003) 13 ab e6 (in the endgame after 13...♗xc3 14 bc ♕xd5 15 ♕xd5 ♘xd5 16 c4 ♘b4 17 ♖xe7 White possibly also retains a microscopic advantage) 14 d6 ♗d7 15 ♗g5 f6 16 ♗e3 ♘c8 17 ♗c5 b6 18 ♗a3 the chances of the two sides look equal. True, in the game Glek – Szabolcsi (Paris 2000) Black blundered – 18...♖e8?, and after 19 ♘d5! was forced to resign at once. However how to approach Black's position in the event of 18...♖f7 – is unclear.

More promising is **12 ♗g5!? ♗g4 13 h3 ♗xf3 14 ♕xf3** Straightforward exchanges in this position do not lead to anything good – 14...♘xb3?! 15 ab, and then:

15...♗xc3 16 bc ♕xd5 17 ♕xd5

♘xd5 18 c4 ♘f6 19 ♖fe1 ♖fe8 20 ♗xf6 ef 21 ♖xe8+ ♖xe8 22 ♖xa7. In this rook endgame White has practically an extra pawn;

15...h6 16 ♗e3 ♗xc3 17 bc ♕xd5 18 ♕xd5 ♘xd5 19 ♗xh6 ♖fd8 20 ♖fe1! e6 21 ♗g5 f6 22 c4! and though it is small, White still has a 'plus'.

15...♕d7 16 ♖fd1 ♘c8 17 ♕e3 ♖e8 18 ♗f4 a6?! 19 ♘a4 ♕f5 20 ♖ac1 b5 21 g4 ♕f6 22 ♖c6, and it is already very bad for Black (Nunn – Seirawan, London 1984).

The conclusion is obvious: after 12 ♗g5!? ♗g4 13 h3 ♗xf3 14 ♕xf3 Black should temporarily abstain from exchanges. For example, **14...♕d7!? 15 ♖fe1 ♖fe8 16 ♖e2 h6 17 ♗d2 ♖ad8** (Brunner – Miral, Zug 1987). The bishop b3 has nowhere to escape from the black knight; Black's own weaknesses are covered, there is a square of invasion – c4. Chances are mutual.

2) **7 ♕b3** (considered a 'tougher' move than 7 ♗c4) **7...♘b6** For a long time the exchange 7...♘xc3!? was denounced without exception by all the theoreticians – on the basis of the game Tal – Pohla (USSR 1972). However it was the analysis of the St.Petersburg master Konstantin Agapov that first shook this assessment, and then the Norwegian grandmaster Simen Agdestein finally convinced us that Black was more or less okay.

Critical for the variation 7...♘xc3 is the position after 8 ♗c4! e6 9 bc ♘c6 10 ♘f3 ♗g7 11 ♗a3 ♗f8! A possible continuation is:

12 ♗xf8 ♔xf8 13 0-0 ♘a5!? (this is more accurate than 13...♔g7 14 ♗b5 ♗d7 15 ♕b2 ♘a5, Kochiev – Agapov, Leningrad 1987, after which White, in the opinion of Agapov, could maintain a minimal advantage by 16 ♗e2 ♖c8 17 ♖ac1) 14 ♕b4+ ♔g7 15 ♗e2 b6 16 ♖fd1 ♗b7 17 c4 ♖c8 18 c5 ♗d5 and Black even has the more promising position (van der Sterren – Agdestein, Germany 1998);

12 ♗c1 (trying to find another plan of play) 12...♗g7 13 ♗b5 ♗d7 14 ♗a3 ♗f8 15 ♗xf8 ♔xf8 16 0-0 ♔g7 17 ♗e2 b6 18 c4 ♕f6 and Black has no problems (Botvinnik – Petrosian, Moscow 1963);

12 0-0 ♘a5! (after 12...♗xa3? 13 ♕xa3 ♕e7 14 ♕c1 Tal placed the queen on h6 and won with a direct attack against Pohla) 13 ♗b5+ ♗d7 14 ♕a4 ♗xa3 15 ♗xd7+ ♕xd7 16 ♕xa3 (16 ♕xa5 ♗d6) 16...♘c4 17 ♕c5 ♕d5 18 ♕xd5 ♕xd5, and Black, even after giving up the d5 pawn, saved this endgame (Lukin – Kalinin, Medzibrozhe 1991).

So, in all probability, playing 7...♘xc3 is possible, even if in such a way Black also backs himself into a corner. Far more possibilities for

counterplay remain for him after 7...♘b6!? In reply White usually chooses between 8 ♗b5+ and 8 d5.

a) **8 ♗b5+ ♗d7** (dubious is 8...♘8d7?! because of 9 a4!? a6 10 ♗e2 ♘f6 11 a5) **9 ♘f3** The Romanian grandmaster Levente Vajda decided to run to the edge: 9 a4. It turned out favourably: 9...♗g7 10 a5! ♘c8 11 ♘f3 ♘d6 12 ♗xd7+ ♘xd7 13 ♗f4 0-0 14 ♗xd6 ed 15 0-0, and Black had no compensation for his pawn weaknesses (Vajda – Taylor, Budapest 2003). But in reply to 9 a4?! more concrete (and stronger) is 9...♘c6! 10 ♘f3 ♗e6!?, and if 11 d5?! (11 ♕c2 ♗f5 with equality), then 11...♘xd5 12 ♘d4 ♘c7! The extra pawn proves useful (de Jong – Pilen, Wijk aan Zee 1990).

However, besides the idea a2-a4-a5 in this or that variation, there is nothing else for White.

9...♗g7 10 ♘e5 One more example with the plan of advancing the edge pawn: 10 ♗xd7+ ♕xd7 11 a4 0-0 12 a5 ♘c8 13 d5 ♘a6 14 0-0 ♘d6 15 ♖e1 ♖fe8 16 ♗e3 ♕c8 17 ♗g5 ♘c5 18 ♕c2 e5! with a comfortable game (Nureev – Evseev, Tula 1999).

10...0-0

65

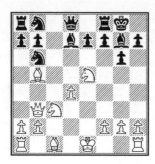

The advantage of the two bishops is the most that White can get out of the position. But this is too small to fight for a real advantage:

11 ♘xd7 ♘6xd7!? (also sufficient for equality is 11...♘8xd7 12 ♗e3 ♘f6 13 0-0 ♘g4 14 ♗e2 ♘xe3 15 fe e5!, Gdanski – Urban, Brzeg Dolny 1996) **12 0-0 ♘c6** (Osinovsky – Evseev, St.Petersburg 2002).

We get the impression that nowadays the variation 8 ♗b5+ has become obsolete. If White does not push the d4 pawn, then it automatically becomes a weakness. And for what in return? Only the possibility of driving the knight from b6 by a2-a4-a5. This is very little.

b) **8 d5!?** (now the struggle moves to more interesting territory) **8...♗g7 9 ♗e3 0-0 10 ♖d1** Somehow Black needs to unravel the cluster of pieces on the queen's flank. And he cannot always achieve this. Thus extremely dubious is 10...♘8d7?! (with the idea of capturing the c4 square) in view of 11 ♗e2! ♘e5 12 h3! and the game is up for Black: 12...♕c7 13 ♘b5 ♕b8 14 ♖c1 e6 15 d6 ♘d5 16 ♘c7 winning the exchange (Pavasovic – Burmakin, Ljubliana 1997).

10...♘a6!? This looks the most sensible. Thus Black does not duplicate the function of his knights (one heads for c4, the second – for c5) and does not obstruct the pathway of the bishop c8.

The critical position of the 8 d5 variation.

b1) **11 ♗xa6** A principal decision. Now there is a devaluation of the black pawns on the queen's flank and a weakening of the c6 square, which at an opportune moment can be occupied by a white knight. On the other hand, the loss of the bishop is deeply felt by White, and if its black counterpart gets to a6, the whole diagonal will be under its control.

This struggle of 'for and against' prompts all the following moves.

11...ba 12 ♘ge2 a5! The remaining moves are weaker:

12...♗d7?! 13 0-0 ♖b8 14 ♗f4 ♖c8 15 ♘d4 ♗g4 16 f3 ♗d7 17 ♖fe1 ♖xc3? (a mistaken combination; Black obviously did not see White's 20th move) 18 bc ♗a4 19 ♕a3 ♗xd1 20 ♘c6! Sveshnikov – Garcia, Cienfuegos 1979) or

12...♗b7?! 13 0-0 ♕d6 14 ♖d2 ♖fd8 15 ♖fd1 a5 16 a3 a4 17 ♘xa4

♗xd5 18 ♕b5 e6 19 ♘xb6 ab 20 ♘f4, and White will soon be a pawn ahead (Kuijf – Pilen, Amsterdam 1987).

13 ♕b5 (not allowing the bishop to a6) **13...♕d7!?** Having his own way. The alternative is 13...a4!? (but not 13...♖b8 because of 14 ♘d4!) 14 ♗d4 ♗d7 15 ♕b4 ♖c8 16 0-0 ♖c4. In the game Sveshnikov – Seres (Nova Gorica 1997) Black made a few more very decent moves: 17 ♕a5 ♕b8 18 b3 ab 19 ab ♖c7 20 ♘e4 ♗f5 21 d6 ed 22 ♘xd6 ♗c2 23 ♗xg7 and after 23...♔xg7 was able to fully count on a draw.

14 ♕xa5 ♘c4 15 ♕b4 ♗a6

Black is a pawn down, but compensation can be seen with the naked eye: two splendid bishops, and for White – problems with his king and on the queen's flank. In the game Pavasovic – Slipak (Pinamar 2002) Black quickly established parity: **16 ♗f4 ♘xb2!? 17 ♕xb2 ♗xe2 18 ♕xe2 ♗xc3+ 19 ♗d2 ♗g7 20 ♗e3 ♗c3+ 21 ♗d2 ♗g7** and it still seems that he has got a bad deal out of it.

b2) After **11 ♘f3** Black likewise has the right to reckon on

counterplay. All will depend on the next few moves.

11...♕d6!? It is important to activate the knight a6 quite quickly. A supplementary idea is to exchange queens on b4 at an opportune moment. In the event of the passive 11...♗d7 White exchanges the dark-squared bishops and obtains an obvious advantage: 12 ♗e2 ♖c8 13 ♗d4! ♕c7 14 0-0 ♖fd8 15 ♗xg7 ♔xg7 16 ♖fe1 ♘c5 17 ♕b4 ♕d6 18 ♗b5 ♕f6 19 ♗xd7 ♖xd7 20 ♘e5 (Suba – Jaime, Malaga 2002).

12 ♗e2 And why not the prophylactic 12 a3, preventing the exchange of queens? The whole point being that Black has the tactical resource 12...♘c5 13 ♕b5 ♘ca4!

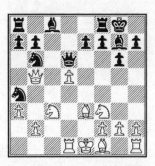

If 14 ♘xa4, then 14...♗d7, while after 14 ♘e4 ♕d7 15 ♕b3 ♘xb2! 16 ♗b5 ♕g4 17 ♘g3 ♘xd1! 18 h3 ♘xe3 19 hg ♘xg2+ 20 ♔f1 ♘f4 and White's position is like a ruin (Barle – Adorjan, Reykjavik 1988). We must say that Adorjan's play in this game makes a powerful impression.

12...♘c5 13 ♕b5 ♘ca4! (a familiar blow) **14 ♘e4 ♕d7 15 ♕b3** It seems that White has already lost control over the position. Black has at least a draw 'in the pocket'.

15...♘xb2!? 16 ♘c5 ♕f5 17 ♖d2 ♕b1+ 18 ♖d1 ♕f5 (Sermek – Sax, Bled 1999).

On the whole, at the present time the variation 6...♘xd5 looks quite reliable for Black. True, a great extent of knowledge is required in order not to land in a difficult position – but who can say that in other schemes less knowledge is required? But, objectively, nowhere – neither upon 7 ♗c4 nor 7 ♕b3 – can White count on a serious advantage.

B

6...♗g7

What to do with the extra pawn on d5? Cling on to it with all his might (7 ♗c4), advance it in order to spoil the opponent's 'coiffure' (7 ♗b5+ ♘bd7 8 d6) or simply carry on with his development (7 ♘f3)?

Continuing his development will not be a success. Or rather it will in itself be a success, but White's advantage will then be irretrievably lost: 7 ♘f3 ♘xd5 8 ♗c4 ♘xc3 9 bc ♕c7 10 ♕e2 ♗e6! 11 ♗b5+ ♘c6 12 0-0 0-0 13 ♖e1 ♗d5 (Lugovoi – S.Ivanov, St.Petersburg 2000). However the remaining two moves hold good:

1) **7 ♗c4!? 0-0 8 ♘ge2** Finally making a claim on the extra material – when the knight gets to f4, recovering the pawn will be considerably more complicated.

There is less sense in 8 ♘f3 ♘bd7, and then:

9 d6!? ed 10 0-0 ♘b6 11 ♗b3 ♗f5 12 ♖e1 ♖c8 13 ♗f4 a6 14 ♖c1 ♘c4 15 ♗xc4 ♖xc4 16 ♕b3 b5 17 a4 ♗e6. Black has happily solved his problems and is ready to adequately deal with the complications:

18 ab!? ♖xd4! 19 ♕xe6! ♖xf4! (19...fe?! 20 ♘xd4) 20 ♕e3 ♖b4 with equal chances;

9 0-0 ♘b6 10 ♗b3 ♘bxd5 11 ♖e1 b6 12 ♘e5 ♗b7 13 ♗g5 ♖c8 14 ♕f3. White's piece formation looks highly aggressive, however in the game Aleksandrov – S.Kasparov (Minsk 2000) the aggression was successfully quelled: 14...♖c7! 15 ♕h3 ♘xc3! 16 bc ♕c8! 17 ♕xc8 ♗xc8 etc.

The idea 8 ♕f3!? ♘bd7 9 h3!? ♘b6 10 ♗b3 a5 11 a3 a4 12 ♗a2 has been insufficiently tested in practice to be able to make any kind of definite judgement. We mention only the game Spangenberg – Ricardi (Buenos Aires 2000) in which Black reacted with an interesting exchange sacrifice: 12...♖a5!? 13 ♗d2 ♘bxd5!? 14 ♘xd5 ♘xd5 15 ♗xa5 ♕xa5+ 16 ♔f1 ♗e6 17 ♖d1 ♖c8 18 ♗b1 ♕b6 with compensation.

After 8 ♘ge2 Black can choose between two march routes of the knight b8: d7-b6 or a6-c7.

a) **8...♘bd7 9 ♘f4 ♘b6 10 ♗b3 ♗f5** Weak is 10...♗g4?, since this only helps White to create an attack on the king's flank: 11 f3 ♗f5 12 g4! ♗d7 13 h4! ♖c8 14 h5 (Agdestein – T.Hansen, Kiel 2000).

Few chances of equality are offered by 10...♕d6 11 0-0 ♗d7 12 ♖e1 a5 13 a4 ♖fc8. The future invasion of the knight on c4 was countered by White in a totally surprising way... with a rook on e5: 14 h3 h6 15 ♖e5! ♘c4 16 ♕e2! (Tal – Wade, Tallinn 1971).

11 0-0 ♗e4!? Black made a poor redeployment in the game Kobalija – Turov (Kolontaevo 1997): 11...♘c8 12 ♖e1 ♘d6 13 h3 ♖c8 14 ♕f3!? b5?! 15 ♘d3! a5 16 a3 ♕b6 17 ♘e5 b4 18 ♘a4. As a result of all the manoeuvring White's knights obtained outposts, but Black's – did not.

12 ♘xe4 ♘xe4 13 ♕d3 ♘d6 14 ♗e3 ♕d7 15 ♖fc1 ♖fc8 16 h3 ♘f5 17 ♖c5 ♕d6 18 ♖ac1

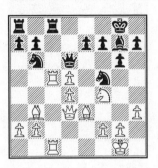

This is how the game Kuijf – Hodgson (Margate 1984) developed. Black's position looks very uneasy, but tactics come to his aid: **18...♗xd4! 19 ♖xc8+ ♖xc8 20 ♖xc8+ ♘xc8 21 ♘xg6! ♕f6! 22 ♘f4** (22 d6 ed! 23 ♗xd4 ♘xd4) **22...♘xe3 23 fe ♗xb2 24 ♗c2 ♕h4 25 ♔h2 ♘d6** with a probable draw.

b) **8...♘a6!? 9 0-0 ♘c7 10 ♘f4** Both sides have included virtually all their reserves in the struggle for the d5 pawn. And yet there are more black reserves to come! He can bring up the bishop (to b7) and the rook (to d8), whereas White has only a queen – to go to b3 (hardly to f3, where it has to put up with the bishop b7). Is the struggle for the d5 pawn being lost by White? Apparently, yes, but how long can the moment of realisation be delayed?

10...b6 11 ♖e1 (after 11 a4 ♗b7 12 ♕b3 ♖b8 13 ♗e3 a6!? the queen on b3, faced with the imminent break b6-b5, is starting to feel uncomfortable, Conquest – Bronstein, Bayswater 1989) **11...♗b7**

12 ♖e5?! Stubborness will cost White dear! It was necessary to reconcile himself to giving back, finally, that cursed pawn: 12 a4 ♘cxd5 13 ♘fxd5 ♘xd5 (Galkin – Burmakin, Oberwart 1999).

12...♘d7 13 ♖e2 ♘f6 14 ♕b3?! ♖b8 15 a4 a6 16 ♗d2 b5! 17 ab ab 18 ♗d3 g5! 19 ♘h3 h6 20 ♖ae1 b4! And with energetic play Black took over the initiative (Velimirovic – Drazic, Pogorica 1996).

2) **7 ♗b5+ ♘bd7** On 7...♗d7 very convincing play was demonstrated by the English grandmaster John Nunn (in a game against Hickl, Dortmund 1987): 8 ♗c4 0-0 9 ♕b3! ♗f5 10 ♕xb7 ♘bd7 11 ♗f4 ♘e8 12 ♘f3 ♘b6 13 ♗b3 ♗c8 14 ♕c6 ♘d6 15 ♕c5 ♗a6 16 ♘e5 ♖e8 17 0-0-0!

8 d6! Strictly speaking, this makes sense of the check on b5: Black has been forced to cover the d-file and thereby oblige him to take on d6 with a pawn.

Black can join the opponent's cause (8...ed), but can also be obstinate (8...0-0 or 8...e6).

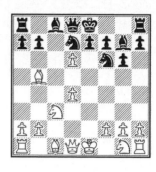

a) **8...0-0!?** An interesting pawn sacrifice, first played in the game Canal – Opocensky (Sliac 1932). Black's idea has its points: he intends to carry out a7-a6, b7-b5, blockade the queen's flank on the light squares and transfer the whole heavy struggle to the weak isolated d4 pawn. And it is not possible to say what is the right way for White to deal with this plan!

9 de ♕xe7+ 10 ♘ge2 Here we have an excellent example that shows how Black's idea can work: 10 ♗e2 a6! 11 ♘f3 b5! 12 a3 ♗b7 13 0-0 ♕d6 14 ♗g5 h6 15 ♗h4 ♘h5! The compensation is evident (Hendriks – van Mil, Antwerp 1995).

10...a6 11 ♗xd7 Even after 11 ♗d3 b5 12 0-0 ♗b7 Black has repeatedly managed to demonstrate that his aspirations are well-founded:

13 ♗g5 ♘b6 14 ♕d2 ♖fe8 15 ♘g3 ♕d7 16 ♘ce2 ♘e4 17 ♗xe4 ♗xe4 18 b3 ♘d5 (Bronstein – Gurgenidze, USSR 1972);

13 ♘g3 ♖fe8 14 a3 ♘b6 15 ♗g5 h6 16 ♗e3 ♘fd5 17 ♖e1 ♕h4 (Alabkin – Turov, Krasnodar 1997).

11...♛xd7!? Black has the firm intention of establishing his bishop on b7. Therefore inconsistent is 11...♗xd7?! 12 ♗g5 ♛d6 13 ♗f4 ♛b6 14 ♗e5 ♖fd8 15 0-0 ♗c6 16 ♛d2 ♘e4 17 ♛f4 ♘xc3 18 bc and chances of realising his extra pawn appear for White (Sveshnikov – Gipslis, USSR 1975).

12 0-0 b5 13 ♗f4 ♗b7 14 ♗e5 ♖fe8 15 ♛b3 ♘g4!? 16 ♗xg7 ♛c6 17 d5 (also in the event of 17 f3 ♚xg7 18 ♖ac1 ♘f6 the weakness of the d4 pawn, together with the weakening of the e3 square, gives Black chances of obtaining counterplay) **17...♛d6 18 ♘g3 ♚xg7 19 ♛d1 ♛f4** Winning this position is of course difficult for Black but it is fully possible to make a draw (Frolyanov – Malofeev, St.Petersburg 2002).

And so if you do not want to sit in the trenches – boldy play 8...0-0. It's worth it!

b) **8...e6?!** As distinct from 8...0-0, this is not a gambit – Black is hoping to win back the pawn. But he intends to capture on d6 with a piece so as to leave Black again with a weak isolani on d4.

9 ♘f3 Impetuosity – 9 d5?! – here is completely out of place: 9...e5! 10 ♘f3 0-0 11 0-0 ♘e8 12 ♖e1 f6 13 ♘e4 a6 14 ♗a4 ♖f7 15 ♗e3 ♗f8, and suddenly Black's plan has succeeded (Djuhuis – L.-B. Hansen, Groningen 1986).

9...0-0 10 0-0 ♘b6 Even worse is 10...a6?! 11 ♗d3. Now if 11...♘b6, then after 12 ♗f4 Black will not get the d6 pawn: 12...♘bd5 13 ♘xd5 ♘xd5 14 ♗g3 ♛b6 15 ♗c4! ♛xb2 16 ♖e1 ♘c3 17 ♛c1 ♘b4 18 ♖e3 with great chances of victory (Jansa – Kucera, Usti nad Labem 1994). While on 11...b5 12 a4!? b4 13 ♘e4 ♗b7 14 ♘c5! looks very good (Jansa – Burovic, Eupen 1996).

11 ♗f4 ♘h5 12 ♗e5! a6 13 ♗d3 f6 14 ♗g3 ♘xg3 15 hg ♛xd6 16 ♛b3 ♘d5 17 ♖fe1 Black has in the end won the d6 pawn. But he will not like the suspect position he has reached (Meduna – Lipka, Czech Republic 2002).

c) **8...ed** (the main continuation) **9 ♛e2+.** If Black does not want to transfer to an endgame so soon, then he is forced to play 9...♚f8. Though he will spend some time castling artificially (h7-h6, ♚f8-g8-h7), it is not so easy for White to obtain the advantage:

10 ♘f3 h6 11 0-0 ♘b6 (or 11...♔g8, Shirov – Vizhmanavin, Tilburg 1992; in Shirov's opinion, White retains a minimal advantage by 12 ♗c4 ♘f8 13 ♖e1 ♗e6 14 d5 ♗g4 15 h3) 12 ♗d3 ♔g8 13 ♗f4 ♔h7 (...and once again the king's journey has a happy ending) 14 h3 ♖e8 15 ♕d2 ♘fd5 16 ♗g3 ♘xc3 17 bc ♗e6 18 ♖ab1. This is how the game Lautier – Yusupov (Baden Baden 1992) continued. After 18...♗d5!? there are chances for both sides.

9...♕e7 The critical position of the system with 7 ♗b5+. Now the exchange of queens cannot be avoided; and the endgame is not easy to play.

10 ♗f4 ♕xe2+ 11 ♗xe2!? The light-squared bishop transfers to f3, making it difficult for the opponent to develop his queenside pieces.

The other idea – to place the rook on e1 a little earlier and try to exploit the enemy king – 11 ♘gxe2 ♔e7, and then:

12 0-0 ♘b6 13 ♖fe1 ♗e6 14 ♖ad1 a6 15 d5!? ♘fxd5! 16 ♘xd5+ ♘xd5 17 ♗c4 ♘xf4 18 ♘xf4 ♗e5 19 ♘xe6

fe 20 f4 ♗xf4 21 ♖xe6+ ♔d7 22 g3 ♖ac8! (Nunn – Stean, Hastings 1980) or

12 0-0-0 ♘b6 13 ♖he1 ♗e6 14 ♔b1 a6 15 ♗d3 ♔d7 16 ♘e4 ♘bd5 17 ♘g5 ♖ac8 (Georgadze – Bagirov, Tashkent 1984). As we see, the minor pieces (mainly the bishop on e6) are unable to defend their king.

11...♔e7 12 ♗f3 Premature is 12 0-0-0 ♘b6 13 ♗f3, upon which the pawn sacrifice 13...♗e6!? 14 ♗xb7 ♖ab8 is worth considering. The position of the king on c1 gives Black a target for counterplay on the b and c files.

12...♘b6 13 ♘ge2 It is worth mentioning the prophylaxis carried out by White in the game Miles – Belyavsky (Biel 1991): 13 b3!? Immediately 'clipping' the knight b6, indeed the standard pawn sacrifice 13...♗e6 no longer has the same effect. Belyavsky was restricted to the modest 13...♖b8 (13...♖d8!?), but after 14 ♘b5 ♘e8 15 ♘e2 a6 16 ♘bc3 ♘c7 17 0-0-0 h5 18 ♖he1 ♗g4 19 ♗e4 ♖hc8 20 ♔b1 ♘e8 21 h3 ♗d7 22 ♖d3 ♔f8 23 ♖e3 he did not achieve full equality.

After 13 ♘ge2 Black has several plans to choose from.

The slowest is 13...a6 (Black denies the white knight the b5 square, but is it worth spending time on this?) 14 0-0 ♖b8 15 ♖fe1 ♗e6 16 ♘g3 ♔d7 17 ♘ge4 ♘xe4 18 ♘xe4 (Smagin – Vizhmanavin, Tashkent 1984), and the d6 pawn falls all the same: 18...♘c8 19 ♘c5+!

However, at times purely defensive tactics give not a bad result. As, for example, in the game Miezis – Jonkman (Bad Worishofen 1999): 13...♖d8!? 14 0-0 ♖b8 15 ♖fe1 a6 (just like it all went in Smagin against Vizhmanavin but with a single exception: the position of the rook on d8 allows the king to hide on f8, and the knight to come up to defend the d6 pawn) 16 ♘g3+ ♔f8! 17 ♘ge4 ♘e8! 18 ♖ad1 ♗f5 19 g4 ♗xe4 20 ♗xe4 ♘c7 21 ♗g3 ♘e6 22 ♘e2 ♖d7! (the same excellent manoeuvre: Black frees the rook b8 from menial work) 23 b3 ♖e8, and there is hardly anything left of White's initiative.

In contrast to the slow 13...a6 and 14...♖b8 – there is the impatient 13...♗e6?! 14 ♗xb7 ♖ab8 15 ♗f3 ♘fd5. The intermediate 16 ♗g5+! (remember this moment) severely complicates Black's counterplay: 16...f6 17 ♗c1 ♘b4 18 0-0 ♖hc8 19 b3! f5 20 ♗g5+! ♔d7 21 ♖fd1. There is no real compensation for the pawn (Rasic – Salai, Slovakia 1998).

Australian grandmaster Ian Rogers treated this variation rather well. One can fully emulate the following example of his creative work.

13...h6!? Threatening to win a piece by g6-g5-g4! If the opponent notices this threat, he will be forced

to spend time on prophylaxis (14 h3 or 14 h4), but then Black can already sacrifice a pawn – 14...♗e6!? You see the g5 square (we recall 16 ♗g5+! in the game Rasic – Szallai) is now reliably covered!

14 h3 In the game Smerdon – Rogers (Canberra 2002) after 14 h4 ♗e6!? White did not risk taking the offered pawn and played 15 ♖c1?! It is clear that he is not fighting for the advantage; but what was Black thinking about in reply to 15 ♗xb7 ? Analysis shows that even in this case he has compensation, sufficient for equality: 15...♖ab8 16 ♗f3 ♘fd5! 17 ♖d1 ♖hc8 18 0-0 ♘xf4 19 ♘xf4 ♖c4 20 ♘b5!? ♘c8 21 b3 ♖c2 22 ♘xe6 fe 23 ♖c1 ♖xa2 24 ♖c7+ ♔f8 etc.

14...♗e6 15 ♗xb7 ♖ab8 16 ♗f3

When Rogers met this position for the first time, he, so to speak, 'muffed it': 16...♘bd5?!, and did not obtain compensation for the pawn (Zifroni – Rogers, Agios Nikolaos 1995). But then a year later it all fell into place:

16...♘fd5! (by linking up with the bishop g7, Black thereby overloads the knight e2, which makes the move 17 b3 impossible) **17 ♗d2 ♘xc3**

18 ♗xc3 ♘a4 19 0-0 ♖hc8!
(Bergstrom – Rogers, Gausdal 1996).
The arising position somehow
resembles the Volga Gambit. Like
there, the pawn sacrifice bears a
purely positional character, like there,
Black will not only fight with less
material in the endgame, but even
urges on the opponent towards this!
The activity of the rook on the b and
c-files together with powerful minor
pieces (the bishop g7 is particularly
good) means he will have an
enduring initiative.

II
6 ♕b3!?

Less popular is the other way of
pressurising the d5 pawn: 6 ♗g5.
There are several reasons for this.

Firstly, it is possible to react with
the sharp 6...♘e4!? After 7 ♗e3
♘xc3 8 bc ♗g7 9 cd ♕xd5 10 ♕b3
♕d6 11 ♘f3 0-0 12 ♗e2 ♘c6 13 0-0
b6 14 ♖ad1 ♗g4 15 c4 ♖ab8 Black's
position is in no way worse
(Ljubojevic – Kamsky, Monaco
1995).

Secondly, there is the quiet move
6...♗g7. White can win a pawn; but
this does not bring him an advantage.

7 ♗xf6 ♗xf6 8 cd (long ago
Botvinnik advised against taking the
pawn on d5 with the knight in view of
8...♗g7 9 ♘f3 ♘c6 followed by
♗c8-g4 and e7-e6) 8...0-0 9 ♗c4
♕b6!? 10 ♘ge2 ♕xb2 11 ♖b1 ♕a3
12 0-0 ♘d7 with the better chances
(Krasenkov – Svidler, Madrid 1998).

So hardly anyone departs from the
theoretical verdict on the non-topical
6 ♗g5. Quite another matter is
6 ♕b3!?

6...♗g7 Black is forced to sacrifice
a pawn, since other possibilities are
unattractive:

6...dc?! 7 ♗xc4 e6 8 ♘f3 or
6...e6?! 7 ♘f3 ♗g7 8 cd ed 9 ♗g5. In
the present situation the combination
of the moves g7-g6 and e7-e6 does
not make the slightest impression;

6...♘c6?! 7 cd ♘a5 8 ♕a4+ ♗d7
9 ♗b5 a6 10 ♗xd7+ ♘xd7 11 ♘ge2
b5 12 ♕d1 ♘f6 13 ♘f4 ♗g7 14 0-0.
Chances are small that Black will
obtain compensation for the
sacrificed material (Noskov –
Katalymov, USSR 1973).

A stand alone idea is 6...♘bd7!?
7 cd ♘b6. It is worthwhile for White
to look for something else apart from
the experimental 8 ♗e2?! ♘fxd5
9 ♗b5+?! ♗d7 10 ♘xd5 ♘xd5
11 ♗c4 ♗c6 12 ♘f3 ♗g7 13 0-0 0-0
14 ♘e5 e6 15 ♘xc6 bc 16 ♖d1 ♖b8.
Black has weaknesses, but he also has
his own trumps (Smeets – Seirawan,
Dordrecht 2003).

7 cd 0-0 Before us lies the tabiya of
the variation 6 ♕b3.

It is clear that all White's plans are linked to the defence of the d5 pawn. But how best to defend it? Just one light-squared bishop can defend the pawn from three positions: c4, f3 and g2. But how best to go to work: first to move out the bishop, and then the knight, or first to develop the knight along the march route g1-e2-f4, and only then think where to post the bishop?

For convenience the further layout of material is examined in three parts: 8 ♘ge2 (A), 8 g3 (B) and 8 ♗e2 (C). It goes without saying, however, that in many variations these ideas cross over, and similar positions are reached by transposition of moves.

A

8 ♘ge2 He will not succeed in defending the pawn in the more natural way: 8 ♘f3 ♘bd7 9 ♗g5 ♘b6 10 ♗c4, as Mikhail Tal twice tried to do in the XXIX USSR Championship (Baku 1961). After 10...♗f5 sooner or later Black will bring the bishop to the c4 square (by means of ♖a8-c8):

11 ♗xf6 ♗xf6 12 ♖d1 ♖c8! 13 ♗d3 ♗g4 14 ♗e4 ♘c4 15 h3 ♗xf3 16 ♗xf3 ♕a5 (Tal – Lein) or

11 ♖d1 ♘e4 12 0-0 ♘xc3 13 bc ♖c8! 14 ♗b5 h6 15 ♗h4 g5 16 ♗g3 ♕xd5 (Tal – Bronstein).

After 8 ♘ge2 Black usually chooses between two moves of the queen's knight: to d7 or a6.

1) **8...♘bd7 9 g3** The alternative – 9 ♘f4 ♘e8 (the position on 9...♘b6 10 ♗e2 is looked at within the variation 8 ♗e2) 10 ♗e3 ♘d6 11 ♗e2 ♘b6 12 a4 a5 13 0-0 ♗d7 with a very complicated struggle. Thus the game Yakovich – Miroshinchenko (Noyabrisk 2003) continued 14 ♘d3 ♘bc4 15 ♘c5 ♘xe3 16 fe ♗c8 17 ♗d3 b6 18 ♘5e4 ♘f5 19 ♖ae1 e6 20 de ♗xe6 and the game still did not veer to one side or the other.

9...♘b6 10 ♗g2 ♗f5 It is not clear whether it is worth Black including 10...a5 11 a4 and only then play 11...♗f5. It is important that after 12 0-0 ♗d3?! White has the jab 13 d6!, when the doubled weak extra pawn is converted to one in top condition: 13...ed 14 ♗xb7 ♖b8

15 ♗f3 ♖e8 16 ♕d1 ♗a6 17 ♖e1 ♕d7 18 ♘f4 (Hubner – Smyslov, Tilburg 1984).

11 ♘f4!? Starting concrete play, the point of which becomes clear later.

Of course, 11 0-0 is also played. After 11...♕d7, with just a single move White cannot prevent the transfer the bishop to d3 or h3 (11 ♘f4 g5!), but it is possible to prepare himself for the bishop sortie:

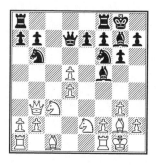

12 a4!? ♗d3 13 d6! ed 14 a5! ♗c4 15 ♕b4 ♗xe2 16 ♘xe2 ♘bd5 17 ♕b3 ♖fe8 18 ♘c3 with tangible pressure on the long diagonal (Liberzon – Gurgenidze, Alma Ata 1968) or

12 ♖d1!? ♗h3 13 ♗h1! ♗g4 14 ♖e1 ♗xe2 15 ♖xe2 ♖ad8 16 ♗f4, and in view of the weakness on e7 Black will hardly win the d5 pawn in the near future (Brodsky – Mittelman, Rishon-le-Zion 1997).

11...♕d7 While White has not castled short, it is dangerous to play 11...g5. However the attempt to prepare this move by 11...h6!? did not succeed in the game A.Sokolov – Ziganova (Helsinki 1992): 12 h4!

♖c8 13 0-0 ♕d7 14 a4 ♘c4 15 a5 ♖fd8 16 ♖a4! ♘d6 17 ♖d1 ♘fe4 18 ♖b4.

12 h4! The point of the idea 11 ♘f4 – now the construction ♕d7+ ♗f5 loses all sense. The bishop has simply nowhere to go!

12...♖ac8 13 0-0 h6 14 ♖e1 ♘c4 15 ♕a4!

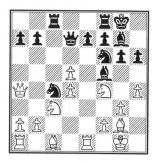

Making the opponent 'an offer he can't refuse'. However, with the exchange of queens, the last possibilities of striking up, if you like, some kind of counterplay are extinguished (Korneev – Novitsky, Minsk 1998).

2) **8...♘a6!?** (it is logical to exploit the fact that the f1-a6 diagonal is temporarily obstructed) **9 g3** The endgame after 9...♕b6?! 10 ♕xb6 ab 11 ♗g2 ♘b4 12 0-0 ♖d8 has been investigated at the very highest level. The conclusion, confirmed by the authority of four world champions, is that 13 d6! guarantees White a serious advantage:

13...♖xd6 14 ♗f4 ♖d7 15 ♖fd1 ♘bd5 16 ♗e5 (Spassky – Petrosian, Moscow 1966);

13...ed 14 ♗g5 ♖e8 15 a3 ♘c6 16 ♖fe1 ♗g4 17 ♗xf6! ♗xf6 18 ♘d5 ♗d8 19 ♘ec3 (Tal – Botvinnik, Moscow 1966).

In recent times Black has pinned his hopes entirely on another idea: **9...b5!?**

Black will not object to an exchange of the b-pawn for the d-pawn. But he will offer the exchange now, while the white pieces have poor interaction with one another.

It is of course possible to reject the capture on b5, but then he has to abandon any dreams of an advantage: 10 a3 ♖b8 11 ♗f4 ♖b6 12 ♗g2 b4 13 ♘a4 ♖b7 14 0-0 (risky is 14 d6 ed! 15 ♗xb7 ♗xb7 16 0-0 ♖e8 – the light squares around the king g1 are extremely weak, and any intrusion by the queen spells trouble) 14...ba 15 ♕xa3 ♘xd5 (Shulman – Abdullah, Dacca 1999).

10 ♘xb5 Also after 10 ♕xb5 ♖b8 11 ♕a4 ♘b4 Black, in the opinion of Slovakian grandmaster Ljubomir Ftacnik, has quite a few chances of generating an initiative.

10...♘xd5 11 ♗g2 ♗e6 12 ♕d1 ♕a5+ 13 ♘bc3 ♘xc3 14 bc ♖ad8 (also interesting is 14...♖ab8!? 15 0-0 ♗c4) **15 0-0 ♗c4 16 ♗d2**

In the encounter Adams – Granda (Madrid 1998) Black rushed to establish material parity: 16...e5?! With the loss of the d4 pawn the white bishops become active; shortly after Black miscalculated a simple variation and resigned.

Michael Adams himself also pointed out the right direction of counterplay: **16...♖b8!** (no rush!) **17 ♖e1 ♖b2 18 ♗f1** (not possible is 18 ♘c1? ♗xd4!) **18...♖fb8** Black's initiative is worth a pawn, though it would be unjust if White complained about his position.

As we see, upon both 8... ♘bd7 and 8...♘a6 White does not hurry to deploy the knight to f4. With two moves – 9 g3 and 10 ♗g2 he takes both the h1-a8 diagonal as a whole, and the b7 pawn (with the idea d5-d6!) in particular. Therefore it is worthwhile for Black to think about a line of play that is especially directed against g2-g3.

3) 8...♖e8!? 9 g3 e6!

The same motive as in the variation 8...♘a6 9 g3 b5!? – the undeveloped, uncoordinated state of the white pieces. But the carrying out of the idea by 8...♖e8!? 9 g3 e6! is perhaps even better.

Dangerous now is 10 de?! ♗xe6 11 ♕xb7 ♘bd7 12 ♗g2 ♖b8 13 ♕xa7 in view of 13...♗c4 14 ♗f3 ♘d5 15 ♕a4 ♘7b6 16 ♕c2 ♕f6 with an attack (Beim – Shereshevsky, Kharkov 1967).

But also upon the careful **10 d6 ♕xd6 11 ♗g2 ♘c6 12 0-0** there do not appear to be any problems for Black. Possible, if nothing else, is **12...♘d5 13 a3 ♘xc3 14 bc e5!? 15 d5 ♘a5 16 ♕a4 ♕d8 17 ♗g5 f6 18 ♗e3 ♗d7 19 ♕b4 ♗f8 20 d6 b6** (M.Tseitlin – Bukhman, Leningrad 1973).

The idea of 8...♖e8 works even if White does not play 9 g3. For example, 9 ♘f4 e5! or 9 ♗g5 e6! 10 de ♗xe6 11 d5 ♗f5 12 0-0-0 ♘bd7 13 ♘d4 ♘c5 14 ♕b5 (Zude – Schmittner, Geissen 1991) 14...♕c8!? 15 ♘xf5 ♕xf5 16 ♗e3 ♖ac8! with an attack.

It has to be acknowledged that the move 8 ♘ge2 is too slow and therefore inaccurate.

B

8 g3 Suggested by the Soviet master and theoretician Vasily Sozin in 1932. We will not digress from the usual moves such as 8...♘bd7, but will immediately pass on to a couple of counterattacking ideas: 8...e6!? and 8...♘a6 9 ♗g2 b5!?

1) **8...e6!?** White can refuse the sacrifice – 9 ♗g2 ♘xd5 10 ♘ge2 ♘c6 11 0-0.

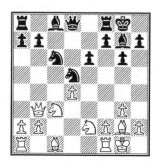

Black retains chances of gradually equalising the game:

11...♘xd4 12 ♘xd4 ♗xd4 13 ♘xd5 ed 14 ♗h6 ♖e8?! (after 14...♗g7 White has a purely symbolic advantage) 15 ♖ad1 ♕f6? (a blunder; there is still nothing terrible after 15...♗f6 16 ♗xd5 ♕e7 17 ♖de1 ♗e6) 16 ♕a4! (Timofeev – Petzold, Retymnon 2003);

11...♕b6 12 ♕xb6 ♘xb6 13 ♖d1 with an endgame which Black, in the game Tukmakov – Dydyshko (Rostov on the Don 1967), clearly overestimated: 13...♖d8 14 ♗f4 ♘d5 15 ♗g5! f6 16 ♗d2 ♘db4 17 ♖ac1 ♘d3 18 ♖b1 ♘xd4?! 19 ♘xd4 ♖xd4 20 ♗e3 ♖d7 21 ♖d2 ♘e5 22 ♖bd1 ♖xd2 23 ♖xd2 ♘f7? (23...♗f8!?) 24 ♘b5! winning;

11...♘b6 12 ♖d1 ♕e7 13 ♗e3 ♕b4 14 ♕c2 ♘e7! 15 a3 ♕c4 16 b3 ♕c7 17 ♖ac1 ♕d7, and equality is not far off (Gipslis – Selezniev, USSR 1961).

So that the adherence to principles, shown by White with his capture on e6, can only be welcomed by Black in the present concrete case.

9 de ♞c6 Upon 9...♗xe6 10 ♛xb7 ♞bd7 11 ♗g2 ♖b8 12 ♛xa7 ♖e8 13 ♞ge2 ♗c4 14 ♗f3 ♞d5 by transposition of moves we have reached a position identical to that which we met in the game Beim – Shereshevsky (page 78).

Here we have yet another example, showing that White, despite his extra pawn, risks far more than the opponent:

15 0-0 (Beim, we recall, played 15 ♛a4) 15...♞xc3 16 ♞xc3 ♗xf1 17 ♚xf1 ♞f8 18 ♞d5?! (it seems he can still make a draw: 18 d5 ♗xc3 19 bc ♛f6 20 ♗f4 ♛xc3 21 ♗xb8 ♛xa1+ 22 ♚g2) 18...♞e6, and Black eventually won (Heidgesetter – Evseev, Norway 1998).

10 ef+ ♚h8 (again Black is 'minus three', and again virtually without risk) **11 ♞ge2 ♛e7** The key d4 pawn is hanging. He cannot defend it by 12 ♗e3: 12...♞g4 13 ♗d2 ♗e6 14 d5 ♗xf7 – with the king on d2 he will not live long (Gheorghiu – Johannessen, Havana 1966). It means that White is forced to retreat with

virtually his only developed piece: **12 ♛d1!?**

The main thing for Black in this position – is not to overestimate it. Thus on 12...♞g4?! 13 ♗g2 ♞xd4 'surprisingly' it becomes clear that White has still not lost the right to castle: 14 0-0. Try to get at the king on g1!

The Canadian grandmaster Kevin Spraggett suddenly decided to play 'in brilliant style':

12...♞xd4? 13 ♛xd4 ♞g4 14 ♛e4 ♛xf7. But after 15 f4 ♗d7 16 ♛b4 a5 17 ♛b6 ♗c6 18 ♖g1 ♖fe8 19 ♗d2 ♞xh2 20 0-0-0 the attack came to an end (Hennigan – Spraggett, Lugano 1988).

So is there a win for Black? As a matter of fact, no, but there is a precise draw: **12...♗f5!? 13 ♗g2 ♞b4 14 0-0 ♞c2 15 ♖b1 ♞b4** with a repetition of moves.

2) **8...♞a6 9 ♗g2 b5!?** We have already given a rough idea of what happens after the capture of the pawn: 10 ♛xb5?! ♖b8 11 ♛a4 ♞b4 or 10 ♞xb5 ♗b7 11 ♞c3 (in the variation 11 ♞c7?! ♛xc7! 12 d6 ♗xg2 13 dc ♞xc7 Black has a whole set of pieces for the queen) 11...♖b8 12 ♛c4 ♛b6 13 ♞ge2 ♞b4 14 0-0

♖fd8 with more than enough compensation for the sacrificed material.

Prudence should take precedence: **10 ♘ge2**, but then **10...b4!**

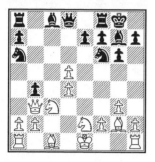

It is dangerous to win the exchange: 11 d6?! bc! 12 ♕a3 (even worse is 12 ♗xa8 because of 12...♗e6! 13 de ♕xa8!) 12...♖b8 13 de ♕d7 14 ef♕+ ♗xf8 15 b4 ♗xb4 16 ♕b3. True, there is no mate, but there is an initiative, and an enduring one: 16...c2+ 17 ♔f1 ♕f5 18 ♕e3 ♗d6 etc.

In the game Stanec – Krivoshey (Oberwart 2000) White again refused the Greek gift: **11 ♘d1 ♗b7 12 ♘e3 ♖b8 13 0-0 ♘c7 14 ♕xb4 ♘cxd5 15 ♕a3 ♘xe3 16 ♕xe3 ♗xg2 17 ♔xg2 ♕d5+ 18 ♕f3** Draw.

If up to now the variations 8 g3 e6!? and 8 g3 ♘a6 9 ♗g2 b5!? have not been the focus of attention (at least, officially), then it is only because White has been wary of continuing the discussion.

C

8 ♗e2 The main continuation. Incidentally, the moment White picks up the bishop he finds it necessary to place it precisely on e2. After

8 ♗c4?! ♘bd7 9 ♘ge2 ♘b6 10 0-0 there are still some questions after 10...♘xc4 11 ♕xc4 b6 12 ♗g5 ♗b7 13 ♘f4 ♕d7 14 ♖fe1 ♖fd8 15 ♕b4! And in the famous game Alekhine – Euwe (Berne 1932) White even managed to carry out a nice combination: 15...♕g4 16 ♗xf6 ♗xf6 17 ♖e4 ♕f5 18 g3 e6 19 ♘xe6!

But the more accurate 10...♗f5!? ends all questions: 11 ♘g3 ♗c2! or 11 ♘f4 ♘xc4 12 ♕xc4 ♘e8!, and White is not destined to gain the advantage.

After 8 ♗e2 none of the jabs (e7-e6!? or b7-b5!?) work. There are two main continuations: 8...♘bd7 and 8...♘a6, but first of all we deliberately get shot of the side-lines:

Dubious is 8...b6?! 9 ♗f3 ♗b7 10 ♘ge2 ♕d7 in view of 11 ♗f4 ♖d8 12 ♖c1 ♘a6 13 ♕a3! (analysis by Boleslavsky).

The transfer of the knight to d6, suggested by the Soviet master Nikolai Kopylov, does not bring equality. In the game Vasyukov – Doda (Belgrade 1961) White refuted this manoeuvre in the simplest way: 8...♘e8?! 9 ♘f3 ♘d6 10 ♗f4 ♗g4 11 ♖d1 ♗xf3 12 ♗xf3 ♘d7 13 0-0 ♘b6 14 ♖fe1 ♘bc4 15 ♘b5! ♕d7

16 ♘xd6 ♘xd6 17 h3 ♖fe8 18 ♗g4.

Bronstein suggested 8...a5?!, but Botvinnik responded: 9 ♗f3 ♘a6 10 a3! Later, two Scandinavian grandmasters also decided to take a look at it: so what happened next? This: 10...♘c7 11 ♘ge2 ♕d7 12 0-0 a4 13 ♕c4 ♖a5 14 ♗d2 b5 15 ♕c5 ♕d8 16 ♘a2! ♖a8 17 ♘b4 and Black's game is simply bad (C.Hansen – Hector, Vejle 1994).

1) **8...♘bd7 9 ♗f3** In the game Janosevic – Hort (Copenhagen 1965) White, quite frankly, complicated his development unnecessarily: 9 ♘h3?! ♕b6 10 ♕d1?! And after 10...♘e8! he immediately began to have difficulty finding moves. He played 11 ♗e3, but then came 11...♘df6 12 ♘f4 ♕xb2 with advantage.

9...♘b6 The tabiya of the variation 8 ♗e2.

He needs to develop, but how? Obviously, 10 ♗f4, 10 ♗g5 or 10 ♘ge2.

a) **10 ♗f4** Apart from everything else, this is excellent prophylaxis against 10...e6?! – 11 d6! ♗d7 12 ♗e5!, and Black already has major problems: 12...♘bd5 13 ♘ge2 ♗c6 14 ♘xd5 ♘xd5 15 0-0 etc.

(Sveshnikov – Gipslis, Naberezhny Chelny 1988).

10...♗f5 Also possible is 10...♗g4 but its main defect is Black's complete lack of counterplay after 11 ♗xg4 ♘xg4 12 ♘f3 ♘f6 13 d6! ed 14 0-0. He can hardly get moving, e.g. 14...♘h5 15 ♗g5 ♕d7 16 a4! ♖ae8 17 a5 ♘c8 18 ♖fe1 (Gulko – Delaney, New York 1998).

11 ♖d1 ♕d7 V.V. Smyslov treated this position quite riskily: 11...♕c8 12 h3 ♕c4?! After 13 ♘ge2 ♕xb3 14 ab ♗c2 15 ♖a1 ♖xb3 16 d6 ♘fd5! 17 de ♖fe8 18 ♗d6 ♗f6 19 0-0 ♗xe7 it all came together pretty well (Bhend – Smyslov, Tel Aviv 1964). On the other hand we don't know how Black intended to reply to 13 d6! ed 14 ♗xd6 ♖fe8+ 15 ♘ge2.

12 h3 h5 13 ♘ge2 White resolved the problems of defence of the d5 pawn more simply in the game Gulko – Tukmakov (Vilnius 1978): 13 ♗e5 ♖fd8 14 ♗xf6 ♗xf6 15 ♘ge2 However this didn't bother his opponent: 15...h4!? 16 0-0 ♖ac8 17 ♖fe1 ♘c4 18 ♘f4 ♕d6 with sufficient counterplay.

13...♖fd8 (Black has successfully completed his development and there is nothing left for White but to 'shed' the extra pawn – and not in the most favourable light for him) **14 d6!? ed 15 0-0 d5** He could have waited with this move. But nor should he drag it out as Black did in the game Ehlvest – Timman (Riga 1995): 15...♖ac8 16 ♘g3 ♖c4? (16...d5) 17 ♗g5 ♖dc8 18 ♗e2 ♗e6? 19 d5! winning.

After 15...d5 White arrives at a crossroads.

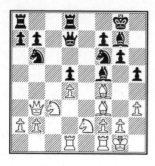

It is possible to win a pawn –
16 ♘g3 ♗e6 17 ♘b5 ♘e8 18 ♘xa7,
but **18...♘c4!** forces White to allow a
repetition of moves: **19 ♘b5 ♘a5
20 ♕a4 ♘c4** (Pavasovic – Ivacic,
Portoroz 1996). Incidentally,
Botvinnik advised Black not to hurry
to force a draw, but consolidate by
means of 16...♖ac8!? 17 ♗g5 ♗e6.

However after 16 ♗g5 or 16 ♗e5
Black 'unloads' his counterplay with
the help of one or other tactical
operation:

16 ♗e5 ♗g4! 17 hg hg 18 ♗xf6
♗xf6 (Sveshnikov – Burovic, Torcy
1991) or

16 ♗g5 ♗g4! 17 ♗xg4 hg 18 h4
♖e8 (Georgadze – Vaganian, USSR
1983), and both times achieved the
better position. Therefore today the
move 10 ♗f4 has rather fallen into
the shade.

b) **10 ♗g5**

Despite the fact that the variation
has had extensive practice, it is
difficult to give any kind of clear
cut recommendation as to its
performance.

Thus, even the extravagant
10...h6?! 11 ♗xf6 ef!? is apparently
possible: 12 ♘ge2 f5 13 0-0 ♗d7
14 ♖fd1 ♕b8 15 a4 ♘c8 16 d6 ♘xd6
17 ♘f4 ♔h7 18 ♖ac1 h5. White has
space and comfortable squares for his
minor pieces, while Black has two
bishops and a huge amount of
optimism (Potkin – Novik,
St.Petersburg 2003).

It is also possible to say the very
same about 10...a5?! On general
considerations the move ought not to
be particularly good; in practice,
however, Black frequently achieves a
game with fully equal rights.

11 ♖d1 a4 12 ♕b5 ♘e8 13 ♘ge2
♘d6 14 ♕b4 ♗d7 15 0-0 ♘bc8
16 ♘g3 ♖e8 17 ♖fe1 h6 18 ♗f4 ♕b6
(Pinter – Bronstein, Budapest 1977);

11 ♗xf6 ef!? 12 ♘ge2 ♗f5 13 0-0
♗d3 14 ♘a4 ♗xe2 15 ♗xe2 ♘xa4
16 ♕xa4 f5 17 ♗f3 ♕b6 18 ♖fd1
(Vasyukov – Ermenkov, Cienfuegos
1975) 18...♖fd8!? 19 ♖ab1 ♕b4 with
a draw.

It has to be established that Black
will find some way (transfer of the
knight to d6, bishop to d3, again
occasionally prodding the queen with
the edge pawn), and White – not
quite.

Usually Black (as also upon
10 ♗f4) will choose between two
moves with the bishop – to g4 or f5.

b1) 10...♗g4 11 ♗xf6 ♗xf3 12 ♘xf3

Botvinnik rejected 12...♗xf6?! in view of 13 a4 ♕c7 14 0-0 ♖fd8 15 a5 ♕c4 16 ♖a3! He assessed the endgame as being in White's favour.

Subsequent generations of grandmasters have transformed Botvinnik's idea in this variation: 12...♗xf6?! 13 0-0 ♕d6 14 a4 a5 15 ♖a3! ♖fd8 16 ♘e4 ♕b4 17 d6! ♘c4 18 ♕xb4 ab 19 ♖b3 ♖xa4 20 ♘c5. We single out the games Hebden – Arkell (London 1988); King – Arkell (London 1988). And why not? The endgame actually proves to be in White's favour!

It turns out that the idea **12...ef!? 13 0-0 ♕d7** is not an alternative.

The further continuation might be:

14 ♖fe1 ♖fd8 15 a4 ♗f8 16 ♘e4 ♔g7 17 d6 ♗xd6 18 ♘c5 ♕c6 White is effectively left with an extra d-pawn, but all the other factors are not in his favour. The most probable outcome of the game will be a draw (Kosten – Arkell, Hastings 1991).

b2) 10...♗f5 11 ♖d1

Compared to analogous positions from the variation 10 ♗f4 ♗f5 11 ♖d1 this is not quite appropriate: the continuation 11...♕d7 12 h3 h5 13 ♘ge2 ♖fd8, considered the main line when the bishop is on f4, here is dubious in view of 14 ♗xf6! ♗xf6 15 0-0 ♘c8 16 ♘g3 ♘d6 17 ♖fe1 ♖ac8 18 ♖e2 and White's chances are still superior (Sermek – Ivacic, Slovenia 1993).

Therefore Black returns to the plan with the advance of the a-pawn: **11...a5!? 12 ♘ge2 a4 13 ♕b5 h6** It is worth turning our attention to the game Dolmatov – Gurgenidze (Kutaisi 1978): 13...♗d7!? 14 ♕b4 ♖e8 15 0-0 h6 16 ♗xf6 ef 17 d6 ♗f8! 18 ♗xb7 ♖b8 19 ♗f3 f5 20 d5 ♕f6. For the present Black is two pawns down, but there is no doubt that he will win back both the one on d6 and (a little later) that on b2.

14 ♗xf6 ef!? 15 0-0 ♖e8

A position has been reached in which there is, as they say, 'dynamic equality': any one of three results is possible. White could extinguish the opponent's initiative and steadily realise his extra pawn, he can return the material and force a draw by exchanges, but might 'overdo' things and lose, even with the extra pawn.

c) **10 ♘ge2** Black's standard choices are: 10...♗g4 or 10...♗f5.

c1) **10...♗g4 11 ♗xg4 ♘xg4** Obviously, with the loss of the d5 pawn, White's chances of an advantage are also lost. He must somehow manage to do something before Black plays ♘g4-f6 or ♕d8-d7 and ♖f8(a8)-d8. But what?

12 a4! (and here is the reply – it is necessary to pester the knight b6) **12...♘f6!** Weaker is 12...a5?! 13 0-0 ♕d6 14 ♗f4 ♕b4. After 15 ♕d1! the black queen starts to feel uncomfortable.

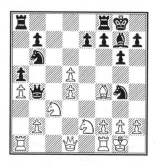

15...♘f6? 16 d6! ed 17 ♘b5 ♘e8 18 b3 d5 19 ♗c1!, and there is no defence against 20 ♗a3 (Ricardi – Glavina, Buenos Aires 1987);

15...♖fd8 16 ♗c7! ♖d7 17 d6! ed 18 ♗xb6 ♕xb6 19 ♘d5 ♕a7 20 ♘ec3 ♕xd4 21 h3 ♘h6 22 ♕xd4 ♗xd4 23 ♘b5 ♗xb2 24 ♖a2 ♗g7

25 ♘b6 (J.Polgar – Skembris, Corfu 1990).

13 ♘f4 (13 a5?! ♘bxd5 14 ♕xb7 is too early in view of 14...♕d6 15 ♕b3 ♖ab8 16 ♕d1 ♖fc8 17 0-0 ♕a6! 18 ♕d2 e6 19 ♖d1 ♖b3 20 ♕c2 ♕c4 with colossal compensation, Sabyanov – Burmakin, Kstovo 1997) **13...a5!?** The only move. Weak is 13...g5? 14 ♘fe2 h6 – White has still not castled kingside and therefore can allow himself to play 15 h4!

However if Black defends b7 – 13...♕d7, then he risks falling into an extremely passive position after 14 a5 ♘c8 15 0-0 ♘d6 16 ♖d1 ♖ac8 17 ♘d3!? ♘fe4 18 ♗e3 ♘xc3 19 bc ♕b5 20 ♖a3 ♖c4 21 ♘e5 (Kobalija – Ponomarev, Rimavska Sobota 1996).

14 0-0 ♕d6! (Black has made three best moves in a row and ought to be rewarded for his efforts) **15 ♖d1** The immediate 15 ♘b5 ♕d7 16 d6 ed has been encountered. In the game S.Polgar – Gipslis (Brno 1991) White did not manage to consolidate his claim to an advantage: 17 d5 ♖fc8 18 ♕d3 ♘e8 19 ♖a2 ♘c4 20 b3 ♘e5 21 ♕d1 ♘c7! with the unstoppable break b7-b5.

15...♖fd8 16 ♘b5 ♕d7 17 d6 ed 18 ♘c3 ♖a6 19 ♗e3 A critical position has arisen.

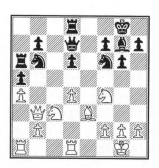

The fact that even very early on Black can be unnerved is shown by the game Sax – Gipslis (Valbo 1994): 19...♖c8 20 h3 ♖c4?! 21 ♘d3 ♕d8 22 ♘e5! Probably Black missed this shot but even upon the more appropriate 20...♘c4 21 ♘fd5 ♘xd5 22 ♘xd5 White has the more pleasant position.

We dare say the moment has come for a sortie into the opponent's camp: **19...♕f5!? 20 d5 ♘g4!** After **21 ♗xb6** (and what else?) **21...♕xf4** Losing is 22 ♗xd8? because of 22...♕xf2+ 23 ♔h1 ♕f4! with unavoidable mate. There remains **22 g3**, but then **22...♕h6 23 h4 ♖e8**, and we do not think that Black risks losing this position. This is how further events might develop:

24 ♕b5 ♖aa8 25 f4 ♕h5 26 ♖e1 ♘f6 27 ♔g2 ♕f5 28 ♖xe8+ ♖xe8 29 ♖f1 (or 29 ♖c1 h6!? followed by g6-g5!) **29...♘d7 30 ♗xa5 ♗d4!** with a threatening initiative.

c2) **10...♗f5** The idea is clear: while the knight is not standing on f4, the bishop will be ferried over to d3, and from there to c4, winning a pawn.

The knight, incidentally, can hardly be maintained on f4: 11 ♘f4 g5! 12 ♘fe2 g4! Continuing the forcing

variation – 13 ♘g3 ♗g6 14 ♗e2 ♘bxd5 15 0-0 (Botvinnik recommended 15 h3!?, but this is by now another story) 15...♕a5 16 ♗d2 ♖fd8 17 ♕xb7 ♖ab8 18 ♘xd5 ♕xd5 19 ♕xd5 ♘xd5, we reach a position in which the activity of the black pieces should be enough for a draw (Batakov – Volchok, correspondence, 1987).

After 11 d6 ed 12 ♗xb7 ♖b8 13 ♗f3 Black likewise obtains sufficient compensation for the pawn – 13...♘bd5 14 ♕d1 ♘b4 15 0-0 ♘c2 16 ♖b1 ♘b4 17 ♖a1 ♘c2 18 g4 ♗xg4 19 ♗xg4 ♘xa1 20 ♗f3 ♕d7 with very sharp play (Ulibin – Bagirov, Vilnius 1997).

11 0-0 It goes without saying that even here Black can (indeed in several ways) exchange the b-pawn for the d-pawn. That he obtains compensation for the material is confirmed by statistics. But it is still not sure that it is worth giving up b7!

For example, we examine the programmed 11...♗d3!? 12 d6 ed 13 ♗xb7 ♖b8 14 ♗f3 ♕d7 15 ♕d1 ♗a6 16 b3 ♖fe8 17 ♖e1 ♖bc8 18 ♗a3.

In the game Milos – Kamsky (Palma de Mallorca 1989) Black

played 18...d5 and soon won (White put a piece en prise). Also encountered is 18...g5!?, likewise with good results.

On the other hand, perhaps White's king is weak? Or he has pawn weaknesses? Or a poor development of pieces? You see none of these things. And a pawn...is a pawn.

Or 11...a5 12 ♗f4 ♗d3!? 13 d6 ed. This is a trap – Black invites a capture on b7: 14 ♗xb7? ♖b8 15 ♗f3 ♘bd5!, actually with good play. But even here it is not certain that Black's construction is without defects. Thus in the game Dolmatov – Adams (Hastings 1989) followed 14 ♕d1!? ♗a6 15 b3! h6 16 h3 ♘h7 17 g3 ♖c8 18 ♗g2 ♖e8 19 ♖e1 ♘f6 20 ♖c1 and Black's minor pieces on the queen's flank find themselves unemployed until the end of the game.

The most accurate move appears to be **11...♕d7!?** – both to defend b7 and also to bring up the rook to d8. And the idea ♗f5-d3-c4 has not gone away.

12 a4!? ♗d3 (on 12...♖fd8 unpleasant is 13 d6! followed by a4-a5) **13 d6 ♗c4** Possibly the most accurate move here is 13...e6!? 14 ♗f4 ♗c4 15 ♕a3 ♖fd8 16 ♖fc1

♗f8 17 ♗e5 ♗xd6 18 ♗xd6 ♕xd6 (de Vries – Rogers, Wijk aan Zee 2003).

14 ♕b4 e6 The alternative, as is not difficult to imagine, is again a pawn sacrifice: 14...♕xd6!? 15 ♕xd6 ed 16 ♗xb7 ♖ab8 with compensation.

15 ♗g5 ♘fd5 16 ♗xd5 ed 17 ♗e7 ♖fe8 18 ♖fe1 ♘c8 19 ♘f4 a5 20 ♕a3 ♘xe7 21 de ♗h6 22 b3 ♗xf4 23 bc dc 24 ♘e4 ♔g7 We have failed to prove that the capture on d4 is bad. The maximum White gets after 24...♕xd4 is a complicated heavy piece endgame: 25 ♖ad1 ♕g7 26 ♘c3 ♕h6 27 h3 ♗d2 28 ♖e4 ♗xc3 29 ♕xc3 ♕g5 30 ♖d7 etc.

25 ♕f3 ♕f5 We have left the opening problems quite far behind but on the other hand the whole variation hardly looks forced.

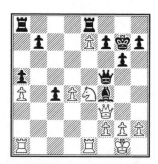

In this position White cannot transpose into the endgame – 26 g3?! – in view of 26...♖xe7! 27 ♕xf4 ♕xf4 28 gf ♖ae8. In the game Kornev – Alabkin (St.Petersburg 2003) White defended the rook e1 – **26 ♔f1!?**, at the same time setting a trap: on the capture of the e7 pawn follows 27 g4! with an immediate win. But such a side-step with the king also has its flip side: it allows

26...♗xh2!? 27 ♕xf5 gf 28 ♘c3 ♗d6 29 ♘d5 ♖ac8 with equality. Therefore worth considering is 26 ♔h1!?

Drawing a line under the variation 8...♘bd7, it should be mentioned that it develops with noticeable pressure from White. It takes a lot of effort for Black to maintain equality, and this obliges him to look for a roundabout way.

2) **8...♘a6!?** The knight goes not to c7, as one might first think, but to b4 (after ♕d8-b6).

There are three paths: 9 ♗g5, 9 ♗f4 or 9 ♗f3.

a) **9 ♗g5** This was played long ago by Robert Fischer, true, without particular success: **9...♕b6 10 ♕xb6 ab 11 a3** (directed against ♘a6-b4) **11...♖d8 12 ♗xf6 ♗xf6 13 ♖d1 ♗f5 14 ♗c4 ♖ac8 15 ♗b3 b5! 16 ♘f3 b4 17 ab ♘xb4 18 ♔e2 ♗c2 19 ♗xc2 ♘xc2 20 ♔d3 ♘b4+** with equality (Fischer – Yanofsky, Netanya 1968);

b) **9 ♗f4** Superficially – a simple developing move, but in fact – a trap: if 9...♕a5?, then 10 d6! ♗e6 11 ♕b5!, and Black remains a pawn down, and without compensation for it. For example: 11...♕b4 12 de ♕xe7 13 ♘f3 ♘b4 14 0-0 ♖fd8 15 a3 ♘c2

16 ♖ad1 ♖ac8 17 d5 ♗d7 18 d6! (Cherniaev – Dunnington, London 1999).

9...♕b6!? 10 ♕xb6 ab 11 d6 More cunning would be to wait until the knight jumps to b4, and only then carry out the break: 11 ♖c1!? ♘b4 12 d6! The pawn cannot be taken, and the exchange occurs without hindrance: 12...♖e8 13 de ♖xe7 14 ♗e5 (Inkiov – Hodgson, Palma de Mallorca 1989). White won this game; true, Venzislav Inkiov himself regarded his plan with scepticism. The Bulgarian grandmaster considered that after 14...♘fd5!? 15 ♘xd5 ♘xd5 16 ♘f3 ♗xe5 17 de ♘f4 Black would retain possibilities of fighting for the initiative.

11...ed 12 ♗xd6 ♖d8

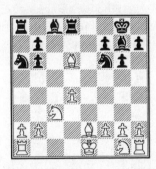

Yet another position with 'dynamic equality'. White has – a pawn, Black has – development. In the game Ulibin – Evseev (St.Petersburg 1998) White tried to hang on to the material – 13 ♘b5, but after 13...♗d7!? (a recommendation of Karsten Muller) he might have run into difficulties. Apparently the right strategy lies in an immediate return of the pawn and eradicating his lag in development: **13 ♗a3!? ♖xd4 14 ♘f3 ♖d8**

15 0-0 ♗e6 (15...♘c5!? 16 ♖ad1 ♗d7) **16 ♘g5 ♘d5 17 ♘xe6 ♘xc3 18 ♗xa6 fe 19 ♗c4 ♘d5 20 ♖ad1** White's superiority has increased noticeably (Shaked – Perelstein, Seattle 2003). Probably, not without help from the opponent.

c) **9 ♗f3** (considered the strongest) **9...♕b6** It is not clear whether it is worth first exchanging the light-squared bishops: 9...♗g4 10 ♗xg4 ♘xg4 11 ♘ge2 ♕b6. True, the d5 pawn is weakened, but in any case White intends to give it up. The game Wahls – Lutz (Cologne 1989) bore witness to the fact that Black was probably wrong: 12 ♕xb6 ab 13 0-0 ♘f6 14 ♗f4 ♖fd8 15 d6! ed 16 ♘b5 ♘e8 17 ♘ec3 ♘ac7 18 ♖fd1 and White has the advantage.

After 9...♕b6 the choice, as before, is to exchange yourself (10 ♕xb6) or allow this to be done for you.

c1) **10 ♕xb6 ab 11 ♘ge2** (Botvinnik's idea, to take under control the c2 square, has not received recognition: 11 ♗f4 ♘b4 12 ♔d2!?) **11...♘b4 12 0-0 ♖d8 13 d6!?** Practice has shown that only in this way is it possible to fight for the advantage.

13...♖xd6 14 ♗f4 ♖d7 15 ♖fd1

(worth considering is 15 ♗e5!? ♖a5 16 ♖fd1, Dolmatov – Evseev, Novgorod 1999) **15...♘fd5** Slightly weaker is 15...♘bd5 – after 16 ♗e5 ♖d8 17 ♘f4 the knight f6 and the bishop g7 will remain for some time, as it were, 'out of play':

17...♘xf4 (incorrect is 17...♘xc3 18 bc g5?! – White obtains a great advantage by force: 19 ♗xf6! ♗xf6 20 ♘d5 ♖d6 21 ♖db1 ♖a6 22 ♘c7 ♖a4 23 ♘e8!, Potkin – Burmakin, St.Petersburg 2000) 18 ♗xf4 ♗g4 19 ♗xb7 ♗xd1 20 ♗xa8 ♗g4 21 ♗f3!? ♗xf3 22 gf ♖xd4 23 ♗e3 ♖d6 24 ♘b5 ♖d8 25 a4! All captures have been made and it must be acknowledged that White has chances of victory (Marin – Slovinianu, Romania 2000).

Therefore practice turns to the side of 15...♘fd5 – now both the knight b4 and the bishop g7 themselves take an active part in the play.

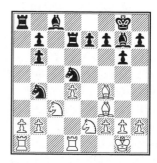

Weak is 16 ♗e5?! ♘xc3 17 bc ♗xe5 18 de ♘d3 19 ♗g4 e6 20 f4 ♖a4! 21 ♗f3 (21 g3 ♘xe5!) 21...♘xf4 (Galdunts – Burmakin, Graz 2001).

Therefore if White wants to establish a bishop on e5, it is necessary first to exchange: 16 ♘xd5

♘xd5 17 ♗e5. Yet another trap, this time a positional one: 17...♖d8?! 18 ♗xd5! ♖xd5 19 ♘c3 ♖d8 20 ♗xg7 ♔xg7 21 d5!, and once again it is White who is playing for a win (Sveshnikov – Adorjan, Moscow 1989).

But if Black sees through the trick, then he should not have a problem: 17...♘b4! (avoiding the exchange) 18 ♗xg7 ♔xg7 19 a3 ♘c6 20 ♖ac1 ♖d6 21 d5 ♘e5 22 ♖c7!? (22 ♗e4 b5) 22...♘xf3+ 23 gf (Zavgorodny – Evseev, Alushta 2002) 23...e6 24 ♖dc1 ♗d7 25 de ♗xe6 26 ♘f4 ♗f5, and the game is close to a draw.

If we forget about the idea ♗f4-e5 then there remains **16 ♗g3 ♘xc3!? 17 bc ♘c6 18 ♘f4 ♖a5 19 h4** Black's redoubt in this endgame is defended by the St.Petersberg grandmaster Denis Evseev.

At first he tried 19...♔f8 20 ♖ab1!? e5 (weaker is 20... ♖xa2?! 21 ♘d5 ♖d8 22 ♗c7 ♖e8 23 ♖xb6), but after 21 de ♘xe5 22 ♗d5 ♖c5 23 ♗b3 ♖xd1+ 24 ♖xd1 ♖xc3 25 ♘d5 it must be said that all Black's problems are behind him (Voitsekhovsky – Evseev, Tula 1999). Evseev lost this game, not finding the correct order of moves: 25...♖c6! 26 ♘xb6 ♗e6!

But the next time he was ready with an important improvement: **19...e5!?** (not spending time on the unnecessary king move) **20 de ♘xe5** There is full equality: **21 ♗d5 ♘c6 22 ♖ac1 ♗e5** etc. (Vokarev – Evseev, Toliatti 2003).

c2) **10 ♘ge2!?** How strange that his own doubled pawns on the b-file give White far more chances than the other side's!

10...♕xb3 11 ab ♘b4 12 0-0 ♖d8

Finally, however, White can fall back on the standard method – 13 d6, and then:

13...ed?! 14 h3!? (preventing the exchange of the light-squared bishops) 14...♘c2 15 ♖a4 ♗d7 16 ♖c4 ♖ac8 17 ♗f4 d5 18 ♖xc8 ♗xc8 19 ♗e5 ♗e6 20 ♘f4 with appreciable pressure;

13...♖xd6!? 14 ♘b5 ♖d8 15 ♘c7 ♖b8 16 ♗f4 ♗g4 17 ♗xg4 ♘xg4 18 h3 ♘f6 19 ♖xa7 ♘c6 20 ♖aa1 ♖bc8 21 ♘b5 ♘d5 22 ♗d2 (Ehlvest – Yagupov, Batumi 2002) 22...e6!? White's chances of success are not great.

But exploiting the open a-file is too great a temptation: **13 ♖a5!?** Even if this brings White nothing in particular, the freshness of the resulting positions makes them attractive. In the game Gelfand – Morozevich (Wijk aan Zee 2002) Black replied 13...h6!? Taking under control not only the g5 square, but also the neighbouring one – f4, since on 14 ♗f4?? follows 14...g5!, and White loses one of the bishops.

After the forced 14 h4 Morozevich easily created counterplay after: 14...♘d3!? 15 ♖d1 ♘xc1 16 ♖xc1 b6 17 ♖a4 ♗b7 18 d6 ♗xf3 19 de ♖d7 20 gf ♖e8. The weakness of the white pawns on the king's flank guarantees him a not insignificant material advantage. Meanwhile instead of 13...h6!? more popular is **13...a6**, which is also probably enough for equality.

14 ♗g5 Also tried is 14 ♗f4, but Black manages to extinguish some of the opponent's activity: 14...♗g4!? 15 ♗xg4 ♘xg4 16 ♖c5 ♘f6 17 d6!? (obviously, the only chance) 17...ed 18 ♖c7 ♖ab8 19 ♗g5 ♖dc8 20 ♖c4 ♘d3 (Acs – Smetankin, Rimavska Sobata 1996).

14...h6 15 ♗xf6

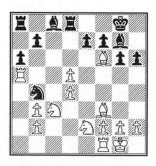

15...ef!? The whole idea, though also quite possible is 15...♗xf6 16 ♖a4 ♘d3 17 ♗e4 ♗f5 18 ♗xf5 gf 19 ♖b1 b5 20 ♖a5 ♘b4, and Black equalises (Bauer – Okhotnik, Alberville 2002).

16 ♘a4 b5!? 17 ♘c5 ♖b8 18 ♖c1 f5 19 g3 ♖b6 In this complicated position Black's chances are in no way worse (Charbonneau – Perelstein, Bermuda 2002).

The system 1 e4 c6 2 d4 d5 3 ed cd 4 c4 ♘f6 5 ♘c3 g6!? is a difficult, heavy-going variation in which from the very first moves Black must work intensively and put every effort into dealing with its intricacies.

Black sacrifices a pawn – but what does he get in return? Either compensation, which (at least, at first) does not look quite sufficient, or an inferior endgame, in which he still needs to earn a draw. Variations, where White risks no less than the opponent (for example, 6 ♕b3 ♗g7 7 cd 0-0 8 ♘ge2 ♘a6!? 9 g3 b5!? or 8...♖e8!? 9 g3 e6!?) – an exception which only proves the rule.

Such a variation cannot be a 'pass' in our opening repertoire. It needs either to be studied properly, examined and understood with all its fine points, so as to feel it, so to speak, with the tips of one's fingers – or not to play it at all.

Index to Chapter Three

1 e4 c6 2 d4 d5 3 ed cd 4 c4 ♘f6

5 ♘c3 g6   62

I. 6 cd   62

  A. 6...♘xd5   62

    1) 7 ♗c4   62

    2) 7 ♕b3   64

    7...♘b6

      a) 8 ♗b5+   65

      b) 8 d5   66

      8...♗g7 9 ♗e3 0-0 10 ♖d1 ♘a6

        b1) 11 ♗xa6   66

        b2) 11 ♘f3   67

  B. 6...♗g7   68

    1) 7 ♗c4   68

    7...0-0 8 ♘ge2

      a) 8...♘bd7   69

      b) 8...♘a6   69

    2) 7 ♗b5+   70

    7...♘bd7 8 d6

      a) 8...0-0   70

      b) 8...e6   71

      c) 8...ed   71

II. 6 ♕b3   74

6...♗g7 7 cd 0-0

A. 8 ♘ge2   75

  1) 8...♘bd7   75

  2) 8...♘a6   76

  3) 8...♖e8   77

B. 8 g3   78

  1) 8...e6   78

  2) 8...♘a6   79

C. 8 ♗e2   80

  1) 8...♘bd7   81

  9 ♗f3 ♘b6

    a) 10 ♗f4   81

    b) 10 ♗g5   82

      b1) 10...♗g4   83

      b2) 10...♗f5   83

    c) 10 ♘ge2   84

      c1) 10...♗g4   84

      c2) 10...♗f5   85

  2) 8...♘a6   87

    a) 9 ♗g5   87

    b) 9 ♗f4   87

    c) 9 ♗f3   88

    9...♕b6

      c1) 10 ♕xb6   88

      c2) 10 ♘ge2   89

Chapter Four

1 e4 c6 2 d4 d5 3 ed cd 4 c4 ♘f6
5 ♘c3 e6 6 ♘f3 ♘c6

The main move is 6 ♘f3, but first we look at the sidelines. There are three of them: 6 a3 (A), 6 c5 (B) and 6 ♗g5 (C).

A

6 a3!? Pursuing a concrete aim – not to allow the bishop to b4; however in many variations of the Panov Attack the move a2-a3 is useful also in its own right (for example, as part of the pawn chain a3-b4-c5-d4). Black's task is to find an order of moves upon which the very early advance of the a-pawn turns into a waste of a tempo.

6...♗e7 More rarely encountered is 6...dc, and this is understandable – it is more logical to take on c4 after White has developed the light-squared bishop. Upon 7 ♗xc4 ♗e7 8 ♘f3 0-0 9 0-0 the game (with an

increase in move numbers by one) transposes into a corresponding variation of the Nimzo-Indian defence – 1 d4 ♘f6 2 c4 e6 3 ♘c3 ♗b4 4 e3 d5 5 a3 ♗e7 6 ♘f3 0-0 7 ♗d3 dc 8 ♗xc4 c5 9 0-0 cd 10 ed.

Let us turn our attention to the fact that Black can exploit the absence of the knight on c6 and carry out the manoeuvre ♗c8-d7-c6-d5, which is useful for the blockade of the d4 pawn. Thus, in the game Topalov – Yudasin (Pamplona 1995) was played 9...♗d7!? 10 ♕e2 (harmless is 10 d5 ed 11 ♘xd5 ♘xd5 12 ♕xd5 ♘c6 13 ♕h5 in view of 13...♖a5! 14 ♘g5 ♗xg5 15 ♕xg5 ♖fe8! with ♗e6 to follow) 10...♗c6 11 ♖d1 ♗d5!

Play continued 12 ♘xd5 ♘xd5 13 ♗d3 ♘d7!? (more solid than the routine development of the knight to c6) 14 ♕e4, and now, in the opinion of Yudasin, Black equalises by means of 14...♘7f6 15 ♕h4 ♕b6.

7 ♘f3 With the knight on g1, 7 c5!? 0-0 8 ♗d3 b6 9 b4 a5 10 ♘a4 has independent significance. This is because the tempo saved on the development of the king's knight has been spent by White on the erection of a pawn wall – from 'a' to 'd'. The idea is interesting but clearer than daylight is also its 'painful spot': no knight on f3 – no control over the e5 square.

From this also comes the decision: 10...bc 11 bc ♗a6 12 ♗c2 (it is clear that after the exchange of light-squared bishops Black has a good game) 12...♕c7! 13 ♘e2 e5! (the pawn wall is wrecked and all White's efforts turn to dust) 14 de ♕xe5 15 ♗f4 ♕e6 16 ♘b6 ♖a7 17 ♗e3 ♗xe2 18 ♕xe2 ♘bd7 and Black's position is better.

7...0-0 8 ♗d3 dc 9 ♗xc4 A position is reached, analogous to that which occurred in the game Topalov – Yudasin. Analogous, but not identical – White has brought the bishop to c4 in two moves, and not one, and therefore has not managed to castle kingside.

9...b6 Sharper is 9...a6!? 10 0-0 b5 11 ♗a2 ♗b7. Events developed interestingly in the game Zhang Penxiang – Galkin (Erevan 1999):

12 ♗g5 ♘bd7! Since the pawn is already on a3, there is no point thinking about the manoeuvre ♘b8-c6-b4. Therefore the knight is better developed on d7 and then (depending on White's play) to decide where to transfer it. The best square is b6, but it is quite possible that the knight has to transfer to f8 for defence of the king.

13 ♗b1!? (not spending time on bringing the queen's rook into play) 13...♖e8 14 ♕d3 ♖c8 15 ♖d1 ♕c7 16 ♗h4 ♖ed8 17 ♗a2 ♕b8. It is possibly worth simplifying the position: 17...♘c5!? 18 ♕e2 ♘ce4 19 ♘xe4 ♗xe4, and it is not clear how White can generate further threats.

18 ♕e2 ♘b6 19 ♗g3 (the tempting piece sacrifice 19 ♗xe6?! does not work because of the intermediate 19...♗xf3! and Black repulses the attack: 20 gf fe 21 ♕xe6+ ♔f8 22 ♘e4 ♕c7! 23 ♗xf6 gf 24 ♘xf6 ♔g7! 25 ♖ac1 ♕d6) 19...♕a7! 20 ♘e5 ♘bd5 with a very complicated, double-edged struggle.

10 0-0 ♗b7 At the very least, no worse is 10...♗a6!?, but this continuation has still not been successfully instilled into practice with the same credibility as the usual development of the bishop on the long diagonal.

The idea of 10...♗a6 lies in the fact that Black effects an exchange of the opponent's most dangerous attacking piece – the light-squared bishop. The downside of the plan is the weakening of the c6 square, but Black can live with this:

11 ♗xa6 ♘xa6 12 ♘e5 ♘c7 13 ♘c6 ♕e8 14 ♘xe7+ ♕xe7 15 ♗g5 h6 16 ♗h4 ♖ad8 17 f4 ♕d7! (an unconventional but successful decision) 18 ♗xf6 gf 19 ♕h5 (also in the case of 19 ♕g4+ ♔h7 20 ♖ad1 ♖g8 21 ♕f3 f5! Black risks nothing) 19...♕xd4+ 20 ♔h1 ♔h7 and White has yet to prove that his initiative is worth the sacrificed pawn (Rozentalis – Speelman, Esbjerg 2001).

11 ♖e1 ♘c6 The position has the look of the tabiya of the Queen's Gambit or, more accurately, the Semi-Tarrasch defence. Opening reference – D40, but with the following order of moves: 1 d4 d5 2 c4 e6 3 ♘f3 ♘f6 4 ♘c3 c5 5 e3 ♘c6 6 a3 cd 7 ed ♗e7 8 ♗d3 0-0 9 0-0 dc 10 ♗xc4 b6 11 ♖e1 ♗b7.

12 ♗a2 ♖c8 13 ♕d3 ♖e8 In the game Stein – Peterson (Kiev 1964) Black transferred the rook to d7 – 13...♖c7!? 14 ♗g5 ♖d7, but this did not bring a radical change. After 15 ♖ad1 ♕c8 16 ♗b1! g6 17 ♗a2! ♖e8 18 ♕e3 White continued to hold the initiative.

14 ♗g5 ♘d5 15 h4!? ♘xc3 16 bc g6 17 ♖ad1 ♘a5 18 ♖e5

This is how the game Bernt – Dettling (Germany 2001) continued. After **18...♗xf3 19 ♕xf3** Black hurried with an exchange on g5. More solid looks **19...♕d6!?**, when neither 20 ♕e2 ♗xg5 21 hg ♘c6 22 ♖e3 ♘e7!, nor 20 ♗xe7 ♖xe7 21 ♕f6 ♘c4 22 ♗xc4 ♖xc4 23 d5 ♕d8! are so terrible.

It is not worth spending time preventing the threat of 6...♗b4 at such an early stage of the game. The move 6 a3 is experimental and on the whole narrows down White's possibilities.

B

6 c5 A normal development of events would be 6...♗e7 7 ♘f3, but we will meet this position in Chapter Six (under a different order of moves – 6 ♘f3 ♗e7 7 c5). But first we stop at **6...b6?!**, though the idea is premature (the undermining of the c5 square is better undertaken after castling).

We are mainly interested in the position after **7 b4 a5 8 ♘a4 ♘fd7** (in the game Delchev – Pyankov, Saint Affrique 2002, Black first exchanged on c5 – 8...bc 9 bc, and only then played 9...♘fd7, but White all the same easily obtained the advantage: 10 ♘f3 ♗e7 11 ♗f4 0-0 12 ♖c1 ♘c6 13 ♗b5 ♗b7 14 0-0 ♗f6 15 ♖e1 ♖c8 16 ♗f1 ♘e7 17 ♕b3 ♗c6 18 ♘b6) **9 ♗b5 bc 10 bc ♗a6 11 ♕e2**

If Black has a way to equality then this must be by some kind of refined trickery. But this is something we do not see. And he could even lose at once here: 11...♗e7? 12 ♘b6 ♖a7 13 ♘xd7 ♗xb5 14 ♕xb5 ♖xd7 (14...♘xd7 15 c6) 15 ♗f4! 0-0 16 ♖b1 (Popovic – Wells, New York 1984). Not much better is 11...♕c7 12 ♘b6 ♖a7 13 ♗xa6 ♘xb6 14 ♗b5+ (Netzel – Hazelhorst, Germany 1996).

Apparently it is necessary to play **11...♗xb5 12 ♕xb5 ♕c7 13 ♘b6 ♖a7**, though after **14 ♖b1** Black's position inspires no confidence at all.

C

6 ♗g5 This move is an original test for Black's understanding of the nuances of the Panov Attack. This can be expressed in an even more concrete way: Black must understand why he should not play 6...♘c6?!

1) **6...♘c6?! 7 c5!** Only so! Unconvincing is 7 cd ed 8 ♗b5 ♗e7 9 ♘f3 0-0 10 ♗xc6 bc 11 ♘e5 if only because of 11...h6!? He can win a pawn – 12 ♘xc6, but after 12...♕e8 13 ♘xe7+ ♕xe7+ 14 ♗e3 (Sveshnikov – Peresipkin, Chelyabinsk 1975) 14...♗a6! White, quite frankly, is taking a risk.

Ulibin, in a game against Morovic (Pula 1999), did not take the pawn and play quickly led to a draw: 12 ♗e3 ♗d6 13 0-0 c5 14 ♗f4 ♗b7 15 ♖c1.

After 6 ♗g5 ♘c6?! 7 c5!, because of the pin, Black is deprived of his main resource – the jump of the knight to e4. Strategically he has nothing to counter White's claw of pawns on the queen's flank.

Nothing helps, and 7...b6?! only plays into White's hands because of 8 b4!

7...h6?! enjoys a dubious reputation: 8 ♗xf6 ♕xf6 9 ♗b5 g6 10 ♘f3 ♗g7 11 ♕d2 ♗d7 12 ♖d1 0-0 13 0-0 ♕d8 14 ♖fe1!, and all the key dark squares find themselves under the control of white pieces and pawns. In the game Ehlvest – Granda (Erevan 1996) play continued 14...b6

15 ♗xc6! ♗xc6 16 b4 bc 17 bc ♖b8 18 ♘e5 ♗e8 19 f4! with a solid advantage.

When everything is bad, tricks come into play. Here we have just such a case: instead of 14...b6 he could try 14...♕a5!?

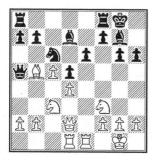

If White decides that Black has blundered a pawn, and plays 15 ♗xc6?! ♗xc6 16 ♘xd5?, then he loses all his advantage: 16...♕xd2 17 ♘e7+ ♔h7 18 ♘xd2 (18 ♖xd2? ♗xf3 19 gf ♖fe8 – the knight falls) 18...♗xd4.

But if White is adamant about having his own way – 15 a3!, then Black's position again becomes worthless. Incidentally, after 15 a3! there is the immediate threat of 16 b4, and on a3 he cannot take because the queen would then be trapped by ♖a1 and ♖eb1.

Objectively, the strongest path is 7...♗e7 8 ♘f3, and this position too we will look at in detail in Chapter Six (6 ♘f3 ♗e7 7 ♗g5 ♘c6 8 c5). But in the meanwhile let's stop at the move **7...♗d7**, upon which Black places the opponent under the obligation to decide how exactly to carry out b2-b4.

8 a3!? Less promising is 8 ♗b5 b6 9 ♗xc6 ♗xc6 10 b4 in view of 10...bc 11 bc ♕a5! (the black queen undertakes counterplay all by herself) 12 ♗d2 ♕a6! In the game Topalov – Gulko (Elenite 1995) there followed 13 ♘f3 ♘d7 14 ♕e2 ♕xe2+ 15 ♔xe2 ♗e7 16 ♗e3 f6!? 17 ♘e1 0-0 18 ♘d3 ♖ab8 19 ♖ab1 a5 20 f4 g5!, and White did not manage to win this endgame.

8...b6 9 b4 bc 10 dc h6 11 ♗e3 a6 (on anything else he cannot slow down the advance of the pawns) **12 ♗e2 g6!? 13 ♖c1 ♗g7 14 ♘f3 0-0 15 0-0 ♔h7** (up to this moment we have been following the game Damjanovic – Stojanovic, Bela Crkva 1996, but White was not able to detect the right plan in this position) **16 ♘d4!** On the queen's flank White has got everything he wants; now he needs to realise the dark-squared strategy in the centre. The exchange of knights is the first, but extremely important step. Then – the advance f2-f4, establishing d4 for the knight or the bishop, with a complete blockade.

16...e5 (or 16...♕c7 17 f4! ♖fd8 18 ♘xc6 ♗xc6 19 ♗d4!) **17 ♘xc6 ♗xc6**

18 f4! e4 Black is forced to let go of the key d4 square. In the opposite case everything turns out worse: 18...d4? 19 fe de 20 ♕xd8 ♖fxd8 21 ef or 18...ef?! 19 ♖xf4.

19 f5! Far more energetic than the direct 19 ♗d4 ♘e8 20 a4, after which Black, tempo by tempo, succeeds in generating counterplay: 20...♗xd4+ 21 ♕xd4 ♘g7 22 b5 ♘f5 23 ♕d2 ab 24 ab d4 25 bc e3!

19...♘e8 20 fg+ fg 21 ♖xf8 ♗xf8 22 ♗g4! (the e2 square is needed by the knight as a point of transfer on the way to its main objective – d4!) **22...♗g7 23 ♘e2!** White has an unquestionable positional advantage.

2) **6...♗e7 7 ♘f3 0-0!** Without the target on c6 the plan with c4-c5 and b2-b4-b5 loses half its strength. Moreover, having reliably tucked away his king into safety as well, Black can without difficulty undermine the opponent's pawn chain: 8 c5 b6! 9 b4 a5! 10 a3 ♘e4!? 11 ♗xe7 ♕xe7. If White continues to be stubborn – 12 ♘a4?, then he risks losing: 12...ab 13 ab bc 14 bc ♕a7 15 ♗d3 ♕a5+ 16 ♘d2 ♗d7 17 ♗c2 ♗b5 (Kan – Makogonov, Leningrad 1939).

Pushing the c-pawn to c5, without having the target of a black knight on c6, is foolish. Therefore once again it all comes down to the pawn pair c4-d5. Either White exchanges on d5 – when a position arises with symmetrical pawns on the d-file, or else Black takes on c4 – and continues the eternal debate about the 'isolani' on d4.

8 ♗d3 Choosing the 'isolani'. In the game Oral – Burmakin (Koszalin 1999) White took the first path – 8 ♖c1 b6 (incidentally, even here 8...dc!? 9 ♗xc4 ♘c6 10 0-0 ♘d5 is quite possible with favourable simplification) 9 ♗xf6 ♗xf6 10 cd ed 11 ♗e2 ♘c6 12 ♕a4 ♗b7 13 0-0, but after 13...a6!? 14 ♖fd1 b5 15 ♕c2 ♖c8 16 ♕f5 ♘e7 17 ♕g4 ♕d6 18 ♗d3 g6 Black does not achieve more than enduring equality.

8...dc 9 ♗xc4 a6 10 0-0 He can also prevent the thrust b7-b5 – 10 a4. However the accurate move 10...♗d7! (a well-known nuance – if the knight does not develop to c6, this square will be exploited by the bishop) brought the game Sharapov – Ovseevich (Alushta 2000) to a perfectly even endgame: 11 0-0 ♗c6 12 ♗a2 ♘bd7 13 ♕e2 ♖e8 14 ♖fd1 ♘d5 15 ♗xe7 ♕xe7 16 ♗xd5 ♗xd5 17 ♘xd5 ed 18 ♕xe7 ♖xe7 19 ♖ac1 ♘f8 etc.

10...b5 11 ♗d3 ♗b7 12 ♕e2 ♘c6 13 ♖ad1 ♘b4 14 ♗b1 ♘bd5 Black has done everything in a competent fashion and now should not experience any particular problems. Of course the whole game still lies ahead but for the time being he can have no complaints. The game J.Polgar – Inkiov (Stara Zagora 1990) continued: **15 ♘e4 ♘xe4 16 ♕xe4 g6 17 h4**

17...♖a7!? 18 ♕g4 ♘f6. The chances are mutual.

1 e4 c6 2 d4 d5 3 ed cd 4 c4 ♘f6 5 ♘c3 e6 6 ♘f3

We go over to the tabiya of the Panov Attack. Chapter Five will be devoted to a look at the continuation 6...♗b4, Chapter Six – to a look at 6...♗e7. But in this chapter we stop at the least favourable (among the main lines) move – **6...♘c6?!** You have probably already guessed what is the right reaction: **7 c5!**

It is precisely the position of the black knight on c6 that makes the

idea of the closed centre promising. Catching on to the knight (whether by b2-b4-b5, or the simple exchange ♗f1-b5xc6), White invariably seizes the e5 square. And it is this that determines his advantage.

As distinct from the position upon 6 ♗g5 ♘c6?! 7 c5!, here we glance at counterplay for Black, linked to the manoeuvre ♘f6-e4 and a subsequent advance of the kingside pawns (f7-f5 and even g7-g5). All the same, as shown by practice, White's chances are preferable.

We look at two replies for Black: 7...♗e7 (A) and an immediate 7...♘e4 (B).

A

7...♗e7 8 ♗b5! 0-0 Black can reserve the right to take on c6 with the bishop, and not the pawn: 8...♗d7. But after 9 0-0 0-0 10 ♖e1 a6 11 ♗xc6 ♗xc6 12 ♘e5! it becomes obvious that this does not change the evaluation of the position. The game Sadvakasov – Kobalija (Calicut 1998) continued: 12...♘d7 13 ♘xc6 bc 14 ♗f4! ♖e8 15 ♕a4 ♕c8 16 ♖e2! (in no case allowing the e5 square out of his hands) 16...f6 17 ♖ae1 and White has play on both flanks. Black – nowhere.

9 0-0 ♘e4! The only way of generating counterplay. That such play is generally possible is made clear upon the superficial 10 ♗f4?! After 10...g5! 11 ♗e3 ♗d7 12 ♖c1 f5! White, in the game Smirin – Olafsson (Istanbul 2003), managed, only with difficulty, to extinguish the opponent's initiative: 13 ♗xc6 ♗xc6

14 ♘e5 ♗f6 15 ♘xc6 bc 16 f3 ♘xc3 17 ♖xc3 f4 18 ♗f2 e5 19 ♕d3 ed 20 ♗xd4 ♕d7 21 ♗xf6 ♖xf6 with a quick draw.

Hardly particularly favourable is 10 ♖e1 ♘xc3 11 bc – White voluntarily spoils his pawn structure, for what? A possible continuation is:

11...♕c7 12 ♗d3 b6! 13 cb ab 14 ♘g5 ♗xg5 15 ♗xg5 ♗a6! (Brunell – Henkin, Stockholm 1996);

11...♗d7 12 ♖b1 b6! 13 c4 ♘a5 14 cb dc 15 ba ♖xa7 (Martin – Bagirov, Dieren 1990).

As we see, the simple resource b7-b6 exposes White's pawn weaknesses on the a- and c-files.

10 ♕c2! The most promising continuation. White bothers the knight e4, and also defends himself against doubled pawns on the c-file.

10...f5!? The game takes shape in a more simple way after 10...♘g5 11 ♗xg5 ♗xg5 12 ♘xg5 ♕xg5 13 ♖ad1 ♗d7 14 f4! ♕f6 15 ♕d2 g6 16 a3 ♖ad8 17 b4 ♘e7 18 ♗e2 (Zakhartsov – Lunev, Krasnodar 1999). White, as promised, controls the dark squares in the centre, though it remains unclear whether he missed a propitious moment to exchange on c6?

11 ♘e2!? A very important and fine moment. It seems there is a simple solution to the position: 11 ♗xc6 bc 12 ♘e5. But after 12...♕c7! it becomes clear that the white knight on e5 is still uncomfortable – a capture is threatened on c5, while 13 ♗f4, as we already know, is poor because of 13...g5! In the game Delchev – Henkin, (Pardubice 1997) there followed 13 ♘xe4 fe 14 f4 ♗a6 15 ♖f2 ♗h4 16 g3 ♗f6 17 ♗e3 ♗xe5 18 de ♗d3 19 ♕c3 ♖ab8, and White obtains no advantage at all.

So the attempt to resolve the position by the really quite simple method of ♗f1-b5xc6, followed by ♘e5, is far from always being a success!

11...♗f6?! Too timid. Once again, as in the previous examples, he should venture 11...g5!? 12 ♗xc6 bc 13 ♘e5 ♕c7! White can then fight for the advantage by 14 b4!? (defending the c5 pawn and threatening to expel the enemy knight) 14...f4 15 ♖e1 a5 16 f3! ♘f6 17 ba ♖xa5 18 ♗d2 ♖a8 19 ♘c1!

12 ♗f4 ♗d7 13 ♗xc6 bc 14 ♗e5 ♘g5 15 ♘xg5 ♗xe5 16 de ♕xg5 17 f4 The position is clearly favourable for White (Velimirovic – Solmundarsson, Reykjavik 1974).

B

7...♘e4!? More concrete than 7...♗e7. Black places his hopes on the fact that he succeeds in distracting the opponent from play on the dark squares.

8 ♕c2! As in the variation 7...♗e7 8 ♗b5 0-0 9 0-0 ♘e4, this is the best reaction to the thrust of the knight. The point lies in the fact that White does not spoil his pawn structure.

It is more natural to look at the development of the light-squared bishop, but then, by exchanging on c3 and undermining the c5 pawn with the move b7-b6, Black obtains counterchances, e.g. 8 ♗d3 ♘xc3! 9 bc ♗e7 10 0-0 b6! 11 cb ab 12 ♗b5 ♗d7 13 c4 dc 14 ♗xc4 ♘a5 15 ♗e2 0-0 16 d5 ed 17 ♕xd5 ♗e6 18 ♕xd8 ♖fxd8 19 ♗e3 ♗c5 (Grosar – Dautov, Altensteig 1995).

Incidentally in the variation 8 ♗d3 ♘xc3! 9 bc, apart from play with b7-b6, it is necessary to remember the idea of grandmaster Alexei Vizhmanavin: 9...e5!?

The idea is obviously 'non-classical' (Black is too badly developed to open the centre at such an early stage of the game), but it seems that there is no direct refutation.

Encountered is 10 ♘xe5 ♘xe5, and then:

11 ♕e2 ♗xc5! 12 ♕xe5+ ♕e7 13 ♗f4 ♗d6 14 ♕xe7+ ♔xe7 15 ♗xd6+ ♔xd6 16 ♔d2 ♗d7 17 ♖he1 ♖he8 18 ♖xe8 with a draw (Smirin – Vizhmanavin, Elenite 1993);

11 de ♗xc5 12 ♕h5! g6 13 ♕h6 ♗f8 14 ♕f4 ♗c5 15 ♗b5+ ♗d7 16 ♗xd7+ ♕xd7 17 ♕f6 ♖g8 18 ♖b1 with a minimal advantage (Dolmatov – Vizhmanavin, Novosibirsk 1993).

We return to 8 ♕c2. The knight on e4 is hanging, and Black must decide what to do about it: exchange (8...♘xc3), consolidate (8...f5) or sharpen the position even further (8...♕a5).

1) **8...♘xc3** A routine move. By exchanging his only active piece, Black deprives himself of any counterplay: 9 ♕xc3 a5 (in order to forestall the advance of the pawns on the queen's flank, quite bad is 9...♗e7 10 ♗b5 ♗d7 11 0-0 0-0 12 ♖e1 ♘e5?! 13 ♘xe5 ♗xb5 14 a4 ♗e8 15 b4, Jansa – Kolarov, Lugano 1968) 10 ♗b5 ♗d7 11 0-0 ♗e7 12 ♗f4 0-0 13 ♖fe1 ♗f6 14 ♕d2 ♖e8 15 ♖ac1 a4 16 ♗xc6 ♗xc6 17 ♖c3! ♗e7 18 ♘e5 ♗b5 19 ♖h3 ♗f8 20 ♕c2 In view of the fact that bad is 20...g6 21 ♘xf7! (Gulko – Contreras, Cali 2001), White will hold the initiative for a long time.

2) Occasionally **8...f5** is met. The general opinion is that upon accurate play White obtains a positional advantage. Here are a few examples from practice: 9 ♗b5 ♗d7 10 0-0 ♗e7 11 ♗xc6 ♗xc6 (or 11...bc 12 ♘e5 0-0 13 f3 ♘xc3 14 ♕xc3 ♗e8 15 b4 ♗f6 16 ♖e1, Schmidt – Lechtynsky, Bavaria 1998) 12 b4 0-0 13 ♗f4 g5 14 ♗e5 f4 15 ♘d2 ♘xd2 16 ♕xd2 f3 17 g4! (Gdanski – Bartel, Warsaw 2002).

3) **8...♕a5!?** Out of three possibilities for Black – it goes without saying this is the most intriguing. Nevertheless, the right recipe for White was prescribed as long ago as 1908!

9 a3! Here already it is necessary to cast off general considerations and simply accurately calculate variations. Thus upon 9 ♗b5 ♘xc3 10 ♗xc6+ bc 11 ♗d2! ♕a6 12 ♗xc3 f6! Black retains the capability to continue the struggle. For example, 13 b4 ♗e7 14 a4 0-0 15 ♕e2 ♖b8 16 ♕xa6 ♗xa6 17 ♔d2 e5! (Vasyukov – Lutikov, Kiev 1964).

But here, upon 9...♘xc3 10 ♗d2! the black queen already cannot retreat along the f1-a6 diagonal. Another idea is the move 9 a3! shown by the variation 9...♗d7 10 ♖b1! with the threat of b2-b4. In the game Reti – Duras (Vienna 1908) White continued to act in exemplary fashion: 10...f5 11 b4 ♕c7 12 g3! (securing the f4 square for the bishop) 12...a6 13 ♗f4 ♕c8 14 ♘a4!

The taste of old games, like old wine, becomes all the richer and finer with the years.

9...♗e7 10 ♖b1 f5 11 b4 ♕c7 This is how the game Gdanski – Henkin (Osterskar 1995) continued. The Polish grandmaster without further ado played 12 b5 and achieved victory after a great fight. But, in our view, strongest in this position is the decision 'à la Reti':

12 g3! If 12...♗f6, then after 13 ♗f4 ♕f7 14 ♗b5 ♗d7 15 ♗xc6 ♗xc6 16 b5 White has an obvious advantage.

And in the case of **12...g5** White should exploit the fact that he has still not castled kingside: **13 ♗b5 0-0 14 h4!** with a menacing initiative.

Thus Black still has to find an antidote to the plan 7 c5! Therefore the variation 6...♘c6?! is an infrequent guest in modern chess practice.

Index to Chapter Four

1 e4 c6 2 d4 d5 3 ed cd 4 c4 ♘f6
5 ♘c3 e6   92
  A. 6 a3   92
  B. 6 c5   94
  C. 6 ♗g5   95
    1) 6...♘c6   95
    2) 6...♗e7   97

1 e4 c6 2 d4 d5 3 ed cd 4 c4 ♘f6
5 ♘c3 e6 6 ♘f3   98
6...♘c6 7 c5
  A. 7...♗e7   98
  B. 7...♘e4   99
8 ♕c2
    1) 8...♘xc3   100
    2) 8...f5   101
    3) 8...♕a5   101

Chapter Five

1 e4 c6 2 d4 d5 3 ed cd 4 c4 ♘f6
5 ♘c3 e6 6 ♘f3 ♗b4

After these moves arises a position that is characteristic for the Nimzo-Indian defence. We will look only at those continuations which have a direct relationship with the Panov Attack, although drawing a boundary line between them is very difficult.

The main move in this position is 7 cd, upon which White insures himself against the loss of a tempo (unavoidable, for example, after 7 ♗d3 dc 8 ♗xc4). But before we set about an analysis of the capture on d5, we need to stop at the side lines. There are four of them: 7 ♕b3 (A), 7 ♕a4+ (B), 7 ♗g5 (C) and 7 ♗d3 (D).

A

7 ♕b3 ♘c6! If White places the queen on b3 in order to immediately obtain the advantage of the two bishops – 8 a3?! ♗xc3+ 9 ♕xc3, then a cruel disappointment awaits him: 9...♘e4 10 ♕c2 ♕a5+ 11 ♗d2 ♘xd2 12 ♕xd2 ♕xd2+ 13 ♔xd2 ♘a5! and the endgame is much better for Black (Velikov – Groszpeter, Plovdiv 1982).

8 ♗g5 dc Probably played through fear of losing a pawn. However analysis shows that after 8...0-0!? 9 cd ed 10 ♗xf6?! ♕xf6 11 ♕xd5 ♖e8+ 12 ♗e2 ♗e6 Black's initiative is worth a pawn.

9 ♗xc4 As we see, once again it all comes down to the 'isolani'. True, White loses a tempo but the position of his queen on b3 is not easy to justify, for example:

9...0-0 10 ♖d1 ♗e7 11 ♗d3 (trying to return to the usual 'battery' play by means of ♗b1, a3, ♕c2) **11...b6 12 0-0 ♗b7 13 ♗b1 g6 14 ♘e5 ♖c8 15 ♖fe1 ♘a5 16 ♕b5 ♘d5 17 ♗h6 ♘xc3 18 bc ♖e8** (Barua – Rogers, Hastings 1994). The game is complicated, but no way does Black risk more than his opponent.

B

7 ♕a4+ ♘c6 8 ♘e5?! A rather different theme – White tries to raise the level playing field to a position with forcing variations. But Black has a retort:

8...♗d7!? The simpler 8...♛a5 is also appropriate. In the endgame after 9 ♛xa5 ♗xa5 10 ♘xc6 bc 11 cd cd White does not have even a shade of advantage.

9 ♘xc6 9 ♘xd7 ♛xd7 10 a3 ♗xc3+ 11 bc 0-0 also suits Black. In the game Melnikov – Shaposhnikov (St.Petersburg 2001) the knights surprisingly quickly came to dominate the bishops: 12 ♗e2 dc! 13 ♛xc4 ♖ac8 14 0-0 ♘a5 15 ♛d3 ♘d5 etc.

9...♗xc3+ 10 bc ♗xc6 11 ♛a3 dc 12 ♗xc4 ♛c7! (Oswald – Orlov, Vancouver 2001). It is already clear that White has achieved nothing. g2 is hanging, the bishop on c4 is also under threat; his development is backward. It remains for Black to play 0-0-0 and e6-e5 in order to finally turn the position to his favour.

C

7 ♗g5 We break up the further play, separating variations which have no connection with each other: 7...0-0 (quiet), 7...♛a5 (sharp) and 7...h6 (middling).

1) 7...0-0 8 cd (8 ♖c1 ♘bd7 9 c5!? looks richer in ideas) **8...ed 9 ♗xf6 ♛xf6 10 ♗e2 ♘c6 11 0-0 ♖d8 12 ♛b3 ♗e6 13 ♖ad1 ♖ab8 14 h3 a6 15 ♖fe1 ♗a5** On the board we have a simple position with a slight advantage for Black (Hedke – Dreev, Bad Wiessee 1998).

2) 7...♛a5!? 8 ♗d2 ♘e4!?

Reminiscent of the variation 7 ♛a4+ ♘c6 8 ♘e5, but here already Black is asking for trouble.

9 ♘xe4!? Only this principled move leaves White chances of victory. More conciliatory are 9 cd or 9 a3 breaking the tension in the position, but only just:

9 cd ed 10 ♗d3 ♗f5 11 0-0 0-0 12 ♛c2 ♘c6 13 ♗e3 ♗xc3 14 bc ♗g6! (Gulko – Smyslov, Moscow 1976);

9 a3 ♘xd2 10 ♛xd2 dc 11 ♗xc4 0-0 12 0-0 ♗xc3 13 bc ♘d7 14 ♗d3 b6 (Barua – Adianto, Shakti 1996). Black is not threatened with anything.

9...de 10 a3 ♗xd2+ 11 ♘xd2 ♘c6 12 b4 ♛f5 13 ♘b3 a6 This is how the game Hracek – Dautov (Germany 1997) went. It looks like Black's early activity has turned out a mess. The e4 pawn is weak and White has good prospects of an attack on the queen's flank. This is how Dautov himself suggested playing: **14 ♗e2 0-0 15 0-0 b6 16 ♕d2 ♗b7 17 a4 ♕g6 18 ♕c3 f5 19 f4! ♕f6 20 b5** with an unquestionable advantage.

3) **7...h6 8 ♗xf6 ♕xf6 9 ♕b3 ♕e7?!** We are following the game Ivanchuk – Dreev (Linares 1997). Black was riveted to the pursuit of the 'advantage of the two bishops', and probably wrongly. Later Dreev proposed 9...♗xc3+ 10 ♕xc3 dc 11 ♗xc4 ♘c6 12 0-0 ♗d7 with equality.

10 c5 ♗a5 11 ♗b5+ ♗d7 12 ♘e5! (the heart of the position lies in the control of this square) **12...♘c6 13 ♗xc6 ♗xc6 14 0-0** Dreev played 14...♗c7 here, but after 15 f4! he ran into difficulties. It seems it would be more practical to simplify the position: **14...0-0 15 ♘xc6!? bc 16 ♕a4 ♗xc3 17 bc ♕c7**, but even in this case it is White who is conducting the play – **18 ♖fb1 ♖fb8 19 ♖b3!**

D
7 ♗d3 dc 8 ♗xc4 ♕c7!?

An idea of the Czech grandmaster Miroslav Filip, which he first tried in

a Candidates tournament (Curacao 1962) against Benko.

It will not be easy for Black to exploit the enemy pieces on the c-file; no, his idea is far deeper. The light-squared bishop is developed on the long diagonal and after White castles short, a cloud hangs over his king's position: ♘f6-g4, and then an attack on f3 – after which h2 is undefended. Filip's idea has stood the test of time as White has not found a complete antidote.

Meanwhile c4 is hanging. 9 ♕a4+?! Not very productive – after 9... ♘c6 10 0-0 ♗xc3 11 bc 0-0 it is obvious that the white pieces are not where they need to be.

Nor is there any particular sympathy for 9 ♕b3?! – the queen and the bishop are deliberately subjected to the threat of ♘b8-c6-a5! The Dutch grandmaster John van der Wiel pointed out a convincing variation: 9...♘c6 10 0-0 ♗xc3! 11 bc ♘a5 12 ♗b5+ ♗d7 13 ♗xd7+ ♕xd7! 14 ♕b4 ♘c6 and it is only White who has problems.

So there isn't a big choice: 9 ♕d3 or 9 ♕e2.

1) **9 ♕d3 0-0 10 0-0**

The further choice of plan depends

on how Black regards his own light-squared bishop. If like a son (who he wants to quickly bring out to b7), then he must give up his stepbrother: 10...♗xc3 11 bc b6. But if like a stepson, then he can leave the bishop on c8 and for the time being play 10...♘bd7.

However, playing 10...b6 at once is dangerous in view of 11 ♘b5 ♕d8 12 ♗f4. True, it should be mentioned that in the original game Black extricated himself with honour from the difficulties: 12...a6 13 ♘c3 ♗b7 14 ♖ad1 ♘bd7 15 a4?! ♗xc3 16 bc ♕c8 17 ♗b3 ♗e4 18 ♕e3 ♗d5 19 ♗c2 ♕b7 (Benko – Filip, Curacao 1962). But nobody wanted to repeat Filip's exploits – which in itself gives us clues for reflection...

At first glance, also dubious is 10...♘bd7 – for roughly the same reason: 11 ♘b5 ♕b6 12 a3 ♗e7 13 ♗e3.

14 ♘c3, but after 14...♕d6 15 ♘g5 b5 16 ♗a2 ♗b7 17 ♖ad1 ♖ad8 18 ♘ge4 ♕b8 19 h3 ♘xe4 20 ♘xe4 ♘f6 he was forced to go over to defence – the weakness of the d4 pawn did not offer compensation.

If the above mentioned discussion is right and the jump of the knight to b5 is harmless, it means that there is no particular need to hurry with the exchange on c3. Nevertheless **10...♗xc3 11 bc b6** remains the most popular variation. Incidentally, it is better to begin precisely with 11...b6; if the moves are transposed – 11...♘bd7 12 ♖e1 b6, then after 13 ♗a3!? ♖d8 (even worse is 13...♖e8 14 d5!) White has available the unpleasant resource 14 ♗e7! Continuing the variation – 14...♖e8 15 ♗xf6 ♘xf6 16 ♘e5 ♗b7 17 ♖e3!? (Florean – Nisipeanu, Romania 1997) revealed that the black king began to feel uncomfortable.

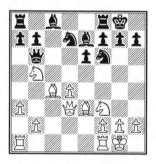

But here it all comes together – for the queen sacrifice Black acquires three minor pieces: 13...a6! 14 d5 ab! 15 ♗xb6 bc.

In the game Reindermann – Ivanchuk (Wijk aan Zee 1999) in reply to 13...a6 White reacted in another (and more modest) way:

But once again everything comes together tempo by tempo: 17...♘d7! 18 ♘xd7 ♕xd7 19 ♖h3 g6, and the white queen will not manage to join up with the rook on the deadly h-file: 20 ♕d2? ♗xg2! or 20 ♗b3 ♕c6 21 ♕g3 ♖ac8 (analysis by Nisipeanu and Stoica).

**12 ♗b3 ♗b7 13 ♖e1 ♘bd7
14 ♗g5** Black is not scared at all of
14 c4 ♖fd8 15 ♗g5 in view of
15...♘c5! 16 ♕e2 ♘ce4 17 ♗xf6
♘xf6 with a comfortable game
(Vajda – Groszpeter, Gyula 2000).

14...♖ac8 15 ♖ac1 ♕d6! Yet
another standard device for such a
position: while threatening ♘d7-c5,
Black transfers his queen to a3, from
where it keeps 'under surveillance'
the c3 pawn.

16 ♗c2 ♖fd8 17 ♗h4 (or 17 ♕e2
♖e8 18 ♗b1 h6 19 ♗xf6 ♘xf6 – it
must be conceded that it is more far
pleasant to play Black in this
position, Vajda – Nisipeanu,
Bucharest 1997) **17...♕a3 18 ♗b3**
On 18 ♗b1?! Black had prepared
18...♗e4! and, in view of the fact that
the rook on c1 is 'in the sights' of the
queen, White cannot take on e4.

But also on b3 the bishop gets no
rest: **18...a5! 19 ♘d2 a4! 20 ♘c4
♕f8 21 ♗xf6 ♘xf6**

22 ♘xb6 (after 22 ♗xa4 ♗a6 the
knight c4 definitely will not survive)
22...ab 23 ♘xc8 b2! After the forcing
variation ends (White eats up b2, and
Black – c8), there should not be any
doubt about the evaluation of the
position: the two minor pieces are

considerably stronger than the rook
and two pawns (Kraut – Schlusser
Germany 1996).

2) **9 ♕e2 0-0 10 0-0 ♘bd7** The
alternative is 10...♗xc3 11 bc ♘bd7,
and then:

12 ♗g5 b6 13 ♗xf6?! ♘xf6
14 ♘e5 ♗b7. The black pieces are
placed so harmoniously that they are
ready to meet any counterattack
(Schpenger – Dautov, Germany
2003);

12 ♗d2 b6 13 ♗d3 ♗b7 14 ♖ac1
♖ac8 15 ♖fe1 ♖fd8?! (an
unconvincing move which White
exploits) 16 ♗g5 h6 17 ♗h4! ♖e8
(forced) 18 ♗g3 ♕d8 19 ♗b5 ♘e4
20 ♘e5 with advantage (Karpov –
Morozevich, Prague 2002);

12 ♗a3!? ♖e8 (as distinct from the
variation 9 ♕d3, here this move is
possible since the position of the
queen on e2 deprives White of the
break d4-d5) 13 ♖ac1 b6 14 ♘e5
♗b7 15 f4!? (upon the presence of
the dark-squared bishop such an
attack has chances of success; this is
why Schpenger was wrong to
exchange on f6) 15...♖ad8?! (this and
the following moves by Black are
extremely passive) 16 ♗d3 ♕b8
17 ♖ce1 ♕a8 18 ♕c2 g6 19 ♘c4
♗a6 20 ♘d6 ♗xd3 21 ♕xd3 ♖e7
(21...♖f8 22 ♘b5!) 22 f5! (Speelman
– Richardson, England 2001).

11 ♘b5 The knight, staying alive,
starts to show its tenacity. It seems
that Black is in for it, but as shown by
the games Benko – Filip and
Reindermann – Ivanchuk, concrete
variations appear quite naturally for
him.

In the game de la Riva – Magem (Terrasa 1995), after 11...♕d8 12 a3 ♗a5 (taking measures against ♗c1-f4) 13 b4 a6! 14 ♘c3 ♗c7 15 ♗g5 h6 16 ♗h4 b5 the opponents agreed to a draw although the position is somewhat preferable for White.

More accurate is **11...♕c6!? 12 ♘e5 ♕e4!** The game Karpov – van der Wiel (Saloniki 1988) transposed to a complicated endgame in which both sides had chances:

13 a3 ♗e7 14 ♗g5 ♕xe2 15 ♗xe2 h6 16 ♗h4 g5! 17 ♗g3 ♘e4 18 ♖fd1 ♘xg3 19 hg ♖d8 20 ♘g4 ♘f6 21 ♘c7 (little is offered by the immediate 21 ♘xh6+ ♔g7 22 ♘g4 ♘xg4 23 ♗xg4 ♗d7, but also the intermediate move does not change anything) **21...♖b8 22 ♘xh6+ ♔g7 23 ♘g4 ♘xg4 24 ♗xg4 e5!** A draw was soon agreed.

Let us go over to an analysis of the main continuation **7 cd** It depends on Black, whether he will adopt play with a symmetrical pawn structure – 7...ed (I), or continue with a typical 'isolani' on d4 – 7...♘xd5 (II).

I
7...ed

With the bishop on b4 we have a more lively position than with the bishop on e7. Besides this, Black has no problems with the development of his light-squared bishop. Yet, for all that, the symmetrical pawns usually favour the one who has an extra tempo at his disposal – in the present case White.

There are three strategies of immediate development for White: a deployment (8 ♗g5 or 8 ♘e5), introduction of the queen (8 ♕b3; 8 ♕a4+) or the bishop f1 (8 ♗e2; 8 ♗b5+; 8 ♗d3).

A

8 ♗g5 (this move offers no advantage, but of course the whole game still lies ahead) **8...0-0 9 ♗e2 ♕d6 10 ♖c1 ♘e4 11 0-0 ♗xc3 12 bc ♘c6?!** He should do away with the enemy bishop – 12...♘xg5 13 ♘xg5 h6 14 ♘f3 ♘c6, when Black will not in the least be worse.

13 ♗h4 f5? (after this serious positional mistake Black's position becomes uneasy; why not 13...♗g4!?) **14 c4!** Now the a2-g8 diagonal (and as a consequence of this also other lines) starts to 'whistle'. But Black has brought this misfortune upon himself.

14...dc 15 ♗xc4+ ♔h8 16 ♖e1 h6 17 d5 ♘a5 18 ♕d4 b6 19 ♘e5 ♔h7 20 ♗d3

The position is already very bad, but to lose in one move – 20...♘f6? 21 ♖xc8! (Aleksandrov – Zhukova, Batumi 2001) nevertheless means nothing. The same motif also occurs in the variation 20...♗e6 21 ♖cd1! ♕xd5? 22 ♖xe4!, but after 20...♔g8 it would still be possible to put up a stubborn resistance.

B

8 ♘e5 (again by-passing the advantage) **8...0-0 9 ♗d3 ♘c6** The quietest. He could attack the c3 square but usually he leaves well alone:

9...♘e4 10 ♕b3 ♕b6 11 0-0 ♗xc3 12 bc. According to an analysis by Erling Mortensen, the pawn is untouchable: 12...♕xb3 13 ab ♘xc3? 14 ♗a3 ♖d8 15 ♖fc1 ♘e4 16 ♗e7 ♖e8 17 ♗b5! In the game Mortensen – Danielsen (Copenhagen 1997) Black played more modestly: 12...♘c6 13 ♗a3 ♕xb3 14 ab. The endgame is in White's favour: he has two bishops and a more flexible pawn structure.

10 0-0 ♗d6 In a quiet and approximately equal position

everything is decided by an imperceptible nuance. How, for example, to drive away the knight from the outpost on e5? Possibly with the bishop, but also possibly with the rook – 10...♖e8. After 11 ♘xc6 bc Black, in the game S.Polgar – Zelcic (Portoroz 1994), gradually took over the initiative: 12 ♗f4?! ♗xc3 13 bc ♕a5 14 ♗e5 ♘d7 15 ♕c2 h6 16 f4 ♗a6! etc.

11 ♘xc6 bc 12 ♗g5 ♖b8 13 b3 h6 14 ♗h4 ♖e8 15 ♖c1 ♗f4 16 ♖c2 ♖b4 17 ♗g3

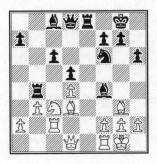

We are following the game Shamkovich – Mureshan (Palma de Mallorca 1989). The position has not moved a jot away from equality and this can be most simply confirmed by means of **17...♗xg3 18 hg** (or 18 fg ♗g4 19 ♕d2 ♕e7) **18...♔h8 19 ♘e2 ♕b6 20 ♕d2 a5 21 ♖fc1 ♗d7**

C

After **8 ♕b3 ♘c6 9 ♗b5** Black (if only he had not put his bishop b4 en prise) has generally nothing to fear. For example, **9...0-0 10 0-0 ♗xc3 11 ♕xc3 ♘e4 12 ♕a3 ♗d7 13 ♗e3 ♕b6 14 ♗xc6** with a draw (Renet – Vizhmanavin, London 1996).

D

More interesting is **8 ♕a4+ ♘c6 9 ♗b5** After **9...0-0** White can force the game (10 ♗xc6) or wait (10 0-0).

1) **10 ♗xc6 ♗xc3+.** The intermediate 10...♕e7+?! leads to nothing. After 11 ♘e5 bc 12 0-0 c5 13 ♗g5! ♗xc3 14 bc (Yagupov – T.Ivanov, Zhavoronky 1995) only the accurate 14...♕e8! leaves White chances of equalising.

11 bc bc 12 0-0 ♕b6 (sharper is 12...♘e4!? 13 ♕xc6 ♖b8 14 c4 ♗b7 15 ♕a4 dc 16 ♕xc4 ♕a5 with compensation, Oral – Kharitonov, Koszalin 1999) **13 ♗a3 ♖e8 14 ♘e5 ♘e4 15 ♕xc6 ♕xc6 16 ♘xc6 ♘xc3 17 ♖fe1 ♗a6** The game is even (Marin – Volkov, Romania 2001).

2) **10 0-0 ♕a5** Absolute symmetry should be in White's hands, but... actually too many pieces are standing 'under exchange'.

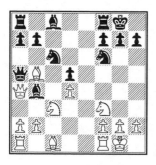

First we mention that it is not possible to win a pawn – 11 ♗xc6 bc 12 ♕xc6?? in view of 12...♗d7.

White can count on a minimal 'plus' after 11 ♗d2 ♕xa4 12 ♗xa4 ♗f5 13 ♗xc6 bc 14 ♘a4 ♗d6 15 ♖fc1 (Peresipkin – Bagirov, Baku 1977). With normal defence Black

ought to achieve a draw without problems.

A similar scenario developed in the game Miladinovic – Bras (Korinth 1998), with the only difference that White managed to achieve victory: **11 ♕xa5 ♗xa5 12 ♘a4 ♗g4?!** An instructive mistake! Black wants to spoil the opponent's pawn structure on the king's flank but does not take into account that the main defender of the c6 pawn will leave the board. Incidentally, it is incomprehensible how Black intends to attack the pawns on f2 and f3 – as he will be riveted to the defence of his own pawn weaknesses. After **13 ♗xc6 bc 14 ♗e3 ♗xf3?! 15 gf** White in the end will gobble up both the c- and a-pawns. And easily win the game.

In order to avoid problems with weak pawns, on 11 ♕xa5 it was necessary to reply 11...♘xa5! Then, generally speaking, we cannot see how White can obtain the advantage. For example: 12 ♗d2 a6 13 ♗d3 ♘c4 or 12 ♗g5 ♗xc3 13 bc a6 14 ♗d3 ♘e4.

E

8 ♗e2 0-0 9 0-0 ♗xc3 The game Liberzon – Petrosian (Erevan 1965) ended in an anaemic draw: 9...♕a5 10 ♕c2 ♗g4 11 ♗g5 ♘bd7 12 ♘e5 ♗xe2 13 ♘xe2 ♖fe8 14 ♗xf6 ♘xf6 15 ♘g3 ♕b6 16 ♘f3 g6.

10 bc ♘e4 11 ♗b2 (Black also has no problems after 11 ♕b3 ♘c6 12 ♗e3 ♘a5 13 ♕b4 ♗e6 14 ♖ac1 ♖c8, Bosboom – Douven, Hilversum 1988) **11...♗g4 12 c4 ♘c6 13 ♖e1 ♖c8**

White has two bishops, Black – a strong position in the centre. There is a complicated game in prospect with chances for both sides (Dolmatov – Kharitonov, Sochi 1978).

F

8 ♗b5+ ♗d7 9 ♕e2+. Grandmaster Stanislav Voitsekhovsky tried playing 9 ♗d3, but without great success:

9...♘c6 10 0-0 ♗g4 11 ♖e1+ ♗e7 12 ♕b3 ♗xf3 13 ♕xb7 ♕c8 14 ♕xc8+ ♖xc8 15 gf ♘xd4 (Voitsekhovsky – Dreev, Novgorod 1999);

9...0-0 10 ♘e5 ♘c6 11 0-0 ♖e8 12 ♖e1 ♘g4! 13 ♘f3 ♖xe1+ 14 ♕xe1 (Voitsekhovsky – Kharitonov, Ekaterinberg 1999) 14... ♕c7!? 15 h3 ♖e8 16 ♕d1 ♘f6.

9...♘e4 Another line of defence is 9...♕e7 10 ♘e5 ♘c6!? 11 ♘xd7 ♕xe2+ 12 ♔xe2 ♔xd7. The game Franco – Romero (Dos Hermanas 2001) continued 13 ♗e3 ♖he8 14 ♖hd1 ♗xc3 15 bc ♘e4 16 ♖dc1 ♘d6, and Black should hold.

10 0-0 Definite problems are set by 10 ♘d2!? 0-0 11 ♘dxe4 (Ashley – Vadasz, Budapest 1997). Black must play very clearly, in order not to drift

into the worse position. In particular, instead of taking on e4, worth considering is 11...♖e8!? and then: 12 ♗e3 de 13 0-0 ♘c6 14 d5 (or 14 ♖fd1 a6 15 ♗a4 ♕h4 16 h3 b5 17 ♗c2 ♗d6 with counterplay) 14...♘e5 15 ♘xe4 ♘g4 16 ♗d4 (more careful is 16 ♗xd7 ♕xd7 17 ♕c4) 16...♕h4 17 h3 ♘h2! 18 ♔xh2 ♖xe4 19 ♗e3 ♗d6+ 20 ♔g1 ♗xh3! with a decisive attack.

10...♗xc3 11 bc 0-0 12 ♗d3 On the board is the tabiya of the variation.

1) First we should discuss **12...♘xc3!?** Thus – do not be afraid of ghosts! – plays the Czech grandmaster Eduard Meduna.

13 ♕e5! 13 ♕b2?! is unprincipled. White does not attempt a pawn storm on the king and his double attack on c3 and b7 is easily repulsed: 13...♕c8 14 ♕b3 ♗a4 15 ♕a3 ♗b5 16 ♗xb5 ♘xb5 17 ♕b3 ♕c4 (Sveshnikov – Meduna, Sochi 1986).

13...♗g4 14 ♘g5!? h6 15 ♘h7 (in such positions you don't move backwards) **15...♖e8 16 ♘f6+ gf 17 ♕g3** All this looks highly dangerous for Black, but... only at first sight. In fact the attack is easily repulsed:

17...f5 18 f3 ♕f6 19 fg ♕xd4+

20 ♔h1 ♕xg4 21 ♕c7 ♘c6 22 ♕xb7 ♕g6 23 ♗f4 ♘e4 (Janev – Meduna, Budapest 2000). The handsome knight on e4 single-handedly cements Black's position. At an opportune moment it will also be ready to go over to a counterattack: **24 ♗b5 ♘a5 25 ♕c7? ♖ec8! 26 ♕xa5 ♖c2!**

2) On the other hand, do not look at **12...♗f5?!** The base of the knight e4 is confirmed as unstable: the d5 pawn can be undermined (c3-c4), the bishop f5 – driven away (♘f3-h4).

But what is the accurate order of moves? Most promising looks **13 ♕b2!? ♕c8** (now the queen does not control the h4 square) **14 ♗f4 ♘d7 15 ♘h4!** (undermining the right) **15...♗e6 16 c4!** (undermining the left) **16...♘b6 17 ♖ac1 ♕d7 18 ♘f3 f6 19 c5** White has an unquestionable advantage (Sveshnikov – Kalinichev, Norilsk 1987).

3) Interesting is **12...♖e8!? 13 ♘e5 ♘c6**, practically forcing White to sacrifice a piece.

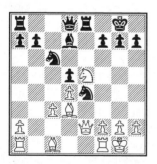

After **14 ♘xf7!? ♕f6** (considered the only move; bad is 14...♘xc3? 15 ♕h5) **15 ♘e5 ♘xe5 16 de ♕xe5!** and Black equalises (Sveshnikov – Savon, Moscow 1991).

But, frankly speaking, we do not see why he cannot grab the material – **14...♗xf7!? 15 ♕h5+ ♔f8** If **16 ♕xd5**, then simply 16...♘f6 17 ♗a3+ ♘e7 18 ♕xb7 ♕a5 – the attack is over, and the three pawns for the piece will allow White (after successful deployment) to escape defeat. If however **16 ♗a3+**, then in this case there is no clarity at all: **16...♘e7!? 17 ♗xe4 de 18 ♕xh7 ♖c8 19 ♖ae1 ♕a5 20 ♗b4** (or 20 f3 ♕xa3 21 fe+ ♘f5!) **20...♕f5 21 ♕xf5+ ♗xf5 22 f3 e3!**

G

8 ♗d3 Among all seven candidates – the healthiest and probably the strongest move.

8...0-0 The intermediate 8...♕e7+ counts on the fact that White has weaknesses – 9 ♗e2?!, is met by 9...♘e4! 10 ♕b3 0-0 11 ♗e3 ♘c6 12 0-0 ♗e6 (Turov – Virovlyansky, St.Petersburg 1998). But if White is not afraid to sacrifice a pawn – 9 ♘e5! ♘c6 10 0-0 ♘xd4, then instead he could gain a very strong initiative: 11 ♖e1 ♘e6 12 ♗b5+ ♔f8 13 ♗e3 etc.

9 0-0 And here we have a branch. Other moves most frequently met are 9...♗g4 and 9...♘c6.

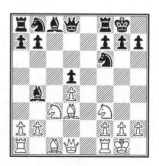

1) **9...♗g4 10 ♕b3!?** Hinting to the opponent that his last developing move was not with the right piece.

10...♗xc3 (Poluljahov recommended 10...♘c6 11 ♘e5 and only now 11...♗xc3) **11 bc ♗xf3 12 gf** In two moves Black has given up his two bishops, and for what? It must be out of a great love of knights.

But in the position there is also a third factor – the partially open b- and g-files. And both can fall into the hands of the white rooks, as occurred in the game Poluljahov – Wells (Balatonbereny 1992): 12...♕c7 13 ♔h1!? ♘bd7 14 ♖g1 (one!) 14...♔h8 15 ♖b1 (two!) 15...♖ac8 16 ♗d2 ♘b6. In the opinion of grandmaster Aleksander Poluljahov, White consolidates his advantage by 17 a4! ♘c4 18 ♗xc4 ♕xc4 19 ♕xc4 ♖xc4 20 a5 ♖a4 21 ♖b5.

Black was more successful in the following game: **12...♕d7!? 13 ♔h1 ♕h3 14 ♕d1 ♘bd7 15 ♖g1 ♖fe8 16 ♗g5 ♕e6 17 ♖b1 b6! 18 ♕d2 ♘h5 19 ♕c2 g6!**

files (Spraggett – Zelcic, Geneva 1995).

2) **9...♘c6** (appears more reasonable than 9...♗g4) **10 ♗g5 ♗xc3 11 bc ♗g4** It looks very much like this natural move is not the best. The intermediate 11...h6!? 12 ♗h4, and only now 12...♗g4, gives Black, in the variation 13 ♕d2 ♗xf3 14 gf ♕d6 15 ♔h1 ♘h5!, the possibility of laying claim to the f4 square.

12 ♕d2! As is clear from the games Poluljahov – Wells and Spraggett – Zelcic, White should not fear an exchange on f3 since this gives him the chance to break through on the g-file.

Harmless is 12 ♖e1 ♕d6 13 h3 ♗h5 14 ♗xf6 ♕xf6 15 ♖e3 ♖fe8 16 ♕d2 ♖xe3 17 fe (Sveshnikov – Vizhmanavin, Elista 1995) 17...♖e8 with equal chances.

12...♗xf3 13 gf ♕d6 14 ♖ab1 b6 15 ♔h1 ♘h5 16 ♖g1 (now the usefulness of the move 11...h6 becomes apparent) **16...♘a5?! 17 ♗h4!**

Quite another matter! Now there is little use for the rooks on the b- and g-

The position is ripe for all sorts of combinations. Black should not even think about the f4 square: 17...♘f4?

113

18 ♗g3 or 17...♕f4? 18 ♖xg7+!
♔xg7 19 ♖g1+ ♔h8 20 ♕xf4 ♘xf4
21 ♗f6 mate! In the game Rantanen –
Ornstein (Ekso 1981) Black
carelessly played **17...h6?** and after
18 ♗e7! he was left the exchange
down. Necessary was 17...♔h8,
though even in this case it is White
who is definitely conducting the
game.

On the whole the system with 7...ed
is fully viable. Nowhere does Black
lose at once, more than this, in nearly
every variation theory fails to
promise White even a minimal
advantage.

The main defect of this, as indeed
every other symmetrical system, lies
in the fact that play frequently
proceeds, as chessplayers say, 'with
two possible results'. White either
wins or obtains a draw. No other is on
offer.

But we would very much like it to
be.

II
7...♘xd5

In positions with an isolated d4
pawn Black has more 'chances' of
being subjected to an attack, but also
more chances of taking over the
initiative. There are two main moves:
8 ♕c2 (A) and 8 ♗d2 (B). Besides
this, it is worth mentioning **8 ♕b3**. At
one time this was a main move in the
repertoire of Judit Polgar, but after
her game with Smyslov (Aruba 1992)
she no longer played it. This is how
the game went:

8...♘c6 9 ♗d3 ♕b6! The clearest
decision. With the exchange of
queens disappear White's chances of
an attack – and the weakness on d4
remains...

**10 ♗d2 ♗a5! 11 0-0 ♕xb3 12 ab
♗b6 13 ♗c4** More careful is
13 ♘xd5 ed 14 ♗c3, though even in
this case Black's problems are over:
14...0-0 15 b4 ♖e8 16 ♖fe1 ♗d7
17 b5 ♘e7 18 ♗b4 ♗f5!
(Christiansen – Schwartzmann, Wijk
aan Zee 1993).

13...♘de7 14 ♘a4!? ♗c7
(avoiding the trap: 14...♗xd4?
15 ♘xd4 ♘xd4 16 ♘b6!) **15 b4 a6
16 ♘c3!? 0-0** (also the second pawn
is not very edible: 16...♘xb4?!
17 ♘b5! ♘bd5 18 ♖fc1 ♗b8
19 ♗xd5 ed 20 ♘c7+ ♗xc7 21 ♖xc7
with the initiative) **17 b5 ♘a5
18 ♗a2 ab 19 ♘xb5 ♗b6 20 ♘e5
♘ac6** That's it: Judit Polgar played
this endgame very enterprisingly. But
nevertheless White did not have even
a hint of advantage.

The conclusion is clear: Smyslov's
discovery 9...♕b6! and 10...♗a5!
closes down the whole variation with
8 ♕b3.

A

8 ♕c2 This continuation was first
met in the game Najdorf – Portisch

114

(Varna 1962) and up to the present day it has not lost its topicality.

1) Already, right from the start, definite accuracy is required of Black. Thus on **8...0-0?!** follows **9 ♗d3!**, forcing the opponent either to weaken his castled position or remove his king from the centre.

9...g6 10 0-0 ♘c6 11 a3 ♗e7 12 ♗h6 ♖e8 13 ♖fd1 ♗f6 (Kobalija – Turov, Sochi 1998) 14 ♗e4!, increasing the pressure;

9...♘f6 10 0-0 ♗d7 11 ♘e5 ♗c6 12 ♖d1 h6 13 ♗e3 ♗d6 14 ♕d2. Once again the position of the black king inspires no confidence at all (Bologan – Rausis, Tallinn 2000).

2) Also unconvincing is **8...♕c7 9 ♗d2 ♘d7** in view of yet again **10 ♗d3!?** After **10...♗xc3 11 bc ♘5f6 12 0-0** in the game Potkin – Asrian (Moscow 2002) the careless 12...0-0?! was met by 13 ♖ae1 b6 14 ♘e5 ♗b7 15 f4 ♖fe8 16 ♖e3 ♘f8 17 f5! ef 18 ♗xf5 ♘g6 19 ♖h3! and White was close to his objective.

Black should delay castling till later: **12...b6 13 ♖fe1** (or 13 ♖ae1 ♗b7 14 ♘e5 ♘xe5 15 ♖xe5 0-0 16 ♖fe1 ♖fc8 17 ♖5e3 a5 18 ♖h3 h6 19 ♕c1 ♔f8 20 c4, and White's prospects are superior, Sveshnikov –

Sasikiran, Dubai 2002). **13...♗b7 14 ♘e5 ♘xe5 15 ♖xe5 0-0**

In the game Sveshnikov – Schweizer (Cap d'Agde 2003) White decided that the position was already ripe: **16 ♗g5?** Punishment followed swiftly: **16...♘g4! 17 ♗xh7+ ♔h8 18 ♕e2 ♕xc3 19 ♖d1 ♘xe5 20 de** (20 ♕h5 ♘f3+!) **20...♕c6**, and Black won. It is not hard to see that 16 ♖ae1 returns us to the game Sveshnikov – Sasikiran. Incidentally, on 16 ♖ae1 no good is 16...♘g4? 17 ♗xh7+ ♔h8 because of 18 ♖h5.

3) **8...♘d7** (the idea of this move lies in the transfer of the knight to f6) **9 ♗d3** Worth considering is 9 ♗e2!? – the bishop heads for f3, paralysing the queen's flank. In the game Voitsekhovsky – Donchenko (Tula 1999) White realised his idea: 9...♘7f6 10 0-0 0-0 11 ♗g5 ♗e7 12 ♘e5 h6 13 ♗xf6 ♗xf6 14 ♗f3! ♘xc3 15 ♕xc3 ♖b8 16 ♖fd1 ♕d6 17 ♖ac1 etc. But only because the opponent did not counter White's plan. Instead of 11...♗e7 stronger is 11...h6 12 ♗h4 ♘f4! 13 ♗c4 ♘g6!, scattering White's bishops around the board. Possible then is 14 ♗g3 ♘h5! 15 a3 ♗xc3 16 bc ♗d7 17 ♖fe1 ♖c8 18 ♗a2 (Howell – Speelman, London

2003) 18...♘xg3 19 hg ♕a5 with a pleasant game.

9...♘7f6 10 0-0 ♗e7 Noticeably weaker is 10...♗d7?! in view of 11 ♘xd5 ♘xd5 12 ♘e5 ♗d6 13 ♗c4 ♖c8 14 ♕b3! ♗c6 15 ♕g3! (Benjamin – Seirawan, Seattle 2000).

Tempting is 11 ♗b5+?! ♗d7 12 ♗xd7+ ♕xd7 13 ♘e5. It seems that the queen must move but then follows an unpleasant check on a4... But as a matter of fact he has a better move: 13...♘b4! 14 ♕d1 ♕d6 15 a3 ♘c6 with equality (Kaidanov – Yermolinsky, Modesto 1995).

Conclusion: launching raids on Black's position will not work; he needs to carry out a systematic siege – **11 a3 0-0 12 ♘e5**, and then:

12...h6 13 ♕e2 ♕d6 14 ♖d1 b6?! (it is surprising but in this way Black loses control over the d5 square) 15 ♘xd5 ♕xd5 16 ♗c4 ♕e4 17 ♕xe4 ♘xe4 18 d5! (Potkin – Vescovi, Linares 2001) or

12...♕d6 13 ♗g5 (more elastic is 13 ♖d1!? ♗d7 14 ♘xd5 ♕xd5 15 ♗c4 ♕d6 16 ♗f4) 13...h6 14 ♘xd5 ♕xd5 15 ♗e3 ♗d7 16 ♗c4 ♕d6 17 ♕d3 ♗c6 (Ivanovic – Yermolinsky, Erevan 1996).

And so the plan ♘b8-d7-f6 can be recommended in practice as being

sufficiently reliable. But the development of the knight to c6 is incomparably more popular. Why? The same principle: Black does not want to play passively for a draw, he wants to struggle for three results!

4) **8...♘c6**

There are two main plans for White. The first – with the development of the bishop to d3, when it is necessary to be prepared for the sacrifice of the d4 pawn. Secondly, with the bishop going to e2.

a) **9 ♗d3!?** By stopping the opponent castling, White hopes to prevent the members of the diagonal battery changing places with a transfer of the queen to e4.

It depends on Black which course the further play will take: quiet and moderate (9...♗e7; 9...h6) or forcing and explosive (9...♘xc3; 9...♗a5).

a1) **9...♗e7 10 a3** A knight threatened to jump to b4, but now Black must decide how to avoid losing h7 or else put the king to work.

a11) **10...♘f6?!** Voluntarily retreating from the centre should not be partcularly good.

11 0-0 There is an interesting but hardly positionally based plan with long castling: 11 ♗e3 0-0 12 0-0-0?! In the encounter Anand – Adams (Groningen 1997) followed 12...♗d7 13 ♘g5 (the break 13 d5 ed 14 ♘xd5 is inappropriate, namely because his king has gone to the left: 14...♖c8! 15 ♔b1 h6 16 ♘xe7+ ♘xe7 17 ♕b3 ♘ed5) 13...h6 14 ♘ge4 ♖c8 15 ♔b1 ♘a5 16 ♘c5. By continuing 16...♗c6 17 ♕e2 b6 18 ♘5e4 ♘xe4 19 ♘xe4 ♘c4!, Black obtains the better game.

11...0-0 (losing is 11...♘xd4? 12 ♘xd4 ♕xd4 13 ♘b5) **12 ♖d1** The retreat of the knight from d5 begins to tell. Thus, on 12...a6? there is the decisive 13 d5! ed 14 ♘xd5! ♘xd5 15 ♗xh7+ ♔h8 16 ♗e4 ♗e6 17 ♗xd5 ♗xd5 18 ♕f5, and White remained with an extra pawn (Topalov– Gausel, Moscow 1994).

12...♗d7

In this position Topalov rejected the immediate break with d4-d5 in favour

of 13 ♘e5 a6 14 ♗e3 ♕c7 15 ♘xd7 ♕xd7, and only now 16 d5 (Topalov – Yudasin, Groningen 1993).

In fact, there are no grounds for delay: after **13 d5! ed 14 ♘xd5! h6 15 ♘xe7+ ♘xe7 16 ♘e5 ♘ed5 17 ♘xd7 ♕xd7 18 ♗f5 ♕b5 19 b4 ♖fd8 20 ♗b2** the two powerful bishops and open position defines White's advantage (Estremera – Izeta, Leon 1997).

a12) **10...♗f6 11 0-0 h6** Preparing castling whilst retaining pressure on the d4 pawn. Objectively this is the right path but nevertheless psychologically there is the fear: will White suddenly find how to exploit the tempo spent on h7-h6?

Instead of 11...h6 he has other tries:

11...♗xd4?! (too risky) 12 ♘xd5 ed 13 ♗b5 ♗f6 14 ♗xc6+ bc 15 ♕xc6+ ♗d7 16 ♖e1+ ♔f8 17 ♕xd5 ♗e6 18 ♕c5+ ♕e7 19 ♕h5 (Brodsky – Berg, Groningen 1994);

11...♘de7?! 12 ♗e3 h6 13 ♖ad1 0-0 (Topalov – Gulko, Moscow 1994) 14 ♘e5!? ♘f5 15 ♗xf5 ef 16 f4! with a strong initiative.

12 ♖d1 0-0

Apropos White's plan, there is no discord at all – the queen ought to transfer to e4 via e2. But theoreticians and practical players are by no means in agreement about the correct order of moves.

Here is one harmless attempt to set up a 'queen + bishop' battery with the necessary range: 13 ♕e2?! ♘xd4 14 ♘xd4 ♗xd4 15 ♕e4? (recklessly played; 15 ♗h7+ would lead to a draw) 15...♘f6 16 ♕h4 e5 17 ♗xh6 ♘g4 18 ♗g5 ♗xf2+ 19 ♕xf2 ♕xg5 with an extra pawn (Velimirovic – Garcia, Rio de Janeiro 1979).

More interesting is the idea of the German grandmaster Karsten Muller: **13 ♗c4!?** The bishop not only offers the possibility of the queen going to e4, but also itself 'strains' the d5 square. And yet, in the opinion of Muller, Black has the right to count on equality: **13...♘ce7 14 ♕e4 b6!? 15 ♗d3 ♘g6 16 ♘e5 ♗xe5 17 de ♗b7** etc.

a2) **9...h6 10 0-0 0-0 11 a3 ♗e7** A modification of the previous variation, with the only difference that Black intends to defend against the threats on the b1-h7 diagonal by means of g7-g6.

Acceptable is 11...♗d6 – then the knight on c6 goes to e7, reinforcing the outpost on d5 and heading for f5 or g6:

12 ♕e2 ♘ce7! 13 ♘e5 ♘f5 14 ♖d1!? ♘xd4 15 ♕e4 ♘f5 16 ♘xd5 ed 17 ♕xd5 ♗c7! (Bologan – Epishin, Germany 1999);

12 ♖d1 ♘ce7! 13 ♕e2 ♗d7 14 ♘e5 ♗xe5 15 de ♘xc3 16 bc ♘g6 17 ♗xg6 fg 18 ♗e3 (18 ♕d3 ♗c6) 18...♕e8 19 ♖d6 ♗c6 20 ♕g4 ♖f5 (Kindermann – Lobron, Dortmund 1983).

12 ♕e2 ♖e8! A cool and absolutely correct reply, whereas the panicky 12...♘f6?! gave White a very strong attack in the game Naiditsch – Cvitan (Oberwart 1998): 13 ♖d1 b6 14 ♘e4 ♘d5 15 ♗b1 ♗f6 16 ♕d3 ♘ce7 17 ♘e5 ♘f5 18 g4! ♘e7 19 ♘g3.

13 ♗c2 ♗f8 14 ♖e1 ♗d7 15 ♕d3 (by lingering a move, White risks not setting up the battery at all: 15 ♘e4 ♕b6! 16 ♕d3 ♕a6!, Korneev – Assmann, Werfen 1993) **15...g6**

In the game Malaniuk – Aleksandrov (Wisla 1992) White, by playing 16 ♗d2?, fell into a well-known tactical trap: 16...♘cb4! 17 ab ♘xb4 18 ♕e4 ♗c6 19 d5 ed.

There is no alternative to h2-h4-h5 – otherwise he will not break through to the g6 pawn. The question only is whether Black will allow this march to be carried out to the end. In the game Kunte – Sasikiran (Kelambakkam 2000) he allowed – **16 h4 ♘f6?!** 17 ♘e5 ♘e7 18 h5! ♘xh5 19 ♕f3! with a double attack on f7 and b7. But only a year later the same opponents followed the right version: **16...h5** Kunte – Sasikiran, New Delhi 2001). The game is even.

a3) **9...♘xc3?! 10 bc ♘xd4?** This was played by Black in the stem game Najdorf – Portisch (Varna 1962), probably wishing to refute White's whole plan beginning with 8 ♕c2.

However it cannot be refuted with anything but it is possible to lose here – and quite quickly.

11 ♘xd4 ♕xd4 12 ♗b5+! Weaker is 12 ♕a4+? ♗d7 13 ♕xb4 ♕xd3 14 ♗a3 because of 14...0-0-0!

12...♔e7 13 0-0 ♕xc3 14 ♕a4!? Najdorf attacked in another way: 14 ♕e2 ♗d6 15 ♗b2 ♕a5 16 ♖fd1 ♖d8 17 ♕h5 f6 18 ♕xh7, and soon achieved victory. Instead of 17...f6 there is no salvation in 17...h6 18 ♗xg7 ♗d7 19 ♕h4+ ♔e8 20 ♗xd7+ ♔xd7 21 ♗xh6, but the consequences of 14...♖d8!? are not clear until the end.

Now however on 14...♖d8 follows 15 ♖b1, and on the retreat of the bishop b4 – 16 ♕h4+ and 17 ♕xh7.

14...♗d6 15 ♗f4 ♗xf4 (or 15...e5 16 ♖ac1 ♕d4 17 ♖c4 ♕d5 18 ♖d1 ♕e6 19 ♗c1!) **16 ♕xf4 ♕c5 17 a4 g5 18 ♕g3 ♖d8 19 ♖ac1 ♕d5 20 f4!** White's attack is virtually irresistible (Nunn – Lobron, Biel 1982).

a4) **9...♗a5!?** A correction to Portisch's plan – Black wins a pawn when the bishop is not on b4, but on

a5 (which in many variations it is), and, what is no less important, White is obliged to place a pawn on a3, depriving himself of the manoeuvre ♗c1-a3.

10 a3!? White has no right to display faint-heartedness and returns to his chosen path. Pieces not allowed:

10 ♗e4?! ♘xd4 11 ♘xd4 ♘xc3 12 bc ♕xd4 13 0-0 ♕xc3 14 ♕b1 f5! 15 ♕b5+ ♔f7, and Black is ready to castle artificially (Hubner – Hracek, Batumi 1999);

10 ♗xh7? ♘xc3 11 bc ♖xh7! 12 ♕xh7 ♗xc3+, remaining with extra material;

10 0-0?! (by allowing the exchange of one of his key attacking pieces, White reduces his prospects) 10...♘db4! 11 ♕d1 ♘xd3 12 ♕xd3 f6!? 13 ♖d1 0-0 14 ♗f4 ♘b4 15 ♕c4 ♘d5 16 ♗d2 ♗xc3 17 bc ♘b6 18 ♕b3 ♕d5 19 ♖ac1 ♘c4 with advantage (Rechlis – Henkin, France 1999).

10...♘xc3 In contrast to White, Black can allow himself to deviate: 10...h6 11 0-0 0-0. The feeling of course is that this play is strange, but a refutation of such chess 'cowardice' has not yet been found:

12 ♗c4 ♘ce7 13 ♗d2 ♗d7 14 ♘xd5 ed 15 ♗d3 ♗b6 (Gdanski – Luther, Istanbul 2003);

12 ♖d1 ♗c7 13 h3 ♘ce7 14 ♘e5 ♗d7 15 ♘xd5 ♘xd5 16 ♗h7+ ♔h8 17 ♗e4 ♗e8 18 ♕e2 f6 19 ♘d3 ♗c6 (Ehlvest – Yudasin, New York 2003).

11 bc ♘xd4!? (they're off!) **12 ♘xd4 ♕xd4 13 ♗b5+!** In Najdorf mould. Weaker is 13 0-0 ♕e5 14 ♗e3, and Black can in some way extinguish the opponent's initiative:

14...♗d7 15 ♗d4 ♕h5 16 ♗e4 ♗c7 17 f4 0-0 18 ♗xb7 ♖ab8 19 ♗e4 ♗b6 (Ervich – Podgaets, Hoogeveen 1999) or (what is even stronger)

14...♗b6!? 15 ♖fe1 ♕c7 16 ♖ab1 ♗d7 17 ♖b4 ♗xe3 18 ♖xe3 ♗c6 (Kindermann – Speelman, Plovdiv 1983).

After 13 ♗b5+! arises a critical position for the variation 9 ♗d3.

What carries more weight – a pawn or the initiative? The evaluation has changed time and again. At the present moment the conclusion is this: Black has deployed sufficient resources for the defence. Let's look at all the possibilities: 13...♔f8, 13...♔e7 and 13...♗d7.

a41) 13...♔f8 (a rare but interesting move) **14 0-0 ♕xc3 15 ♕e2** (it is

worth thinking about 15 ♕b1!? followed by a3-a4 and ♗c1-a3) **15...a6 16 ♗d3!? ♕xa1 17 ♗b2 ♕xf1+ 18 ♔xf1 ♗d8**

In the game Gipslis – Albert (Berlin 1995) White decided not to risk anything and forced a draw by perpetual check: 19 ♗xg7+ ♔xg7 20 ♕g4+ ♔f6 21 ♕h4+ ♔g7 22 ♕g4+ ♔f6.

Taking into account that it is not easy for Black to put right the coordination of his pieces, White can, without particular risk, continue the struggle. For example: **19 ♕c2 ♗d7** (19...f6 20 ♗xa6! ♔f7 21 ♗b5, and it is not clear how Black can complete his development) **20 ♕c5+ ♔g8 21 ♕b4 ♗c6 22 ♕g4 g6 23 ♕h3!** (threatening 24 ♗xg6) **23...f6 24 ♕xe6+ ♔g7 25 ♗c4 ♖f8 26 a4!** with an attack.

a42) 13...♔e7 14 0-0 ♕e5 If Black's life is without risk, which is food without salt, then it is worth trying 14...♕xc3?! 15 ♕e4!? f6 (Rogers – Effert, Altensteig 1988) 16 ♗f4!? e5 17 ♖fd1!

15 a4! ♗b6 16 ♗a3+ ♗c5 17 ♕e2!? (weaker is 17 ♖fe1 ♕c7 18 ♕f5 ♗xa3 19 ♕g5+ ♔f8 20 ♖xa3 ♕e7, and Black has almost defended himself, Rogul – Zelcic, Pula 2000) **17...♕c7 18 ♕g4 ♔f8** In the game Kotronias – Kurkunakis (Athens 1996) White slightly lowered the tempo of attack – 19 ♗b4, and after 19...e5 20 ♕c4 b6 21 a5 ♖b8 the opponent consolidated his forces.

Therefore worth considering is **19 ♕c4!? b6 20 ♖fd1**, with the pin on the bishop c5 drawing fire in the direction of the only open d-file. Losing now is 20...♕e7 in view of 21 ♗xc5 bc 22 ♖ab1! ♖b8 23 ♗a6! ♖xb1 24 ♖xb1 ♕c7 25 ♗xc8 ♕xc8 26 ♕f4 – the position of the rook h8 is indeed humble. Nor is there any relief in 20...a6 21 ♕h4 f6 22 ♗xc5+ bc 23 ♗c4.

20...g6 21 ♕e4!? ♖b8 Inferior is 21...♗b7 22 ♗xc5+ bc 23 ♕e3 with a great advantage for White.

22 ♗c1! f6!? (useless is 22...♗b7 in view of 23 ♕h4! ♔g8 24 ♖d7 ♕e5 25 ♗h6) **23 ♕f4 ♕xf4 24 ♗xf4 ♖b7** (material loss is inevitable also on 24...e5 25 ♖d8+ ♔g7 26 ♗h6+! ♔xh6 27 ♖xh8) **25 ♗a6 ♔e7 26 ♗xb7 ♗xb7** White wins the exchange but it is not easy to realise it.

It goes without saying that all the analysis starting with 19 ♕c4!? needs to be carefully tested in practical play.

a43) **13...♗d7!?** In the variation 9...♘xc3?! 10 bc ♘xd4? 11 ♘xd4 ♕xd4 12 ♗b5+! this move would in principle not be possible, since after 12...♗d7? 13 ♗xd7+ ♔xd7 14 ♕a4+ Black loses a bishop; here however this is, generally speaking, the main line!

14 0-0 A time for reflection approaches for Black...

He would like to cut the Gordian knot at once: 14...♖c8!? 15 ♖d1 ♕xd1+ 16 ♕xd1 ♗xb5. The king is no longer threatened, while the rook and light-squared bishop can construct a quite impregnable fortress. Nevertheless the game Topalov – Magem (Pamplona 1995) showed that Black does not succeed in achieving full equality: 17 ♕h5 a6 18 ♗b2! 0-0 19 c4! ♖xc4 20 a4.

14...♗xc3?!, as always, – is an extra shot of adrenalin to the game: 15 ♗xd7+ ♔xd7 16 ♕e4 ♕c6 17 ♕d4+ ♔e8 18 ♗b2 f6 19 ♕g4 ♔f8 20 ♖ac1 h5 21 ♕f4 ♕b5 22 ♗xf6 ♕f5 23 ♕d6+ ♔g8 (Ikonnikov – Nureev, Perm 1997), and here White did not notice 24 ♗xg7! ♔xg7 25 ♖c5.

A rare guest in tournament practice is 14...♕e5!?, and it is not quite clear why. After 15 ♗xd7+ ♔xd7 16 ♕a4+ ♔e7 17 ♗f4 there is 17...b5! 18 ♕xa5 ♕xf4 (Bersma – Gyimesi, Groningen 1999). As soon as the rook h8 enters the game, all Black's problems will be over.

14...♕d5 15 c4 ♕f5! The queen must transfer to a defensive square. Otherwise, as for example in the game Boyle – Purich (correspondence, 1992), he might be left material down: 15...♕h5? 16 ♕a4! ♗xb5 17 ♕xa5.

16 ♗xd7+ ♔xd7 17 ♕b2 The most promising continuation, but here are the others:

Weak is 17 ♕d1+?! ♔e7 18 ♖b1 b6 19 ♕e2 ♖hd8 20 ♖b3 ♖ac8, and White has neither pawn nor attack (Pavlovic – Tukmakov, Biel 1997);

Interesting is 17 ♕b3 b6 18 ♖d1+ ♔e7 19 a4!, however in the game Aleksandrov – Dautov (Germany 1999) after 19...♖hd8 20 ♗a3+ ♔f6 21 ♗d6 Black found a defence: 21...g5! 22 ♖d3 ♔g7;

Finally, there is no promise of advantage in 17 ♕a4+ ♔e7 18 c5!? in view of 18...b6! 19 ♗f4 e5! (Wahls – Dautov, Germany 1997).

17...b6 Now again White has a great choice – but that does not mean to say it is a very rich one.

It is possible to establish parity – 18 ♗e3 ♔e7 19 ♖ad1 ♖hd8 20 ♖xd8 ♖xd8 21 ♕xg7, but after 21...♗d2! there is no reason for White to think about an advantage (Vratonjic – Stojanovic, Niksic 1996).

18 c5!? looks very rich in ideas.

The problem for White is that his opponent is not thinking of extra pawns but simply about artificial castling: 18...♔e7 19 cb ab 20 ♗e3 ♖hd8 21 ♖ad1 ♔f8 22 ♖xd8+ ♖xd8 with full equality (Aronian – Asrian, Erevan 2001).

The most natural move in the position is of course 18 ♖d1+. But also here, Black easily fulfils the obligatory programme: 18...♔e7 19 ♗e3 (19 ♕xg7?! ♖hg8 20 ♕d4 ♖ad8 21 ♕h4+ f6 22 ♖xd8 ♖xd8 23 ♗e3 ♗c3) 19...♖ad8!? (there is no need to be distracted by the defence of the g7 pawn: 19...f6?! 20 c5!, Topalov – Tukmakov, Groningen 1993) 20 ♖xd8 ♖xd8 21 ♕xg7 ♗d2 22 ♗d4 ♕g6 The advantage seems already to lie with Black (Trabert – Henkin, Holland 1998).

The only means of complicating the evacuation of the black king is by **18 a4!?**

On the simple-minded 18...♔e7 follows 19 ♕a3+ ♔f6 20 ♕g3 e5! (even worse is 20...♖hd8 21 ♖a3! ♔e7 22 ♖f3 ♕g6 23 ♗a3+ ♔e8 24 ♕h4, and the king is left in the centre) 21 ♗b2 ♔e6 22 ♖ad1 ♖hd8 23 ♖d5! Though the attack with the white pieces in no way looks deadly, it is not easy to withstand the pressure (Kunte – Prakash, Calcutta 2001).

Totally unconvincing is also 18...f6?! 19 ♖d1+ ♔c6 20 c5! (Al. Karpov – Ovechkin, Smolensk 2000), and on 19...♔e7 follows 20 ♕a3+ ♔e8 (or 20...♕c5 21 ♕g3) 21 ♕d6, and the harmony in Black's camp is not what it was.

Obviously, it is necessary to place the rook on d8. But which rook? In the game Calzetta – Kakhiani (Istanbul 2000) Black prescribed 18...♖hd8, but she was not able to guarantee the safety of her own king: 19 ♖a3! f6 20 ♖g3 g6 21 ♖h3 h5 22 c5!

It is worth trying **18...♖ad8!?**, and if White acts along the lines of the old scheme – **19 ♖a3 f6 20 ♖g3**, then he can add the rook to the defence of the pawn: **20...♖hg8** After **21 ♕b3 ♔e7 22 c5 bc 23 ♗a3 ♕d5** Black can at last breathe freely (Bergstrom – Taylor, York 2000), though it is hardly appropriate to consider this game as the last word.

In the variation 9 ♗d3 time after time there arises a very interesting 'frontier' situation. The evaluation continually fluctuates, and theory cannot give a guarantee that the next novelty that comes along will not turn upside down the current verdict on the position.

Not every practitioner is happy with this. To play such a variation is like sitting on a barrel of gunpowder! For those who feel best in a quiet, peaceful backwater, there is the variation 9 ♗e2.

b) 9 ♗e2

White does not intend to sacrifice more pawns (9...♘xc3?! 10 bc ♘xd4? 11 ♘xd4 ♕xd4 12 ♕a4+ and 13 ♕xb4), so making the move 9...♗a5?! pointless – the jump of the knight to b4 is no longer a fork.

White does not quite reject attacking play – after ♕c2-e4 and ♗e2-d3 the battery is once again in place (though, of course, there is also the march route to f3 for the bishop). In short, everything is the same as 9 ♗d3, only... quieter.

9...0-0 Before castling he did not attempt to make any critical moves, but recently there has been a tendency to do precisely this:

9...♘ce7!? 10 0-0 ♗d7 11 ♘e5 (or 11 a3 ♗d6 12 ♘e4 ♗c6 13 ♘e5 h6 14 b4 a6 15 ♘xc6 ♘xc6 16 ♗b2 ♖c8 17 g3 0-0 18 ♕b3 ♗e7 with roughly equal chances, Kobalija – Ovechkin, Moscow 1999) 11...0-0 12 ♕b3 ♗c6 13 ♗g5 ♕a5 14 ♗f3 ♗xc3 15 bc ♗a4 (15...♘f5!?) 16 ♕a3 f6 17 c4 ♕b4 18 ♗c1 ♕xa3 19 ♗xa3 fe 20 cd ♖xf3!? 21 gf ♘xd5 22 de with a very complicated endgame (Ulibin – Ovechkin, Toliatti 2003).

10 0-0 We have reached the tabiya of the variation 9 ♗e2.

After 10...♘f6?! White can obtain a favourable version of the Queen's Gambit. This is achieved in the following way: 11 ♖d1 ♗e7 12 a3 ♗d7 13 ♗c4 ♖c8 14 ♕e2 ♕c7 15 ♗a2 ♖fd8 16 h3 ♗e8 17 ♗e3 (Razuvaev – Kelecevic, Berne 1995).

That leaves just two moves: 10...♗e7 and 10...♖e8

b1) **10...♗e7** Black transfers the bishop to f6 where it will occupy a more favourable position, and to be exact: it will create a threat to the d4 pawn and take part in the consolidation of the king's position along the well-known scheme: g7-g6, ♘c6-e7, ♗f6-g7.

11 ♖d1 ♗f6! Every other move, slowing down (or more so, excluding) the above mentioned regrouping of forces, is noticeably weaker:

11...♘cb4 12 ♕b3 b6 (in case of 12...♘f6 White, as shown by the game Sveshnikov – Olafsson, Stockholm 1998, will force the opponent away from the d5 square: 13 ♘e5 ♕b6 14 ♘c4! ♕d8 15 ♗f3! ♘fd5 16 ♘e3! ♘xc3 17 bc ♘c6 18 ♗b2 ♕c7 19 c4) 13 a3 ♘xc3

14 bc ♘c6 15 c4?! (in too much of a hurry; he should make the developing move 15 ♗e3 and only after 15...♗b7 play 16 c4 with advantage) 15...♘a5 16 ♕e3 ♗a6! 17 ♘e5 ♖c8 (I.Gurevich – Seirawan, San Francisco 1999);

11...♗d7?! (counting on a trap) 12 ♘xd5 ed 13 ♕b3 ♗e8 14 ♘e5! (not possible is 14 ♕xb7? because of 14...♖b8 15 ♕a6 ♘b4 – this is the whole trap) 14...f6 15 ♘g4 ♕b6 16 ♕xb6 ab 17 ♘e3 with a steadily improving position (Ulibin – Asrian, Krasnodar 1998);

11...♖e8?! (not very successfully combining two plans) 12 a3 a6 13 ♗d3 g6 14 ♗h6 ♗d7 15 ♗e4 ♘xc3 16 bc (Gdanski – Grabarchik, Plok 2000);

11...♕d6?! 12 ♘g5! g6 13 ♕e4! (threatening to transfer the queen to h4) 13...f6 (forcing measures) 14 ♘f3 ♗d7 15 ♗c4 ♘cb4 16 ♖e1 ♖fe8 17 ♗d2 ♗f8 18 ♗b3 (Sveshnikov – Spraggett, Palma de Mallorca 1989);

11...♕b6 (Black will deploy his pieces – queen on b6, rook on d8, bishop on f6 – so they occupy themselves in real earnest with the d4 pawn, but who will be defending his king?) 12 ♕e4!

The model game Ulibin – Tukmakov (Pula 1999): 12...♖d8 13 ♗d3 g6 14 ♗c4! (going over to a siege of the d5 square) 14...♘f6 15 ♕e2 ♘d5 (acknowledging that the plan to pressurise the d4 pawn was a failure – 15...♘xd4? 16 ♖xd4! ♖xd4 17 ♗e3 ♗c5 18 ♘a4 ♕b4 19 ♘xd4 ♕xa4 20 ♗b5, and White somehow or other is left with an extra piece: 20...♕a5 21 ♘b3; 20...♕b4 21 ♘c2) 16 ♗h6 ♗f6? (a blunder, but also after 16...♘xc3 17 bc ♕c7 18 ♗b3 White has an obvious advantage) 17 ♗xd5. And not waiting for 17...ed 18 ♘xd5!, Black resigned.

In the encounter Kharlov – Prakash (Calcutta 2001) Black returned to the right plan: 12...♗f6! 13 ♗d3! (there was no sense in taking the pawn – 13 ♘xd5 ed 14 ♕xd5, since the black pieces come alive after 14...♗g4) 13...g6 14 ♗c4 ♘ce7 15 ♘e5 ♗g7 16 ♗b3 ♕d8. But the loss of two tempi (♕d8-b6-d8) in such a position cannot fail to leave a trace – and after 17 ♕f3 White held the initiative for a long time.

Black does not have the right to delay the plan ♗e7-f6, g7-g6, ♘c6-e7; there is no alternative to 11...♗f6.

12 ♕e4 ♘ce7 13 h4!? Slightly more flexible than 13 ♗d3 g6 14 ♗h6 ♖e8 15 h4. With such an order of moves White might have perhaps still been able to carry out h4-h5, but at this moment the brilliance of the attack loses its lustre, for example: 15...♗d7 16 ♗g5 ♗c6 17 ♕g4 ♘f5 18 ♘e4 h6 19 ♘xf6+ ♘xf6 20 ♗xf6 ♕xf6 (Adams – Magem, Debrecen 1992).

13...♗d7 14 ♗d3 The moment of truth has arrived.

How to save himself from mate – 14...g6 or 14...♘f5 ? Surprisingly, modern theory permits both possibilities!

14...g6 looks dangerous as it allows the opponent more freedom of action. For example: 15 h5 ♗c6 (Black demonstrated a new plan of defence in the game Sveshnikov – Malakhov, Moscow 2003: 15...♖c8!? 16 hg hg 17 ♗h6 ♘xc3 18 bc ♗c6 19 ♕f4 ♘d5 20 ♕g4 ♗g7 21 ♗xg7 ♔xg7 22 ♘e5 ♕f6, and after 23 c4 ♘f4 24 ♗f1? ♖h8 25 ♘xc6 ♖h4! he took over the initiative) 16 ♕g4 ♘f5 17 hg hg 18 ♘e4 ♗g7, but what then? White has completed his 'obligatory programme' of work, but the way to complete such a well-begun attack is somehow not apparent. Matters might be concluded by a repetition of moves – 19 ♘fg5 ♖e8 20 ♕h3 ♘h6 21 ♘f3 ♘f5 22 ♘fg5 ♘h6 (Ionov – Danialov, Wijk aan Zee 1998), whereas the attempt to continue the struggle – 19 ♕h3 ♖e8 20 ♘eg5 ♘f6 21 ♘e5 ♖e7 – in the game Sveshnikov – Ryzntsev (Moscow 2002) turned out badly: in the end Black won.

So that for the time being 14...g6 has not been refuted. However **14...♘f5!** is tough and even stronger! The tactical basis of the move lies in the fact that on 15 g4?

...follows 15...♗c6! 16 ♘xd5 ♗xd5 17 ♕f4 ♘xd4! 18 ♘xd4 ♗xd4 19 ♕xd4 ♕xh4 20 f3 ♗xf3 21 ♖d2 f5! with threats difficult to repulse.

Also incorrect is 15 ♘e5?! Black simply exchanges half of his opponent's active pieces – but the other half of them are no worse: 15...♘xc3! 16 bc ♗xe5! 17 de ♗c6 18 ♕g4 ♕a5 19 ♗xf5 ef 20 ♕g3 ♖fe8 (Renet – Speelman, France 2001).

Finally, the attempt to provide himself with material – **15 ♘xd5 ed 16 ♕xd5** likewise finds a tactical refutation: **16...♗a4! 17 ♕xd8** (inferior is 17 ♕xf5 g6 18 ♕h3 ♗xd1 19 ♗h6 ♗xf3 20 ♗xf8 ♗xg2!) **17...♖fxd8 18 b3 ♘xd4!,** and a draw is not far off.

b2) **10...♖e8** Obviously Black intends to dispatch the bishop to the long diagonal, not via f6, but via g7. But this is not the only feature of his plan. First, by remaining on b4, the bishop prevents White from setting up a battery '♕e4+♗d3' – while the

c3 pawn is hanging and the queen immobile. And there is an almost imperceptible nuance: if White wants to oust the knight from the d5 square, he must somehow or other uncover the e-file. And then the bishop on e2 looks bad!

After **11 ♖d1** the most logical move seems to be 11...♗f8, but first we look at how the struggle turns out on 11...♗d7.

b21) **11...♗d7!?**

If White wants at all costs to set up a battery, he has to spend time on 12 a3. But with the extra tempo Black will not even fear the devil: 12...♗f8 13 ♕e4 g6 14 ♗g5 ♕a5 15 ♖ac1 h6 16 ♗d2 ♕d8 17 ♘e5 ♘xe5 18 de ♗c6 19 ♕g4 ♗g7 (Howell – Wells, Edinburgh 2003).

More interesting is **12 ♘g5!? g6 13 ♘ge4** In the game Kharlov – Izoria (Batumi 2002) the sharp 13 h4 was encountered. The correct reply consists of 13...♖c8! 14 h5? ♗xc3 15 hg hg 16 bc ♘cb4!

13...♖c8!? Not hurrying with 13...♗f8, Black retains the tension in the position.

14 ♗g5 ♗e7 15 ♗xe7 ♘cxe7!? 16 ♘d6 Even if White sees the opponent's counterplay coming, he must play like this otherwise 16...♗c6 follows with consolidation.

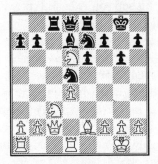

16...♗a4! 17 ♕xa4 ♕xd6 18 ♕xa7 ♕b4 19 ♗f3 (or 19 ♘xd5 ♘xd5 20 b3 ♘c3 21 ♖e1 ♖ed8, winning back the pawn) **19...♕xb2 20 ♘xd5 ♘xd5 21 ♖ab1 ♕c2 22 ♗xd5 ed 23 ♕xb7 ♕f5** In view of the activity of the black pieces, it is extremely complicated for White to realise his material advantage.

b22) **11...♗f8 12 ♕e4** There is no serious alternative to this move, though, (dissatisfied with the following course of events) White has repeatedly tried to deviate:

12 ♗d3 g6 13 ♗e4 ♘xc3 (he can also maintain the tension in the centre – 13...♗g7!? 14 ♗g5 f6 15 ♗h4 ♘ce7 with a double-edged game, for example: 16 ♖e1 ♗d7 17 ♘xd5 ♘xd5 18 ♕b3 ♗c6 19 ♘e5 ♕b6 20 ♘xc6 bc 21 ♖ac1 g5! 22 ♗g3 f5) 14 bc ♗d7 15 ♗f4 (stronger is 15 ♖b1!?, when some problems remain for Black: 15...♕c7 16 ♗g5 ♖ac8 17 ♕d2 ♘a5 18 ♘e5 ♗a4 19 ♖dc1 ♗g7 20 ♗f4) 15...♖c8 16 ♕d2 b6 17 d5 ed 18 ♗xd5 ♗e6 19 c4 ♗g7 20 ♖ac1 ♕e7 with approximate equality (Wolf – Lutz, Groningen 1993);

12 a3 ♗d7 13 ♗g5 ♕b6 14 ♘a4 ♕c7 15 ♖ac1 h6 16 ♗h4 ♖ac8 17 ♕b3 ♕f4!? (Christiansen – Miton, Bermuda 2003),

...and here, 18 ♗g3!? leads to interesting complications: 18...♕e4 19 ♕xb7 ♕e2 20 ♖e1 ♕d3 (20...♘e5 21 ♘xe5 ♗xa4 22 ♕xf7+) 21 ♕xd7 ♕a6 22 ♗c7 ♕xa4 23 ♘e5 ♘xe5 24 ♕xa4 ♘d3 25 ♔f1 ♘xe1 26 ♔xe1 ♖xc7 27 ♖xc7 ♘xc7 28 ♕xa7 ♘d5;

12 ♘e5 (the most active of the sub-variations, but even now Black gradually extinguishes his opponent's initiative) 12...♘xc3 13 ♕xc3 ♗d7 14 ♕b3 (or 14 ♗f3 ♖c8 15 ♕h3 ♘xe5 16 de b6 17 ♗e3 ♖c7 18 ♕d3 ♕b8 19 ♗e4 h6 20 f4 ♖ec8, Sveshnikov – Tukmakov, Budapest 1996) 14... ♘xe5 15 de ♕c7 16 ♗e3 ♗c6 17 ♕c3 a5 18 ♗d4 ♖ec8 19 ♕e3 ♗d5 20 a3 ♗c5 (Sveshnikov – Zontakh, Vrnjacka Banja 1999).

After **12 ♕e4** the above-mentioned nuance comes into effect: the vis-a-vis of the rook e8 and bishop e2 provides an opportunity for the unhindered development of the bishop c8.

12...♗d7!? Black played without cunning in the game Sveshnikov – Oll (Vilnius 1997): 12...g6 13 ♗g5 (White is a little better also in the event of 13 ♗c4 ♘xc3 14 bc ♗d7 15 ♗g5) 13...f6 14 ♗d2 ♗g7 15 ♗b5 ♘de7 16 ♗f4 g5 17 ♗g3 ♘d5. After 18 ♕g4 White's chances are preferable.

13 ♗g5 ♗e7!? On 13...♕a5 lay in store 14 ♗d3 g6 15 ♕h4 ♗g7 16 ♘e4 ♕b6 17 ♗c4!, and the f6 square is on the verge of a bad crash (Ulibin – Henkin, Koszalin 1999).

With the move 13...♗e7 Black invites the opponent to win a pawn: 14 ♘xd5 ed 15 ♕xd5 ♗g4 16 ♕xd8 ♖axd8 17 ♗e3. But after 17...♗f6 Black has sufficient counterplay. In this way the idea of the move 13 ♗g5 (covering over the e-file and without difficulty gobbling up d5) is repudiated.

14 ♗d2 f5 15 ♕c2 ♗f6 16 ♘xd5 ed 17 ♗c3 ♕b6 18 ♗d3 g6 The game is even (Kindermann – Bareev, Germany 2000).

The variation 8 ♕c2 will satisfy the taste of chessplayers of every style and temperament. If you want complications – after 8...♘c6 play 9 ♗d3!?, and you will have more

than enough excitement. If you want a strictly positional struggle – place the bishop on e2 and prove the advantage of the 'isolani'. Moreover the attack (with help of the battery ♕c4+♗d3) has by no means been removed from the agenda.

Indeed it is difficult here – the queen on c2 (as is clearly seen from the variations given above) is far from always being capable of quickly setting up a battery. On the other hand, most frequently he has to reorganise the combination '♕c2+♗d3' by playing ♕c2-e2-e4. But, you see, the queen could tread the same path from the d1 square!

From there comes the idea – not to spend time on 8 ♕c2, but defend the knight c3 with the bishop from d2, and bring the queen (after ♗f1-d3, of course) to e4 by the short march route: d1-e2-e4. Thus was born the variation 8 ♗d2.

B

8 ♗d2

8...0-0 There is a reason to wait a while with castling. Why? If White plays conventionally (♗d3, ♕d1-e2-e4), without paying attention to his opponent's moves, he can get caught out. For example: 8...♘c6 9 ♗d3

♗e7 10 ♕e2 ♕b6!? 11 0-0 0-0 12 a3 ♖d8 13 ♖ad1? ♕xb2! 14 ♘b5 a6 15 ♖b1 ♕a2 16 ♖a1 ♕b3 17 ♖fb1 ♕a4 18 ♘c3 ♕a5 19 ♘b5 ♕b6 20 ♘d6 ♕c7 with a healthy extra pawn (Cherniaev – P.H. Nielsen, Hastings 2004).

In reply to 8...♘c6 9 ♗d3 ♗e7 it is better to secure himself early against hostility – 10 a3!? Now, matters are clearer, no good is 10...♕b6 11 0-0 ♕xb2? 12 ♘a4, as the d4 pawn is inedible: 10... ♗f6 11 0-0 ♗xd4?! 12 ♘xd4 ♘xd4, and then:

13 ♘xd5 ♕xd5 (13...ed 14 ♖e1+ ♘e6 15 ♕h5) 14 ♕g4 0-0 15 ♗h6 ♕e5 16 f4! (Vaisser – Sveshnikov, Moscow 1989) or

13 ♕a4+ ♘c6 14 ♘xd5 ♕xd5 (14...ed 15 ♖fe1+ ♗e6 16 ♗b4!?) 15 ♗e4 ♕d7 16 ♖ad1 ♘e7 (16...f5? 17 ♗g5!, King – Korchnoi, Switzerland 1999) 17 ♕c4 ♘d5 18 ♗xd5 ♕xd5 19 ♕g4!

9 ♗d3 ♘c6 10 0-0 After castling, analogous thoughts can arise for White. Indeed, while the black knight can cover the h7 square in one move, the combination 10 ♗xh7+ ♔xh7 11 ♘g5+ ♔g8 12 ♕h5 (or 12 ♘xd5 ♕xd5 13 ♕h5 ♕f5) does not work – 12...♘f6. But it is possible to step up

the pressure! In the game Lanka – Prysikhin (Germany 2000) followed 10 a3 ♗e7 11 h4!?

White commences active play on the king's flank. The threat is ♘g5, and in certain variations – the manoeuvre ♖h1-h3-g3. Moreover the rook enters the game at once, the saved tempo on castling is somehow very relevant. However when faced with operations on the flank, according to all the rules of warfare you must look for counterplay in the centre: 11...e5!? 12 de ♘db4 13 ♗e4 ♘d3+ 14 ♗xd3 ♕xd3 15 ♕e2. By continuing 15...♕xe2+!? 16 ♘xe2 f6!, Black obtains sufficient compensation for the pawn.

10...♗e7 Fully acceptable is 10...♘f6!? Here the reckless pawn sacrifice 11 ♕e2?! ♘xd4 12 ♘xd4 ♕xd4 13 ♖ad1 is obviously unsatisfactory in view of 13...♕h4! 14 ♘e4 ♗xd2 15 ♘xf6+ ♕xf6 16 ♖xd2 e5.

In the game J.Polgar – Karpov (Dos Hermanas 1999) in reply to 10...♘f6 there followed 11 ♗g5 h6!? 12 ♗e3 ♗d6 13 ♖c1 e5!? In positions with an 'isolani' at d4, it is not often that you come across such an advance, but in the present case it all turns out nicely for Black: 14 h3 ♗e6 15 ♕d2 ♕a5 16 ♗xh6!? ed 17 ♘b5 ♕xd2 18 ♗xd2 ♗b8 19 ♘bxd4 ♘xd4 20 ♘xd4 ♗xa2 with equality.

From the other continuations, after 10...♘f6 we see 11 a3 ♗c7 12 ♗c3!? In such positions this kind of development of the dark-squared bishop was recommended as long ago as Nimzowitsch. Here are two examples from contemporary practice – 12...b6 13 ♕e2 ♗b7, and then:

14 ♖ad1 ♖c8 15 ♘e5 ♘d5 16 ♗e4 (Vysochin – Sergeev, Cappelle la Grande 2003);

14 ♖ac1 ♖c8 15 ♖fd1 ♕d6 16 ♘g5 (Vysochin – Abdelnabi, Cairo 2003) 16...♘a5 17 d5!?

As we see, the Ukrainian grandmaster Spartak Vysochin was twice able to obtain a highly promising position. But returning to 10...♗e7, White has a huge number of possibilities.

The general line of course is ♕d1-e2-e4, it is necessary only to decide whether to play 11 ♕e2 at once or first make the move 11 a3 which is useful in every respect. Besides this, on principle one can reject the idea of placing the queen on e4 and play something else.

1) **11 ♘xd5 ed 12 ♕b3 ♗f6 13 ♗c3 a5 14 a3 ♗g4 15 ♗e2 ♖e8 16 ♖fe1** (Lputian – Bologan, Poikovsky 2003) 16...♕d6;

2) **11 ♖e1 ♗f6 12 ♘xd5 ed 13 ♘e5 g6 14 ♗c3** (Mirumian – Asrian, Erevan 1996) 14...♕b6!? 15 ♕f3 ♗g7 16 ♕xd5 ♗e6 17 ♕b5 ♖fd8

3) **11 ♗e3** (how can he lay claim to an advantage by simply giving up his dark-squared bishop in this way?) **11...♘xe3 12 fe b6 13 ♗e4 ♗b7 14 ♘e5 ♘xe5 15 ♗xb7 ♖b8 16 ♗a6 ♘g6 17 ♘b5 ♗g5** (Agdestein – Henkin, Germany 2000);

4) **11 ♗e4 ♘f6 12 ♗xc6 bc 13 ♘a4 ♗a6 14 ♖e1 ♗c4! 15 ♕c2 ♗d5** (Vaganian – Schussler, Germany 1994).

It is obvious that Black is not posed serious problems by 11 ♘xd5, 11 ♗e3, 11 ♗e4 or 11 ♖e1.

5) **11 ♖c1** The idea of the move is shown by the variation 11...♘db4 12 ♗b1! ♘xd4 13 ♘xd4 ♕xd4 14 ♘b5 ♕f6

15 ♖c3! e5 16 ♘c7 ♖b8 17 ♖g3 ♕c6 (Onischuk – Polak, Vienna 1996) 18 ♗c3! with a very strong attack. However if Black is not tempted by the d4 pawn, the benefits, so to speak, from playing 11 ♖c1 are not obvious.

11...♗f6! 12 ♕e2 ♕b6! (double attack) **13 ♗e3 ♘xe3 14 fe g6 15 ♘e4 ♗g7 16 ♘fg5 ♕d8** If anyone is taking risks in this position then it can only be White (de Vries – Ionov, Wijk aan Zee 1999).

6) **11 ♕c2 ♘db4?!** It goes without saying that stronger is 11...g6. After 12 ♗h6 ♖e8 13 a3 by transposition of moves we arrive at the game examined above, Kobalija – Turov, but! with an extra tempo for Black (Kobalija's bishop went to h6 in one move, and not two as here).

12 ♗xh7+ ♔h8 13 ♕b1 ♘xd4 (on 13...g6 White had the pleasure of sacrificing a bishop; also 13...f5 failed to make an impression, 14 ♗g6 ♘xd4 15 ♘e5 ♘e2+ 16 ♘xe2 ♕xd2 17 ♗h5!) **14 ♘xd4 ♕xd4 15 ♗e3 ♕h4 16 ♗e4 e5 17 a3 ♘c6 18 f4!** The initiative is on White's side (Elianov – Ionov, St.Petersburg 1999).

7) **11 a3** Preventing ♘db4, but at the cost of a tempo. Black's task is to generate counterplay in the region of the a3 pawn.

11...♗f6

Surprising: after the programmed 12 ♕e2 Black step by step achieves equality. This is what the extra (on account of 11 a3) tempo means!

First, it is possible to gobble up the pawn. Only he should not do this with the bishop – after 12...♗xd4?! 13 ♘xd5 ♕xd5 (13...ed 14 ♗xh7+!) 14 ♗e4 and further exchanges on c6 and d4, the 'opposite coloured bishops' give White a strong attack (P.Cramling – Korchnoi, Biel 1984) – but with the knight!

This is why: 12...♘xd4!? 13 ♘xd4 ♗xd4 14 ♗xh7+ ♔xh7 15 ♕e4+ ♔g8 16 ♕xd4 ♘b6!? 17 ♗e3 ♕xd4 18 ♗xd4 ♘c4 with an equal endgame (Adams – Speelman, Hastings 1991).

Secondly, the idea of changing the pawn structure is also not a bad recommendation: 12...♘xc3!? In the game Wahls – Karpov (Baden Baden 1992) Black had no problems at all: 13 bc g6 14 ♗e4 ♗d7 15 ♖ab1 b6 16 ♘e5 (16 c4 ♖e8!?) 16...♖c8 17 f4?! ♗g7. Perhaps the 'hanging' pawn pair c3+d4 looks even worse than the isolani on d4, and together with the weakness on a3 – particularly so.

Here we also have the only tempo-gaining move in reply to 11...♗f6 – this is **12 ♕c2** But then the queen does not get to e4, so why then was 8 ♗d2 played?

12...g6 Incidentally, it is unclear how White can prove his advantage upon 12...h6. After 13 ♖ad1 there are two ideas to choose from:

13...♘xd4!? 14 ♘xd4 ♗xd4 15 ♘xd5 ♕xd5 16 ♗c3 c5 (IIracek – Groszpeter, Kecskemet 1992);

13...♘xc3!? 14 ♗xc3 ♘e7 15 ♕e2 ♗d7 16 ♕e4 g6 17 ♘e5 ♗a4. We are following the game Illescas – Dorfman (France 1991), which White lost. Even though it is possible to force a draw:

18 d5!? ♗xd1 19 de ♗b3 20 ♘xf7 ♖xf7! 21 ef+ ♔xf7 22 ♗xf6 ♔xf6 23 ♖e1 ♗d5 24 ♕e5+ ♔f7 25 ♕f4+ ♔g7 26 ♕e5+ (analysis by Dorfman).

13 ♗h6 ♗g7 14 ♗xg7 ♔xg7 White's position is more pleasant, but no more than that. He can commence an attack – 15 ♖ad1 ♘ce7 16 h4, or proceed more carefully – 15 ♗e4 ♘ce7 16 ♖ac1!? b6 17 ♘xd5 ♘xd5 18 ♕c6; in each case Black has sufficient resources to lead the game to a draw.

8) **11 ♕e2** This move is not only in itself natural but is also objectively the strongest in the present position. Which is not possible to say about 11...♘f6. This reply is seen most frequently (Black prevents the deployment of the queen to e4), but not exclusively – and Black could play more inventively. However, everything is still in order.

a) Winning a pawn by **11...♘db4 12 ♗e4 ♘xd4 13 ♘xd4 ♕xd4** is suspect, though similar to another version that is favourable for Black. Developing the bishop c8 is complicated and White's advantage in force gives him the initiative: **14 ♗e3 ♕e5 15 ♕f3** etc. (Yudasin – Uldashev, Erevan 1996).

He could try to win the exchange – 12...♗f6 13 ♖ad1 b6, but White is alert: 14 ♗b1! ♗a6 15 ♕e4 g6 16 ♖fe1 ♘e7 17 ♗h6 with advantage (J.Polgar – Magem, Las Vegas 1999).

b) It is better to give up the d4 pawn in another way: **11...♕b6!?** (the patent of certain Dutch players). Possible then is:

12 ♖ad1 (12 a3?! ♖d8 13 ♖ad1 ♕xb2! by transposition of moves leads to the game Cherniaev – Nielsen, looked at above) 12...♖d8 13 ♗g5 ♗xg5 14 ♘xg5 h6 (Zude – van Wely, Germany 1998) or

12 ♕e4 g6 13 ♘a4 ♕d8 14 ♖ac1 ♘f6 15 ♕e3 ♘b4 (van den Doel – de Vries, Rotterdam 2000).

c) And, finally, the main line. There is a hypnotist at work indicating that the strongest move in the position is **11...♗f6!?** If now White makes all the 'obligatory' active moves – 12 ♕e4 g6 13 ♗h6 ♖e8 14 ♘e5, then after 14...♘de7! it becomes clear that it is time for him to beat a retreat: 15 ♗b5 a6 16 ♘xc6 bc 17 ♗xc6 ♘xc6 18 ♕xc6 ♖b8. Black wins back the pawn and begins to play for a win (Vajda – Nisipeanu, Budapest 1996).

He needs to be more attentive – **12 ♖ad1**, and then **12...♕b6!**, when again concrete threats appear. After 13 ♗b1 ♘xd4 14 ♘xd4 ♕xd4 15 ♗g5 ♕e5 16 ♕d3 ♕f5! Black has nothing to fear (Vajda – Berescu, Romania 2000).

White should make a tempo move, in order to divert the opponent away from the d4 pawn: **13 ♕e4 g6 14 ♗h6** (Sermek – Lopez Martinez, Leon 2001), but then follows **14...♖d8!**

The position has still not been met in practice, but this phenomenon is probably temporary. By not removing the knight from the centre, Black, with three moves (11...♗f6, 12...♕b6 and 14...♖d8), is able to properly pressurise the d4 pawn and thereby

guarantee himself worthwhile counterplay. Possible then is:

15 ♖fe1!? (intending a double capture on d5 and then mate on e8) **15...♗d7 16 ♗g5 ♗xg5** (losing is 16...♕xb2? 17 ♘xd5 ed 18 ♕h4 ♗xg5 19 ♘xg5 h5 because of 20 ♘xf7! ♔xf7 21 ♕g5 with mating threats) **17 ♘xg5 ♕xd4 18 ♘xd5 ed 19 ♕xd4 ♘xd4 20 ♗xg6 hg 21 ♖xd4 ♖e8 22 ♖ed1 ♖e2 23 ♖xd5** Black develops activity that is sufficient for a draw after 23 ♖b4 ♗c6 24 ♘f3 a5 25 ♖b6 d4! 26 ♘xd4 ♖d8 27 f3 ♖c2 28 ♖b3 ♗a4! 29 ♖xb7 ♖c4.

23...♗c6 24 ♖5d2 ♖ae8 25 f3 f6 26 ♘e4 ♖xd2 27 ♘xd2 ♖e2 It is not possible to realise such an extra pawn. It will be a draw.

d) **11...♘f6** At first sight, all very logical: one knight strikes the e4 square and thereby prevents the battery ♕e4+♗d3, while the second knight (travelling via b4) takes up a position on d5.

And yet 11...♘f6 does not equalise – **12 ♘e4!**

An unpleasant move. Firstly, White wants to exchange the knight f6 before his stepbrother transfers to d5 – then nothing will stop the queen occupying the principal square e4. The other idea for White is purely positional: to grab space on the queen's flank by means of a3, b4 and a future ♘c5.

The tactical basis of 12 ♘e4! lies in the variation 12...♘xd4? 13 ♘xd4 ♕xd4 14 ♗c3, when White develops a very strong attack for the pawn:

14...♕d8 15 ♘xf6+ ♗xf6 16 ♖fd1 ♕e7 17 ♕e4 g6 18 ♗b4;

14...♕b6 15 ♘xf6+ ♗xf6 (or 15...gf 16 ♕g4+ ♔h8 17 ♕h5) 16 ♕e4;

14...♕d5 (the most tenacious) 15 ♘xf6+ ♗xf6 16 ♗xf6 gf 17 ♖ac1!? ♕e5 (17...f5 18 ♗b1) 18 ♕d2 ♕g5 (trying to prevent the invasion of the queen on h6) 19 f4 ♕d5 20 ♖f3 ♖d8 21 f5!

Since the manoeuvre ♘c6-b4-d5 (12...♘b4? 13 ♘xf6+) is not possible and since he cannot play 12...b6? because of the double attack 13 ♘xf6+ ♗xf6 14 ♕e4, the question arises: how can Black complete his development? Worth considering is the simple 12...♘xe4 13 ♕xe4 f5!? 14 ♕e3 ♗f6 followed by ♘c6-e7-d5. This order of moves appeared quite recently and up to now White has achieved nothing in this variation:

15 ♗c3 ♘e7! 16 ♗c4 ♘d5 17 ♗xd5 ♕xd5 18 ♖fe1 ♖e8 19 ♘e5 b6 20 ♘d3 ♗b7 (Yakimov – Al. Kharitonov, Haldikiki 2001) or

15 ♖ad1!? ♘e7! (not to be distracted by the capture of the d4 pawn) 16 ♗c4 ♘d5 17 ♕b3 ♕b6 (Smeets – Rogers, Wijk aan Zee 2002).

The prospects for 12...♘xe4!? will become apparent in the near future but, for the present, practitioners (and home analysts) are concentrating on two directions: 12...♗d7 and 12...♕b6.

d1) **12...♗d7 13 ♖ad1** Black put off his problems for a move, but now it is necessary to make some kind of decision.

Playing with a view to a repetition of moves – 13...♖c8 14 ♖fe1 ♘d5 15 ♘c3 ♘f6 is mistaken in principle, because White has resources to improve his position: 16 a3 ♕c7 17 ♗g5. In the 2nd game of the match for the FIDE world championship Kamsky – Karpov (Elista 1996) play continued 17...♕a5? 18 d5! ed 19 ♗xf6 ♗xf6 20 ♗xh7+! ♔xh7 21 ♖xd5 and though Black gave up his queen he was unable to save the game.

On the other hand, Black equalised with apparent ease in the game Barua – Sasikiran (Calcutta 1998): 13...♖e8 14 ♖fe1 ♕c7 15 ♗g5 ♘d5 16 ♘c3 g6 17 ♕e4 ♘cb4 18 ♗xe7 ♖xe7 19 ♕h4 ♕f4. It is strange that White did not even try to exploit the position of the queen on c7: 15 ♖c1!? (instead of the insipid 15 ♗g5), and if

15...♘d5 16 ♘e5 f6, ôî 17 ♘g5! fe 18 ♗xh7+ ♔f8 19 de with a decisive attack.

The ideal place for the queen in the present scheme is the b6 square. However in the game de Vries – Gyimesi (Ohrid 2001) after **13...♕b6 14 ♗g5 ♘d5 15 ♘e5** the queen was forced to return home – **15...♕d8** But what to do? The threats on the king's flank are increasing and 15...♘xd4? is dubious because of 16 ♕h5 g6 17 ♕h3.

A few moves later White's advantage became visibly quite distinct: **16 ♕h5 g6 17 ♕h4** (nothing is offered by 17 ♕h6?! ♘xd4 18 ♗xe7 ♕xe7 19 ♘xd7 in view of 19...♘f5) **17...f6 18 ♘xc6 ♗xc6 19 ♗h6 ♖f7 20 ♘c5**

d2) **12...♕b6!?** Epishin's idea, worked out after an unfortunate development of events for us in the second game of the Kamsky – Karpov match.

At the time it seemed to us that this move was the most accurate – by threatening to capture on b2, the queen does not allow White to improve the arrangement of his forces. But much water has flowed under the bridge since then... The

plan which we did not fear at the time (a2-a3 and b2-b4), as will become clear, actually places in doubt 12...♕b6. And on the other hand – the deployment which we feared most of all, now does not look so dangerous at all.

d21) **13 ♖fd1** It was precisely this move that we feared most of all during the match with Kamsky. The threat to the b2 pawn, as becomes clear, is illusory. After 13...♕xb2? 14 ♖db1 ♕a3 15 ♖b3 ♕a4 16 ♘xf6+ both captures on f6 are equally bad: 16...♗xf6 loses the queen after 17 ♕e4 g6 18 ♗b5, while 16...gf also clearly leads to mate: 17 ♗xh7+! ♔xh7 18 ♘g5+! fg 19 ♕h5+ ♔g7 20 ♖h3.

Black can link the move 13...♗d7 to ideas that are well known to us from the games Yakimov – Al. Kharitonov and Smeets – Rogers: 14 a3 ♖ad8 15 b4 ♘xe4 16 ♕xe4 f5!? 17 ♕e3 ♗f6 18 ♗c3 ♘e7!

Stronger is 14 ♘e5!? and problems remain:

14...♗e8 15 ♘c4 ♕c7 16 ♘xf6+ ♗xf6 17 ♕e4 g6 18 ♗h6 ♘xd4 (or 18...♗g7 19 ♗f4 ♕d7 20 ♗d6 f5 21 ♕e1 ♖f7 22 ♗e5) 19 ♗xf8 ♔xf8 20 ♖ac1 ♗c6 21 ♕e3 ♖d8 22 ♗e4. It will be difficult to realise the extra exchange but White still remains on top.

14...♖ad8 15 ♘xf6+ ♗xf6 16 ♕e4 g6 17 ♗h6 ♗g7 (weaker is 17...♖fe8 because of 18 ♕f4! ♕xd4 19 ♕xd4 ♘xd4 20 ♘xd7 ♖xd7 21 ♗b5!) 18 ♗g5 ♕xd4 (also in this situation the sacrifice of the exchange seems the best chance for Black – and it is necessary to sacrifice it precisely in this way: worse is 18...♕xb2?! 19 ♗xd8 ♖xd8 20 ♖ab1 ♕xd4 21 ♘f3) 19 ♕xd4 ♘xd4 20 ♗xd8 ♖xd8 21 ♘xd7 ♖xd7 22 ♖ac1. A draw is probable though it will be agonising for Black.

However after **13...♖d8!** the d4 pawn can be taken without any sacrifice!

14 ♘xf6+ ♗xf6 15 ♕e4 g6 16 ♕f4 On 16 ♗c3 it is not necessary to hurry with 16...♘xd4?! 17 ♘e5 ♕d6 18 f4, when White exerts unpleasant pressure. Correct is 16...♗d7! Only by reinforcing the f7 square by 17...♗e8, can Black occupy himself with the d4 pawn.

The position has suddenly become sharp and general considerations are no use. To be sure, even here he would like to wait a while with the capture on d4, but after the 'conciliatory' 16...♗g7?! White is ready with 17 ♘g5! The f7 pawn is hanging and 17...f6 loses in the long but uncomplicated variation 18 ♘xh7! ♔xh7 19 ♕h4+ ♔g8 20 ♗xg6 ♔f8 21 ♕h7 ♕xd4 22 ♗h5! (defending the rook on d1 and creating the threat 23 ♗h6) 22...♕xd2 23 ♖xd2 ♖xd2 24 ♕g6 ♔g8 25 ♕e8+ ♔h7 26 ♗g6+ ♔h6 27 ♗e4.

There remains 17...f5 18 ♗c3 ♘xd4 (upon 18...h6 19 ♘f3 g5 20 ♕e3 g4 21 ♘e5 Black suffers for nothing) 19 ♗c4 h6 20 ♘f3 and White's compensation far outweighs the sacrificed material.

And here upon the immediate **16...♗xd4!** the compensation, so to speak, is not obvious: **17 ♗c3** (17 ♘xd4 ♖xd4!) **17...e5 18 ♕h4 h5 19 ♗c4 ♔g7 20 ♘g5 ♗g4!** There is no attack, but there is an extra pawn.

It is interesting that there are no practical trials of the move 13...♖d8!. Nevertheless one fine day White, as if by command, will stop for a moment and play 13 ♖fd1...

d22) **13 a3!** By rejecting a direct attack on the king, White makes a sort of compromise. In fact the move has a healthy positional basis. Firstly, it radically prevents the manoeuvre ♘c6-b4-d5. Secondly, it organises pressure on the queen's flank by means of b2-b4 and ♘e4-c5 (at the same time the knight on c5 shields the d4 pawn against the queen). It is not apparent where Black's counterplay is coming from.

13...♗d7 As before, 13...♕xb2? is not possible because of 14 ♖fb1 ♘xd4 15 ♘xf6+ ♗xf6 16 ♕e4!

14 ♖fd1 Possibly the most accurate order of moves is the following: 14 b4! ♖ad8 15 ♘c5!? In the game Palac – Hermansson (Panormo 2001) White continued to play convincingly: 15...♗e8 16 ♖fc1 a6 17 ♖ab1 (threatening b4-b5) 17...♘a7 18 a4 ♗c6 19 ♘e5! And White's advantage is obvious; he won this game.

14...♖ad8 Black rightly rejects 14...♘xd4?, calculating the variation 15 ♘xd4 ♕xd4 16 ♗c3 ♕a4 17 b3! ♕c6 (not possible is 17...♕xb3 because of 18 ♘xf6+ ♗xf6 19 ♕e4!) 18 ♘xf6+ ♗xf6 19 ♗xf6 gf 20 ♗xh7+! with a mating attack.

15 ♘xf6+ ♗xf6 16 ♕e4 g6 17 ♗e3 ♘e7 18 ♘e5 ♘f5 19 ♘c4 ♕a6 20 a4 ♗c6

We are following the 4th game of the match for the world championship Kamsky – Karpov (Elista 1996). It can be seen that Black has not only equalised the game but his chances are perhaps already preferable. However the improvement 14 b4! ♖ad8 15 ♘c5 forces one to treat the whole variation 11...♘f6 with a fair deal of scepticism.

The system 6...♗b4 in the Panov Attack 1 e4 c6 2 d4 d5 3 ed cd 4 c4 ♘f6 5 ♘c3 e6 6 ♘f3 has managed to accumulate so many ideas and nuances that it is not easy to deduce any kind of general conformity to established chess wisdom.

Take, for example, just the last variation – 7 cd ♘xd5 8 ♗d2 0-0 9 ♗d3 ♘c6 10 0-0 ♗e7 11 ♕e2. In some variations Black should capture the d4 pawn at once, when the opportunity presents itself. In others – it is necessary to be patient and defer any win of a pawn, sometimes he even rejects the idea of taking on d4 on principle. But only calculation of concrete variations can help the practical player make the right choice; any deviation from pure reasoning may lead him far away from the truth.

A startling lack of chess laws can also be observed in the present system. Once again we return to the last variation. Statistics bear witness to the fact that 11...♘f6, as before, is the most popular reply to 11 ♕e2. Meanwhile from our previous variations it follows that this move is out of date. Stronger is 11...♗f6!?, but who would give a guarantee that when this idea gets into the head of some analyst or other, he will not find a stronger move?

The search for truth in the system 6...♗b4 is continuing day by day. This means that the variation is alive, here there and everywhere.

Index to Chapter Five

**1 e4 c6 2 d4 d5 3 ed cd 4 c4 ♘f6
5 ♘c3 e6 6 ♘f3 ♗b4**   103

A. 7 ♕b3   103
B. 7 ♕a4+   103
C. 7 ♗g5   104
  1) 7...0-0   104
  2) 7...♕a5   104
  3) 7...h6   105
D. 7 ♗d3   105
  7...dc 8 ♗xc4 ♕c7
  1) 9 ♕d3   105
  2) 9 ♕e2   107

**1 e4 c6 2 d4 d5 3 ed cd 4 c4 ♘f6
5 ♘c3 e6 6 ♘f3 ♗b4 7 cd**   108
I. 7...ed   108
A. 8 ♗g5   108
B. 8 ♘e5   109
C. 8 ♕b3   109
D. 8 ♕a4+   110
  8...♘c6 9 ♗b5 0-0
  1) 10 ♗xc6   110
  2) 10 0-0   110
E. 8 ♗e2   110
F. 8 ♗b5+   111
  8...♗d7 9 ♕e2+ ♘e4 10 0-0 ♗xc3
  11 bc 0-0 12 ♗d3
  1) 12...♘xc3   111
  2) 12...♗f5   112
  3) 12...♖e8   112

G. 8 ♗d3   112
  8...0-0 9 0-0
  1) 9...♗g4   113
  2) 9...♘c6   113
II. 7...♘xd5   114
A. 8 ♕c2   114
  1) 8...0-0   115
  2) 8...♕c7   115
  3) 8...♘d7   115
  4) 8...♘c6   116
  a) 9 ♗d3   116
  a1) 9...♗e7   117
  10 a3
  a11) 10...♘f6   117
  a12) 10...♗f6   117
  a2) 9...h6   118
  a3) 9...♘xc3   118
  a4) 9...♗a5   119
  10 a3 ♘xc3 11 bc ♘xd4
  12 ♘xd4 ♕xd4 13 ♗b5+
  a41) 13...♔f8   120
  a42) 13...♔e7   120
  a43) 13...♗d7   121
  b) 9 ♗e2   123
  9...0-0 10 0-0
  b1) 10...♗e7   124
  b2) 10...♖e8   126
  11 ♖d1
  b21) 11...♗d7   126
  b22) 11...♗f8   127

B. 8 ♗d2   128
    8...0-0 9 ♗d3 ♘c6 10 0-0 ♗e7
    1) 11 ♘xd5   130
    2) 11 ♖e1   130
    3) 11 ♗e3   130
    4) 11 ♗e4   130
    5) 11 ♖c1   130
    6) 11 ♕c2   131
    7) 11 a3   131

8) 11 ♕e2   132
    a) 11...♘db4   132
    b) 11...♕b6   132
    c) 11...♗f6   133
    d) 11...♘f6   133
    12 ♘e4
    d1) 12...♗d7   134
    d2) 12...♕b6   135
    d21) 13 ♖fd1   135
    d22) 13 a3   136

Chapter Six

1 e4 c6 2 d4 d5 3 ed cd 4 c4 ♘f6
5 ♘c3 e6 6 ♘f3 ♗e7

The most popular branch in the Panov Attack. White has three replies to choose from: 7 c5 (I), 7 ♗g5 (II) and 7 cd (III).

I
7 c5!?

Never very popular, and now a virtually forgotten continuation. The plans of the two sides are clear: White intends to construct a pawn chain b4-c5-d4 and on the basis of this carry out an advance on the queen's flank, while Black will set about undermining this pawn chain (a7-a5 and b7-b6) and also undertake counterplay in the centre: ♘f6-e4 and f7-f5.

Practice shows that Black can reckon not only on equality but also something more. Upon this it is very important that the second knight is not yet standing on c6. And it does not need to! There it only becomes a target for the white pawns (b4-b5).

We add that the prophylactic 7 a3 is not necessary here; White then would be making an excess of pawn moves. For example, 7...0-0 8 c5 ♘e4 9 ♕c2 f5 10 b4 ♗f6 11 ♗b2 ♘c6 12 ♖d1 ♗d7 and Black's chances are in no way worse (analysis by Botvinnik).

After **7...0-0** (also interesting is an immediate 7...♘e4!?) arises the tabiya of the variation 7 c5. White can play directly – 8 b4 (A), 8 ♗g5 (B) or 8 ♗f4 (C), and can prevent the manoeuvre ♘f6-e4: 8 ♕c2 (D) or 8 ♗d3 (E).

A

8 b4 Black has two active retorts: 8...b6 and 8...♘e4.

141

1) **8...b6!? 9 ♗b2** Likewise encountered is 9 ♖b1!? bc 10 bc ♘e4 11 ♘xe4 de 12 ♘e5 ♕c7 13 ♗f4 ♖d8 14 ♕a4 (14 ♕d2!?) 14...g5! 15 ♗d2 ♗d7 16 ♗b5 ♗xb5 17 ♕xb5 ♖xd4 18 ♕e8+ ♗f8 19 ♗c3 ♕xe5 (Morozevich – Bareev, Dortmund 2002). Here White should concede a draw by 20 ♖b7 ♘d7 21 ♕xa8 ♕xc5 22 ♗xd4 ♕c1+.

9...a5 10 a3 ab 11 ab ♖xa1 12 ♗xa1 bc 13 dc It seems that Black is playing into his opponent's hands, giving him connected and far advanced passed pawns. But this impression is deceptive. White lags seriously behind in development and while he is making up for his neglect, Black will manage to generate counterplay.

13...♘c6 14 ♕a4 (14 b5 ♘b4 15 c6 d4) **14...♕c7 15 ♗e2**

We are following the game Pilgaard – Ngyen An Dung (Budapest 1999). Black, by playing **15...♗d7?!**, showed his determination to sacrifice a piece. Such tactics justified themselves; soon he won. However analysis showed that the sacrifice was incorrect. He should play simply 15...♗b7!? 16 0-0 ♖a8 17 ♕b3 ♘g4 18 g3 ♘ge5 19 ♘b5 ♘xf3+ 20 ♗xf3 ♕b8 with sufficient chances.

16 b5 ♗xc5 17 bc ♗xc6 18 ♘b5 ♘e4 A critical moment in the game. By choosing 19 ♗d4?, White made a blunder. There followed 19...♗xb5 20 ♗xb5 ♗xd4 21 ♘xd4 ♕c3+, and he had to resign because of the unstoppable mate.

The refutation lies in **19 0-0! ♕b6 20 ♗d4 ♖a8 21 ♗xc5 ♘xc5 22 ♕b4** Black apparently thought that by playing **22...♖a2** (22...♘e4 23 ♕d4), he would obtain sufficient compensation for the piece. But **23 ♖b1! ♖xe2 24 ♘bd4 ♕xb4 25 ♖xb4 ♘a6 26 ♖b1!** dispels all his illusions.

Despite setbacks in individual games, on the whole the reliability of playing 8...b6 and 9...a5 is beyond doubt.

2) **8...♘e4!?** He can defend the knight on c3 in two ways: 9 ♕c2 and 9 ♗b2.

a) **9 ♕c2?!** looks completely natural but after the game Estrin – Bergrasser and Berta – Bergrasser the desire of players to play this was something we did not see...

9...♘c6! In conjunction with the following combination – the most resolute, though also not bad is 9...f5 10 ♗d3, and then:

10...♘c6 11 a3 ♗f6 12 ♘e2 g5! 13 ♗b2 (or 13 b5 ♘e7 14 ♘e5 ♗xe5

15 de ♘g6 16 ♗b2 ♕a5+ 17 ♔f1 ♗d7) 13...g4 14 ♘e5 ♕c7 15 f3 ♗h4+ 16 g3 ♘xe5 17 de gf 18 gh fe 19 ♕xe2 b6. The struggle is very sharp, but Black is in no way worse;

10...b6 11 ♖b1 ♗f6 12 h4!? (preventing the thrust g7-g5, inevitable after 12 0-0; for example, 12...♘c6 13 ♘e2 a5 14 a3 ab 15 ab bc 16 dc g5!, Estrin – Zagoryansky, Moscow 1944) 12...♘c6 13 ♘e2 a5 14 a3 ab 15 ab bc 16 dc e5 17 0-0 ♕e7 18 ♗b5 (inferior is 18 b5 ♘xc5! 19 bc e4) 18...♘d8 19 ♗g5 ♗xg5 20 hg f4! 21 ♕b3 ♗e6. White has a difficult position (Estrin – Konstantinopolsky, correspondence, 1950).

After 9...♘c6! the break e6-e5 is threatened. White's reply is forced – **10 b5**, but it is then that followed Bergrasser's combination:

10...♘xd4! 11 ♘xd4 ♗xc5 For the piece Black has a total of two pawns. On the one hand, not much, but on the other – the pawns are in the centre and very difficult to blockade. Besides this, White is again behind in development.

12 ♘xe4 ♗xd4 13 ♘c3 (according to an analysis by Boleslavsky, weaker is 13 ♘g5 g6 14 ♖b1 e5 15 ♘f3 ♗b6)

13...e5 An important moment. Bergrasser himself suggested for the present not to touch the centre pawns: **13...♗d7!?** This is how a couple of his games went:

14 ♗b2 ♖c8 15 ♕d2 ♗b6 16 ♔d1?! (really it was best to return the piece – 16 ♗e2 d4 17 0-0, rather than suffer) 16...a6! 17 ba d4 18 ♘b5 ba 19 ♘xd4 ♗a5 20 ♕d3 e5 with a decisive advantage (Estrin – Bergrasser, correspondence, 1980);

14 ♕d2 ♗b6 15 ♗a3 ♕f6! 16 ♗b4 (on 16 ♗xf8 ♖xf8 Black is for the time being a rook down but in the end it will all come together in his favour: 17 ♖c1 ♗a5 18 ♗d3 ♖c8 19 0-0 ♗xc3 20 ♕e3 b6) 16...♖fc8 17 ♖c1 a5 18 ba ba with serious compensation for the piece (Berta – Bergrasser, correspondence, 1987).

In correspondence play it is quite possible that the move 13...♗d7 is strongest. However in practice it is clear that simpler is 13...e5.

14 ♗b2 ♗e6! (weaker is 14...♗b6 15 ♗e2 d4 16 ♘e4 ♗a5+ 17 ♔f1 ♗f5 18 ♗d3 ♖c8 19 ♕e2 ♕e7 20 g4!, and White quite surprisingly has somehow managed to blockade the pawns, Estrin – Zagorovsky, correspondence, 1974) **15 ♕d2 ♖c8**

Detailed analysis of this position was made in his day by Isaac Boleslavsky. Here is his conclusion.

16 ♗e2 (bad are both 16 ♖c1 ♗b6 17 ♘a4 ♗a5 18 ♗c3 ♖xc3!, and 16 ♘a4 ♗f5 17 ♖c1 ♖xc1+ 18 ♗xc1 ♕h4 19 ♘c3 ♖c8 20 ♗b2 ♗xc3 21 ♗xc3 ♕e4+ 22 ♗e2 d4) **16...♗b6 17 0-0 ♗a5 18 ♕d3 d4 19 ♘a4** In the event of 19 ♘e4 Black replies 19...f5 20 ♘g3 ♗b6 and then e5-e4; however the position after 19 ♘d1 ♗c4 20 ♕e4 ♗xe2 21 ♕xe2 ♖e8 was assessed by Boleslavsky as equal.

19...♗c4 20 ♕e4 ♗xe2 21 ♕xe2 ♕d5 White has retained the extra piece and avoided a rout. But he is not in a position to slow down the e- and d-pawns, therefore Black has full compensation for the piece.

b) **9 ♗b2** Essentially a natural move.

9...f5 10 ♗d3 This position arose in the game Matulovic – Petrosian (Belgrade 1961). It has decisive significance for understanding the play in such situations.

Black needs to tackle the pawn wedge b4-c5-d4. An immediate 10...a5 is weak because of 11 b5. Therefore correct was 10...b6!, preparing the break a7-a5. Petrosian

committed an inaccuracy by playing 10...♗f6?! There followed 11 b5! It becomes clear that it is practically impossible to shake the foundations of White's pawns on the queen's flank. Black has to look for chances in an attack on the enemy king, but even here his possibilities are not great: 11...♗d7 12 0-0 ♗e8 13 ♖b1 ♘d7 (13...♘h5!?) 14 ♘e2 g5 15 ♘e1 ♗g7 16 f3 ♘ef6 17 ♗c2 ♖c8 18 ♘d3 ♗g6 19 a4 ♘h5. By continuing 20 ♘b4!, Matulovic had every chance of breaking through first.

However after the correct **10...b6!** Black, in all variations, achieves his objective – shaking the opponent's pawn wedge on the queen's flank.

11 a3 bc 12 dc There is also a defect in 12 bc. It opens the b-file, and Black does not fail to exploit this: 12...♘c6 13 ♕a4 ♖b8 14 ♖b1 ♗d7, and if 15 ♗b5, then 15...♘a5!

12...a5! 13 0-0 ♗f6 14 ♖c1 ab 15 ab ♘c6! Black provokes the further advance of the b and c-pawns, endeavouring to prove that without due support of the pieces the passed pawn will be weak, not strong.

16 b5 ♘b4 17 c6 (or 17 ♗xe4 fe 18 ♘e1 ♘a2!? 19 ♖c2 ♘xc3 20 ♗xc3 d4).

The previous phase of the struggle has turned out in Black's favour. But how should he proceed further?

Dubious is 17...♗xc3?! 18 ♗xc3 ♘a2, since after 19 ♗d4 White has good compensation for the exchange. On the other hand, worth considering is 17...♘a2!? 18 ♘xa2 ♗xb2 19 ♖c2 ♗f6 20 ♕e2 ♕c7 21 ♖b1 ♖b8 22 ♕e3 ♖b6 with a blockade on the dark squares.

However the strongest is the following path: **17...♕b6!? 18 ♗b1 ♘xc6 19 ♘xd5 ♕xb5 20 ♗xf6 ed** Black will hardly manage to realise the pawn (particularly after 21 ♘d4!), but in this way he fully insures himself against hostile action.

It is no great exaggeration to say that the idea of an immediate 8 b4 is obsolete.

B

8 ♗g5?! In principle, the exchange of the dark-squared bishop in a situation where there is a skirmish going on around the c5, d4, e5, squares, should be favourable for Black. But the manoeuvre ♘f6-e4 enters into his plan. Does White then allow his bishop to be exchanged?

8...b6 9 b4 Now Black has two plans, approximately equal in strength – either to further undermine the pawn chain by means of a7-a5, or immediately offer an exchange of bishops: 9...♘c6 10 b5 ♘e4 or 9...♘e4. In each case, in order to defend his pawns on the queen's flank, White is forced to spend extra time, which means that castling will be delayed. In reply follows the break

in the centre e6-e5, and with the king on e1 White might as well think about equality.

1) **9...a5!? 10 ♘a4** The position after 10 a3 was studied in Chapter Four under the following order of moves: 1 e4 c6 2 d4 d5 3 ed cd 4 c4 ♘f6 5 ♘c3 e6 6 ♗g5 ♗e7 7 ♘f3 0-0 8 c5 b6 9 b4 a5 10 a3 To what was said there we can add that after 10...♘e4 11 ♗xe7 ♕xe7 12 ♘a4 ab 13 ab bc 14 ♘xc5 (we remind you that bad is 14 bc? in view of 14...♕a7! 15 ♗d3 ♕a5+ 16 ♘d2 ♗d7 17 ♗c2 ♗b5, Kan – Makogonov, Leningrad 1939) 14...♖xa1 15 ♕xa1 e5!? (also interesting is 15...♘c6 16 ♕b2 e5!? – Makogonov) 16 de ♘c6 17 ♘d3 ♘xb4 18 ♕b2 ♘xd3+ 19 ♗xd3 ♗g4 20 ♗xe4 de 21 ♘d2 e3! 22 fe ♕h4+ 23 g3 ♕h3 24 ♘e4 ♕h6 and White, despite the limited material, can expect a difficult defence (Gergel – Podgaets, Odessa 1967).

10...♘fd7 11 ♗xe7 ♕xe7 12 ♗b5 ab 13 c6 ♘f6 14 ♖c1 (14 ♘xb6 ♖a5) **14...♖a5 15 c7 ♘a6 16 ♗xa6 ♖xa6 17 ♘e5** This is how the game Matulovic – V. Sokolov (Sarajevo 1958) went. In it Black retreated but the position has not just one, but two solutions:

17...b5 18 ♘c5 ♖xa2 19 ♘c6? ♕xc7 – analysis by Rellstab. True, it is not quite clear what he intended on 19 0-0;

17...♗b7!? (the simplest) 18 ♘c6 (or 18 0-0 ♖c8) 18...♕d7 19 ♘b8 ♕xa4 20 ♘xa6 ♕xa6.

2) 9...♘c6!? 10 b5 ♘e4 An interesting idea, sounded out in the game Vallejo – van der Wiel (Elgoibar 1998).

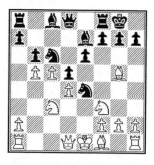

By continuing 11 ♘xe4!? de 12 bc, White retained slightly better chances. Here are some sample variations:

12...♗xg5 (or 12...ef 13 ♗xe7 ♕xe7 14 ♕xf3 bc 15 ♕a3 ♕h4 16 dc ♕e4+ 17 ♗e2 ♕xg2 18 ♕f3) 13 c7 ♕d5 14 ♘xg5 ♕xg5 15 ♕d2 ♕xd2+ (also in the event of 15...♕e7!? White is in a position to force the opponent to exchange queens: 16 ♕f4 ♗b7 17 ♕d6 ♕g5 18 h4 ♕d5 19 ♕xd5 ed 20 ♖c1) 16 ♔xd2 bc 17 dc (weaker is 17 ♔e3 f5 18 ♖c1 f4+ 19 ♔xe4 ♗b7+ 20 ♔d3 ♖ac8 21 ♖xc5 ♖f7) 17...a6. With accurate play Black can apparently achieve a draw, but the general vector of the position is determined in White's favour.

However Vallejo played 11 ♗d2?!, allowing van der Wiel to seize the initiative: 11...♘a5 Now it is already too late for 12 ♘xe4 de 13 ♗xa5 ef 14 ♕xf3 ba, and if 15 ♕xa8, then 15...♕xd4 16 ♖d1 ♕c3+ 17 ♔e2 ♕e5+ 18 ♔f3 ♗xc5 with a decisive attack.

In the game, play continued 12 c6 ♘xd2 13 ♕xd2 a6 14 ♖c1 ♗b4 15 ♕c2 ab 16 ♗xb5 ♗a6 17 0-0 ♗xc3 18 ♗xa6 ♖xa6 19 ♕xc3 ♕d6 20 ♘e5 ♖c8 Later on, the fact that Black had only one pawn weakness against three of the opponent began to tell. Eventually Black won.

3) 9...♘e4! The most natural way. The theoretical basis of this move was given by Genrikh Kasparian a long time ago. This is how events could develop:

10 ♗xe7 ♕xe7 11 ♘a4 (11 ♘xe4 de 12 ♘e5 ♖d8 13 ♕d2 ♗b7 14 ♗e2 f6 15 ♘c4 ♘c6 16 ♘d6 a5! – Kasparian) 11...♗d7 (11...bc 12 ♘xc5 ♘c6 13 a3 a5 14 ♗b5 ♘c3 15 ♕d3 ♘xb5 16 ♕xb5 ♕c7 – Kasparian) 12 ♗d3 ♘c6 13 b5 ♘b4 14 0-0 bc 15 dc ♘xd3 16 ♕xd3

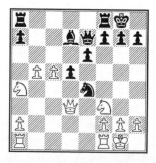

16...a6! 17 c6 ab 18 ♘b6 ♖a3! 19 ♕xb5 ♘c3! winning (Barlov – Christiansen, Tjentiste 1975).

146

C

8 ♗f4 Containing more ideas than 8 ♗g5, but also not without its downsides. The bishop, standing on f4, can come under the tempo-gaining attack g7-g5.

8...b6 Let us also look at 8...♘e4. After 9 ♗d3?! Black's plan would be justified: 9...♘xc3 10 bc b6! The pawn outpost on c5, cramping his position, is removed from the board, allowing counterplay against the weaknesses on a2 and c3. Besides this, it is useful to exchange the bishop d3 in order to deprive White of vistas for attack. In this sense it is very pertinent that the knight is still b8, since White cannot prevent an exchange on a6. Here are some sample variations:

11 cb ab 12 ♕c2 h6 13 0-0 ♗a6!;

11 h4 ♗a6!, and no good is 12 ♗xh7+? ♔xh7 13 ♘g5+ ♔g8 14 ♕c2 (14 ♕h5? ♗d3) 14...♗xg5 15 hg f5!;

11 ♖b1 ♘c6 (11...♗a6!? 12 c6 ♗d6 13 ♗xd6 ♕xd6 14 ♗xa6 ♘xa6 15 ♕a4 ♘b8 16 ♖xb6 ab 17 ♕xa8 ♕xc6) 12 cb (in the present situation 12 h4!? looks more well-founded) 12...ab 13 ♕c2 h6 14 0-0 ♗a6!, and Black's position deserves the

preference (Pioch – Kostro, Poland 1974).

The idea of an immediate 8...♘e4 can be placed in doubt only by the reply 9 ♕c2!? After an exchange on c3 White will recapture with the queen, leaving his pawn structure intact and secure. And 9...♕a5 can be parried by 10 ♗d3 f5 11 ♗xb8! ♖xb8 12 a3 ♘xc3 13 b4!

9 b4 Black has a pleasant choice between 9...bc, 9...a5 and 9...♘e4.

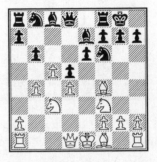

1) **9...bc 10 bc** Inferior is 10 dc. In the game Sliwa – Pomar (Varna 1962) Black, with very elementary moves, secured himself the better game: 10...a5 11 a3 ab 12 ab ♖xa1 13 ♕xa1 ♘c6 14 ♕a4 d4 15 ♘d1 ♕d5 etc.

10...♘e4 11 ♘xe4 de 12 ♘e5 f6 13 ♘c4 ♘c6 14 ♘d6 g5! 15 ♘xc8 ♕xc8 16 ♗e3 ♖d8 In the encounter Urbanec – Meduna (Hlohovec 1993) White blundered: 17 ♗c4?, and, after 17...♔h8, one of his pawns – c5 or d4 – must be lost.

The only possibiity of continuing the struggle was **17 ♕a4 a6! 18 ♖b1 ♖b8 19 ♖xb8 ♕xb8 20 ♗e2 ♕b1+ 21 ♗d1 ♕b5** The game in unclear.

2) **9...a5!?** A higher ranking move than 9...bc.

147

10 ♘a4 Possible is 10 a3 – since the white bishop is on f4, and not on g5, the jump 10...♘e4 will be without tempo (compared with the games Kan – Makogonov and Gergel – Podgaets). However Black still has the tempting possibility of complicating the game: 10...ab!? 11 ab ♖xa1 12 ♕xa1 ♘c6 13 ♕a4

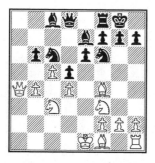

13...bc!? In the game Spal – Lechtynsky (Klatovy 1998) White did not risk accepting the piece sacrifice. Possibly he was right. After 14 bc ♗d7 15 ♗b5 ♕a8 16 0-0 ♘e4 starts a quiet, approximately equal game.

However what awaits White if he takes the piece? The variations show that from his point of view the risk is hardly excessive: 14 ♕xc6 ♗d7 15 ♕a6 (bad is 15 ♕c7? because of 15...♕xc7 16 ♗xc7 cd 17 ♘a2 ♖c8 with a decisive advantage) 15...cb 16 ♘b5 (also on 16 ♘d1 ♕a8 17 ♕d3 ♕a2 18 ♗e2 ♖a8 he will probably have to give up a piece for the b-pawn) 16...b3 17 ♘d2 (17 ♗d3 ♗b4+ 18 ♗d2 ♕a8 with compensation) 17...♕c8 18 ♘c7 (after 18 ♕xc8 ♖xc8 19 ♘xb3 ♗b4+ 20 ♗d2 ♗xd2+ 21 ♔xd2 ♘e4+ 22 ♔e1 ♗xb5 23 ♗xb5 ♖b8 Black

recovers the material with interest) 18... ♘h5 19 ♗e5 f6 20 ♕xc8 ♖xc8 21 ♗a6 ♖b8 22 ♘xd5 fe 23 ♘xe7+ ♔f7 with good chances of victory.

10...♘bd7 11 ♖c1 After 11 c6? Black is ready to sacrifice not just one, but two pieces in a row – 11...♗xb4+ 12 ♘d2 ♘e4! 13 cd ♗xd7 14 ♘b2 ♕f6 15 ♘d3 ♘xf2! – and all this with great benefit to himself.

11...♘e4 12 ♗b5 ab! 13 c6 ♗a6!

In the game Rogul – Cvitan (Porec 1998) White lost ignominiously: 14 ♗xa6? ♖xa6 15 cd ♕xd7 16 ♖c7 ♕xa4 17 ♕xa4 ♖xa4 18 ♖xe7 b3!

The essence of the combination undertaken by the Croatian grandmaster Ognien Cvitan is revealed on other replies by White. And namely – upon **14 c7!?** After **14...♕c8 15 ♗xd7 ♕xd7 16 ♘xb6 ♕b5 17 ♘xa8 ♖xa8** arises a critical position. White is the exchange up and has a strong passed pawn on c7, And Black – just one threat: 18...b3! 19 ab ♗b4+ 20 ♗d2 ♘xd2 21 ♘xd2 ♕d3! and a further check on the e-file.

And suddenly it becomes clear that it is difficult to find a defence against this threat, if indeed it is in general possible! Even on the very strong 18 ♘d2 ♘c3 19 ♕f3 Black's initiative is very strong. For example, 19...♗c8 20 ♖c2 ♖xa2 21 ♖xa2 ♘xa2 22 ♕e2 ♕c6 23 ♘f3 ♘c3 etc.

3) **9...♘e4 10 ♕c2** (nothing good comes from 10 ♘xe4?! de 11 ♘e5 f6 12 ♘c4 ♘c6) **10...♘c6!?** Following in the footsteps of Bergrasser, but with different ideas.

11 ♖b1 bc 12 bc In the game Pilgaard – Schandorff (Greve 2002) White, unconcerned, played 12 ♘xe4 de 13 ♕xe4.

There followed a completely unforeseen tactical blow: 13...♘xd4! He cannot take the rook in any way: 14 ♕xa8? ♘c2+ 15 ♔e2 ♗a6+ or 14 ♘xd4 ♕xd4 15 ♕xa8?! ♕xf4 16 ♗e2 ♕c7. Pilgaard chose 14 ♗d3, but after 14...♘xf3+ 15 ♕xf3 ♗d7 16 0-0 cb 17 ♖fd1 ♕e8 18 ♗e4 ♗a4! he was not able to equalise.

12...♕a5 13 ♗d2 A position is reached which you would definitely like to play as Black. However for the present no reliable path to an advantage has been found.

The simplifying manoeuvre 13...♘xd2 14 ♕xd2 ♗a6? is no good because of 15 ♘xd5! In the game Balashov – Galkin (Tomsk 1997) was

seen a piece sacrifice typical for this position: 13...♘xd4?! 14 ♘xd4 ♘xd2 15 ♕xd2 ♕xc5. In our view, in the present situation there was no need for this. The above-mentioned game continued 16 ♖c1 (16 ♗d3!?) 16...♗f6 17 ♘f3 ♕a3 18 ♗e2 ♖b8 19 ♘b5 ♕a4 20 ♘bd4 ♗a6, and soon the opponents repeated moves.

Worth serious consideration is **13...♘b4!? 14 ♕b2 ♘xd2 15 ♕xd2 ♖b8**

In the event of 16 ♗e2 unpleasant is 16...♘c2+! 17 ♔d1 ♖xb1+ 18 ♘xb1 ♘b4 19 a3 ♕a4+ 20 ♔c1 ♘c6.

No use is 16 ♖b3 ♗a6 17 ♘xd5? ed 18 ♗xa6 because of 18...♘c2+ 19 ♔d1 ♕xa2; and even after 17 ♘e5 ♖fc8 Black has the better game.

White could stabilise the position with the help of an exchange of queens: **16 ♘b5!? ♘c6 17 ♕xa5 ♘xa5 18 ♗d3 ♘c6 19 0-0** (if White seriously decides to 'dry up' the game, he should not stop half way; after 19 ♔d2?! e5! 20 de ♗g4 Black again gets chances) **19...♗f6 20 ♖fd1 ♗d7** The endgame is approximately equal.

Drawing conclusions from the three continuations (8 b4, 8 ♗g5 and

8 ♗f4), to a greater extent focusing on White's play and to a lesser extent on the anticipated play of the opponent (♘f6-e4), it is possible to draw the conclusion that the strategy itself is not justified. Black's plan is also more in the centre and requires fewer tempi to realise. Even after creating a pair of passed pawns on the queen's flank, White, convinced that his own king is in a lamentable state, is forced go over to defence.

D

8 ♕c2!? An ideal move (White prevents the jump of the knight to e4), we just don't understand why he can't do the same by placing the bishop on d3? Therefore 8 ♕c2 will probably be played rarely, and up to now there exists no connection with theory. After **8...b6 9 b4** he can reply in different ways:

9...a5 10 ♘a4 ♘bd7 11 b5! (learning the lesson taught by the game Ciolovic – Zelcic, San Vincent 2002: 11 c6? ♗xb4+! 12 ♔d1 ♘e4 13 a3 ♗d6 14 cd ♗xd7 15 ♔e1 ♖c8 16 ♕d1 ♕c7 17 ♗d2 e5! 18 ♗e2 ed 19 ♔f1 d3!, and Black won) 11...bc 12 dc e5 13 ♗e2 d4 14 0-0 ♘d5 15 c6

(Ciolovic – Fonteine, Pancevo 2002);
9...♘c6 10 a3 bc 11 bc e5 12 de ♘g4 13 ♗e2 ♘gxe5 14 ♘xe5 ♘xe5 15 ♗f4 ♘g6 16 ♗g3 ♗xc5 17 0-0 ♗e6 18 ♖fd1 ♕g5 19 ♗f3 ♖ac8 20 ♕d3 h5!? with chances for both sides (Nataf – Palo, Istanbul 2003).

E

8 ♗d3! The most natural and objectively the strongest move. White develops, prepares castling and prevents the knight jump to e4. One could not wish for more. As regards the plan to advance the queenside pawns, Black now actually forces White to occupy himself with this.

8...b6 9 b4 a5!? Black's chances lie in intensifing the situation on the board to the maximum. It is worth giving Black a couple of tempi in development – and not even stop at that. Here are a few examples:

9...♗d7?! 10 ♗e3! (so as to meet 10...a5 with 11 b5) 10...♘g4 11 0-0 a5?! (Botvinnik recommended 11...bc 12 bc ♘xe3 13 fe ♘c6) 12 ♘a4! bc 13 bc ♗xa4 14 ♕xa4 ♘xe3 15 fe ♘a6 16 ♖ab1 with an overwhelming positional advantage (Botvinnik – Golombek, Moscow 1956);

9...bc?! 10 bc ♘c6 11 0-0 ♗d7 12 h3 ♘e8 13 ♗f4 ♗f6 (Fischer – Ivkov, Buenos Aires 1960) 14 ♗c2!? ♕a5 (not possible is 14...♘xd4? 15 ♘xd4 e5 in view of 16 ♗xe5 ♗xe5 17 ♗xh7+!) 15 ♕d3 g6 16 ♕d2. Thanks to the protected passed pawn on c5 White has the initiative.

After **10 ♘a4** a critical position arises.

The b6 square (and this means also the tension on the queen's flank as a whole) can be held by 10...♘fd7 or 10...♘bd7. Let us look at both moves.

1) **10...♘fd7** In his turn, White can choose between 11 a3, 11 b5, 11 h4 and 11 ♕c2.

a) **11 a3?!** Listless and allowing equalisation with help from the standard **11...ab 12 ab bc 13 dc ♘c6 14 ♖b1 e5** But in the game Nuevo – Campora (Seville 1999) the desire to acquire an extra pawn led Black to the verge of a catastrophe:

15 ♗b5 ♗b7 16 ♕xd5 ♕c7 17 0-0 ♘f6 18 ♕b3?! Not the best move, since the black knight attacks the queen with tempo, but in any case Black holds the initiative. For example, 18 ♕c4 e4 19 ♘d2 ♘g4 20 g3 ♕e5 with a subsequent transfer of the queen to h5.

18...e4 19 ♘d2 ♘d4 20 ♕c4 ♘g4 21 g3 ♖ad8 22 ♘b3 ♘f3+ 23 ♔g2 ♗d5 24 ♕e2 e3! etc.

b) **11 b5!?** Thought up by Botvinnik, which in itself gives the move a mark of quality. However on correct play there is no danger for Black.

11...bc 12 dc e5! 13 c6 e4 14 cd ♘xd7 15 0-0 ef Everything is in order for Black after 15...♗f6 16 ♖b1 ed 17 ♕xd3 ♘e5 18 ♘xe5 ♗xe5 19 ♗b2 (19 f4!?) 19...♗xh2+! 20 ♔xh2 ♕h4+ (Kopaev – Sokolsky, correspondence, 1950).

16 ♕xf3 ♘e5 17 ♕g3 ♘xd3 18 ♕xd3 d4! An important improvement. In the original game, Botvinnik – Pomar (Munich 1958), was played 18...♗d6, which is noticeably weaker in view of 19 ♗a3!

19 ♗f4 ♗b7 20 ♖ac1 ♗g5 21 ♗xg5 ♕xg5 22 f3 ♖ac8 23 ♖xc8 ♖xc8 24 ♖e1 h5

Botvinnik succeeded in blockading the opponent's central pawns on the d5 square, and the light-squared bishop remained 'blunt'. Here, however, the bishop is almost the strongest piece on the board and in any case it is not Black who has to equalise the game (Sokolsky – Simagin, correspondence, 1964).

c) **11 h4!?** Leading to a very sharp game. Black needs to be on the alert since after an exchange on b6 the bishop sacrifice on h7 is threatened. Apart from this, White wants to transfer the rook to g3.

In the game Stisis – Burmakin (Aika 1992) Black varied and ran into danger: 11...bc 12 bc ♗a6 13 ♗f4 ♖e8? He will not have to wait long for his punishment: 14 ♗xh7+! ♔xh7 15 ♘g5+ ♔g8 16 ♕h5 ♘f6 17 ♕xf7+ ♔h8 18 h5. It goes without saying that it was necessary to play 13...♗xd3 14 ♕xd3 ♘c6, though after 15 ♖b1 White had an unquestionable advantage.

Nor was everything alright for Black after 11...h6 12 ♖h3!? ♗f6 13 ♖g3 e5 14 ♗xh6 e4 15 ♘g5. In the game Keller – Pomar (Lugano 1968) there was a downright massacre: 15...♘c6? 16 ♕h5 ed 17 ♗xg7! ♖e8+ 18 ♔f1 ♗xg7 19 ♕xf7+ ♔h8 20 ♕h5+ ♔g8 21 ♕h7+ ♔f8 22 ♘e6+! ♖xe6 23 ♖xg7.

Stronger is 15...ed! 16 ♕xd3 ♖e8+ 17 ♔d2 ♘f8 (Blatny – Adams, Oakham 1990), but even here White's attack is menacing.

11...f5!? The most reliable continuation. Now the b1-h7 diagonal is reliably covered and the way for the rook to g3 prohibited.

12 ♘g5 ♕e8 13 ♔f1 Necessary since any raids by White are easily repulsed: 13 ♘xe6 ♗xc5 14 bc ♕xe6+ or 13 ♗b5 ab!? 14 ♘xb6 ♖a5 15 ♕e2 ♗xg5 16 hg ♗a6 17 ♗xa6 ♘xb6 18 ♗d3 ♘a4 19 ♗f4 ♘c3.

13...♗f6 14 ♗b5 ab 15 ♘xb6 ♗a6! **16 ♗xa6** (upon 16 ♘xa8 ♗xb5+ 17 ♔g1 ♘a6 18 ♘b6 ♘dxc5! Black's initiative cancels out his material deficiency) **16...♘xb6 17 ♗e2 ♘a4** with the better game (Barberis – Profumo, Bratto 1997).

d) **11 ♕c2!?** Undeservedly, theoreticians have devoted little attention to this move. On the basis of an interesting, if debatable recommendation of Kasparian (see below), the queen move is considered insufficient to obtain an advantage. But how is it that the statistics are so depressing for Black?

Let us look at this continuation in detail.

d1) The trappy **11...b5!?** (reckoning on 12 ♗xb5? ab 13 a3 ♕a5 14 ♕e2 ♗a6!, Haba – Jung, St.Ingbert 1991) is not so easy to refute. For example, 12 ♗xh7+ ♔h8 13 ♘b2 ♘c6 14 ♗d3 ♘xb4 15 ♕e2 ♘xd3+ 16 ♘xd3 b4

17 ♗f4 ♘f6 leads to a position in which it is difficult to say what carries more weight: White's attack or the pluses at Black's disposal.

Apparently, the best reply is **12 ♘c3!?** Possible then is:

12...♘c6!? 13 ♗xb5! (more reliable than 13 ♗xh7+ ♔h8 14 ♘xb5 ♘xb4 15 ♕b1 g6 16 ♗xg6 fg 17 ♕xg6 ♖f6 18 ♕h5+ ♔g7 19 0-0 ♗a6 20 a4, and once again it is unclear how strong White's attack is) 13...♘xb4 14 ♕e2 ♗a6 15 ♗xa6 ♘xa6 16 ♗f4 with a small but stable 'plus';

12...ab 13 ♘xb5 ♘f6 (13...h6 14 c6 b3 15 ♕c3!) 14 0-0 ♘c6 15 a4! Here White's advantage is more clearly visible.

d2) 11...ab This move has still not been met in practice. Analysis takes us to an endgame with better prospects for White:

12 c6 (the complications after 12 ♗xh7+ ♔h8 13 c6 ♘xc6 14 ♕xc6 ♗a6 15 ♕c2 ♖c8 16 ♕b1 ♕c7 17 ♘b2 f5 18 ♗g6 ♖f6 19 ♗h5 g6 20 ♗g5 gh 21 ♗xf6+ ♗xf6 lead to absolutely nothing for White) **12...♘xc6 13 ♕xc6 ♗a6 14 ♘b2 ♕c8 15 ♕xc8 ♖fxc8 16 ♗xa6!?** After 16 0-0 Black manages to establish a fortress, which is very hard to breach: 16...♗c4! 17 ♗g5 ♗d6 18 ♖fc1 b5.

16...♖xa6 17 ♘d3 This is an endgame White has been seeking but his advantage is not great.

d3) 11...♘c6 (considered the main move) **12 ♗xh7+ ♔h8 13 b5 ♘b4 14 ♕b1**

The position is very sharp, but what we do not understand is why everybody plays 14...bc?! here. After 15 a3, time after time White is firing at point blank range: 15...cd (or 15...c4 16 ab ab 17 ♗c2 b3 18 ♗xb3 cb 19 ♕xb3 ♘b6 20 ♘e5, and the black king is hopelessly weak, Liberzon – Opocensky, Leipzig 1965) 16 ab ♗xb4+ 17 ♔f1 f5 (after 17...g6 18 ♗xg6 fg 19 ♕xg6 Black is doomed, Alekhina – Sanadze, Beltsy 1972) 18 ♘g5 ♕e8 19 ♕d3 (Bishop – Fitzpatrick, San Mateo 1992).

It goes without saying that stronger is **14...f5!?** This was the position Kasparian also had in mind when he wrote that after 15 a3 bc 16 dc ♘xc5 17 ♘xc5 ♗xc5 18 ♗g6 ♕f6 Black had good prospects.

But firstly, instead of 16 dc, more interesting is 16 ab!? cd 17 ba ♔xh7 18 a6 e5 19 0-0. And secondly, the obvious 16 ♗g6. You see, in order to avoid the headaches associated with calculating the capture of the bishop h7, it is simpler to adopt this order of moves: **15 ♗g6!? bc 16 a3** Now on 16...cd White has every chance of delivering mate, for example: 17 h4 e5 18 ♘g5 ♘b6 19 ab ♗xb4+

20 ♔d1 ♘xa4 21 ♖xa4 ♗d7 22 ♘f7+ ♖xf7 23 ♗xf7 ♖b8 24 ♕b3 ♗xb5 25 ♖xb4! ab 26 ♕f3!

A little stronger is **16...c4 17 ab ♗xb4+ 18 ♔f1 ♕f6 19 ♗h5 g6 20 ♗f4!** ♔g8 (20...gh 21 ♘b6!) **21 ♗xg6 ♕xg6 22 h4 ♕h5 23 ♖h3** White is attacking with equal material but not, it must be said, with equal strength.

Precisely 11 ♕c2!?, in our view places under doubt 10...♘fd7 and confirms one more time that the strongest move is – 10...♘bd7.

2) **10...♘bd7!?**

We look at the following possibilities: 11 c6, 11 a3, 11 ♗f4 and 11 ♕c2.

a) The move **11 c6?!** is interesting as an amusing trick in analysis but not to be played in a serious game. After **11...♗xb4+ 12 ♗d2 ♘b8 13 ♖c1 ♕c7 14 0-0 ♗a6 15 ♗xa6 ♖xa6 16 ♘e5 ♖c8** Black has a great advantage (Muse – Koch, Germany 1993).

b) On **11 a3** Black equalises with the thematic **11...ab 12 ab bc 13 bc e5!** The variation 14 de?! ♘xc5 15 ef ♘xd3+ 16 ♕xd3 ♗xf6 17 ♘d4 ♕e8+ 18 ♗e3 ♖xa4 was investigated

as far back as Botvinnik, while in the game Railich – Groszpeter (Paks 2001) another capture was tested: **14 ♘xe5 ♗xc5! 15 0-0 ♘xe5 16 de ♘e4** In each case Black has nothing to worry about.

c) **11 ♗f4** White's idea is understandable: the bishop must help the pawn to get to c7. In the game Prins – Richter (Teplice 1949) Black replied with a piece sacrifice: 11...ab 12 c6 ♘c5!? 13 dc bc 14 0-0 ♕a5 15 ♘b2 ♗a6 16 ♗e5 ♖ac8 17 ♕c2 ♖xc6. An interesting concept, isn't it?

The position after 11 ♗f4 has been repeatedly refined. Among others, we have the idea 11...ab 12 c6 ♘h5?! Taking the piece now is bad: after 13 cd? ♗xd7 14 ♘e5 ♘xf4 15 ♘xb6 ♕xb6 16 ♘xd7 ♕c6 Black stands to win (Railich – Dettling, Budapest 2001). Considerably stronger is 13 ♗g3, hoping for 13...♘xg3? Then instantaneously an attack on the h-file unfolds.

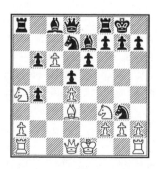

14 ♗xh7+! ♔xh7 15 hg+ ♔g8 16 cd ♗a6 17 ♘e5 g6 18 ♘c6 ♕xd7 19 ♕c1 ♖fc8 20 ♘xe7+ ♕xe7 21 ♕h6 ♕f6 22 ♘xb6 ♕xd4 23 ♕h7+ ♔f8 24 ♕h8+ winning.

In his turn, instead of 13...♘xg3? Black ought to play 13...♘df6!? 14 c7 ♕e8 15 ♘xb6 ♖a7 with a complicated struggle. The process of refinement and substitution of one variation for another is endless...

In itself the idea 11...ab 12 c6 ♘h5?! has little value. On the other hand after the immediate **11...♘h5!**, it looks like the whole undertaking with 11 ♗f4 should be given up as a bad job. It has to be established that White simply loses a tempo and as a consequence cannot count on an advantage:

12 ♗g3 f5!? 13 ♘e5 ♘xg3 14 ♘c6 ♕e8 15 ♘xe7+ ♕xe7 16 hg ab 17 c6 ♘f6 18 ♘xb6 ♖a3 with counterplay (analysis by Konstantinopolsky) or

12 ♗d2 ab 13 c6 ♘b8 (13...♘df6! 14 ♘e5 g6 15 ♖b1 b5 16 ♘c5 ♗xc5 17 dc ♕c7 – Konstantinopolsky) 14 ♘e5 ♘f6 15 ♕b3 b5! 16 ♘c5 ♗xc5 17 dc ♕c7 18 ♗f4 ♘xc6 (L.Vajda – Lupulescu, Romania 1999). In all of these variations there can only be one question – how great is Black's advantage?

d) **11 ♕c2** In the variation 10...♘fd7 the queen move is essentially a double attack – the h7 pawn is hanging as well as the knight on b8 (after c5-c6-c7). However Black is not facing any concrete threats here, therefore he is fighting not for equality – but for the advantage.

11...♕c7!? 12 cb Quite bad is 12 a3 ab 13 ab e5! In the game Golikov – Tikhomirov (correspondence, 1967) play continued 14 c6 ♗xb4+ 15 ♔f1 ♗a6! 16 ♗xa6 ♖xa6 17 ♖b1 b5!, and soon White resigned.

12...♗xb4+ 13 ♗d2 ♕d6 14 ♖b1 ♘xb6 15 ♗xb4 ab 16 ♘c5 ♘bd7 Once again it is Black who is playing for a win (Blatny – Ostenstahl, Trnava 1989).

The last variations certainly represent the back yard of Panov Attack theory, and on them one cannot judge the strength of the 7 c5 system (where one can see that Black has to choose in the region of 10-11 moves to decide what is the easiest way for him to obtain an advantage?!). But on the whole the system 7 c5 is going through a deep crisis. Old ideas are refuted, there are no new ones. What will be its future?

II
7 ♗g5

Variations with this move have been partially examined in Chapters Two and Four.

Less popular is 7 ♗f4 – possibly because in positions with the isolated pawn (and this applies in all cases) it is more usual to see the bishop on g5 or e3, but not on f4. This is how the struggle continued:

7...0-0 8 ♖c1 (8 c5 was looked at above, under the inverted order of moves: 7 c5 0-0 8 ♗f4) 8...♘c6 9 a3 ♘e4 10 ♗d3 ♘xc3 11 ♖xc3 dc 12 ♖xc4 ♕a5+! (usually almost every exchange favours the player fighting against the isolated pawn, and to be really precise – the exchange of queens; therefore White refrains from 13 ♕d2) 13 ♗d2 ♕d5 14 ♕c2 f5! (in principle such a weakening is undesirable but in the present situation it is more important to limit the activity of the bishop d3 and at the same time guarantee the safety of his queen) 15 0-0 ♗d7 16 ♖c1 ♖ac8 17 ♕b1 b5! 18 ♖4c3 a6 19 ♗e3 ♗d6 20 b4 ♘e7 with a very comfortable game (Mishychkov – Sakaev, St.Petersburg 1997).

7...♘c6?! The position after 7...0-0 8 c5 b6! returns us to the games Kan – Makogonov and Gergel – Podgaets.

8 c5! The knight, prematurely developed on c6, will in the future become an object of attack by the b-pawn, though Black loses the struggle for the key e5 square earlier.

8...0-0 An immediate 8...♘e4 9 ♗xe7 ♕xe7 is also played. In order not to spoil the pawn structure, we recommend 10 ♕d3!?, and then:

10...♘xc3 11 ♕xc3 e5!? (essentially the only possibility of getting stuck into the game) 12 de ♗g4 13 ♗b5 ♗xf3 14 gf 0-0 15 ♗xc6 bc 16 0-0-0 ♖ab8 with some compensation (analysis by Dolmatov);

10...f5?! (principled but... dubious) 11 ♕e3 0-0 12 ♗b5 ♘b4 13 ♖c1 ♗d7 14 ♗xd7 ♕xd7 15 ♘e5 ♕e7 16 0-0 ♘c6 17 ♘xc6 bc 18 f3 White has the advantage – mainly because of his possession of the e5 square (Rogers – Kuijf, Wijk aan Zee 1993).

In reply to 10 ♕d3 Black most frequently resorts to a repetition of moves – 10...♘b4 11 ♕b5+ ♘c6. Returning the queen – will be a draw, not returning it – and Black takes on c3 and spoils the opponent's pawns. But there is also a third way – exchanging himself: 12 ♘xe4! de 13 ♘e5 ♕c7 14 0-0-0 0-0 15 ♘xc6 bc 16 ♕e2 ♕a5 17 a3 (Gelfand – Kuczynski, Moscow 1994). In this position Sergei Dolmatov also advised sacrificing a pawn: 17...e5!? 18 ♕xe4 ed 19 ♕xd4 ♗e6.

9 ♗b5 ♘e4 Vladimir Kramnik took in hand 9...h6!?

In the stem game was played 10 ♗xf6 ♗xf6 11 0-0 ♘e7! (retaining the knight for struggle against the e5 square) 12 b4 b6 13 ♕d2 bc 14 bc ♗d7 and Black has no problems at all equalising (Timman – Kramnik, Amsterdam 1996).

If White retreats the bishop to h4, then there arises a position that is analogous to the main line, only with a pawn on h6 ('luft' which might in any case prove useful): 10 ♗h4 ♘e4 11 ♗xe7 ♘xe7, and then:

12 ♕c2 ♕a5 13 ♗d3 ♘xc3 14 ♕xc3 ♕xc3+ 15 bc b6! 16 cb ab 17 ♔d2 ♗a6 with a draw (Kobalija – Dychkov, Moscow 1995);

12 ♖c1 b6 13 c6 ♘d6 14 0-0 ♕c7 15 ♘e5 f6 16 ♘g4 a6 17 ♗d3 ♕xc6 18 ♗b1 ♕e8 19 ♕d3 (Korchnoi – Kramnik, Zurich 2001) 19...♘df5 20 ♖fe1 ♗d7. White has definite compensation for the pawn but no more than that.

Gradually White's principal weapon in the struggle against 9...h6 became the move 10 ♗f4!? After 10...♘e4 11 0-0 ♘xc3 12 bc ♗d7 13 ♕a4 (with the idea of making it difficult for Black to advance b7-b6)

brought no advantage in view of 13...♕e8! In the game Magomedov – Klinova (Hoogeveen 2001) Black quickly obtained equality and we will not dwell on this: 14 ♗xc6 ♗xc6 15 ♕b3 f6 16 ♖fe1 ♕d7 17 ♖e3 ♖fe8 18 ♗g3 ♗d8 19 ♘e1 b6! 20 ♘d3 ♗b5.

Instead of 13 ♕a4 stronger is 13 ♖c1!?

The idea is the same – to make difficult the break b7-b6. Nevertheless Black should take a risk and go in for the variation 13...b6!? 14 c4! dc 15 d5! ed 16 ♕xd5 ♕c8 17 cb ab 18 ♖xc4 ♗c5. There does not seem to be any immediate danger (analysis by P.Blatny and C.Hansen).

In the game Kasparov – Anand (Amsterdam 1996) Black played otherwise – 13...♖e8?! After 14 ♖e1 it was already too late for the thematic break: 14...b6?! 15 c4! bc 16 cd ♘xd4 17 ♘xd4 cd 18 ♗c7! ♕c8 19 ♗e5 ♕d8 20 ♗xd7 ♕xd7 21 de ♕xe6 22 ♗xg7! Therefore Anand first went 14...♗f6, and only in reply to 15 ♖b1 played 15...b6. Kasparov replied by sacrificing a pawn – 16 ♗a6 ♗c8 17 ♗b5 ♗d7 18 ♗a6 ♗c8 19 ♗d3!? bc 20 ♘e5

157

♗d7?! 21 ♖b7 – and developed a menacing initiative.

Instead of 20...♗d7 he should immediately exchange on e5. Only not 20...♘xe5? 21 de ♗g5 – when White wins the exchange: 22 ♗xg5 ♕xg5 23 ♗b5 ♖d8 24 ♗c6, but 20...♗xe5! 21 de f5 with chances of a successful defence.

10 ♗xe7 Let us look at both captures: 10...♕xe7 (A) and 10...♘xe7 (B).

A

10...♕xe7 White has a simple choice. Without pity to spoil his pawns on the queen's flank – 11 0-0, or with pity – play 11 ♖c1 or 11 ♕c2.

1) **11 0-0?! ♘xc3 12 bc ♗d7** In the game Kobalija – Fressinet (Calicut 1998) Black somewhat uncertainly played b7-b6: 12...♘a5?! 13 ♗d3 h6 14 ♖b1 ♕c7 15 ♗c2! b6. As a result after 16 ♕d3 White obtained a dangerous initiative. Play continued: 16...g6 17 ♕e3 ♔g7 18 ♘e5 bc 19 ♖b5! (doesn't the position remind us of what we saw in Kasparov against Anand?) 19...♗a6 (defending the extra pawn is foolish, since after 19...♘b7 20 ♖fb1 c4 21 ♕g3 he cannot shake off the trouble around

the g6 square) 20 ♖xc5 ♕d8 21 ♘g4! ♖h8 (21...♗xf1 22 ♕xh6+ ♔g8 23 ♖c7!) 22 ♕e5+ ♔g8 23 ♗xg6! with a win.

13 ♖b1 ♖fc8 14 ♖e1 ♘a5 15 ♗d3 ♖ab8 16 ♘e5 ♘c6! 17 ♕c2 g6 18 ♘f3 b6! 19 cb ab 20 ♕d2 ♕f6 We are following the game Anic – Prie (France 1998). Even after White carries out a favourable exchange – **21 ♗b5 ♗e8 22 ♗xc6! ♖xc6 23 ♘e5 ♖c7**, his position does not improve much. True, in such structures the knight is far stronger than the bishop but, you see, White has twice as many pawn weaknesses! Black should hold.

2) **11 ♖c1 ♘xc3 12 ♖xc3**

12...e5! It is necessary to make this break before White has castled. Otherwise the advantage of the knight over the bishop will become obvious.

13 de d4! Namely so! Insipid is 13...♘xe5 14 ♘xe5 ♕xe5+ 15 ♕e2.

14 ♖c1 Few would risk accepting the pawn sacrifice – 14 ♘xd4 ♖d8 15 ♗xc6 bc, and then:

16 0-0? ♕d7! 17 ♖d3 ♗a6 winning;

16 ♖d3?! ♕xe5+ 17 ♖e3 ♕f4 18 0-0? (the tension is maintained

after 18 g3 ♕f6 19 0-0 ♗e6 20 ♖e4 ♗xa2) 18...♗g4 19 ♘e2 ♕xe3!, when White resigned (Drira – Pomar, Caorle 1972);

16 f4!? (obviously the strongest) 16...♗a6!? (surprisingly White can defend himself in the event of 16...♕d7 17 ♖d3 ♕d5 18 ♖d2 ♕e4+ 19 ♘e2 ♖xd2 20 ♕xd2 ♗a6 21 ♔f2 ♗xe2 22 ♖e1!) 17 ♖c2 ♖d5 18 b4 ♖ad8 19 ♖d2 ♕d7 20 e6!? fe 21 ♘f3 ♖xd2 22 ♕xd2 ♕xd2+ 23 ♘xd2 ♖d4 Black wins back the pawn, retaining chances of victory.

14...♘xe5 15 ♘xe5 ♕xe5+ 16 ♕e2 In the final account it all comes down to a quiet position in which neither White nor Black has particular prospects.

16...♕d5 17 0-0 ♗f5 (why, incidentally, does he not take the pawn – 17...♕xa2!? 18 ♗c4 ♕a5 19 ♕e7 ♕b4 20 b3, and here if only 20...♗e6!?) **18 b4 ♖ad8 19 ♖fd1 d3 20 ♕d2 a6** The game is even (Paoli – O'Kelly, Teplice 1949).

3) **11 ♕c2!? ♘g5 12 ♘xg5 ♕xg5 13 ♗xc6 bc 14 0-0 e5**

15 f4! Very strong. White determines the right pawn structure for himself. He could only reckon on a minimal advantage in the event of

15 de ♕xe5 16 ♖fe1 ♕f6 17 ♖ad1 ♖b8 18 ♕d2 ♗g4 19 f3 ♗e6 20 b3 (Keres – Alekhine, Amsterdam 1938).

15...ef 16 ♕d2 ♖b8 17 b3 ♗h3 18 ♖f2 ♖be8 19 ♕xf4 In sight is an endgame in which Black has no antidote to the charge of the a and b-pawns (Ivkov – Bergrasser, Leipzig 1960).

B

10...♘xe7! Considerably stronger than 10...♕xe7. Black realises that he should at all costs avoid a position in which a handsome knight on e5 will be facing a pitiful light-squared bishop.

11 ♖c1!? Clearly unfavourable is 11 0-0 in view of 11...♘xc3! 12 bc b6! 13 cb ab 14 a4 ♕c7 15 ♕b3 ♗a6 (Suba – Rogers, Malta 1980). But why can't he play 11 ♕c2 (after all, it is precisely this move that appears in the main line with 10...♕xe7)? Because in reply there follows 10...♕a5! (here we see just one benefit of taking on e7 with the knight), and White's pawn mass once again becomes worthless – 12 ♗d3 ♘xc3! 13 bc h6 14 0-0 b6!

11...b6 12 c6!?

The passed pawn on c6 – is this a strength or a weakness? Let's have a look at 12...♘d6 and 12...♕d6.

1) **12...♘d6 13 0-0!?** Attentive readers will detect the difference in comparison to the game Korchnoi – Kramnik (Zurich 2001). The black pawn is standing not on h6, but on h7! If now 13...♕c7 ('à la Kramnik'), then after 14 ♕c2 a6 15 ♗d3 White gains an important tempo to successfully defend his passed pawn: 15...h6 16 ♘e2.

In the game Yurtaev – Ivanchuk (Tashkent 1985) Black played **13...♘xb5 14 ♘xb5 a6**, and after **15 ♕a4** embarks on a mistaken tactical operation:

15...♘xc6?   16   ♖xc6   ♗d7 Ivanchuk did not notice that on **17 ♘d6 ♖a7 18 ♖fc1 ♖c7** a blow awaits him: **19 ♘xf7!** White won shortly.

Instead of 15...♘xc6? worth considering is 15...♗d7!? 16 cd ab 17 ♕xb5 ♖a5 18 ♕b3 ♕xd7. The advantage remains with White but Black can successfully defend himself: 19 ♕xb6 ♖xa2 20 ♖c7 ♕d8 21 ♖fc1 ♘f5 or 19 a3 ♕d6 20 ♖c3 ♖aa8 21 ♖fc1 ♖fc8.

2) **12...♕d6!? 13 0-0 a6**

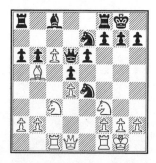

How strange that this position is easily transformed into one with an isolani: 14 ♗d3!? ♘xc6 (taking on c3, and then on c6 is not possible because of the standard blow on h7) 15 ♘xe4 de 16 ♗xe4 ♗b7 17 ♘e5. After 17...♖ac8 (it is possible that the most accurate defence lies in 17...♖a5!? 18 ♗xb7 ♘xb7 19 ♖c6 ♕d8) 18 ♕d3 h6!? (only not 18...♘xe5? 19 ♗xh7+ ♔h8 20 ♕h3!) 19 ♗xc6 ♗xc6 20 ♕xa6 ♕d5 21 ♘xc6 ♖xc6 22 ♖xc6 ♕xc6 and it is difficult for White to realise his material advantage. However it is a pleasant kind of difficulty.

In the game Christiansen – Henkin (Biel 1994) White preferred 14 ♕a4 Black should force the play: **14...♗d7!? 15 cd ab 16 ♕xb5 ♘xc3 17 ♖xc3 ♖xa2** White's passed pawn comes closer to promotion, move by move, but the resources of the defence are far from exhausted. There might follow 18 ♘e5 ♖a5 19 ♕b3 ♖a6 20 ♖fc1 f6 21 ♖c8 ♖a8 22 ♖xa8 ♖xa8 23 ♕b5 ♔f8! (losing is 23...fe? 24 de ♕b8 25 ♖c8+!) 24 b4! Not an obvious move. The basis of this idea is to defend the knight by b4-b5. How important this is can be shown by the variation 24 h3 ♖d8 25 ♘c6 ♕xd7 26 ♕xb6 ♖c8.

24...fe 25 de ♕xe5 26 ♕xb6 ♕b8 It all hangs by a very fine thread; let's stop and take a look.

27 ♖c8+! ♔f7 28 ♕d4! (after
28 d8♘+? ♔e8 White loses!)
**28...♕xb4 29 d8♘+! ♔e8! 30 ♘c6+
♖xc8 31 ♕xb4 ♖xc6** An excellent
finish to an imaginative game. Black
constructed a fortress and waited for
the draw offer.

III
7 cd

The main continuation. Black can
take on d5 with the pawn or the
knight.

A

7...ed A passive move, which
cannot be recommended. The
position now reached makes a
curiously depressing impression –
symmetrical, with almost a complete
lack of counterplay for Black.

Let's look at 8 ♗d3 and 8 ♗b5+.

1) **8 ♗d3** (in this case Black is
considered to have an easier defence)
8...♘c6 After 8...0-0 9 h3 Black
should not develop the bishop on b7.
He will not succeed in fighting for the
e4 square and there could be even
more trouble. As, for example, in the
game Mukhytdinov – Burmakin
(Cappelle la Grande 1995): 9...b6?!
10 0-0 ♗b7 11 ♗f4 a6 12 ♖e1 b5

13 ♖c1 ♘c6 14 ♗b1 ♖e8 15 ♕d3
♘a5? (a blunder but Black's position
is in any case suspect) 16 ♗c7!

9 h3 0-0 10 0-0 h6 Quite often
10...♗e6 is played, and then:

11 ♖e1 ♖e8 12 ♗f4 ♗d6 13 ♗e5
♘h5 14 ♕d2 f6 15 ♗xd6 ♕xd6
16 ♖e3 ♘f4 (Spassky – Pomar,
Palma de Mallorca 1969).

11 ♗e3 ♖c8 (dubious is 11...♘d7?!
12 ♘e2! ♕b6 13 ♘f4 ♖ac8 14 ♕b1
h6 15 ♗h7+ ♔h8 16 ♗f5, Vaganian –
van der Wiel, Rotterdam 1989)
12 ♕e2?! (stronger is 12 ♖c1, in
order to hide the bishop d3 in his
'pocket' on b1) 12...♘b4 13 ♗b1
♘e4 (Balashov – Larsen, Buenos
Aires 1980);

11 ♗f4 ♖c8!? 12 ♖e1 ♕b6!?
13 ♘a4 ♕d8 14 ♘c5 (14 ♖c1 ♘e4)
14...♘xd4 15 ♘xd4 ♗xc5 16 ♘xe6
fe 17 ♖xe6 ♕d7 18 ♗f5 ♘e4 19 ♖f6
♗xf2+ 20 ♔h2 ♕xf5!, and Black
obtained compensation for the queen
which was enough for a draw
(Portisch – Larsen, Niksic 1983).

As we see, there is nothing
particularly terrible for Black. And
yet it cannot suit him that there is
absolutely no possibility of
displaying activity in all these
examples (perhaps with the exception
of the game Portisch – Larsen).

11 ♗f4! This came into fashion
following the example of Vishy
Anand. Previously 11 ♗e3 was
played.

11...♗e6 (11...♗d6 12 ♗e5! –
Anand) **12 ♖e1 ♖c8** He could drive
away the bishop from f4 – 12...♘h5
13 ♗e3 ♗d6, but after 14 ♘g5! ♘f6
15 ♘xe6 fe the position transforms

161

into one that is favourable for White. He has two bishops and pressure over the whole board. The game Gulko – Barhagen (Berne 1995) continued 16 ♖c1 ♖c8 17 a3 ♗b8 18 ♖c2 ♘e7 19 ♗c1. White's advantage can only get bigger.

13 ♕d2 ♖e8 14 ♖ad1 ♗b4?! 15 a3 In the game Anand – Ravi (India 1988) Black conceded that his last move was a loss of tempo and retreated: 15...♗f8. In Anand's opinion, White's advantage is consolidated by 16 ♗b1 ♘d7 17 ♖e2.

But certainly Ravi originally intended to play **15...♗xc3 16 bc ♘e4** (16...♘a5 17 ♗xh6!) **17 ♗xe4 de 18 ♖xe4 ♕d5** (weaker is 18...♗d5 19 ♖xe8+ ♕xe8 20 ♘h2! with the idea 21 ♘g4 – Anand) **19 ♖e3 ♘a5** (19...♗d7?! 20 c4! ♕xc4 21 d5!) with a blockade on the light squares in return for the sacrificed pawn.

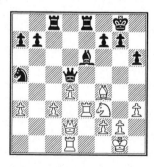

But why did he at the last moment reject his own idea? The solution lies in the variation **20 ♘e5 f6 21 ♖g3! fe 22 ♗xe5 ♔f8 23 ♕f4+ ♗f7 24 ♗xg7+ ♔e7 25 ♗xh6** with a decisive attack.

2) Black is also set serious problems by **8 ♗b5+**. We examine all

three defences against the check: 8...♘c6, 8...♘bd7 and 8...♗d7.

a) **8...♘c6 9 ♘e5 ♗d7 10 0-0 0-0 11 ♖e1** In the game Hubner – Petrosian (Seville 1971) White played 11 ♗g5!? Hubner's deep calculation is admirable: after 11...♘xe5 12 de ♘e4 13 ♗xe7 ♘xc3 14 ♗xd8 ♘xd1 15 ♗xd7 ♖fxd8 16 e6! Black's position, despite the small number of pieces, is very difficult.

However later was found the improvement 11...♖c8, when nothing is offered by 12 ♗xf6 ♗xf6 13 ♘xd5 in view of 13...♗xe5 14 de ♘xe5 15 ♗xd7 ♘xd7 (Sermek – Rogers, Moscow 1994).

11...♖c8 (White has a minimal advantage after 11...♗b4 12 ♗xc6 ♗xc6 13 ♗g5 h6 14 ♗h4 ♕d6 15 ♕b3, Tal – Meduna, Lvov 1981) **12 ♗g5 ♖e8** Black made a positional mistake in the game Velimirovic – Benko (Vrnjacka Banja 1973): 12...♗e6?

Now with the clear cut 13 ♗xc6! bc 14 ♘a4 White established a blockade on the dark squares.

13 ♖c1!? Taking into consideration the fact that Black has no means of gaining counterplay, assuming that

White himself does not help his cause, it is useful to play in an unhurried way. On the other hand, the attempt to immediately extract an advantage from the present situation runs the risk of defeat: 13 ♗xf6? ♗xf6 14 ♘xd5? (White wins a pawn, but... loses a piece) 14...♘xe5 15 de ♗xb5 16 ef ♖xe1+ 17 ♕xe1 ♕xd5.

13...a6 14 ♗xc6 ♗xc6 15 ♕f3 ♕d6 16 ♖e3 ♗d7 17 ♘xd7 ♕xd7 18 ♖ce1 The character of the struggle has not changed over the course of the last ten moves or so. It is better for White to maintain a stable position just as it is for Black to wait patiently for the chance to offer a draw (Brunell – Li, Gausdal 2001).

b) **8...♘bd7** The point of the move lies in the transfer of the knight to b6 where, firstly, it defends the d5 pawn and, secondly, at an opportune moment it will take up an active position on c4. But, as shown by practice, even this plan is insufficient for equality:

9 0-0 0-0 10 ♖e1 ♘b6 11 ♘e5 ♗e6 12 ♕e2 (with the threat of 13 ♘xf7!) **12...a6 13 ♗d3 ♖e8 14 ♗g5 ♘bd7 15 ♖ad1 ♘f8 16 ♕f3 ♖c8**

17 ♗c2! (a class manoeuvre – the bishop transfers to b3) **17...♕d6**

18 ♗b3 ♖cd8 19 ♗f4 with unpleasant pressure (Tal – Chistiakov, Kharkov 1967).

c) **8...♗d7 9 ♗xd7 ♘bxd7 10 ♕b3 ♘b6 11 0-0 0-0 12 ♗g5** We underline the strict way Kasparov played against the computer 'Mephisto' (Hamburg 1985): 12 ♘e5 ♖c8 13 ♖e1 ♖e8 14 ♗g5 ♘h5 15 ♗e3 ♗d6 16 h3 ♗xe5 17 de ♖xe5 18 ♗xb6 ♖xe1+ 19 ♖xe1 ♕xb6 20 ♕xb6 ab 21 ♘xd5, and yet he still achieved quite a large advantage in the endgame.

12...h6 13 ♗h4 ♖c8 14 ♖fe1 ♖c6 15 ♖e2 g5 16 ♗g3 ♘h5 17 ♖ae1 Thus continued the game Adams – Granda Zuniga (Elenite 1993). The position is just right for Michael Adams – a solid advantage with mimimum chances of interference from the opponent.

B

7...♘xd5 The tabiya not only for the present system – but for the whole Panov Attack. Hundreds, thousands of games have come streaming down to this position.

We divide the further material into three parts: 8 ♗b5+, 8 ♗c4 and 8 ♗d3.

1) **8 ♗b5+** This old move does not pose Black problems.

8...♘c6 By driving his knight into a pin, Black maintains some sort of intrigue. There was absolute calm on the board after 8...♗d7 9 ♗xd7+ ♕xd7 (or 9...♘xd7 10 ♘xd5 ed 11 ♕b3 ♘b6 12 0-0 0-0 13 ♗f4 ♗d6 14 ♗xd6 ♕xd6, Alekhine – Eliskases, Buenos Aires 1939) 10 ♘e5 ♘xc3 11 bc ♕b5 12 ♕b3 ♕xb3 13 ab ♘d7 14 ♘xd7 ♔xd7 (Boleslavsky – Suetin, Minsk 1957).

9 ♕a4 It is also possible to pile up on the knight c6 in another way – 9 ♘e5, but after 9...♗d7 there is no advantage: 10 ♘xd7 ♕xd7 11 ♕b3 ♖d8! 12 ♘xd5 ♕xd5 13 ♕xd5 ♖xd5 14 ♗xc6+ bc (Minic – Holmov, Skopje 1967).

9...0-0 Konstantinopolsky suggested sacrificing a pawn: 9...♘xc3!? 10 ♗xc6+ (10 bc ♗d7) 10...bc 11 ♕xc6+ ♗d7 12 ♕xc3 ♗b5! One can agree: there is unquestionable compensation.

10 ♗xc6 ♘b6 11 ♕a5 bc 12 0-0 ♘d5 13 ♕xd8 ♖xd8 14 ♘e5

Thus continued the game Pachman – Kotov (Moscow 1946). It can be shown that White will gradually lay his hands on the c6 pawn. But in fact

there is a concrete idea: **14...♘b4! 15 ♗e3 f6 16 ♘f3 c5! 17 dc ♘c2** Passing the stage of equalisation, Black immediately proceeds to a struggle for the advantage.

2) **8 ♗c4** This was frequently played by Botvinnik. As distinct from 8 ♗b5+, the thrust of the bishop to c4 has not lost its topicality to this day.

White encourages the opponent to exchange on c3. If this happens, a strong pawn pair is created in the centre 'c3+d4'. Then, under cover of the pawns (and exploiting the absence of an enemy knight on d5), the bishop on c4 transfers to the b1-h7 diagonal. As a result of all these manoeuvres, White has good chances of an attack.

Black's basic plan of defence is as follows: reinforcing the king's flank by the reconstruction ♗f6, ♘b8-c6-e7, a timely fianchetto of the light-squared bishop and engaging in counterplay in the centre and on the queen's flank.

8...0-0 For a long time the authors of this book had, so to speak, a cool regard to the voluntary exchange on c3. We studied attentively 8...♘xc3!? during our preparations for the superfinal Candidates match against

Andrei Sokolov (Linares 1987) and came to the conclusion that the way to equality for Black was thorny and long. Over the course of many years the assessment of 8...♘xc3!? no longer looks so categorical... After 9 bc ♕c7 10 ♕e2 and 10 ♕d3 should be examined.

Against 10 ♕e2?! the key can be found quite easily:

12 ♖d1 ♗d6 13 ♗g5 b6 14 d5 ♘c5 15 ♘d4 ♘e4! 16 ♘b5 ♗xh2+ 17 ♔f1 (17 ♔h1 ♘xf2+!) 17...♕e5 18 ♗e7 ♕f4 19 ♕f3 ♘g3+ 20 ♔e1 ♕xc4 21 ♗xf8 ♕f1+ 22 ♔d2 ♕xb5 winning;

12 ♗b2 b6 (inaccurate is 12...♘f6?!, allowing the knight to e5) 13 ♗d3 ♗b7 14 c4 ♖fe8 15 ♕e3 (Alterman – Khlian, Rostov-on-the-Don 1993) 15...♗d6! with equal chances;

12 ♖e1 ♗d6! 13 ♗d3 b6!, ignoring the threat of 14 ♕e4 in view of 14...♘f6 15 ♕xa8 ♗b7 16 ♕xa7 ♖a8 17 ♕xa8+ ♗xa8 18 ♘e5 ♕xc3 19 ♗e3 ♗b7 with better prospects for Black.

Far more dangerous looks 10 ♕d3 (with unambiguous designs on the h7 square). After 10...♘d7 11 0-0 0-0 we were troubled by the plan proposed by Igor Zaitsev: 12 ♘g5!? ♘f6 13 f4. But now it does not seem so dangerous. By playing 13...♗d7 14 ♗b3 (14 f5 ♖ac8!) 14...b5!, Black blockades the c3 pawn and obtains good counterplay.

It remains to add that the computer 'Fritz', in a game against Kasparov (Munich 1994), suggested playing 12 ♗g5!? instead of 12 ♘g5.

There followed 12...♗xg5 (preferable is 12...♗f6!? 13 ♗b3 b6 with the idea, after 14 ♖ae1 ♗b7 15 ♗c2 g6 16 ♗xf6 ♘xf6 17 ♘e5, to reply 17...♘d5!, but the desire of the man, in a struggle against the machine, to simplify the position is understandable) 13 ♘xg5 ♘f6. In the further play – 14 ♖ae1 ♗d7 15 ♗b3 h6 16 ♘e4 ♘xe4 17 ♖xe4 ♖ac8 18 ♖e3 ♔h8 19 ♗c2! f5 20 ♗b3! – White obtained some advantage.

9 0-0 ♘c6 10 ♖e1 White passed over the win of a pawn – 10 ♗xd5 ed 11 ♕b3, and we can confirm this was done deliberately. With the move 11...♗g4! Black can offer the choice of either of two pawns, but both are completely 'inedible'.

12 ♕xb7 ♞b4! 13 ♞e5 ♖b8 14 ♕xa7 ♖a8 The queen cannot hide from perpetual attack – draw (A.Zaitsev – Tal, Tallinn 1971) or

12 ♞xd5 ♝xf3 13 ♕xf3 ♞xd4 with full equality (Robatsch – Trifunovic, Havana 1963).

After 10 ♖e1 we have a parting of the ways in the variation 8 ♝c4.

Black's problems become clearer if we look closely at the consequences of 10...b6?! White played 11 ♞xd5 ed 12 ♝b5!, and it turned out that it was not at all easy for Black to hold this outwardly slightly inferior position. Here is a classic example: 12...♝d7 13 ♕a4 ♞b8 14 ♝f4 ♝xb5 15 ♕xb5 a6 16 ♕a4! ♝d6 17 ♝xd6 ♕xd6 18 ♖ac1. The knight c6 is lame and both open files belong to White. He has a clear advantage (Botvinnik – Alekhine, Amsterdam 1938).

11 ♞xd5 ed 12 ♝b5! – this is a real threat. He can only defend against it in two ways: either by exchanging himself (11...♞xc3), or covering the b5 square (10...a6). The third way – is to immediately start regrouping the minor pieces: 10...♝f6.

a) **10...♞xc3!? 11 bc b6 12 ♝d3 ♝b7**

If Black has obtained a respite for 2-3 moves and can during this time complete his development, then his counterplay on the light squares, together with pressure on the pawn pair c3+d4, outweighs every other factor. White's chances – lie in attack, which he should commence at once. We look at two ways: standard (13 ♕c2) and sharp (13 h4).

a1) **13 ♕c2 g6 14 ♝h6** It is not possible to combine both ideas – on 14 h4?! ♖c8 15 ♕d2 ♝f6 16 h5 follows 16...♞xd4!, and White's position is wrecked: 17 ♞xd4 (or 17 cd ♝xf3 18 gf ♝xd4 19 ♝a3 ♝xa1 20 ♖xa1 ♕f6) 17...♖xc3! (Poulsen – Farago, Gausdal 1976).

Likewise not justifying itself is the idea 14 ♕d2 ♝f6 15 ♕h6?! (the h6 square is obviously reserved for the bishop and not the queen) 15...♝g7 16 ♕h3 ♞e7 17 ♝a3 (17 ♞g5 h6 18 ♞e4 ♝xe4 19 ♝xe4 ♖c8) 17...♝xf3! 18 ♕xf3 ♕d7 19 ♖ab1 ♖fd8 (Gusak – Podgaets, Odessa 1968).

14...♖e8 15 ♕d2 ♖c8!? Played with extraordinary coolness. Usually the bishop h6 gets on Black's nerves so much that he endeavours to exchange it at once.

Thus in the game Lerner – van Wely (Germany 1998) was played 15...♗f8 16 h4 ♗xh6 17 ♕xh6 ♕f6 18 ♗e4 ♖ac8 19 h5 ♖e7 20 ♖e3!? The rook heads for h3, supporting the attack.

The game Eingorn – Farago (Boblingen 1997), deserves a separate discussion – or rather the following position from the game, reached after 15...♗f6 16 ♕f4 ♖c8 17 ♖e3 ♗g7 18 ♗xg7 ♔xg7.

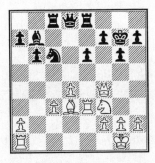

Eingorn played here 19 ♗e4, and Black, move by move, refuted all the threats: 19...♕c7 20 ♕h4 ♘e7 21 ♗xb7 (21 ♘g5 h6 22 ♗xb7 hg) 21...♘f5! 22 ♕e4 ♘d6 23 ♕e5+ f6 24 ♕g3 ♘xb7 25 ♕h3 ♕f7 26 ♖ae1 ♘d6! The partners agreed a draw in view of the following variation: 27 ♖xe6 ♖xe6 28 ♕xe6 ♕xe6 29 ♖xe6 ♖xc3.

An excellent defence but it is hard to shake off the feeling that White did not exploit his attacking potential right up to the end. 19 ♘g5!? suggests itself, and if Black replies as in the game, then he will lose. And to be precise: 19...♕c7? 20 ♕h4 h6 21 ♗xg6! hg (other continuations also do not save him: 21...♔xg6 22 ♘e4; 21...♕d8 22 ♗xf7 hg

23 ♕h5) 22 ♕h7+ ♔f8 23 ♕h6+ ♔e7 24 ♗xf7! ♖h8 25 ♕xe6+ ♔f8 26 ♕f6!

Nevertheless Black has a great supply of ammunition in the position. On 19 ♘g5 there follows the reply 19...♕f6!, and the endgame after 20 ♕xf6+ ♔xf6 can be held:

21 ♘xh7+ ♔g7 22 ♘g5 ♘e7! The extra white pawn is not worth much since the pawns on a2, c3 and d4 are weak;

21 ♘e4+ ♔e7 22 d5 ♘b8! 23 d6+ ♔f8 24 d7 ♘xd7 25 ♘d6 ♘c5! Again there is great positional compensation (now for the loss of the exchange) which should be enough for a draw.

16 h4 Black's plan is revealed brilliantly upon the routine 16 ♕f4?! ♗d6! 17 ♕g4 ♘e7! It becomes clear that all the squares of invasion are covered – which is why there was no need to exchange the dark-squared bishop on the 15th move! The superficially spectacular 18 ♖xe6? loses at once: 18...♖xc3 19 ♗b5 ♗c8! (analysis by Piket).

16...♘a5 17 ♘g5 ♗xg5!? 18 ♗xg5 (18 hg e5) **18...f6 19 ♗f4 ♕d7 20 ♖ac1 ♗d5 21 ♗b1 ♘c4** If White's attack hasn't already landed in a blind alley, then it is very close to it (van Wely – Piket, Wijk aan Zee 1998).

a2) 13 h4!?

A sharp thrust, but only in this way is it possible to break through Black's defence. In his turn, Black has a choice: to stick to principles and accept the pawn sacrifice – 13...♗xh4, or exploit this tempo for another assignment which is to divine the direction of the main blow and try to cushion himself against it – 13...♕d5, 13...♘a5, 13...♗f6 or 13...♖c8.

a21) **13...♗xh4?!** (but in the present case exact adherence to principles can also be false...) **14 ♘xh4 ♕xh4 15 ♖e3** Threatening 16 ♖h3. How to defend?

Possibly too passive is 15...♕d8 16 ♕h5 g6 17 ♖g3 ♕d7 18 ♗h6 ♖fe8, as was seen in the game Poluljahov – Volkov (Tomsk 2001). But after 19 ♖e1 Black's position looks extremely suspect.

Here are some sample variations: 19...e5!? (White wins by direct attack in the event of 19...f5? 20 ♖xg6+! hg 21 ♕xg6+ ♔h8 22 ♗g5 ♖f8 23 ♖xe6 ♕h7 24 ♗f6+ ♖xf6 25 ♕xf6+ ♕g7 26 ♕h4+ ♔g8 27 ♗c4) 20 ♗c4 (not falling into the trap: 20 de ♕xd3!) 20...♕d6 21 ♗d2! (freeing the h6 square for the queen) 21...♔h8! (once again avoiding immediate defeat, inevitable upon 21...♖e7 22 ♕h6 ♔h8 23 ♗g5 f6 24 ♖f3!) 22 ♕h4 ed 23 ♖xe8+ ♖xe8 24 cd. Can Black save this position?

Hardly, and to be really accurate he cannot take the second pawn: 24...♘xd4? 25 ♗c3 ♖e4 26 ♖g4 f5 27 ♖xe4 ♗xe4 28 ♕h6.

On the other hand it is possible to defend actively, even too much so: 15...f5?! Grandmaster Adrian Mikhalchishin assumed that it was not possible to play 16 ♖xe6 because of 16...♘xd4. But analysis does not support this: 17 cd! (there is nothing for White after 17 ♖e3 ♘c6 18 ♖h3 ♕g4 19 ♕xg4 fg 20 ♗xh7+ ♔f7) 17...♕xd4 18 ♗a3! (this is stronger than 18 ♖b1 ♕d5 19 ♕f3 ♕xe6 20 ♕xb7) 18...♕d5 19 ♕f3 ♕xe6 20 ♕xb7 ♖fd8 21 ♗b2 ♕d7 22 ♕xd7 ♖xd7 23 ♗xf5. By force an endgame has arisen with great chances of victory for White.

However most of the time it is best to defend neither passively not hyperactively, but somewhere in the middle:

15...g6 16 ♖g3!? (rather weaker is 16 ♖h3 ♕f6 17 ♗h6 ♖fe8 18 ♕g4 ♖ac8 19 ♗g5 ♕g7 20 ♕h4 f5 21 ♖e1 ♘a5 22 ♖he3 ♕f7 and he has virtually defended himself, Kasparov – Gonda, Cannes 1988) **16...♕e7** There is another idea to transfer the queen to g7 – 16...♕f6, but even here present practice provides evidence in White's favour: 17 ♕g4 ♕g7 18 ♕h4 f5 19 ♗h6 ♕f6 20 ♗g5 ♕f7 21 ♖e1 ♘a5 22 c4 (Anand – Morrison, England 1988). d4-d5 is threatened, and all Black can do if defend, defend...

17 ♗g5 f6 18 ♗h6 ♖f7 (18... ♖fe8? 19 ♗xg6!) **19 ♕h5 f5 20 ♖e1 ♔h8 21 ♕h3 ♕d7 22 ♗c4! ♖e8 23 ♗f4 ♔g8 24 d5!** All the same, White shakes the enemy fortress, though it must be said that it is too fragile (Izoria – Golod, Ohrid 2001).

It is not clear how much partiality he has to have for the other side's pawn to suffer such torment after 13...♗xh4?!

a22) **13...♕d5?!** The reputation of this move is based mostly on an analysis of the game Anand – Timman (Moscow 1992), in which White played 14 ♖b1. The fact of the matter is that Black can calmly take the pawn:

14...♕xa2! While it is not too late, White should force a draw by 15 ♖b5 ♗a6 16 ♗b1 ♕c4 17 ♗d3 ♕a2, otherwise Black will start playing for a win. Here is a sample variation: 16 ♖b2 (instead of 16 ♗b1) 16...♕a5 17 ♗e4 (17 ♘e5, reckoning on 17...♘xe5?! 18 ♖xe5 b5 19 ♕c2 ♖fc8 20 ♗xh7+ ♔f8 21 ♖b3, is parried by the cool 17...♖ac8!?) 17...♖ac8 18 ♕c2 ♕h5 19 ♕a4 ♘a5 20 ♕d7 ♗a3 21 ♖c2 ♗xc1 22 ♖cxc1 ♗b5 23 ♕xa7 ♘c4 etc.

However these and such like analyses are empty. This is because even White's very first move after 13...♕d5 is clearly dubious! Instead of 14 ♖b1, **14 ♘g5!?** suggests itself. After 14...♗xg5 15 ♗xg5 ♘e7 16 ♕g4 h5 17 ♕h3 White holds the advantage in comparatively quiet circumstances, while the sharper **14...h6 15 ♗h7+ ♔h8 16 ♗e4 ♕c4 17 ♕h5 ♔g8 18 ♘h3!?** also turns out in his favour. For example, **18...f5 19 ♗f3 ♕xc3 20 ♗xh6 ♕xd4 21 ♗g5 ♗b4 22 ♖ad1 ♕c4 23 ♖xe6!**

a23) **13...♘a5** There is a story attached to the move 13...♕d5: it is considered reliable but it is not good. About 13...♘a5 one can say exactly the opposite: the move (on the basis of the game Razuvaev – Farago, Dubna 1979) is almost considered to be losing by force, but actually it is wrong to knock it.

In its day the game Razuvaev – Farago actually went the rounds of the world's chess press: **14 ♘g5 h6? 15 ♕h5 ♗d5**

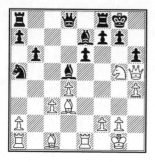

16 ♞h7! ♖e8 17 ♗xh6! gh 18 ♕xh6 f5 19 ♖e3 ♗xh4 20 ♖g3+! ♗xg3 21 ♕g6+ ♔h8 22 ♞f6! In this kind of attack every move deserves an exclamation mark.

However after the elementary 14...♗xg5 (instead of 14...h6?) 15 ♗xg5 (or 15 hg f5! 16 gf ♕xf6 – Pachman) 15...♕d5 16 ♕g4 f5 17 ♕g3 ♖ac8 18 ♗f1 ♕d7 19 h5 ♗d5 (Hernandez – Miguel, Vulka 1984) how big is White's advantage?

a24) 13...♗f6!? 14 ♞g5 g6 15 ♕g4 h5 A forced move; Black cannot allow h4-h5. For example, 15...♞e7?! 16 h5!, and then:

16...♞f5 17 hg hg 18 ♞xe6! fe 19 ♕xg6+ ♗g7 20 ♖xe6 (Poluljahov – Gomez Baillo, Buenos Aires 1998) or

16...♕d5 17 hg ♞xg6 18 ♗e4 ♕d7 19 ♕h3 (Poluljahov – Notkin, Tivat 1995).

The position after 15...h5 looks highly dangerous for Black; however in practice he quite often comes out unscathed.

A sure sign that not everything is going well for White – there is no uniformity in his action. If he were to find an accurate order of moves, somehow he would get his act

together, but for the present the fact that even his queen comes under fire suggests otherwise.

In the game A.Sokolov – Christiansen (Dubai 1986) was seen 16 ♕f4!?, and after 16...e5?! 17 ♕g3 ♕d7 18 ♗a3 ♖fe8 19 ♗c4 ♗xg5 20 ♕xg5 White stood to win. But stronger is an immediate 16...♗xg5!? 17 ♕xg5 (17 hg e5!) 17...♕xg5 18 ♗xg5 ♞a5 19 ♖ac1 ♖ac8. The endgame looks very respectable for Black. There is play against the pawn weaknesses and a blockading strategy on the dark squares.

The other direction is 16 ♕h3. The game Cifuentes – van der Sterren (Holland 1996) did not last long: 16...e5 17 ♗a3 ♖e8 18 ♞e4 ed

19 ♕d7!? ♞e5? 20 ♕xe8+!, and Black resigned.

Which move isn't puzzling here. It is clear that 19...♘e5? is a blunder, and in the event of the correct 19...♖xe4! 20 ♕xd8+ ♖xd8 21 ♗xe4 dc White will be fighting for the draw. And it is not a fact that he will achieve it, for example, 22 ♖ad1 ♔g7!? 23 ♖xd8 ♘xd8 24 ♗xb7 ♘xb7 25 ♖c1 a5 26 ♖b1 ♗d4 27 ♔f1 ♘d8 28 ♔e2 ♘e6 etc.

Cifuentes himself indirectly acknowledged this by suggesting, instead of 18 ♘e4, another means of winning: 18 ♘xf7! ♔xf7 19 ♕g3 ♖g8 20 de ♘xe5 21 ♖xe5 ♗xe5 22 ♕xe5 ♗d5 23 ♗b5!

We agree. But also for Black in this case an improvement – on the 16th and 17th moves – suggests itself. Instead of 17...♖e8 stronger is 17...♗xg5! 18 ♗xf8 ♗d2! 19 ♖ed1 ♗xc3 20 ♖ac1 ed, and instead of 16...e5 – 16...♘e7!? 17 ♗a3 ♖c8, and no good is 18 ♘xe6 fe 19 ♕xe6+ ♖f7 20 ♗xe7 ♕xe7 21 ♕b3 ♕d7 22 ♗xg6 ♗d5. It would seem to be a miniature, plain and simple, but so many questions!

In reply to 15...h5 White most frequently retreats **16 ♕g3** Here there was also once a short game: 16...♕d7?! 17 ♘e4 ♗g7 18 ♗g5 ♘e7?

19 ♕d6! Material loss is inevitable, and after a few moves Black resigned (Onischuk – Magem, New York 1998).

16...♘e7 17 ♗a3 ♕d7! Many times Black has fallen under the blow 17...♖c8? 18 ♘xe6! with a rout – the first time this happened was in the game C.Hansen – Kir. Georgiev (Kiljava 1984).

18 ♘e4 ♗xe4 19 ♗xe4 ♖ac8 20 ♖e3 ♖fe8 21 ♕f4 ♗g7 The position has calmed down, the attack failed to materialise. Black's chances are superior (Banas – Ostendad, Trnava 1989).

a25) **13...♖c8 14 ♘g5** Instant defeat as a consequence of just one mistake is not uncommon in this variation. Here is an example: 14...g6? 15 ♘xh7 ♔xh7 16 ♕h5+ ♔g8 17 ♗xg6 fg 18 ♕xg6+ ♔h8 19 ♖e4! (Matveeva – Intinskaya, Tbilisi 1987).

In the game Chekhov – Honfi (Amstetten 1990) Black cooly played 14...h6, and White was not able to punish him for this: 15 ♗h7+ ♔h8 16 ♗b1 (as pointed out by Chekhov, he rejected 16 ♗c2 in view of the exchange sacrifice: 16...♘xd4! 17 cd ♖xc2! 18 ♕xc2 hg, and Black's light-squared bishop is very strong) 16...♕d5 17 ♕d3 g6 18 ♘f3 (the blow 18 ♘xe6 will rebound... on himself: 18...♘b4! 19 ♕e4 ♕xe6 20 ♕xe6 fe 21 ♗xh6 ♖fd8) 18...♔g7. The position has stabilised, and this means that Black has again escaped.

Analysis shows that also 15 ♕h5 (instead of 15 ♗h7+) does not promise White any particular advantage: 15...♘a5 16 ♖e3 (16 ♘h7? ♖xc3! 17 ♘xf8 ♖xd3) 16...♗xg5 17 hg ♕xg5 18 ♕h2 ♖xc3! 19 ♗h7+ (19 ♗d2 ♘c4) 19...♔xh7 20 ♖xc3 ♕d5 21 ♗e3 ♘c6 22 ♖d1 ♖d8

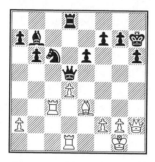

One look at the position is sufficient to understand: here the extra exchange plays no role at all. White has in prospect a hard fight for a draw.

All the same, 14...h6 will play on his nerves. Safer and simpler is **14...♗xg5!? 15 ♗xg5 ♕d5! 16 ♕g4 f5! 17 ♕g3 ♘a5!** Four exemplary moves – and the blockade on the light squares is in place.

In the game Poluljahov – Balashov (St.Petersburg 1998) White rolled up the attack, hastening to secure himself against loss: **18 ♖e5 ♕d7 19 ♗b5 ♗c6** (Black likewise is satisfied with little; otherwise he would have played 19...♕f7!? 20 ♖ae1 a6 21 ♗f1 f4 22 ♕g4 ♗d5) **20 ♗xc6** (20 ♗a6 ♖ce8 and it is difficult for White to improve his position, for example, 21 ♖b1 ♗e4 22 ♗b5 ♗c6 23 ♗d3 ♗d5) **20...♘xc6 21 ♖e2 b5 22 ♖ae1 ♖ce8** Soon a draw was agreed.

Summing up the variation 10...♘xc3!? 11 bc b6 12 ♗d3 ♗b7, it

is possible to say that it is better than its reputation. True, it demands courage of a chessplayer. But if you want to play solidly, do not panic, you have every chance of coming out of the battle with an equal and even better position.

b) **10...a6** With this move Black pursues three objectives: to defend against 11 ♘xd5 ed 12 ♗b5, to prepare an extended fianchetto b7-b5, and in addition, simply to wait for White to show his cards.

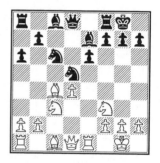

11 ♗b3!? A move which places Black under very great difficulties, but let's also look at other continuations.

A classic example of 11 ♗d3 is the game Polugayevsky – Portisch (USSR – Hungary match, 1969): 11...♘f6 12 ♗g5 b5 13 ♖c1 ♗b7 14 ♗b1 ♖c8 15 ♕d2 ♖e8 16 ♖cd1 ♘b4 17 ♘e5 ♘bd5 18 ♕d3 g6 19 ♕h3 ♘xc3 20 bc ♗d5! 21 ♖d3 ♘h5 with the better prospects for Black.

In his time, Grandmaster Andrei Sokolov suggested 11 ♕e2!? Perhaps the right reaction to this move is to follow the game Stocek – Galkin (Port Erin 2001): 11...♘f6! Logical:

as White has already brought his rook to e1, he does not want to lose time on ♖d1. Stocek replied 12 ♗e3, and obtained a version of the Queen's Gambit Accepted that is comfortable for Black: 12...b5 13 ♗b3 ♘a5 14 ♗c2 ♗b7 15 ♖ad1 ♖c8 16 ♗g5 ♘c4 17 ♗xf6 ♗xf6 18 ♗e4 with equality.

After 11 ♗b3 Black usually exchanges on c3, but a further two ideas are worth considering.

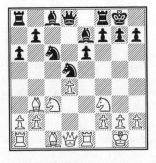

Firstly, all the same 11...b5, despite the fact that the fianchetto here comes without tempo. After 12 ♘xd5 ed 13 ♕d3 (unclear are the consequences of 13 ♘e5 ♘xe5 14 de d4!) and by comparison with the game Tal – Psakhis White still has on the board his light-squared bishop, which is undoubtedly to his advantage. And yet one should not overstate White's superiority.

Possibly even more inetresting is 11...♖e8!?, only it is necessary to link this move not to an exchange on c3, but to a retreat of the knight to f6! As an example we show the game Korneev – Kharitonov (Novgorod 1997): 12 h3 ♘f6! 13 a3 b5 14 d5 ed 15 ♘xd5 ♗e6 16 ♘xe7+ ♖xe7 17 ♕xd8+ ♖xd8 18 ♗xe6 ♖xe6

19 ♖xe6 fe 20 ♗e3 with a minimal advantage in the endgame. And this is only because Black has not secured himself against the break d4-d5: 13...♘a5!? (instead of 13...b5) 14 ♗a2 b5 15 d5 ed 16 ♘xd5 ♘xd5 17 ♕xd5 ♕xd5 18 ♗xd5 ♗b7 with equality.

11...♘xc3 12 bc b5?! Very dangerous! The right order of moves was demonstrated in the game Stocek – Czech (Olomouc 1995): 12...♗f6!? 13 ♕d3 b5 14 ♗c2 g6 15 ♗h6 ♖e8 16 d5 ♘e7! with advantage to Black. Incidentally, why didn't he take on d5? Well, on this White had prepared a beautiful combination: 16...ed? 17 ♕xd5! ♗b7

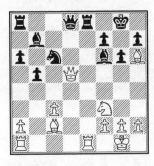

18 ♕xf7+!! ♔xf7 19 ♗b3+ ♖e6 20 ♖xe6 ♘a5 21 ♖xf6+! ♔xf6 22 ♗g5+ ♔g7 23 ♗xd8 ♖xd8 24 ♘d4, remaining with an extra pawn in the endgame.

The position after 11 ♗b3 ♘xc3 12 bc b5?! is usually considered the tabiya of the variation 10...a6, so we assumed that Andrei Sokolov's discovery against Kharitonov (Moscow 1990) had practically closed down the variation. However, without rushing, we will discuss each in turn.

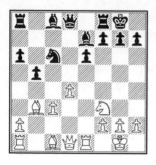

b1) The impatient **13 d5?!** does not give an advantage in view of **13...♘a5** (also sufficient for equality is 13...ed!? 14 ♕xd5 ♗b7 15 ♕h5 ♘a5 16 ♘g5 ♗xg5 17 ♗xg5 ♕d3 18 ♗e7 ♘xb3) **14 de ♗xe6 15 ♗xe6 ♕xd1 16 ♗xf7+ ♖xf7 17 ♖xd1 ♗f6** with serious compensation (pointed out by Anand).

b2) The idea **13 h4!?** After a detailed look at the variations and branches, 10...♘xc3 11 bc b6 12 ♗d3 ♗b7 13 h4 already looks standard. There we did not fear it, and here also we should not worry about it.

Taking on h4, of course, is not necessary; after 13...♗xh4?! 14 ♘xh4 ♕xh4 15 ♖e3 ♗d7 16 ♖h3 ♕f6 17 ♗c2 the pawn is not worth all the suffering.

The main line of the position arises after **13...♗b7!? 14 ♘g5 ♘a5 15 ♕h5** (on 15 ♗c2!? it will be necessary to part with one of the bishops rather more quickly: 15...♗xg5 16 hg f5!) **15...♗xg5 16 ♗xg5 ♕d6 17 ♗f6!?**

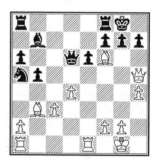

He cannot accept the piece sacrifice: 17...gf 18 ♗c2 f5 19 ♕g5+ ♔h8 20 ♕f6+ ♔g8 21 ♖e3 ♖fc8 22 ♗xf5!

The tempo-gaining side-step is parried by 18 d5! ed 19 ♗c2 g6 20 ♕g5 ♖ae8 21 h5, and the attack is very strong.

And yet there is a defence: **17...♕f4! 18 ♗e5** (or 18 ♗c2 g6 19 ♕g5 ♕xg5 20 hg ♖fc8) **18...♕f5! 19 ♕xf5 ef 20 ♗c2 g6 21 a4 ♘c4** White is a little better but Black should hold the position.

b3) **13 ♕d3!?** This idea was tested in the game A.Sokolov – Karpov (Linares 1987). Black replied 13...♖a7?! and obtained the clearly worse game: 14 ♗c2 g6 15 ♗h6 ♖e8 16 ♕e3 ♖d7 17 h4!? ♗f6 (dangerous is 17...♗xh4 in view of 18 ♘xh4 ♕xh4 19 ♗g5 ♕g4 20 ♗d1 ♕f5 21 g4 ♕d5 22 ♗f3 ♕d6 23 ♗f6) 18 ♗g5 ♗b7 19 ♕f4 ♗xg5 20 ♘xg5

♕c7 21 ♕f6 ♘xd4 22 ♗xg6 hg 23 cd ♖d5 24 ♖ac1 ♕d7

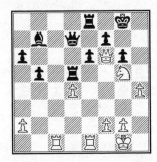

Here, in playing 25 ♖c5, Sokolov did not find the strongest continuation. The game ended with a drawn result. Meanwhile serious problems are posed by 25 ♘e4! For example, in the variation 25...♖h5 26 d5! (this is even stronger than 26 ♕xg6+!? fg 27 ♘f6+ ♔g7 28 ♘xd7 ♖xh4 29 ♖c7 ♗d5) 26...♕xd5 27 ♖c5 ♕xc5 28 ♘xc5 ♖xc5 29 ♖d1 and Black does not have full compensation for the queen.

The correct order of moves was demonstrated by Anand: **13...♗b7 14 ♗c2 g6 15 ♗h6 ♖e8 16 ♖ad1** (G.Kusmin advised trying 16 a4 b4 17 c4) **16...♖c8 17 h4 ♕d5! 18 ♗b3 ♕h5 19 ♕e3 ♘a5!**, and Black's position is already rather more pleasant (Matveeva – Anand, Frunze 1987).

,b4) **13 ♗c2!** In this also lies Andrei Sokolov's idea, found by him three years after his match with Karpov. The variation looked at above shows that Black cannot do without the advance g7-g6. On d3 the enemy queen is lined up against the triad f7-g6-h7, but it really belongs on g4. White can then carry out the pawn advance h2-h4-h5 and under the three attacks from c2, g4 and h5, the g6 square will start to crack.

After **13...♗b7 14 h4!** it is worthwhile for Black to have a good think.

There is no need to explain again in detail how dangerous it is to accept the pawn sacrifice: 14...♗xh4?! 15 ♘xh4 ♕xh4 16 ♖e3 etc.

Also unsatisfactory is 14... ♕d5?! because of 15 ♗g5! In the game Mukhytdinov – Graf (Svidnica 1997) play continued: 15...♖fe8 16 ♕d3 g6 17 ♗b3 ♕d6 18 h5 ♗xg5 (on 18...♗f8 unpleasant is 19 hg hg 20 ♘h2! ♗g7 21 ♘g4) 19 ♘xg5 ♕f4 20 hg! (a very important intermediate move) 20...hg (he will not manage to save the endgame after 20...♕xg5 21 gf+ ♔xf7 22 ♕xh7+ ♕g7 23 ♗xe6+ ♖xe6 24 ♕xg7+ ♔xg7 25 ♖xe6) 21 ♘xe6! with a rout.

In the stem game A.Sokolov – Kharitonov (Moscow 1990) Black also defended poorly: **14...♗f6 15 ♘g5 g6 16 ♕g4 ♖c8 17 h5!** White's plan works 100%. Black's position is indefensible.

There followed **17...♘xd4 18 hg! fg** (allowing the opponent to win beautifully, more tenacious is 18...hg

19 ♕h4 ♗xg5 20 ♗xg5 ♕xg5
21 ♕xg5 ♘xc2).

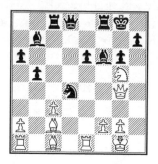

19 ♘xh7! ♘xc2 20 ♕xg6+ ♚h8
(20...♗g7 21 ♘g5) **21 ♗g5! ♗xg5 22
♘xg5 ♕d7 23 ♖xe6 ♖c6 24 ♕h5+
♚g8 25 ♖d1! ♕g7 26 ♖dd6!** A
brilliant attack!

To his great credit, Sokolov's
discovery crosses the plan 11...♘xc3
12 bc b5. However this does not raise
particular alarm, since there is a
worthy alternative – 11...♘f6. This
move leads to the main tabiya of the
Queen's Gambit Accepted (D27), but
to analyse this position properly, in
great detail and within the limits of
the present book, is impossible.

c) **10...♗f6!?** In our view, this is a
very reliable retort (of those which
have a bearing on the Caro-Kann
defence) in the variation 8 ♗c4 0-0
9 0-0 ♘c6 10 ♖e1. Without wavering,
Black immediately sets about
reconstructing his own pieces. The
next move is clear: ♘c6-e7.

11 ♘e4 b6 12 a3 White obtains no
advantage after 12 ♘xf6+ ♘xf6
13 ♗g5 ♗b7 14 ♖c1 ♖c8 15 ♗d3 h6
16 ♗e3 (in the game A.Sokolov –
Schussler, France 2001, White played
impulsively, 16 ♗h4?, not noticing
that then 16...♘xd4! is no good

because of either 17 ♘xd4 ♖xc1, or
17 ♖xc8 ♘xf3+) 16...♕d5 17 ♗c4
♕f5 (Onischuk – Schussler, Germany
1999).

12...♗b7 13 ♕d3

In this position Black has
several continuations worthy of
consideration.

Simplest, certainly, is to play at
once 13...♘ce7. In the game
Korchnoi – Oll (Groningen 1993)
play continued 14 ♗d2 ♘g6 15 ♘eg5
(15 g3!?) 15...♘de7!, and Black
showed he was well prepared for the
tactical struggle: 16 ♖xe6!? (16 ♖ad1
♗d5 17 ♗a6 ♘f5 with equality – Oll)
16...♗xf3! 17 ♖xf6 gf 18 ♘xf3 ♕d7.

Fully recommending itself is the
direction 13...♖c8!? 14 ♘fg5 ♗xg5
15 ♗xg5 f6. After 16 ♗d2 it is
possible to play in the old fashioned
way: 16...♕d7 17 ♖ad1 ♘ce7
18 ♗a2 ♖fe8 19 h4 (after 19 ♗b1?!
♘g6 20 ♕g3 f5! and Black seized the
initiative, Tal – Petrosian, Moscow
1966) 19...♚h8! 20 ♗b1 g6 21 ♕h3
♘f5 (Nikolic – Ribli, Ljubliana
1985). Also it is possible to adopt a
contemporary treatment: 16...♚h8!?
17 ♗b3 ♘c7 18 ♗c3 ♗a6 19 ♕g3
♕d7 20 ♖ad1 ♖cd8 21 ♕h3 ♘d5 22
♗c2 ♘f4 (Acs – Cvitan, Szale 2000).

Most often Black chooses **13...♖e8!?**, absolutely not afraid of the doubling of his pawns: 14 ♘xf6+ gf! 15 ♗b3 ♘ce7 16 ♗a4 ♘c6 17 ♗xc6 ♘xc6 18 ♗h6 ♔h8 (Saravanan – Sasikiran, Nagpur 1999).

More principled is **14 ♗d2 ♘ce7 15 ♖ad1 ♘f5 16 ♗a2 ♘d6** In the game Serper – Kaidanov (Groningen 1993) White rather strayed from the course: 17 ♘g3?! g6 18 ♘e5 ♗g7 etc. Serper himself subsequently indicated the best direction of play: **17 ♘eg5!? g6 18 h4!?** White's plan is clear: he threatens to play 19 ♘e5, then to transfer the queen to h3 and open the h-file. How can Black counter this?

For a start he should repulse White's first threat: **18...♗g7!?** Now 19 ♘e5? loses (19...f6) – so far so good. Obviously White plays **19 h5**, and after **19...♕f6** (in some variations threatening a knight jump to f4) arises a critical position.

Harmless is 20 ♘e5 ♘f4! 21 ♗xf4 ♕xf4, therefore **20 hg** No way should he open the edge files – 20...hg?! It is not easy to show with variations that this move is bad, but all the same the complications must turn out in White's favour. For example: 21 ♘e5

♘f4 22 ♕g3! ♘xg2 23 ♕h3 ♖ad8 24 ♕h7+ ♔f8 25 ♘gxf7! ♘xe1 26 ♖xe1 ♘e4 27 ♗b4+ ♖e7 28 f3 ♖xd4 29 ♘h6 ♔e8 30 ♘hg4!

Obligatory is **20...♕xg6!?**, when a double-edged struggle follows: **21 ♕e2 h6 22 ♘e5** (22 ♗b1 ♕h5 23 ♘e4 ♘f5 with counterplay) **22...♗xe5 23 de ♘f5 24 ♘f3**, and then there is a choice:

24...♔h8 25 ♗b1 ♕g7 26 ♗xf5 ef 27 ♘h4 f4 28 ♕e4 ♕g5 29 g3 ♖ab8 30 ♕d4 ♖e6 31 ♘g2 ♕h5, speculating on threats on the long diagonal;

24...♘d4!? 25 ♕e4 ♕xe4 26 ♖xe4 ♘xf3+ 27 gf ♘e7 28 ♖g4+ ♘g6 29 ♔g2 ♖ad8 30 ♗b1 h5. Thirty moves have already been played but the prognosis on the outcome of the game, as before, presents difficulties.

Nowadays there is not just one direction. After 8 ♗c4 0-0 9 0-0 ♘c6 10 ♖e1 ♗f6!? White has not managed to demonstrate a way to gain even a minimal advantage. Therefore it is possible, in part, that the move 8 ♗c4 will noticeably yield in popularity to 8 ♗d3.

3) **8 ♗d3** Objectively the strongest.

8...0-0 Dubious is 8...b6?! because of 9 ♘e5! The development of the bishop c8 is delayed because of the check on a4, while after 9...0-0 we see that it was wrong to spend a tempo on b7-b6: 10 ♕h5! f5 11 0-0 ♗b7 12 ♗c4 ♘d7 13 ♘xd5 ed 14 ♗b3 ♘xe5 15 de with advantage (Petrosian – Bagirov, Moscow 1967).

9 0-0 In the game Sveshnikov – Kasparov (Tbilisi 1978) was seen 9 h4!? Played with a flourish – like a hussar! For the sake of objectivity let us say that there is no prescription for such an attack (incidentally, if Black wants to avoid it, he can play 8...♘c6, and there is nothing better for White than 0-0). The further continuation of the game was 9...♘c6 10 ♕c2 f5 (simpler is 10...♘f6, intending on 11 ♘e4 to play 11...♘b4 12 ♘xf6+ ♔h8! 13 ♕b3 ♘xd3+ 14 ♕xd3 ♗xf6) 11 a3 b6 12 0-0 ♔h8 13 ♖e1 ♘f6 14 ♕a4 ♗d7 15 ♘g5 ♘g4 16 f3 ♘ce5!? 17 ♕d1 h6 18 fg ♘xd3 19 ♘xe6 ♗xe6 20 ♕xd3 ♗g8, and the rivals concluded peace.

9...♘c6 We look at 10 ♕e2, 10 a3 and 10 ♖e1.

a) **10 ♕e2**

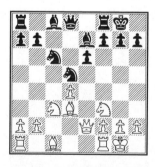

The most reliable is **10...♘f6**, but let us briefly stop at the remaining moves.

There is no sense in accepting the pawn sacrifice by 10...♘db4?! 11 ♗e4 ♘xd4 12 ♘xd4 ♕xd4, since the difficulty with the development of the light-squared bishop outweighs the modest material gain: 13 ♗e3 ♕e5 14 f4 ♕b8 15 ♖ad1 f5 16 ♗f3 ♘c6 17 ♕c4 (Udovcic – O'Kelly, Havana 1964).

Also dubious is 10...♘cb4 11 ♗b1 b6, but not because of 12 ♘xd5? ♕xd5 13 ♗e4, since on that follows 13...♗a6! (Saborido – Portisch, Torremolinos 1961, but simply because of 12 ♕e4! g6 13 a3.

11 ♖d1 ♘b4 12 ♗b1 b6 13 ♘e5 ♗b7 14 a3 ♘bd5 15 ♘e4 ♘xe4 16 ♕xe4

16...f5! 17 ♕f3 ♗f6 18 ♗a2 ♖c8 The game is even (van Wely – Kobalija, Batumi 1999).

b) **10 a3** Black has the choice between 10...♘xc3 11 bc b6 and 10...♗f6.

b1) **10...♘xc3** Upon an analysis of this kind we pick up a peculiar chess principle: nearly always an exchange on c3 justifies itself when the pawn is on a3 and does not justify itself – when the pawn is on a2!

11 bc b6 12 ♕e2 Play in the centre promises White little. For example,

12 ♗e4 ♗b7 13 ♕d3 h6 14 ♖d1 ♖c8 15 ♗f4 ♗d6 16 ♗g3 ♕c7 17 ♖ac1 ♖fd8 18 c4 ♗xg3 19 hg ♘a5 with even chances (Karpov – de Firmian, Oslo 1984).

12...♗b7 13 ♖d1 The arrangement of the rooks is always a difficult choice even if you are something of a fortune teller. White wants to deploy the rooks so that he can combine an attack on the king's flank with play in the centre, for which it is desirable to play c3-c4.

Possible is 13 ♖e1 ♖c8 14 ♗b2 ♗f6 15 ♖ad1 ♘a5! (it becomes clear that the programmed c3-c4 can be carried out only by weakening the kinsgide pawn structure) 16 c4 ♗xf3! 17 gf g6 18 ♔h1 ♗g7 19 ♗c3 ♘c6 20 ♕b2 ♗xd4 21 ♗xg6 ♕f6! (Namyslo – Podgaets, Dortmund 1993).

13...♗f6 14 ♕e4 g6 15 ♗h6

15...♘a5?! An instructive moment. Moving the knight to a5 is quite often seen in such positions and yet it is not worth doing it without particular need. On c6 the knight controls the e5 square and it can make a timely transfer (via e7) to f5, consolidating the position of the king. But on a5 it often find itself out of play.

In the present situation worth considering is 15...♗g7 and only after 16 ♗g5 – 16...♘a5! So when a concrete idea is revealed in the manoeuvre ♘c6-a5, then it is good. On 17 ♗xd8 follows 17...♗xe4 18 ♗e7 ♗xf3; on 17 ♕e3 – 17...♕c7 or even 17...♕d5 with a blockade of the c4 square; on 17 ♕h4 – 17...f6 with an excellent position.

16 ♕f4 ♗g7 17 ♗xg7 ♔xg7 18 ♘e5 ♖c8 19 ♖ac1 ♕d5 20 f3 We are following the game Balashov – Tseshkovsky (Lvov 1978). Black lost his head by playing 20...♕d8 (why does he voluntarily take his queen away from the centre?), and after 21 ♘g4 White develops a dangerous initiative.

Far stronger was **20...f6!?**, intending on 21 ♘g4 to reply 21...g5 22 ♕g3 ♔h8 (mistaken is 22...♖xc3 23 ♖xc3 ♕xd4+ 24 ♔h1 ♕xc3 because of 25 ♕h3). Although even here after 23 ♕h3 White's prospects are superior – namely because Black needs the knight a5 in the region of the f5 square!

However if Black brings the queen to d8 because he fears, on 20...f6, the reply **21 c4**, this is wrong: **21...♕d8 22 ♘g4 g5! 23 ♕e3 h5 24 ♘f2 ♘b3!**

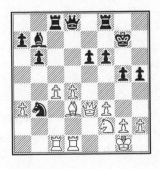

Black, as shown by the following variations, is out of danger:

25 ♗e4 ♘xc1 26 ♗xb7 ♖xc4;

25 ♖b1 ♘xd4 26 ♗e4 ♗xe4 27 ♖xd4 ♗xb1 28 ♖xd8 ♖cxd8;

25 ♖c3 ♕xd4 26 ♕e1 ♘c5 27 ♗e4 ♕e5 28 ♗xb7 ♕xe1+ 29 ♖xe1 ♘xb7 30 ♖xe6 ♖fe8

b2) 10...♗f6 There is not one variation (with the exception of 11 ♗e4 and 11 ♖e1) that does not deserve intensive scrutiny here.

On 11 ♘e4? it is possible to casually capture the pawn: 11...♗xd4 12 ♘xd4 ♘xd4 13 ♕h5 f5 14 ♘g5 h6 15 ♘h3 ♘f6 16 ♕d1 e5 with victory (Osmanovic – Farago, Boblingen 1997).

Advancing the statistics for Black in the branch 11 ♗e3 ♘xc3 12 bc b6, we then have, for example: 13 ♕c2 g6 14 ♗h6 ♗g7 15 ♗xg7 ♔xg7 16 ♖fe1 ♗b7 17 ♖ad1 ♖c8 18 ♕d2 ♕f6 19 ♖e4 ♘e7 20 ♖f4 ♘f5 (Frolyanov – Galkin, Toliatti 2003).

b21) 11 ♗e4 Here the moves 11...♕d6 and 11...♘ce7 are worthy of equal respect.

x) 11...♕d6!? The honour of discovering and working out this branch belogs to Semen Abramovic Furman. Later Hungarian grandmasters took up arms with the system. By reinforcing the d5 square (and not ceding the e5 square which is extremely important for the variation as a whole), Black wants to complete his development by ♗c8-d7.

If White cannot think up something radical in reply, there can be no doubt that Black will achieve an equal game

without difficulty: 12 ♕e2 b6 13 ♖d1 ♗b7 14 ♗g5 ♗xg5 15 ♗xd5 ♗f6 16 ♗e4 ♘d8 17 ♘e5 ♕e7 18 ♕f3 ♖c8 19 ♗xb7 ♕xb7 20 ♘e4 ♗e7 (Korchnoi – Furman, Leningrad 1963).

White links his hopes to the move **12 ♕d3,** and then his further intentions depend on which pawn the opponent advances – **g** or **h**.

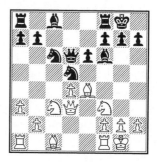

If 12...h6, then White consistently tries to swap the places of the queen and the bishop d3 – you see by now Black cannot play g7-g6, since in this case the pawn on h6 is hanging. And in the event of 12...g6 White tries to shake the pawn triangle f7-g6-h7 with the advance h2-h4 with which we are already familiar.

However practice shows that these hopes (it goes without saying, upon competent play by Black) are destined not to be fulfilled.

12...h6 Considered the main line, though there is apparently also no contra-indication to 12...g6 13 ♗h6 ♖d8 14 ♗xd5 ed 15 ♘b5 ♕d7 (Aratovsky – Furman, Vilnius 1949).

13 ♖d1 Before placing the queen at the head of the battery along the b1-h7 diagonal, White must defend the d4 pawn. The time comes for

Black to find an accurate order of moves.

In his game against Antoshin (Moscow 1970) Furman did not manage this. As a result White achieved the desired reconstruction: 13...♖d8?! 14 ♕e2! b6 15 ♗c2! ♗b7 16 ♕d3 with appreciable pressure.

Otherwise Black plays as in the game Filip – Pinter (Budapest 1977): 13...b6 14 ♕e2 ♗b7 15 ♗c2, and now 15...♘xc3 16 bc ♘e7!? The white queen is not allowed to e4 and in addition the knight is ready to close the weak diagonal, taking up a place on g6 or f5. The game continued 17 a4 ♖fd8 18 ♕d3 ♘g6 19 ♕e3 ♖ac8. Black's position is not bad at all.

The most accurate order of moves seems to be **13...♗d7!? 14 ♕e2 ♖ac8 15 ♗c2 ♘ce7! 16 ♘e4 ♕c7 17 ♘c5 ♖fd8 18 ♕e4 ♘g6!** (Alburt – Sax, Hastings 1983).

y) **11...♘ce7** Also this move has a logical reason: above all Black wants to take care of the defence of the king's flank, putting off for a while the development of the queenside.

12 ♘e5 He could also develop active operations with the help of 12 ♕d3 g6 13 ♗h6. What can Black

do? To exchange the dark-squared bishops – 13...♗g7 14 ♗xg7 ♔xg7 – means allowing himself to be drawn into a tedious and rather worse position. For example: 15 ♕c4 ♘f6 16 ♖ac1 ♘xe4 17 ♘xe4 ♗d7 18 ♘e5 ♗c6 (Makarichev – Tukmakov, New Delhi 1986). Instead of 13...♗g7 more interesting is 13...♖e8, and then 14 ♖fe1 ♗d7 15 ♘e5 ♘xc3 16 ♕xc3.

In the game Podgaets – Kotlerman (Odessa 1971) Black played inaccurately – 16...♘d5 17 ♕f3 ♗c6 18 ♖ac1 ♗xe5 19 de ♕h4 20 ♗d2 ♖ed8 and after 21 ♖c4! ♘b6 22 ♖b4 ♗xe4 23 ♖bxe4 ♕e7 24 ♗h6 ran into difficulties.

Kotlerman rejected 16...♘f5!? because of 17 ♗xf5 ef 18 d5, and wrongly: 18...♖a4! 19 ♕d4 ♕d6! 20 ♗f4 ♗b3 21 ♘c4 ♕a6 22 ♗e5 ♕xc4 leads to an immediate draw.

Incidentally, if Black wants to continue the struggle, he has a way to do this: 19...♗c2!? (instead of 19...♕d6) 20 d6 ♗e4 21 ♗f4 ♕a5 22 d7 ♖xe5 23 b4! ♖e6! 24 ♕xf6 ♕d5 25 ♖ad1 ♕xd7 26 ♖xd7 ♖xf6, and the attempt to restrict the light-squared bishop by 27 b5!? is no good in view of 27...g5! 28 ♗xg5 ♖g6

181

29 f3 ♗xf3 30 gf ♖xg5+ 31 ♔f2 b6 with equality.

After 12 ♘e5 arises a critical position for the assessment of the idea 11...♘ce7!?

Dubious is 12...g6 13 ♗h6 ♗g7 14 ♗xg7 ♔xg7, as was played in the game Smyslov – Ribli (London 1983). The ex-world champion reacted simply and sensibly: 15 ♖c1! b6 16 ♘xd5! ♘xd5 17 ♗xd5 ♕xd5 18 ♖c7 There is no need to exchange pieces, but there is a need – to start to outplay the opponent. After 18...♗b7 19 ♕g4 ♖ad8 20 ♖d1 a5 (20...h5? 21 ♕xg6+) 21 h4 Vasily Vasilievich developed a strong initiative and later won.

Black was more successful with his manouvres in the game Lemmers – Kakhiani (Germany 2000): 12...♘f5!? 13 ♖e1 ♘de7 14 ♗f4 ♘g6!? (probably, Black rightly rejects the offered pawn: after 14...♕xd4 15 ♘g4 ♕xd1 16 ♘xf6+ gf 17 ♖axd1 e5 18 ♗c1 White has serious compensation) 15 ♘xg6 hg. Lemmers played 16 ♗xf5 gf 17 ♗e5 ♗d7 18 d5, but did not achieve a draw: 18...♖e8! 19 ♕d4 ♗xe5 20 ♖xe5 ♕c7 21 ♖ae1 ♕d6 White stands beautifully but that is all.

Instead of 16 ♗xf5 it is interesting to try the immediate 16 d5!?, but also here counterplay appears for Black: 16...e5!? 17 ♗xf5 ef 18 ♗c2 ♕b6 19 ♖b1 ♗f5 (19...♗d7 20 ♖e4) 20 ♗xf5 gf. Retroanalysts will allow themselves to unravel how three black pawns come to be on one file but for practical players, we assume, the arising position must be a matter of taste.

However from the educational point of view we should be mostly interested in the position after **12...♗d7 13 ♕d3 g6 14 ♗h6 ♗g7 15 ♗xg7 ♔xg7 16 ♗xd5 ed 17 ♖fe1**

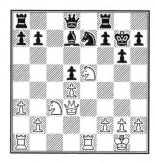

It arose in the game Speelman – Xu Hanbing (Budapest 2000). A position of this kind is typical for the Panov Attack, therefore it is important to understand which method of defence Black should adhere to.

In the above-mentioned game Black played 17...♗e6?!, which is essentially incorrect. The white knight is far more active than the black bishop, and he will not manage to drive it away now (the bishop is hanging on e6). There followed 18 ♖ac1 ♕a5 19 ♕b5! ♕xb5 20 ♘xb5 a6 21 ♘d6 ♘f5 22 ♘xf5+ ♗xf5 23 ♖c7 ♖ab8 24 f3! with an enormous positional advantage in the endgame.

In the diagram position Black, in the first instance, needs to drive away the knight from the e5 square. This is achieved by **17...f6!** After **18 ♘xd7 ♕xd7 19 ♕b5 ♖ad8 20 ♖e2 ♘f5 21 ♖ae1 ♖f7!** (it is important to avoid the weakening of the dark squares by the move a7-a6) the endgame is nowhere near as good for White as before. And if he decides to play on a little with queens – **22 ♕d3 ♖e7 23 ♖xe7+ ♘xe7 24 ♘a4**, then follows **24...b6!** (this is why it was so important not to play a7-a6), and the game is very close to a draw.

b22) **11 ♖e1**

It goes without aying that this move has equal rights to 11 ♗e4. But for the authors there is one problem: variations in the present branch will constantly be crossing over to variations with 10 ♖e1 ♗f6 11 a3 (or with the advance of the a-pawn on the 12th and 13th moves).

Let us deal with it this way: in the present branch we have gathered together all examples with the combination of moves ♖e1 and a3, and analysed 10 ♖e1 ♗f6, refraining from showing games in which at an

early stage the move a2-a3 is seen.

After 11 ♖e1 the first thing that should be made clear is the assessment of the position after 11...♘xd4 12 ♘xd4 ♗xd4 13 ♗xh7+ ♔xh7 14 ♕xd4 ♘xc3 15 ♕xc3. It is not equal – with queens White retains some pressure – but close to equal, for example: 15...f6 16 ♗e3 b6 17 ♕c2+ ♔g8 18 ♖ed1 ♕e7 19 ♕a4 ♗b7 ('Fritz' – Golod, Israel 2000).

Furthermore we make clear what happens on 11...♘xc3. In fact we have already become familiar, in all its details, with the struggle which offers good chances of equalisation for Black: 12 bc b6 13 h4 ♗b7 14 ♘g5 g6 15 ♕g4 h5 16 ♕g3 ♘e7 17 ♗f4 ♖c8 18 ♖ac1

18...♕d7! (18...♘f5?! 19 ♘xe6! is not actually so bad as one might think at first – after 19...♗xh4 20 ♘xd8 ♗xg3 21 ♗xg3 ♖fxd8 22 ♗xf5 Black has only a slightly worse endgame, Makarichev – Meduna, Sochi 1983) 19 ♘f3 ♗xf3 20 ♕xf3 ♘d5 21 ♗h6 ♗g7 22 ♗d2 b5! and already Black is playing for a win (C.Hansen – Ribli, Plovdiv 1983).

Black's most frequent reply to 11 ♖e1 is **11...♗d7!?** A useful developing move, not letting White have control of the e5 square. At the same time is set a mean little positional trick: if White tries to remove the blockade of the d5 square by 12 ♗e4, then Black replies 12...♘ce7, and how then to explain why White played a2-a3?

After 11...♗d7 we look at three dull moves – 12 ♕e2, 12 ♗c2 and 12 ♘e4, not one of them for preference.

12 ♕e2 ♖e8 13 ♘e4 ♘xd4!? (bad is 13...♗xd4? 14 ♘d6 ♖e7 15 ♘xd4 ♘xd4 16 ♕e4 ♘f5 17 ♗g5) **14 ♘xd4 ♗xd4 15 ♘d6 ♕f6 16 ♘xe8 ♖xe8 17 ♗e4 ♗c6 18 a4 g6 19 ♖a3 ♖c8.** For the exchange, a pawn plus a solid position in the centre – this should be more than enough for a draw (Stocek – Meduna, Lazne Bogdanec 1999);

12 ♗c2 ♖c8 13 ♘e4 ♗e7 14 ♕d3 g6 15 ♗d2! (parrying 15...♘cb4 and in his turn preparing b2-b4) **15...♕b6 16 b4 ♖fd8 17 ♗b3 ♗e8 18 ♖ac1** with a space advantage (Gulko– Kaidanov, Key West 1994).

12 ♘e4!? (the pawn sacrifice suggests itself, but in practice its prospects have as yet not been confirmed) **12...♗xd4 13 ♘eg5** (13 ♘xd4 ♘xd4 14 ♗c4 ♕b6 15 ♗xd5 ed 16 ♘c3 ♘e6 17 ♘xd5 ♕d8

with a draw, V. Schmidt – Farago, Baile Herculane 1982) **13...h6 14 ♘xd4 hg 15 ♘f3 f6 16 h4 g4 17 ♘h2 g3! 18 fg ♘e5 19 ♖xe5 fe 20 ♘f3 ♗b5!** White has been completely outplayed (Dreev – Kazimdzhanov, Wijk aan Zee 2002).

c) 10 ♖e1 The main position in the Panov Attack which can also easily be reached by transposition of moves from the Queen's Gambit.

We examine Black's possible moves in increasing order of strength: 10...b6, 10...a6, 10...♘xc3, 10...♘cb4, 10...♗d7, 10...♕d6, 10...♘f6 and 10...♗f6.

c1) 10...b6? (a blunder) **11 ♘xd5 ♕xd5** (11...ed 12 ♗xh7+!, and in any case White wins a pawn, since on 12...♔xh7 follows 13 ♕c2+ and 14 ♕xc6) **12 ♗e4 ♕d6 13 ♘e5!** This is even stronger than 13 ♕c2 ♗b7 14 ♗xh7+ ♔h8 15 ♗e4 ♗f6 (Hebden – Einarsson, London 1987), though even here White has every chance of a win after 16 ♕d1 ♖ad8 17 ♗g5!

13...♗b7 14 ♗f4! ♗f6 15 ♘g6 ♕xd4 16 ♘xf8 ♔xf8 17 ♕xd4 ♗xd4 18 ♖ad1 ♖d8 19 ♗xc6 and without waiting for 19...♗xc6 20 ♗e5, Black resigned (Brodsky – Kobelev, Perm 1997).

c2) **10...a6?!** A shallow move, containing no ideas at all. It is surprisingly played quite often.

11 ♗e4! ♘f6 12 ♗xc6! bc 13 ♘a4 ♘d7 14 ♕c2 ♗b7 15 ♗f4 ♕a5 16 ♘e5 ♘xe5 17 ♖xe5 ♕d8 18 ♖d1 The bishop b7 is outrageously bad, and this determines a positional advantage for White (Matanovic – Portisch, Bled 1961).

c3) **10...♘xc3?!** A poor version of what is generally an interesting idea. Firstly, the bishop gets to d3 in one move, and not two, secondly, White does not spend time on a2-a3. Saving two tempi in this way has a negative influence on the assessment of Black's position.

11 bc b6 Black fell into a plain and simple trap in the game Keres – Sorokin (Parnu 1960): 11...♗d7?! 12 ♗f4!? ♖c8 13 ♕b1! with a double attack on b7 and h7.

12 ♕c2 The diagonal battery can be set up also in reverse order: 12 ♕e2 ♗b7 13 ♕e4. In the game Mukhin – Pavlenko (Irkutsk 1966) play continued 13...g6 14 ♗h6 ♖e8 15 ♕g4, and White's attack was very dangerous.

As always, interesting is 12 h4!?, and then:

12...♗xh4 13 ♘xh4 ♕xh4 14 ♖e3;

12...♗f6 13 ♘g5 g6 14 ♕f3 ♗d7 15 ♘e4 ♗g7 16 h5 ♘e7 17 h6 ♗h8 18 ♗g5 White is close to victory (Lalic – Stefanova, Dos Hermanas 2002);

12...♗b7 13 ♘g5 g6

14 ♘xh7! (the rout begins) 14...♔xh7 15 ♕h5+ ♔g8 16 ♗xg6! fg 17 ♕xg6+ ♔h8 18 ♖e4 ♗f6 19 ♕h6+ ♔g8 20 ♖g4+ ♔f7 21 ♗a3! (Ervich – Koster, Nijmegan 2001).

12...g6 (on 12...h6 White will obviously return to the plan 13 ♕e2 ♗b7 14 ♕e4) **13 ♗h6** We are following the game Winants – Kamsky (Tilburg 1992). White won but Luc Winants was not satisfied with his 13th move, suggesting instead 13 h4!? with the following variations:

13...♗xh4 14 ♗h6 ♖e8 15 ♗b5! ♗d7 16 ♕e4;

13...♗f6 14 h5 ♗g7 15 hg hg 16 ♘g5;

13...♗b7 14 h5 ♗f6 15 hg hg 16 ♗xg6! fg 17 ♕xg6+ ♔h8 18 ♖xe6 winning.

13...♖e8 14 h4 As distinct from the previous variations this is not a pawn sacrifice, since after 14...♗xh4? 15 d5! (he cannot take on d5 as then the queen will be continually preoccupied with the bishop on h4) 15...♘a5 16 ♗b5 White wins immediately.

14...♗f8 15 ♗g5! ♗e7 16 ♗f4 (looking ideal is also 16 ♕d2!? ♗xg5 17 hg followed by ♘f3-h2-g4)

16...♗b7 17 h5 ♔g7 18 ♕d2 ♕d5 19 ♗e4 ♕xh5 20 ♘e5 and then the rook enters the game via the march route e1-e3-h3. To avoid mate Black will have to give up the queen for it, which will merely prolong his defeat.

c4) **10...♘cb4?! 11 ♗b1** It is not clear whether White needs to include the move 11 ♗e4 ♘f6, and only now play 12 ♗b1 (Botvinnik – Flohr, Groningen 1946). Black voluntarily prepares to lead his knight to f6 – otherwise it is difficult to gainfully employ the second knight on b4.

11...♘f6 Also seen is 11...b6 12 a3! ♘xc3 13 bc ♘d5 14 ♕d3, and then:

14...g6 15 ♘e5 ♗g5 16 ♗xg5 ♕xg5 17 c4 ♗a6 18 ♗a2 f6 19 h4! ♕h5 (19...♕xh4 20 ♘xg6!) 20 ♕g3 with a great advantage;

14...♘f6 15 ♗g5 g6 16 ♘e5 ♗b7 17 ♗h6 ♖e8 18 ♕h3 ♕c8 19 ♗a2 ♗f8 20 ♖e3 ♗g7 21 ♖ae1, likewise with a threatening initiative for White (Adams – Seirawan, Wijk aan Zee 1991).

The position after 11...♘f6 presents no little interest for those who habitually play for or against the isolated pawn in the centre.

Which order of moves is the best for White? In the game Keene – Miles (Hastings 1975) White achieved success after 12 ♗g5 b6 13 ♘e5 ♗b7 14 ♖e3 g6 15 ♖g3 ♖c8?! 16 ♗h6 ♖e8 17 a3 ♘c6 18 ♘xg6! hg 19 ♗xg6! fg 20 ♕b1. It was Keene himself who pointed out the correct path for Black: 15...♘c6 16 ♗h6 ♕xd4! 17 ♕xd4 ♘xd4 18 ♗xf8 ♔xf8 with sufficient compensation for the exchange.

We stop for a more detailed examination of the most natural **12 ♘e5 ♗d7 13 ♗g5 ♗c6 14 ♖e3!** g6 (threatening 15 ♗xf6 ♗xf6 16 ♗xh7+! ♔xh7 17 ♕h5+ ♔g8 18 ♖h3) **15 ♖h3** This is how the game Podgaets – Novak (Bratislava 1967) continued. Black replied routinely: **15...♖c8?!**, violating the main principle in such positions: at the first opportunity unload the position by exchanges! Concretely: 15...♘d7! 16 ♗h6 ♖e8 17 ♗f4 ♘xe5! 18 ♗xe5 ♗f8 19 ♕g4. There is a complicated game in prospect with some initiative for White.

16 ♕d2 (with the threat of 17 ♗xf6 ♗xf6 18 ♕h6) **16...♘bd5 17 ♗d3!** (taking the time to include the rook a1 in the game) **17...♘xc3 18 ♗xf6! ♘d5 19 ♗xe7 ♕xe7 20 ♕h6 ♘f6** (losing is 20...f5 21 ♘xg6 hg 22 ♕h8+ ♔f7 23 ♖h7+) **21 ♘g4?!** Easily winning is 21 g4!, but White is enticed by a study-like idea on the theme of 'overloading'.

21...♖fd8

22 d5!! The pawn places itself under fourfold attack but it cannot be taken by anything.

Novak played **22...♗xd5** and after **23 ♕g5!** resigned (23...♔g7 24 ♘xf6 ♕xf6 25 ♖xh7+!).

Also simply losing is 22...♘xd5 23 ♕xh7+ ♔f8 24 ♕h8 mate and 22...♖xd5 23 ♗xg6! fg 24 ♘xf6+ ♕xf6 25 ♕xh7+ ♔f8 26 ♕h8+.

There is a slightly longer continuation upon 22...ed 23 ♗f5! ♖c7 (on 23...♖a8 winning is 24 ♗xg6! fg 25 ♘xf6+ ♕xf6 26 ♕xh7+ ♔f8 27 ♖f3) 24 ♘xf6+ ♕xf6 25 ♕xh7+ ♔f8 26 ♕h8+ ♕xh8 27 ♖xh8+ ♔e7 28 ♖e1+ .

Finally, it is useless to decline the sacrifice: on 22...♗e8 there still follows 23 ♗xg6! fg 24 ♘xf6+ ♕xf6 25 ♕xh7+ ♔f8 26 ♖f3.

c5) **10...♗d7** A passive continuation which cannot be recommended.

11 a3 ♘xc3 12 bc ♕a5 13 ♕c2 g6 14 ♖b1 ♕c7 15 ♗e4! A multi-plan move. Firstly, the rook helps the bishop enter the game via the handy f4 square. Then, waiting until the h-pawn weakens the pawn cover of the enemy king, the rook will go

(depending on circumstances) to the g4 or h4 square.

15...b6 16 ♗f4 ♕b7 17 ♕e2 ♘d8 18 ♘e5! In this game Black did not last to the 30th move. (Malaniuk – Palat, Geneva 1997).

c6) **10...♕d6** Though rarely played, in terms of quality this move is superior to all the previous ones.

11 a3 ♖d8 12 ♕c2 h6

The attempt to get into h7 here leads nowhere: 13 ♘xd5 ♕xd5 14 ♗e3 (Tal advised trying the pawn sacrifice: 14 ♗e4!? ♘xd4 15 ♘xd4 ♕xd4 16 ♗e3) 14...♗d7 15 ♗h7+ ♔h8 16 ♗e4 ♕h5 17 ♘e5 ♘xe5 18 de ♖ac8 19 ♕e2 ♕xe2 20 ♖xe2 ♗c6! (Spassky – Korchnoi, Kiev 1968).

More promising is the plan to grab space on the queen's flank **13 ♘e4!? ♕c7 14 b4**, familiar to us in the Gulko – Kaidanov game seen above.

14...♗d7 15 ♗d2 ♖ac8 16 ♖ac1 ♕b8 17 ♕b3 a6 18 ♗b1 ♗e8 19 ♘c5 White has achieved what he wanted, though Black's position is still very solid (Eingorn – Razuvaev, Tashkent 1980).

c7) **10...♘f6** In the Steiner system (see the final section) we analyse a similar position. But there White succeeded in placing the rook on c1 before starting to set up the battery on the b1-h7 diagonal. Therefore the bishop moved to b1 without detriment to the harmony of the construction.

In the present position White obviously does not succeed in playing ♖c1, ♗b1 and ♕d3. Therefore either the rook a1 remains out of play (after ♗b1) for some time, or the bishop must move to c2.

11 a3 (preventing the knight fork on b4, inevitable upon the construction of the battery) **11...b6**

A critical position. White has four main continuations: 12 ♘e5, 12 ♗g5, 12 ♗b1 and 12 ♗c2. Let's look at them.

c71) **12 ♘e5** From the point of view of opening theory – a move lacking prospects. But it makes some practical sense. If the white pieces are handled by a chessplayer who is a class above his opponent, then with the help of 12 ♘e5 he will secure himself against defeat. A forced variation leads to a rook endgame with an extra pawn for White which,

however, is quite impossible to realise.

12...♗b7 Poor is 12...♘xd4? because of 13 ♗e3 ♘f5 14 ♕f3 ♗d7 15 ♗xf5 ef 16 ♖ad1 ♕c8 17 ♘xd7 ♘xd7 18 ♘d5 ♗d8 19 ♗d4 ♘c5 20 ♘e3!? ♘e6 21 ♗e5 ♗g5 22 ♘xf5 with advantage.

13 ♗a6 ♕c8 14 ♗xb7 ♕xb7 15 ♘xc6 ♕xc6 16 d5 ♕c4 17 de fe 18 ♕e2 ♕xe2 19 ♖xe2 ♗c5 20 ♗e3 ♗xe3 21 ♖xe3 ♘d5 A great number of drawn games have gone this way, the first of them being Ribli – Kavalek (Tilburg 1980).

c72) **12 ♗g5** The motivation for this move is absolutely clear. White is afraid that on 12 ♗c2 or 12 ♗b1 will follow 12...♗a6!?, then the introduction of the white bishop to d3 will have to be put off for an indefinite period. Therefore White simply wants to wait until the black bishop comes out to b7 and only then to choose between ♗c2 and ♗b1.

12...♗b7 13 ♗c2 We also examine 13 ♗b1.

The moves ♗c2 and ♗b1 both free the d3 square for the queen. So what is the principal difference? Well, here it is. If the battery on the b1-h7 diagonal proves to be ineffective then, from its future b1 square, the bishop can go to a2 to support the break d4-d5. However if the bishop at this moment is standing on c2, then it appears logical to transfer it to a4 (particularly with the rook on e8 when the pin on the knight c6 might prove very unpleasant).

Practice has shown that in nearly all the variations Black has an easier game if White moves his bishop to b1. This is how the struggle might continue:

13...♖c8 14 ♕d3 g6 15 ♗a2 ♖e8 (15...♘g4!?, Neamtu – Korchnoi, Bucharest 1966; 16 ♗xe7 ♘xe7 17 ♖xe6!? fe 18 ♗xe6+ ♔h8 19 ♗xg4 with a very unclear game) 16 ♖ad1 ♘d5 17 h4 ♘xc3 18 bc ♘a5 19 ♗xe7 ♕xe7 20 d5 ♕xa3 21 de ♕xa2 22 ♘g5! (Deze – Adamski, Zalaegerseged 1977), and here Black failed to find 22...♗d5!? 23 ♕xd5 ♕xd5 24 ♖xd5 f6 with equality;

13...♖e8 14 ♕d3 g6 15 ♗a2 ♘d5 16 ♗h6 ♘xc3 17 bc ♖c8 18 ♖ad1 ♗f6! (preparing the transfer of the knight to f5) 19 h4 ♘e7 20 g4?! (this move, preventing the transfer of the knight to f5, cannot be recommended since it abruptly weakens the king's flank) 20...♗d5 21 c4 ♗xf3 22 ♕xf3 (Hoffman – Panno, Buenos Aires 1999) and here, if he wants, Black can force a draw by 22...♖xd4 23 ♗b3 ♘c6 24 ♗a4 ♕f6! 25 ♗xc6 ♖xc6! 26 ♕:c6 ♕xf2+ 27 ♔h1 ♕xh4+ etc.

Instead of 20 g4?! worth considering is another, no less sharp operation:

20 ♖xe6!? fe 21 ♗xe6+ ♔h8 22 ♘g5 ♗xg5 23 ♗xg5 h6! 24 ♗f6+ ♔h7 25 h5 ♕d6 26 ♖e1 ♗d5 27 ♗xe7 ♕xe7 28 ♗g8+. However, in this case White can count only on a draw.

After 13 ♗c2 there are two main replies: 13...♘d5 and 13...♖c8.

x) **13...♘d5** If it were so easy to simplify the position, the variation 12 ♗g5 ♗b7 13 ♗c2 would have to be written off and placed in the archives. But, alas: White plays 14 ♕d3, and Black is forced to allow the bishop a loop hole on h6.

He can try to exchange bishops in another way: 13...h6?! 14 ♗h4! (inferior is 14 ♗f4 in view of 14...♗d6!, Dolmatov – Epishin, Moscow 1995) 14...♘h5? But this is a case where the medicine is worse than the disease. White forcibly obtains a great advantage by continuing 15 d5! In the game J.Polgar – Karpov (Budapest 1998) play continued 15...♗xh4? (better really is 15...ed 16 ♕d3 f5 17 ♗xe7 ♘xe7 18 ♘d4 – though White has the initiative, stubborn resistance is still possible) 16 dc ♗xc6 (or 16...♕xd1 17 ♗xd1! ♗xc6 18 ♘e5) 17 ♘e5. Though the game ended in a draw, it is clear that Black is on the brink of defeat.

14 ♕d3! There is still the trappy move 14 h4!?, reckoning on 14...♘xc3?! 15 bc ♗xg5?

Then follows the unforeseen 16 ♗xh7+! ♔xh7 17 ♘xg5+ ♔h6 18 ♕d2 (step by step drawing closer to the enemy king) 18...♔h5 19 ♕e2+ ♔h6 (19...♔xh4? 20 ♘e4!) 20 ♕e3 ♔g6 21 ♕d3+ f5 22 ♕g3 ♕d7 23 ♖xe6+ ♖f6 24 d5! White's attack can hardly be repulsed.

In the game Pigusov – Bareev (Tallinn 1986) Black, suspecting something was wrong, at the last moment backed out: 15...♗a6 (instead of 15...♗xg5?), but after 16 ♕d2 ♗xg5 17 hg ♖c8 18 ♖e4! he came up against insurmountable difficulties.

The very first move of the variation was inaccurate – 14...♘xc3?! He should have played at once 14...♗xg5! To sacrifice on h7 now is senseless (15 ♗xh7+? ♔xh7 16 ♘xg5+ ♔g8 17 ♕h5 ♘f6 or 17 ♘xd5 ♕xd5 18 ♕h5 ♕f5) and otherwise Black forces exchanges

which are favourable for him: 15 ♘xg5 ♘f6 16 ♘ce4 ♘xe4 17 ♗xe4 h6 or 15 hg ♘xc3 16 bc ♘a5 17 ♗e4 ♗xe4 18 ♖xe4 ♖c8 19 ♕d3 ♕d5.

14...g6 15 ♗h6 Also here 15 h4?! does not justify itself in view of 15...♗xg5! 16 ♘xg5 (16 hg ♘xc3 17 bc ♘a5) 16...♘ce7! 17 ♕f3 ♘xc3 18 ♕xb7 ♘cd5 (Salov – Belyavsky, Madrid 1995).

15...♖e8 16 ♗a4 The alternative is 16 ♖ad1, after which it is dangerous to win a pawn by 16...♘xc3 17 bc!? ♗xa3 in view of 18 ♘g5!

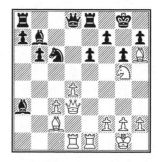

But dangerous – does not mean impossible. Black has two defensive plans worth considering.

Firstly, the fearless 18...♘a5!? Any piece going to e4 can now be exchanged off, while afterwards the queen goes to d5 and from being on the defensive side Black immediately goes over to counterattack. To be concrete: 19 ♗a4 (on 19 ♕h3 strongest is 19...♕f6! and if 20 ♘xh7!? then 20...♕h8! 21 ♘g5 ♗f8! with an exchange of queens and the better position) 19...♖e7 20 ♕h3 f5!? (20...♖c7?! – is already too bold: 21 ♘xh7! ♗e7 22 ♗f4) 21 ♘xe6 ♕d5 22 ♘f4 ♖xe1+ 23 ♖xe1 ♕f7.

The first wave of the attack has been beaten off, and though White's position is more pleasant, Black also has repented for his sins. For example: 24 ♘d3 ♘c4 25 ♗b3 ♗d5 26 ♗xc4 ♗xc4 27 ♘e5 ♕e6 28 ♖e3 ♗d6 29 ♗f4 ♗xe5 30 ♖xe5 ♕d7 31 ♕e3 ♗f7 32 ♖e7 ♕xe7! 33 ♕xe7 ♖e8 with a draw.

In the game Novikov – Kyrkynakis (Mons 1996) Black did not go in for 18...♘a5!?, but made an equally worthy move 18...♗e7!? The mistake on his side followed a move later: 19 ♕g3 ♗f6?!, and after 20 ♕f4 ♘a5 21 ♖e3 ♕e7 22 ♖de1 ♗g7 White already brought matters to a halt:

23 ♘xh7! ♔xh7 24 ♖h3 ♕f8 25 ♗g5+ ♔g8 26 ♕h4 f5 27 ♕h7+ ♔f7 28 ♖h6!

Instead of 19...♗f6?! the move 19...♕d6!? 20 ♕h3 suggests itself, 20...♗xg5 21 ♗xg5 f5!, then the blockade 22...♘a5 and 23...♗d5. Frankly speaking, White's prospects look very hazy.

16...♖c8 16...♘xc3 17 bc ♗f6 does not produce equality in view of 18 ♖ad1, and the centre pawns are very mobile. The game Dolmatov – Burmakin (Novgorod 1999) continued: 18...♕d5 19 c4 ♕h5

20 ♕e3 ♖ed8, and in this position there was no reason at all for White to reject 21 d5!

17 ♖ad1 Interesting is 17 ♘e4 ♘f6 18 ♖ac1 ♕d5 19 ♘eg5!?

19...♘e5! 20 ♗xe8!? (it is still not too late to back down: 20 ♕e2 ♘xf3+ 21 ♘xf3 ♖ed8) 20...♘xd3 21 ♗xf7+ ♔h8 22 ♗xe6 ♖xc1 23 ♘f7+ ♔g8 24 ♗xc1 ♕xe6 25 ♘h6+ ♔f8 26 ♖xe6 ♘xc1 with a better and possibly also winning endgame for Black.

17...a6 18 ♘xd5 ♕xd5 19 ♕e3! A standard method. White, realising that on ♗a4-b3 in any case follows ♕d5-h5, in good time defends the bishop h6. In whose favour? If the queen leaves d5 without a tempo, White gains a tempo for the advance d4-d5!

19...♗f6!? It is useless to counter the inevitable break in the centre with the move 19...♖cd8. In the game Utemov – Lastin (Moscow 1996) White found a forcing way to his objective: 20 ♗b3 ♕h5 21 d5! ed 22 ♕xb6 ♕xh6 23 ♕xb7 ♘a5 24 ♕b6 ♘xb3 25 ♖xe7!

20 ♗b3 It must be acknowledged that in the present branch White finds a move order that is unpleasant for the opponent. All these manoeuvres, reminiscent of a swinging pendulum – ♗c2-a4-b3; ♕d3-e3 – lead to Black losing control both of the d5 square and the position as a whole. His situation is more difficult.

Unsatisfactory is 20...♕h5? 21 d5! ♘d8 22 d6 (Smyslov – Karpov, Leningrad 1971).

Fifteen years later was played 20...♕d7 21 d5 (in the event of 21 ♘e5 Black defended by 21...♘xe5 22 de ♕c6! 23 ♕g3 ♗e7) 21...ed 22 ♕xb6 with advantage (Belyavsky – Karpov, Moscow 1986).

The advantage of the retreat **20...♕d8!?** is that it forces White to think in a non-standard way. If he sees the difference between this move and 20...♕d7 (from d8 the queen cannot move to c6), then he invariably plays 21 ♘e5! Taking on e5 with the knight is not possible for the above mentioned reasons, while after 21...♗xe5 Black, in the game Adams – Dettling (France 2002) waited for the rout: 22 de ♕c7 23 ♖c1 ♕b8 24 ♕xb6 ♘e7 25 ♗xe6!

If however White 'cycles' round the advance d4-d5, then on accurate defence there will be no advantage for him: **21 ♕f4?! ♘a5 22 d5** (or

22 ♗a2 ♘c4 23 d5 e5! 24 ♕e4 b5) **22...e5! 23 ♕e3** (more accurate is 23 ♕b4) **23...♘xb3** (he can also wait with this move; 23...e4!?) **24 ♕xb3 e4 25 d6 ♖e6 26 d7 ♖c5 27 h4**

This is how the game Malinin – Eliseev (St.Petersburg 1999) went. The passed d7 pawn is very strong but White does not have any other trumps. Black can solve all his problems with the sacrifice of the exchange and himself start to play for a win: **27...♖b5 28 ♕a2 ♖e7 29 ♗g5** (29 ♘g5 ♖xd7 30 ♘xf7 ♖d1 31 ♘xd8+ ♗d5!) **29...♖f5** (it is too late to back down: 29...♗xg5?! 30 ♘xg5 h6 31 ♘xf7! ♖xf7 32 ♕e6 or 30...♖xd7 31 ♕xf7+ ♖xf7 32 ♖xd8+ ♖f8 33 ♖d7) **30 ♘d4 ♖xg5! 31 hg ♗xg5 32 ♕b3 e3! 33 fe ♕xd7**

y) **13...♖c8!?** Since the plan with 13...♘d5 proves to be unsound – Black is still not in a position to maintain the d5 square, then it looks logical to try to utilise this tempo to complete his development.

13...♖e8 is also suitable for the same purpose, for example: 14 ♕d3 g6 15 h4!? ♖c8 16 ♖ac1 ♘d5 17 ♘e4 (with his 16th move White defended himself against the thrust b4, but now tactics begin on the other side of the board) 17...f5!? 18 ♘c3 ♗xg5 19 ♘xg5 ♘f4 20 ♕e3 ♕xd4 21 ♘b5 ♕xe3 22 fe ♘xg2! (Reshevsky – Fischer, New York 1961).

14 ♕d3 g6 15 ♖ad1 ♖e8!? Firstly, overprotecting the e6 square, and secondly, preparing the unloading manoeuvre ♘f6-d5 (it is important that White cannot move the bishop to h6 with tempo).

Here we have yet another critical position, with its scarcely perceptible finesses and nuances. The plan with ♗c2-a4 and d4-d5, which recommended itself so well in parallel positions (we recall if only the game Smyslov – Karpov and Belyavsky – Karpov), is no good here: **16 ♗a4** a6 17 ♗xf6 ♗xf6 18 d5 ♗xc3!! This idea was thought up by M.Podgaets during the Karpov – Anand match (Lausanne 1998). With the unexpected exchange Black fully equalises the game: 19 dc (dubious is 19 ♕xc3?! ed 20 ♖xe8+ ♕xe8 21 ♖xd5 b5) 19...♕xd3 20 ♖xd3 ♗xe1 21 cb ♖c1! 22 ♖d1 ♖xd1 23 ♗xd1 ♗a5 24 ♘e5 b5 25 ♘d7 ♗c7. A check on f6 – and on the board arises a drawn 'opposite coloured' endgame.

Black is faced with less difficult problems by **16 ♗b3** In the game Balashov – Hort (Vincovci 1976) play continued 16...♘d5 17 ♘e4 ♔g7!? (Black makes his position more compact and denies the bishop the h6 square) 18 ♗d2 ♘a5 19 ♗a2 ♘f6 20 ♘eg5 ♗d5 21 ♗b1 ♖f8 22 ♘e5 ♘c4 23 ♗c1 ♘xe5 24 de ♘g4 25 ♘e4?! (it cannot be said that the compensation for the pawn is really so obvious) 25...♘xe5 26 ♕g3 ♘d7 27 ♘d6 ♗xd6 28 ♕xd6 and in this unclear position the opponents agreed a draw.

Instead of 25 ♘e4 worth considering 25 ♘f3!? ♗c5 26 ♖d2 (only not 26 ♖e2? ♗c4!) 26...a5 27 h3 ♘h6 28 ♖c2!, and White gradually forced back the enemy pieces with possibly the slightly better game.

Finally is drawn the blueprint of the plan with **16 h4**, likewise not too dangerous in the present situation. Black does not fear the flank attack, but the break in the centre. If he manages to avert or render harmless the advance d4-d5, then the remaining ideas, as a rule, are not capable of causing any harm, for example, 16...♕d6!? 17 ♕e2 ♖cd8 18 ♘e4 ♘xe4 19 ♗xe4 ♘a5 20 ♗xb7 ♘xb7 21 d5 ♗xg5 22 hg ♕b8 23 de ♖xe6 24 ♕c4 ♘c5 25 b4 ♖xd1 26 ♖xd1 ♘e4, draw (Ionov – Klimov, Krasnoyarsk 2003).

Let's go over to coping with the straightforward continuations: 12 ♗b1 and 12 ♗c2

c73) **12 ♗b1 ♗a6!?** It goes without saying, that 12...♗b7 is also played, not fearing 13 ♕d3. With care, it is possible to play like this. For example: 13...g6 14 ♗a2 ♖e8?! (all the same preferable is 14...♕d6!?, so as then to place one of the rooks on d8, to organise pressure on the d4 pawn) 15 h3 ♕d7?! 16 ♗h6 ♗f8 17 ♗xf8 ♔xf8 18 ♖ad1 ♖ad8 19 ♕e3 ♔g7 20 ♘e5 (Suba – Barzelo, Mallorca 2000).

But why? The risk might be excessive. Thus 13...♕d7? loses at once:

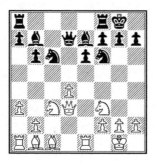

14 d5! ed 15 ♗g5 g6 16 ♖xe7! (Petrik – Masarik, Slovakia 1997). White wins in exactly the same way on 13...♖c8?

It is possible that 12...♗a6!? is no stronger than 12...♗b7, but the idea – is accurate!

13 ♗g5 ♖c8 14 ♕c2 g6 15 ♗h6 ♖e8 16 ♕d1 ♗c4 17 ♗c2 (van Riemsdijk – Campora, Resife 1991). The simplest way for Black to equalise here is by 17... ♘d5! 18 ♘e4 ♘f6.

c74) **12 ♗c2** The main continuation, and with a clear choice of reply – 12...♗b7 or 12...♗a6

x) **12...♗b7 13 ♕d3 g6** From the above mentioned it is clear that 13...♕d7? or 13...♖c8? are both losing because of 14 d5! For the same reason 13...♖e8? is weak. Black does not lose at once – after 14 d5! ed 15 ♗g5 there is 15...♘e4 16 ♘xe4 de 17 ♕xe4 g6, and the bishop e7 is defended. Nevertheless White can penetrate the opponent's defence and in a way that has long been known: 18 ♕h4 ♕c7 19 ♗b3! (threatening a strike on f7) 19...h5 20 ♕e4! ♔g7

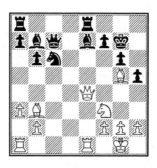

21 ♗xf7! ♔xf7 22 ♗h6! The first time White won in such a way was in the game Stoica – Flis (Polanica Zdroj 1983).

14 ♗h6 (compared to the variations with 12 ♗g5 White has gained a tempo – the bishop went to h6 in one move, and not two) **14...♖e8 15 ♖ad1** If he wants, White can return the tempo so as again to try to carry out the plan with the bishop to g5 and the sprint of the h-pawn 15 h4 ♖c8 16 ♗g5 ♘d5 17 ♖ad1. We have already examined quite a lot of examples on this theme and in the majority of cases Black succeeds in equalising the game. Here is one more: 17...♗xg5 18 ♘xg5 ♘xc3 19 bc (Georgadze – Makarichev, Vilnius 1980) 19...♘e7! 20 c4 ♘f5.

After 15 ♖ad1 arises the tabiya of the system 12 ♗c2. White's plan is to attack the enemy king and this attack has great chances of success, if he begins not on the king's flank, but in the centre (the break d4-d5!).

The general line of defence is to exchange, exchange and exchange again. And the support of the d5 square is like a springboard for these exchanges.

Practical material on this position is more than sufficient, however the exact move order up to now has still not been established. The theory of the variation has not come together as an entity. Therefore Black's possibilities – 15...♗f8, 15...♕c7, 15...♕d6, 15...♘d5 and 15...♖c8 – we will not look at it in their order of strength so much as in their order of popularity.

The manoeuvre **15...♗f8?!** 16 ♗g5 ♗g7 is hardly succesful. If White prevents the freeing h7-h6 by 17 ♕d2!, the pin on the knight f6 becomes very unpleasant. In the game Sher – Mortensen (Hamburg 1992) there followed: 17...♘e7 18 ♘e5 ♘ed5 19 ♘xd5 ♕xd5 20 f3!? (threatening, after the exchange on f6, to win a piece by the move ♗e4) 20...♕d8 21 ♕f4! (White can win the exchange – 21 ♗a4 ♖e7 22 ♕f4 ♘d5 23 ♗xe7 ♕xe7, but he wants more)

21...♕e7 22 ♕h4. In order not to lose the knight, Black pays off a pawn – 22...h6, but it cannot save the game.

15...♕c7 has still not been analysed very much. Black frees the d-file for both of his rooks, while the queen creates threats against the king along the b8-h2 diagonal (in combination with a jump of the knight to g4).

In the game Kharlov – Nisipeanu (Ljubliana 2002) was played 16 ♗b3 ♖ad8 (16...♘g4 17 ♖xe6!) 17 h3, and Black held the position by means of 17...a6 18 d5 ♘a5 – the vis-a-vis of the queen d3 and the rook d8 is obviously in his favour.

More concrete is 16 ♘b5!? ♕d7 17 ♗a4. Interesting things happened (and to be more precise, did not happen) in the game Borik – Seiger (Stuttgart 1979): 17...a6 18 ♘c3 b5 19 ♗b3 ♕c7 (if Black realised the risks he was taking he would have started with 19...♘g4) 20 d5! ed 21 ♘xd5 ♘xd5 22 ♕xd5 ♗f8

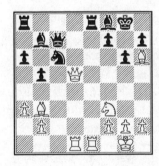

The German master Otto Borik here exchanged on f8; the game soon ended in a draw. It was left to the cadre to play a combination, leading to an endgame with an extra pawn for White: 23 ♕xf7+! ♕xf7 24 ♗xf7+ ♔xf7 25 ♖d7+, and then

25...♔g8 26 ♗xf8 ♖xe1+ 27 ♘xe1 ♖xf8 28 ♖xb7 ♖e8 29 ♔f1 ♘a5 30 ♖a7 ♘c4 31 ♘f3;

25...♖e7 26 ♖exe7+ ♘xe7 27 ♘e5+ ♔e6 28 ♗xf8 ♖xf8 29 ♖xb7 ♖c8 30 ♘d3 ♖c2 31 h4.

In the present position **15...♕d6** looks dubious. As also with 15...♕c7, Black wants to make way for the rook to go to d8, while the queen is tucked away in the region of the b8 and a8 squares.

But after 16 ♕d2!? in the best case he will lose time (16...♖ac8 17 ♗f4 ♕d8), and in the worst – White carries out d4-d5 in favourable conditions for himself: 16...♖ed8?! 17 ♗f4 ♕d7 (Brodsky – Labutin, Kstovo 1994) 18 ♗a4! ♖ac8 19 d5!, and then:

19...♘xd5 20 ♘xd5 ed 21 ♘e5 ♕e8 22 ♖c1, and Black suffers material loss;

19...ed 20 ♗g5 a6 21 ♗xc6! ♗xc6 22 ♕d4 with a double attack on b6 and f6.

For purposes of training we also look at the plan 16 h4!? ♖ad8 17 ♗g5, and more concretely – the encounter Yusupov – Lobron (Nussloch 1996). After 17...♕b8 18 ♗b3 arises the first critical position in this game.

The Slovakian grandmaster Ljubomir Ftacnik preferred here 18...♘a5. An extraordinarily dubious recommendation! With the blow 19 ♗xe6! fe 20 ♖xe6 White tips the balance in his favour:

20...♘d5 21 ♖xg6+! hg 22 ♕xg6+ ♔h8 23 ♘e5 ♖f8 24 ♖d3!;

20...♘g4 (a desperate counter-attack) 21 ♗xe7 ♗xf3 22 ♕xf3 ♕h2+ 23 ♔f1 ♖d7 24 ♕xg4 ♖dxe7 25 d5!, repulses all the attacks;

20...♔f7 21 ♘e5+! ♔g7 (if he takes the rook, the king is mated: 21...♔xe6 22 ♕h3+ ♔d6 23 ♘b5+ ♔d5 24 ♕f3+ ♘e4 25 ♕f7 mate) 22 h5! (apart from other things, he threatens to win back the piece after 23 h6+) 22...♖d6 23 ♖xd6 ♕xd6 24 b4! ♘xh5 (or 24...♘c6 25 ♗h6+!) 25 ♗h6+! ♔g8 26 ba with an attack and material equality;

20...♖d6 21 ♗f4 ♖xe6 22 ♗xb8 ♖xb8 (nominally, for the queen Black obtains sufficient material equivalent, however his disconnected pieces prevent him from putting right his game) 23 b4 ♗xf3 (a forced exchange, since 23...♘c6 is bad because of 24 ♘g5 ♖d6 25 ♕c4+) 24 ♕xf3 ♘c4 25 ♘b5. The threats on the a2-g8 diagonal, together with the advance of the d-pawn, allow us to assess the position in White's favour.

Lobron played 18...a6 and on 19 d5! – 19...♘a5, allowing Yusupov to finish the game brilliantly:

20 de!! ♘xb3 (on 20...♖xd3 follows 21 ef+ ♔g7 22 fe♕ ♕xe8 23 ♖xd3 ♘xb3 24 ♖de3 ♔f7 25 ♗xf6 ♔xf6 26 ♖e6+ ♔f7 27 ♘g5+) 21 ef+ ♔xf7 22 ♕c4+ ♔g7 23 ♘e5! Soon Black resigned.

15...♘d5!? is played quite often. After 16 ♗a4 a6 the plan that suggests itself is to prepare a pawn break in the centre: an exchange on d5, ♕d3-e3, ♗a4-b3 and, finally, d4-d5!

Perhaps there is no great practical interest in the position after 16 h4!? ♘xc3 17 bc!? ♗xa3, but in analysis we cannot ignore it. What carries more weight: the pawn or the attack?

Upon 18 h5 ♕d5 the attack is obviously insufficient:

19 hg hg 20 c4 ♕h5 21 ♕xa3 ♕xh6 22 d5 ed 23 cd ♖xe1+ 24 ♖xe1 ♘a5 25 d6 ♖d8 26 ♗e4 ♕f4!;

19 ♗g5 ♗e7 20 ♕e3 ♘a5 21 hg hg 22 ♗xe7 ♖xe7 23 ♕f4 ♔g7!

More interesting is 18 ♘g5!? ♘e7 19 h5 ♘f5 20 hg hg 21 ♕h3.

White's idea is revealed upon 21...♗e7? 22 ♗g7!! ♔xg7 23 ♕h7+ ♔f6 24 ♕xf7+ ♔xg5 25 ♖xe6 ♖g8 (or 25...♗f6 26 ♖xf6 ♕xf6 27 f4+!) 26 ♖xg6+! ♖xg6 27 ♕xf5+ ♔h4 28 ♕h3+ ♔g5 29 ♕g3+ with unstoppable mate.

A brilliant combination but it did not prompt the right defence: 21...♕f6! The bishop on h6 gets in the way, preventing his pieces from concluding the attack. After 22 ♘e4 (22 ♗f8 ♗b2! 23 f4 ♗xc3) 22...♕h8! 23 ♕f3 ♘xh6 24 ♘f6+ ♔f8 25 ♘d7+ ♔g7 26 ♕xb7 ♘g4 already Black is creating threats against the enemy king.

The most popular reply to 15 ♖ad1 is **15...♖c8** Upon this idea ♘f6-d5 has not been completely taken off the agenda but merely postponed. In several variations (for example, with a black knight on d5 and a white one on e4) the position of the rook on c8 gives Black the possibility of winning a pawn by ♘c6-b4!

16 ♗b3 Of the remaining continuations we see the following:

16 h4!? ♘d5 17 ♘g5 ♗f6 18 ♘xd5 ed (mistaken is 18...♕xd5 19 ♗b3 ♕xd4 in view of 20 ♘xf7!) 19 ♘f3 ♕d7 20 b4 ♖xe1+ 21 ♖xe1 ♖e8 with chances of equalising;

16 ♗f4!? Of course it is hard to believe that White voluntarily played the bishop from h6 to f4. But, firstly, we have already carried out a sufficient examination of positions with the development of the bishop on g5 and h6, and quite a few – with the bishop on f4. And secondly, to be concrete, in this position flow a great number of variations from the Panov Attack and other openings. In order not to make unsubstantiated statements, we take a well-known variation of the Nimzo-Indian defence (A54): 1 d4 ♘f6 2 c4 e6 3 ♘c3 ♗b4 4 e3 0-0 5 ♗d3 d5 6 ♘f3 c5 7 0-0 dc 8 ♗xc4 cd 9 ed b6 10 ♖e1 ♗b7 11 ♗d3 ♘c6 12 a3 ♗e7 13 ♗c2 ♖e8 14 ♕d3 g6 15 ♗f4 ♖c8 16 ♖ad1 – and we have the sought-for position.

We continue the game: 16...♘a5 17 ♘e5 ♘d5 18 ♗d2 ♘xc3 19 ♗xc3 ♗f6 (apparently more accurate than 19...♗d5!? with the aim of exchanging the active white knight by 20...♘c4; the game Mecking – Polugaevsky, Lucerne 1977, ended in a draw by repetiton of moves: 20 ♗a4 ♖f8 21 ♘d7 ♖e8) 20 ♕g3 ♗d5 21 ♕f4 (with the threat of 22 ♗a4) 21...♖f8 22 h4!?

In the game Podgaets – Buturnin (Donetsk 1976) Black decided not to accept the pawn sacrifice: 22...♘c4?! After 23 ♗e4! (it is very important to remove the black bishop from the blockading square d5) 23...♗xe4 24 ♕xe4 ♘d6 25 ♕f3 ♘f5 26 d5! White continued the attack with material equality.

The more principled 22...♗xh4!? 23 ♖d3 (it is necessary for the rook to transfer to the king's flank) 23...♗g5 24 ♕h2 ♘c4 Beginning the second wave of the attack: 25 f4! ♘xb2! (the only defence; losing is 25...♗f6 in view of 26 ♖h3 h5 27 ♖xh5! ♘xa3 28 ♘xg6! fg 29 ♗xg6 ♕d7 30 ♕g3) 26 ♖h3 ♗f6 27 ♖e2 ♘c4 28 ♖xh7! (burning his bridges, White ceases to pay any attention at all to material) 28...♘xe5 29 de ♖xc3

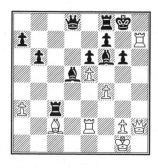

30 ♕h6! Not hurrying to win back the piece, otherwise the attack will remain just a memory. However, objectively Black has sufficient resources to beat off this furious onslaught. There could follow 30...♖g3! (only not 30...♗c6? because of 31 ♗xg6!) 31 ♔h2!? (surrounding the enemy rook) 31...♖g4 32 g3 ♗c4 33 ♖g2! ♗f1 34 ♖f2 ♕d4 (this move forces a

draw) 35 ♖xf1 ♕c3 36 ♖g1 ♕xc2+ 37 ♖g2 ♕f5 38 ef ♕xf6 39 ♖d2 ♕c3 40 ♖d3! ♕f6 41 ♔h3 ♖g5! 42 fg ♕f1+ 43 ♔g4 f5+ 44 gf ♕f5+ 45 ♔h4 ♕xf6+ with perpetual check.

16...♘a5 17 ♗a2 ♘d5 18 ♘e4!? The alternative, and quite a serious one, is 18 ♘e5!? The queen is transferred to the king's flank; Black is forced to be on the alert, since a sacrifice on f7 is in the air.

But it is not all so gloomy. In the game Grigorian – Machulsky (Chelyabinsk 1975) Black found the best defence: 18...♗f8 19 ♕h3 ♘xc3! 20 bc ♗d5! After 21 ♗xd5 Machulsky took on d5 with the pawn; we would prefer 21...♕xd5!? 22 ♗xf8 ♖xf8 23 ♖d3 ♔g7 24 ♕h4 ♘c4 25 ♖h3 h5 26 g4 ♕d8! with approximately equal chances.

18...♘f6 19 ♘eg5 Maintaining the tension around the enemy king. Tempting but weak is 19 ♘xf6+ ♗xf6 20 b4 ♘c6 21 d5 ed 22 ♖xe8+ ♕xe8 23 ♗xd5 ♖d8 24 ♕b3 in view of 24...♖d7! (threatening 25...♘d4!) 25 ♗e3 ♘d8! with equality.

19...♗d5

20 ♘xf7!? An interesting but by no means winning combination. The other thing is that White, with his previous moves, has driven himself into a corner and is now simply forced to sacrifice a knight! Moving the bishop to b1 is not possible – after 20...♘g4 the bishop h6 is lost; nor is there any hint of advantage upon 20 ♗xd5 ♘xd5 21 ♖c1 ♖xc1 22 ♖xc1 ♘b7 23 ♕e2 ♘d6 24 ♘xe6!? (this tactical operation is also forced) 24...♗f6! 25 ♘xd8 ♖xe2 26 ♘c6 ♖xb2 27 ♘xa7 ♗g7 28 ♗xg7 ♔xg7. The activity of the pieces compensates for the small material deficit.

20...♗xf7 21 ♘e5+ ♔g8 22 ♘xg6! (reckoning on 22...♗xa2? 23 ♕g3 ♘h5 24 ♘xe7+ ♔f7 25 ♕f3+) **22...♗d6!** This is how the game Lekhtivara – Gheorghiu (Lenk 1992) went. White, not able to continue to trade blows at a high level, played 23 ♗b1?! and after 23...♖c7! conceded.

He should go in for **23 ♘e5!?** If now 23...♖c7, then 24 ♕g3+ ♔h8 25 ♗g5! ♗xa2 26 ♕h4 with very chance of increasing the attack.

The duel, with an absolutely unpredictable result, proceeded **23...♕c7! 24 ♗b1!** (weaker is 24 ♕g3+ ♔h8 25 ♖c1 ♕e7) **24...♘c6! 25 ♕g3+ ♔h8 26 ♕h4 ♗xe5 27 de ♘g8 28 ♗g5**

The last variation is a model for all systems with 12...♗b7. The resources of attack and defence balance each other out; it is not so much lengthy analysis, the game continues to be balanced in an atmosphere of unstable equilibrium.

y) 12...♗a6!? The idea of this move provokes no doubt at all –

Black prevents the development of the queen to d3.

Let's look at the consequences of the following possibilities: 13 ♘e4, 13 ♕d2, 13 ♗f4, 13 b4 and 13 ♗g5. The last in this series of moves is the main line.

13 ♘e4?! ♖c8 14 ♘eg5 ♕d5 15 ♗f4 h6 16 ♘e4 ♖fd8 17 ♘c3 ♕d7 18 ♗a4 ♕b7 19 ♕d2 ♗f8! 20 ♖ad1 ♗c4 21 ♗e5 ♘xe5 22 ♘xe5 b5 23 ♘xc4 bc 24 ♕e2 ♕b6 (Kolin – Dettling, Aviles 2000). It is possible to draw some conclusions; they are not comforting for White. The loss of a mass of tempi and the fact that the d4 pawn is hanging (and will probably soon be lost) means Black has a great advantage; he played the rest of the game strongly and won.

Why do we show this game? To demonstrate how dangerous planless play by White can be in such positions. In this sense it is easier for Black: he should not allow the break d4-d5, keep his king secure and, indeed, steadily exchange pieces (of course, this is too primitive a scheme, but all the same...). White should be a master of attack, who knows the value of each of his moves. To attack in positions with an isolani – is a lofty art!

13 ♕d2!? An original plan – White intends to transfer the queen to the king's flank, leaving the bishop c1 'in store'.

From Black is required a little bit of prophylaxis: 13...♕d6! (the f4 square is taken under control, while on 14 ♕g5 it is possible to simply gobble up the centre pawns) 14 ♖d1 (insisting on ♕d2-g5) 14...h6! (Black is alert) 15 ♕e1 ♖ac8 16 ♘e4 ♘xc4 17 ♕xe4 f5 18 ♕e1 ♗c4! (the bishop on d5 is not enough to make Black completely happy) 19 ♘e5 ♘xe5 20 de ♕c6. Nothing remains of White's idea.

13 ♗f4 (as distinct from 13 ♗g5, 'loading' Black's king's flank, this move pursues only the aim of a free development) 13...♖c8 14 ♖c1 ♗c4 15 ♗g3!? (Timman – Karpov, Wijk aan Zee 1998) 15...b5! (15...♘d5 16 ♘e4! – this is why earlier White removed the bishop from attack) 16 b3 (it would only be worse after 16 a4?! b4 17 ♘e4 ♘xe4 18 ♗xe4 ♗d5) 16...♗d5 17 ♘xd5 (the pawn is inedible: 17 ♘xb5? a6 18 ♘c3 ♗xf3 19 ♕xf3 ♘xd4) 17...♘xd5 18 ♕d3 g6 19 b4 ♕b6 20 ♗b3 ♖fd8 and Black has no difficulties.

13 b4!? We have probably not come across this plan before in the pages of our book.

In the encounters looked at above White played b2-b4 simply in order to occupy space on the queen's flank (mainly to prop up the outpost on c5). Here the picture is principally different: the c5 square is covered, but White plays 13 b4 to win a piece on the following move!

Possibly because of the fear of falling victim to a pawn fork b4-b5, Black rejected 12...♗a6 in favour of the more modest (but also more safe) 12...♗b7. In fact he does not need to be afraid of 13 b4; there is a reliable way of rendering all threats harmless.

The most natural move 13...♗c4 is just not reliable. After 14 b5 ♘a5 15 ♘e5 ♖c8 16 ♖e3 clouds begin to gather over the black king.

16...♗d6, 16...a6, 16...g6 and 16...♖c7 are all seen. Let's look at these moves in detail.

Bad is 16...♗d6?! 17 ♖h3 all by itself and in combination with 17...♗xe5? (better really is 17...g6, though after 18 ♗h6 ♖e8 19 ♕f3 and White has the initiative) which is linked to a complete miscalculation: 18 de ♕xd1+ 19 ♘xd1 ♗xb5 20 ♘c3 and to avoid the deadly check on h7, Black has to give up the exchange on c3 (Dizdar – Laketic, Kladovo 1990).

Totally unconvincing is 16...a6?! Instead of slowing down the attack on his own king, Black starts to dig in on the opposite side of the board. In addition he loses a pawn: 17 ♖h3 g6 18 ba ♗xa6 19 ♗h6 ♖e8 20 ♗a4 b5 21 ♘xb5 ♕b6 22 ♖b1 ♖ed8 23 ♗g5 ♘c4 (Oral – Zenkluisen, Berne 1998). Of course the outcome of the struggle is still not clear right to the end – the white pieces find themselves in a hanging state.

In connection with this, worth considering is 24 ♘g4!? ♘xg4 (or 24...♘d5 25 ♗xe7 ♘xe7 26 ♕c1! with a very strong attack) 25 ♗xe7 ♗xb5 26 ♗xd8 ♗xa4 27 ♗xb6 ♗xd1 28 ♗c5! White has eaten quite a bit, and will soon eat even more: 28...♗e2 29 ♖e1; 28...♗a4 29 ♖b4; 28...♗c2 29 ♖c1.

Dangerous is 16...g6 when, after 17 ♖h3 ♗d5 (Buturin – Savon, Lvov 1981), the recommendation of Savon 18 ♗h6 ♖e8 19 ♕d2 followed by 20 ♕f4 leads to an advantage for White.

Viswanathan Anand thought up the move 16...♖c7, including the rook in the defence of the f7 square. Though the experiment (in the game Kaidanov – Anand, Moscow 1987) ended in failure, the plan of the Indian grandmaster cannot be underestimated:

17 ♖g3 ♖e8 18 ♗h6 ♗f8 19 ♗g5 ♗e7 20 ♗xf6?! (stronger is 20 ♕f3!, and the d4 pawn is untouchable: 20...♕xd4? 21 ♗xf6 ♗xf6 22 ♕xf6) 20...♗xf6 21 ♗xh7+ ♔xh7 22 ♕h5+ ♔g8 23 ♘e4 ♗d5 24 ♖h3

There is no doubt that White undertook the exchange on the 17th move (and the sacrifice of the piece that followed) because he miscalculated the variations before the diagram position and concluded that he would win. As indeed he did. Black played 24...♔f8? and after 25 ♕xf7+!! resigned in view of 25...♖xf7 26 ♘g6+ ♔g8 27 ♖h8 mate.

Anand blundered into a mate in three moves. These things happen. But objectively the piece sacrifice did not promise White more than a draw. Instead of 24...♔f8? he should play 24...g6!, and after 25 ♘xg6 fg 26 ♕xg6+ ♗g7 27 ♘g5 ♔f8 White should repeat moves: 28 ♘h7+ etc. It is necessary to do this immediately; if he leaves it a move later the chance will have already gone. For example, 28 ♖h4?! ♕d6!, and it is too late to

play 29 ♘h7+ in view of 29...♔e7 30 ♕xg7+ ♔d8 31 ♕g5+ ♔c8 32 ♘f6 ♖d8.

And so the natural move 13...♗c4?! does not justify the trust placed upon it. So reject it. It's no great loss because all problems are solved by 13...♖c8!

If White stubbornly continues 14 b5?! then all Black's pieces will, in order, take up their best positions: 14...♘a5! 15 ♕d3 ♗b7 16 ♘e5 ♕c7 17 ♖e3 g6 18 ♕d1 ♘d5 19 ♘xd5 ♗xd5 etc. (Pukhlya – Ostenstad, Slupsk 1987).

In order to renew the threat of b4-b5, he has to defend the knight c3: 14 ♗b2. In the game Anand – Adams (London 1987) occurred a blunder of yet another great player, only the this time it was not the Indian who suffered: 14...♘d5? 15 b5 ♘xc3 16 ♕d3! (this intermediate move was probably overlooked by Michael Adams) 16...g6 17 ♗xc3 ♕c7 18 ba ♘a5 19 ♗xa5 Black resigned.

Instead of 14...♘d5? the move 14...♗c4! suggests itself. The difference with the branch 13...♗c4?! is obvious: there White's dark-squared bishop was the main spearhead of the attack, whereas here it vegetates on the forgotten (though long) diagonal a1-h8. It is enough to deny this bishop play (and Black does this by firmly maintaining the blockade of the d5 square), and then he can boldly count not only on equalisation but also on taking over the initiative:

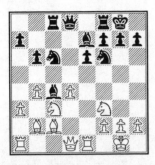

15 ♕d2 ♘d5! 16 ♘e4 a5 17 ba ♘xa5 18 ♕d1 ♗a6 (Mortensen – Ostenstad, Torshaven 1987);

15 b5 ♘a5 16 ♘e5 ♘d5! 17 ♘xd5 ♗xd5, and the piece sacrifice made in the game Lanka – Ostenstad (Trnava 1989) 18 ♗xh7+? ♔xh7 19 ♕h5+ ♔g8 20 ♖e3 was incorrect because of 20...♗h4! 21 f4 (21 ♖h3 ♕g5!) 21...♖c2.

13 ♗g5!? We hope that our review of the previous variations will convince you, to one or other extent, that they are harmless for Black. Quite another matter is the thrust of the bishop to g5. If White is allowed to place his pieces unhindered, according to the scheme: ♕d2, ♖ad1, ♕f4, then the further attack will develop all by itself.

Black should hurry with counterplay!

13...♖c8 14 ♕d2!? Far weaker is 14 ♖c1 ♘d5. Only by 15 h4!? could Black be given some trouble, and

only then if he himself helps the opponent. As, for example, in the game Borge – Danielsen (Denmark 1998): 15...♘xc3?! (usually, if Black reinforces the opponent's pawn centre, then in return he will at least manage to gobble up a3; here however there can be no question of this) 16 bc h6 17 ♗xe7 ♘xe7 (looking very dangerous is 17...♕xe7!? 18 ♗b1 ♖fd8 19 ♕c2 ♕f6 20 ♕h7+ ♔f8, but there is apparently no mate) 18 ♗b1. In this position worth considering is 18...♘f5!? (when so much damage has already been done, he must grab any chance he can) 19 ♗xf5 ef 20 ♕c2 ♗b7 or 19 d5 ♘xh4 20 ♘xh4 ♕xh4 21 ♕c2 g6 22 de ♗c4! with chances of stubborn resistance.

The problem is resolved by the very simple 15...♗c4! 16 ♗xe7 (not dangerous is 16 ♘d2?! ♗xg5 17 hg ♘xd4 18 ♗xh7+ ♔xh7 19 ♘xc4 ♘f4) 16...♕xe7 17 ♘d2 ♘xc3 18 bc ♘a5 19 ♕h5 g6 20 ♕g4 ♗d5! with an excellent position.

The last variation shows that 14 ♖c1 is shown to be a loss of time after 14...♘d5! But also upon 14 ♕d2, more in keeping with the spirit of the position, Black has nothing to fear.

14...♘d5! Simple and reliable. But you will always find creative chessplayers who want to leave the beaten track. For example, instead of the knight, it is possible to try to establish the bishop on d5:

14...♗c4?! 15 ♕f4 ♗d5. After 16 ♕h4 g6 White, in the game Sturua – Kutirov (Erevan 1996), placed his pieces ideally – 17 ♘xd5 ♘xd5 18 ♖ad1 ♕d6 19 ♗b3 – and soon gained victory.

Instead of 16...g6 worth considering is 16...h6!?, rejected as defective by many commentators. Sturua considered that White would gain the advantage by 17 ♘xd5 ♕xd5 18 ♗e3 but he did not notice 18...♘b4! There and then the assessment of the position is changed.

Certainly, on 16...h6 we should first look at 17 ♗xh6!?, but even here the concrete variations are pleasant for Black: 17...♗xf3! (an important intermediate move) 18 ♗xg7 (mistaken is 18 gf? because of 18...♘xd4 19 ♔h1 ♘xc2 20 ♗xg7 ♘h7!) 18...♘h5! 19 ♕h3 ♔xg7 20 ♕xf3 ♘xd4 21 ♕xh5 ♘xc2 22 ♖ad1 (or 22 ♖e4!? ♖c5! 23 ♖g4+ ♗g5 24 ♖d1 ♖h8!) 22...♘xe1 and to avoid worse White must force a draw by perpetual check.

14...♗c4?! cannot be recommended but it is useful to investigate such a variation – this helps us to feel acutely how great are the defensive resources in this kind of position.

Also dubious is 14...♘a5?! 15 ♖ad1 ♘c4. After 16 ♕c1 White is all ready for the break d4-d5, for example, 16...♗b7 17 d5! ♗xd5 18 ♘xd5 ed 19 ♘d4 with a strong initiative.

In the game Novik – Vasyukov (St.Petersburg 1991) Black played more sharply: 16...♕c7 17 d5! ♘xb2!?

There followed 18 d6! ♕xc3 19 de ♘xd1. White hastens to unload this extraordinarily tense situation by taking on f8 and d1. The game ended in a draw. Later Maxim Novik pointed out the possibility 20 ♗xf6! ♕xc2 21 ♕g5! After 21...♕g6 22 ef♕+ ♖xf8 23 ♕xg6 hg 24 ♗e7 Black was forced to part with the exchange since in the event of 24...♖e8? 25 ♖xd1 ♖xe7 26 ♖d8+ ♔h7 27 ♘g5+ ♔h6 28 h4 ♔h5 White weaves a mating net with his limited forces: 29 f3! ♔xh4 30 ♘e4!

15 ♘xd5 Since White cannot avoid exchanges, he should endeavour to produce a more favourable situation for himself.

The encounter Voitsekhovsky – Galkin (St.Petersburg 1998) flowed in dynamic vein: 15 ♖ad1 ♗xg5 16 ♘xg5 h6 17 ♘f3 ♘xc3 (17...♗c4!? does not look bad) 18 bc ♕d6 19 ♕e3 ♘e7 20 ♕e4 g6 21 ♕h4 ♔g7.

Strategically the position is hopeless for White in view of the numerous weaknesses on the queen's flank. Voitsekhovsky exploited his one chance of sharpening the struggle: 22 d5!? ♘xd5 23 ♕d4+. Also here Black falters, making it three inaccurate moves in a row – 23...♔h7 24 ♘e5 ♕c7 25 ♕g4 ♘f6 After 26 ♗xg6+! fg 27 ♕xg6+ ♔h8 28 ♖d7! and by now White could not be stopped.

He needs to defend against the generally transparent threats in another way: 23...♔g8! 24 ♘e5 ♕xa3, and then:

25 ♗xg6 fg 26 ♕g4 ♖f6 27 ♘d7 ♕xc3 28 ♘xf6+ ♕xf6 29 ♖xe6 h5! 30 ♕e4 ♘c3;

25 ♕g4 ♘f6 26 ♕h4 ♕xc3 27 ♕xf6 ♕xc2 28 ♘d7 ♗b7;

25 c4 ♕c3 26 ♗xg6 ♕xd4 27 ♖xd4 fg 28 cd ed. Everywhere the assessment of the position fluctuates from 'good' to 'winning' for Black.

15...♕xd5 16 h4!? Makarichev recommends here 16 ♗e4 ♕d8 17 ♕f4!? But Black's task against this does not change – first of all he needs to induce exchanges of the opponent's pieces: 17...♕d6! 18 ♖ac1 (or 18 ♕h4 h6 19 ♗xe7 ♘xe7) 18...♕xf4 19 ♗xf4 ♘a5.

16...♗xg5 17 hg

This position first arose in the game Novikov – Podgaets (Koszalin 1998). Black did not cope with the problem: 17...♘e7?! 18 ♗e4 ♕d6 19 ♘e5 ♘g6 20 ♗xg6 hg, allowing White to conclude the game beautifully: 21 ♕f4 ♖c2 22 ♖e3 ♖d2 23 ♘xg6! ♕xf4 24 ♘e7+! with mate.

The truth was staring him in the face: **17...♘xd4! 18 ♘xd4 e5** Black wins back the piece, achieving an equal or even slightly better game: **19 ♗f5** (19 ♗b3 ♕xd4 20 ♕xd4 ed 21 ♖e7 ♗c4) **19...♖cd8 20 ♗xh7+ ♔xh7 21 ♕c2+** (Grinfeld – Dettling, Tel Aviv 2001) **21...g6 22 ♘f3 ♗d3 23 ♕c7 e4 24 ♘e5 ♖c8 25 ♕e7 ♖ce8 26 ♘d7! ♖xe7 27 ♘f6+ ♔g7 28 ♘xd5 ♖e5** etc.

The variation 10...♘f6 recommends itself as a solid and reliable line. Because it is not possible to play an immediate 10...b6? in view of 11 ♘xd5 ♕xd5 12 ♗e4!, Black first takes his knight out of the firing line and then develops his queen's flank. We see how this works from the variation 10...♘f6 11 a3 b6 12 ♗c2 where Black's light-squared bishop not only can be developed on b7, but also on a6, delaying the activation of the white pieces. After that the knight will return to d5 and by means of exchanges Black will urge on the position to equality.

Another popular plan is ♗e7-f6 followed by ♘c6-e7. Upon this the light-squared bishop is introduced on the long diagonal via the route d7-c6.

c8) **10...♗f6 11 ♗e4** The idea of sacrificing a pawn – 11 ♘e4!? ♗xd4 12 ♘xd4 ♘xd4 – has arisen quite recently and a general opinion about the correctness of this plan has still not been formed. Up to now Black has mostly succeeded in extinguishing the opponent's initiative, for example: 13 ♕h5 f5 14 ♗g5 ♕e8 15 ♕xe8 ♖xe8 16 ♘d6 ♖f8 (Sulskis – H.Olafsson, Istanbul 2003), and here it is worth giving the preference to 17 ♖ad1!? h6 18 ♗c4 ♘f3+ 19 gf hg 20 ♗xd5 with an unclear endgame.

With the move 11 ♗e4 White tries to remove the blockade on the d5 square. A critical position is reached.

There are two main replies: 11...♕d6 and 11...♘ce7, but the strongest is the last one. Apart from these, we should mention separately 11...h6!? – Black, before bringing the knight to e7, avoids the possible 12 ♗g5 or 12 ♘g5. These are played

very rarely (apparently, in such a tense situation one does not spend time on prophylaxis), but there is no refutation of 11...h6. This is how events could swing about:

12 ♗b1!? (since the early advance of the h-pawn excludes the possibility of covering the b1-h7 diagonal with the move g7-g6, White begins to set up a diagonal battery) 12...♘de7!? 13 ♕d3 ♘g6! (the only but sufficient defence) 14 ♗e3 b6 15 ♕d2 ♗b7 16 ♗e4 ♘a5 17 ♖ac1 ♘c4 18 ♕d3 ♗xe4 19 ♘xe4 (Vaganian – Stangl, Germany 2000) 19...♘xe3 20 ♕xe3 ♘h4 and the game is even.

c81) **11...♕d6** Frankly speaking, no way does this move inspire us with positive emotions. Firstly, the position of the queen on d6 is unstable, which can be underlined by a direct attack – whether from the b5 or e4 square (after the bishop moves away). Secondly, Black loses control over the g5 square. Finally, the main defect of 11...♕d6 is the lack of full value counterplay. In this variation Black does not undertake anything himself – he just repulses the various threats of his opponent.

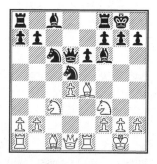

White's replies can be divided into two groups. The first – the obvious continuations 12 ♘b5, 12 ♘g5 and

12 ♗g5, which are also the most popular. In the second group are included moves that are geared towards direct attack – 12 h4, 12 ♕d3 and 12 ♗c2. Though they have been studied less, it is possible that it is precisely these moves that are the way to give Black the most trouble.

x) **12 ♘b5 ♕b8?!** Better to acknowledge his mistake and return to 12...♕d8! Nothing terrible has happened; the knight on b5 is virtually unemployed and will even be forced to retreat.

For a long time the move 12...♕b8?! was considered quite a problem. For example, 13 g3 ♗d7 14 ♘c3 ♘ce7 15 ♗xd5 ♘xd5 16 ♘xd5 ed 17 ♗g5 ♗xg5 18 ♘xg5 ♕d8 (Belyavsky – Portisch, Reggio Emilia 1986). However in an analysis M.Podgaets succeeded in finding a forced way to an advantage for White. All the same the remoteness of the queen from the area of main hostilities cannot but tell!

13 ♘g5! g6 (even worse is 13...h6?! 14 ♘h7! ♖d8 15 ♕g4 e5 16 ♕g3!) **14 ♕f3 ♖d8!?** No help is 14...♘ce7 in view of 15 ♗xd5 ♘xd5 16 ♘c3! ♗xg5 17 ♗xg5 ♕d6 18 ♘e4 ♕b6 19 ♘f6+.

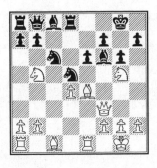

Black defends himself with all his might. If now 15 ♗xd5 ♖xd5 16 ♕xf6, then after 16...♗f5 the trap is shut. True, even without the queen White continues to hold the initiative – 17 ♘e4! ♖xf6 18 ♘xf6+ ♔g7 19 ♘e8+ ♔h8 20 ♘bd6 ♗d7 21 ♘xf7+ ♔g8 22 ♘h6+ ♔f8 23 ♘f6 ♕d6 24 ♘hg4, but it is not fully clear. Instead of 16 ♕xf6 we can look at 16 ♗f4? ♕xf4! 17 ♕xf4 ♗xg5 and 16 ♘d6 ♕xd6 17 ♕xf6 ♕e7, but also this does not lead to its objective.

A clear decision lies in **15 h4! ♘ce7 16 h5! h6 17 ♗xd5 ♘xd5 18 ♘e4** The heavy pieces on b8 and a8 cannot help his king. The outcome of the struggle is predetermined.

y) **12 ♘g5** With the queen on d6 this thrust is not so dangerous:

12...♗xg5?! (excessive caution) 13 ♗xg5 ♗d7 (Rogers – L.-B. Hansen, Malmo 1993) 14 ♕d3 f5 (14...h6!?) 15 ♗xd5 ed 16 ♘b5! ♕g6 (16...♕b8?! 17 ♗e7!) 17 ♗f4 with pressure on the dark squares (analysis by L.-B. Hansen);

12...g6! (12...h6!? 13 ♘h7 ♖d8 has still not been seriously tested) 13 ♘xh7 ♔xh7 14 ♘xd5 ed 15 ♕h5+ ♔g8 16 ♗xg6 fg 17 ♕xg6+ and as shown by the game Kaidanov – Efimov (USSR 1980) it is best for White to be satisfied with perpetual check.

z) **12 ♗g5 ♗xg5** In making this move, it is necessary to be aware of the possible following intermediate bishop sacrifice. In the present position this blow does not work:

13 ♗xh7+ ♚xh7 14 ♘xg5+ ♚g8 15 ♕h5 ♘f6 16 ♕h4 ♖d8 17 ♖ad1 (alas, in reply to 17 ♘ce4 Black simply takes with the queen on d4) 17...♘xd4 18 ♘ce4 (or 18 ♘b5 ♘xb5! 19 ♖xd6 ♘xd6 20 ♖d1 ♖d7) 18...♘xe4 19 ♕xe4 ♚f8 20 ♘h7+ (20 ♕h7 ♕f4) 20...♚e7 with a win.

After **13 ♘xg5 ♘f6 14 d5 ed 15 ♘xd5 ♘xe4 16 ♘xe4** arises a critical position. Though it is clear that Black has virtually achieved equality, the following 2-3 moves from his side must be absolutely accurate – the strength of the centralised white knight in the centre cannot be underestimated.

Best is to transfer immediately to the endgame: 16...♕h6! 17 ♕c1 ♕xc1 18 ♖axc1 ♖d8! 19 ♘d6 (or 19 ♖cd1 ♚f8 20 f3 ♗f5, Kosten – Adams, London 1989) 19...♗e6 20 ♘c7 ♖ab8 21 ♘xe6 ♖xd6 (Kuijf – Dlugy, Amsterdam 1987). In both of the cited games peace was concluded without delay.

Less accurate is **16...♕d8** White replies **17 ♕h5!** Clouds thicken over the black king, but there is still a defence. This is how the game Kargin – Meduna (Chemnitz 1998) continued: 17...f5! 18 ♘ec3 ♗d7

19 ♖ad1 ♖f7! After this the queen transferred to f8, guarding the important d6 square against the enemy knight d6. Though it is more pleasant for White, there is nothing real.

But the second inaccurate move in a row – **17...♗e6?** places Black on the verge of defeat.

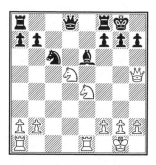

18 ♘df6+! After **18...gf** nothing is offered by 19 ♕h6?! ♚h8 20 ♘xf6 ♗f5 21 ♖ad1 ♘d4! 22 ♘h5 ♖g8 23 ♕e3 ♖e8, but far stronger is an immediate **19 ♖ad1!** In the case of 19...♘d4!? White will perhaps also not deliver mate but he will have an enormous positional advantage: 20 ♕h4 ♚g7 21 ♘g3 ♕a5 22 ♘h5+ ♚g6 23 ♘f4+ ♚g7 24 ♖e3 ♖fd8 25 ♖xd4! ♕f5 (not possible is 25...♖xd4? 26 ♘xe6+ fe 27 ♖g3+) 26 ♘h5+ ♚h8 27 h3!

In the game Guirado – Illescas (Salou 1987) Black chose **19...♕a5?!** and obtained after all a mate in a long and virtually forced variation: 20 ♘xf6+ ♚g7 21 ♖xe6! fe 22 ♖d7+ ♚xf6 23 ♕h6+ ♚e5 24 ♕g5+ ♖f5 25 ♕g3+! ♖f4 26 ♕e3+ ♚f5 27 ♖f7+ ♚g6 28 ♕xe6+ ♚g5 29 ♖g7+ ♚h5 30 ♖xh7+ ♚g5 31 ♖g7+ ♚h5 32 ♕g6+. 'Virtually' – because far more tenacious was 23...♔f5!, and if 24 g4+, then now 24...♔e5 25♕g5+ ♖f5 (there is no check on g3!) 26 gf ♕e1+ with a draw.

Therefore we give a more reliable way of winning: **20 ♕h6 ♔h8** (20...♕f5 21 ♖d3 ♔h8 22 ♖g3 ♖g8 23 ♘d6!) **21 ♕xf6+ ♔g8 22 ♖e3 ♗f5 23 b4 ♖ad8** (23...♕e5 24 ♕g5+ ♔h8 25 ♘d6!) **24 ♖de1 ♘xb4** (24...♕e5 25 ♕g5+ ♕g7 26 ♕xf5) **25 ♕g5+ ♔h8 26 ♘f6 ♘d3 27 ♘h5 ♕c3**

28 ♖e5! Concluding the struggle with a typical combination on the theme of obstruction.

A beautiful attack, but it became possible only as a result of Black's improvement on the 16th-17th moves. The same thing can be said about the moves 12 ♘b5, 12 ♘g5 and 12 ♗g5 as a whole: many beautiful variations, but only thanks to inaccurate play by the opponent.

q) **12 h4!?** An extremely unpleasant plan for Black! Upon the exchange of the dark-squared bishops White intends to take on g5 with the pawn, after which the h-file is opened. In the game Schultz – Meduna (Cologne 1988) Black played with complete unconcern – 12...♗d7 13 ♗g5! ♗xg5 14 hg! ♘f4

15 g3 ♘g6, and after 16 ♔g2! ♘ce7 17 ♖h1 ♗c6 18 ♕g1! ended up in a hopeless position.

Also unsatisfactory is **12...♖d8 13 ♗g5 h6? 14 ♗xd5 hg** (14...ed 15 ♘b5!) **15 ♗xc6 g4 16 ♘e5 bc 17 ♕e2 ♗xh4 18 ♘e4 ♕d5 19 ♕xg4 ♗e7 20 ♕h5** followed by ♖e1-e3-h3 (Wells – Ryan, Dublin 1993. No one has yet shown distinctly how Black should defend against 12 h4!? ...

r) Complicated problems are set by **12 ♕d3!?**:

12...h6 13 ♘b5 ♕d8 14 a3 b6 15 ♘c3 ♘de7 16 ♗f4 ♗b7 17 ♖ad1 ♖c8 18 ♕b5 ♘a5 19 ♗xb7 ♘xb7 (Wahls – Meduna, Germany 1989) 20 ♘e5!? or

12...g6 13 ♗h6 ♖d8 14 ♖ad1 ♗d7 15 ♕d2 ♗e8 16 ♗xd5 ed 17 ♗f4 ♕f8 18 ♗g5 (Belkhodja – Dautov, Nimes 1991). In these games we clearly see the defect of the move 11...♕d6 – a complete lack of active ideas. Black only reacts to threats from the opponent and is not even thinking about a counterattack himself.

w) **12 ♗c2!?** A move with ideas – White plans first to threaten mate by 13 ♕d3 and then, according to the situation, to play either ♘g5, ♗g5 or h4. Black has often found success in this way

12...♘ce7 13 ♕d3 ♘g6 14 ♘e4 ♕b6 15 ♘xf6+ ♗xf6 16 ♗g5 ♘d5 17 ♗b3 ♗d7 18 ♘e5 ♗b5 19 ♕g3 (achieving an ideal arrangement of pieces) 19...♕xd4?! 20 ♖ad1 ♕b4? 21 ♘xg6 hg 22 ♗xd5 ed 23 ♗e7, winning the exchange (Cabrilo – Savon, Belgrade 1988);

12...♘xc3?! (above, we have repeatedly made clear the fatal consequences of this move) 13 bc g6 (no better is 13...♕d5 14 ♕d3 g6 15 ♗f4 b6 16 ♘d2 ♗b7 17 ♘e4 ♗g7 18 ♕g3 ♘e7 19 ♘d6, Ehlvest – Stohl, Groningen 1982) 14 ♘g5!? ♗g7 (Hebden – Hoffman, Vrnjacka Banja 1989) 15 ♕f3!? with strong pressure.

12...♕b4!? A rare case in the 11...♕d6 system – Black attacks something! Besides this, the queen gets the chance to transfer to a more acceptable position – the b6 square.

13 ♕d3 g6 14 ♗h6 ♖d8 15 ♗b3!? In the game Kosten – Barbero (Saint Affrique 1994) Black declined to accept the pawn sacrifice and moved the bishop away to g7. And it is possible he was right: in the variation **15...♘xd4?! 16 ♘e4!** (the tempting 16 ♗xd5 offers nothing in view of 16...♘xf3+ 17 ♕xf3 ♗xc3 18 bc ♕h4!) **16...♗h8 17 ♘xd4 ♕xd4 18 ♕f3 ♕xb2 19 ♖ad1 ♗d7 20 ♖d2 ♕e5 21 ♗xd5 ed 22 ♖xd5!** Black does not survive the pin along the d-file: **22...♕e6 23 ♖ed1 ♖ac8 24 h4** etc.

c82) **11...♘ce7** There can only be one defect of this move: in reinforcing d5, Black loses control of the e5 square.

This is why 11...♘de7?! is rarely employed.

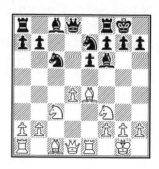

A first glance – an ideal solution: now both central squares – d5 and e5 – are under Black's control. But it is too early to rejoice: by closing in the diagonal view of the queen Black fails to bear in mind 12 ♗g5! On 12...♘f5 follows 13 ♗xf6 ♕xf6 14 d5 ed 15 ♘xd5 ♕h6 (15...♕xb2? 16 ♖b1 ♕xa2 17 ♘c7 ♖b8 18 ♗xc6) 16 ♖c1 with a serious advantage (Neverov – Marcus, Dieren 1998), while 12...♗xg5?! is simply bad in view of the thematic sacrifice 13 ♗xh7+! (surprisingly, in the game Gligoric – Portisch, Madrid 1960, White missed this possibility and after 13 ♘xg5 ♘f5 14 ♗xf5 ♕xg5 15 ♗e4 ♖d8 a draw was agreed) 13...♔xh7 14 ♘xg5+. Neither of the black knights can get to f6 (yet another minus of 11...♘de7?!), therefore he has to go to a clear square with his king: 14...♔g6 15 ♕g4 f5 (15...♕xd4? 16 ♘ge4+ ♔h7 17 ♕h5+ ♔g8 18 ♘g5) 16 ♕g3 ♔f6 17 ♘b5, and then:

17...♘xd4 18 ♕e5+ ♔xg5 19 ♕xg7+;

17...♖h8 18 ♘c7 ♖b8 19 ♘gxe6 ♗xe6 20 ♘xe6 ♕g8 21 d5!;

17...♘d5 (relatively best) 18 ♘d6 g6 19 ♘xc8 f4 20 ♕h4 ♖h8 21 ♘e4+ ♔g7 22 ♕xd8 ♖xd8 23 ♘cd6 with an endgame advantage.

The position after 11...♘ce7 successfully passed the test for durability in the final of the XXXVI USSR championship (Alma Ata 1968) in three games of M.Podgaets: against Tseshkovsky, Vasyukov and Liberzon. Certainly, over the lapse of years the theory of the variation has advanced, but many old assessments remain unshakeable.

Let's look at possible moves for White: 12 h4, 12 ♕b3, 12 ♕c2, 12 ♕d3 and 12 ♘e5. The last two on this list are the strongest, the others are roughly equal in strength to one another.

x) **12 h4** A move which vegetated in the back yard of theory until the world championship match Anand – Karpov (Lausanne 1998).

12...♘f5!? The most concrete continuation. Also played is 12...♗d7, allowing White to start an attack by 13 ♕d3 h6 (if 13...g6, then 14 ♗h6 ♗g7 15 ♗xg7 ♔xg7 16 ♗xd5 ♘xd5 17 ♘xd5 ed 18 ♖e5 with a stable 'plus', Obodchuk – Acs, Budapest 1994) 14 ♘g5!? g6 15 ♘f3

♗g7 16 h5 g5 17 ♘xg5! hg 18 ♗xg5 (Dzhandzhava – Kalegin, Batumi 1991).

13 ♕d3 Anand is absolutely right to reject the tempting 13 ♗xf5 ef 14 ♘xd5 ♕xd5 15 ♗g5. As shown by the game Ziborovsky – Kuczynski (Ksiaz 1998), the change in pawn structure after 15...♗e6!? 16 ♗xf6 gf should not trouble Black.

The main thing is that the excellent outpost on d5 for the queen is now secured. Besides this, prospects for the rooks along the g-file are opened up. And, finally, we must not forget that White has a chronic weakness on d4.

There followed 17 ♕d2 ♔g7 18 h5 h6 19 ♘h2 ♖ad8 20 ♖ad1 ♔h7 and Black has the superior chances.

13...♘xc3?! Not the best choice. He should turn his attention to the order of moves in the game Timman – Portisch (Frankfurt 1998): 13...♘b4! 14 ♕c4 a5 15 ♗g5 ♗xg5 16 hg ♘d6 17 ♕b3 ♘xe4 18 ♖xe4, and here Black equalised by 18... b5! 19 a3 ♗b7 20 ab ab! 21 ♖xa8 ♕xa8.

14 bc h6 15 h5 The alternative is 15 ♗xf5 ef 16 ♗a3 ♖e8 17 ♖xe8+ ♕xe8 18 ♖e1 ♕d8 19 ♕b5 (on 19 c4 it is necessary to sacrifice a pawn –

19...b5!? 20 cb ♗e6) 19...♗e6 20 ♕xb7 ♗d5 21 ♕b5 ♖b8 22 ♕e2 ♕a5 23 ♗b4 ♕xa2 24 ♕xa2 ♗xa2 25 ♗e7 a5 26 ♗xf6 gf with an equal endgame.

15...♘d6 16 ♘e5 White does not create real threats even after 16 ♗h7+ ♔h8 17 ♗a3 ♕c7 18 ♘e5 ♖d8 19 ♖ad1 b6.

16...♘xe4 17 ♕xe4 ♗xe5 18 de (or 18 ♕xe5 ♕d5 19 ♕xd5 ed 20 ♗a3 ♖d8 21 ♖e7 b6 22 f3 ♗e6 with a probable draw).

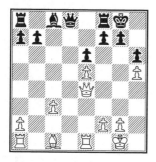

18...f5! Only after this strong move is it possible to say with confidence that Black has equalised the game. In the subsequent struggle, crowned with a fascinating opposite coloured bishops endgame, Black outplayed his opponent and gained victory.

y) **12 ♕b3** Endeavouring to make it difficult for the opponent to develop his queen's flank, White strayed too far from the main objective – attack on the king.

12...♕b6!? Black has a somewhat more difficult task after 12...b6, and then 13 ♗xd5 ♘xd5 14 ♘xd5 ♕xd5 15 ♕xd5 ed 16 ♗g5 ♗xg5 17 ♘xg5 f6 18 ♘f3 with a slightly better endgame (Sveshnikov – Epishin, Biel 1993).

13 ♗xd5 After 13 ♕xb6 ab 14 ♗g5 ♖d8 15 ♖ed1 h6 16 ♗xf6 ♘xf6 17 ♗c2 ♗d7 the game was equal (Chiburdanidze – Ioseliani, Telavi 1988).

13...♘xd5 14 ♘xd5 ed 15 ♗g5 Black cannot fail to obtain compensation for the material in the variation 15 ♕xd5 ♗g4. But after 15 ♕xb6 ab 16 ♗d2 in the game Himmel – Podgacts (Dortmund 1993) a draw was agreed.

15...♗xg5 16 ♕xb6 ab 17 ♘xg5 h6 18 ♘f3 ♗e6

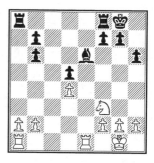

This endgame arose in the game Sveshnikov – Podgaets (Riga 1975) and it is interesting that each of the opponents assessed it in their favour. But it was Black who was closer to the truth: **19 a3 ♖fc8 20 ♖e3 ♖a4 21 h3 b5! 22 ♖b3 b4!** with a serious initiative.

z) **12 ♕c2** Inferior in strength to 12 ♕d3.

12...g6!? Nor did he manage to show any sign at all of an opening advantage after 12...h6!?, for example, 13 ♕e2 ♗d7 14 a3 ♖c8 15 ♗c2 ♘xc3 16 ♕d3 ♘e2+! 17 ♖xe2 ♘g6 (Buturin – Koslov, Sverdlovsk 1987).

On **13 ♗h6** provoking the weakening g7-g6, White could return to the plan with 13 ♕b3. In the game Vasyukov – Podgaets (Alma Ata 1968) Black easily equalised, exploiting the same idea that occurred in the encounter with Sveshnikov: 13...♕b6!? 14 ♗xd5 ♘xd5 15 ♘xd5 ed 16 ♕xb6 ab 17 ♗h6 ♖d8 18 a3 ♗g4 19 ♘e5 ♗e6 20 ♖ad1 ♖dc8 21 ♖d3 ♖a4!

In not a single computer database do we find the game Podgaets – Daskalov (Odessa 1975), but meanwhile it proceeded very instructively. On 13 ♕b3 Black reacted with the move 13...♔g7, and after 14 h4! (so as after the exchange of dark-squared bishops to take the h-pawn) 14...♘c6 15 ♗g5 ♘a5 16 ♕c2 ♗xg5 17 hg arose a critical position.

17...♖h8!? Original play. White opens the h-file, so that after g3, ♔g2 and ♖h1 he can start active operations on it, but Black intends to exploit the file first!

However Daskalov's plan has a flaw and White succeeds in exposing it in a combinational way: 18 ♖ac1! h6 19 ♘xd5 ed 20 ♗xg6! Now losing are both 20...fg 21 ♕c7+ ♕xc7 22 ♖xc7+ ♔f8 23 ♘e5 ♗f5 24 g4 ♗e4 25 f3, and also 20...hg 21 ♗xf7! Black replied 20...♘c6!?, which did

not save him from defeat: 21 gh+! ♖xh6 22 ♗f5 ♕h8 (22...♘xd4 23 ♕c3! ♗xf5 24 ♘xd4) 23 g3 ♖h1+ (23...♘b4 24 ♕xc8! ♖h1+ 25 ♔g2 ♖xc8 26 ♖xc8 ♕h5 27 ♖xh1 ♕xf5 28 ♖c7) 24 ♔g2 ♖xe1 25 ♖xe1 ♕h5 26 ♘h4!, and after a few moves it was all over.

13...♗g7 14 ♗xg7 After 14 ♗g5 f6! 15 ♗d2 ♗d7 16 ♕b3 ♗c6 Black, in the game Spassky – Petrosian (Moscow 1966), managed to achieve an ideal arrangement of pieces, and already White had to take measures to turn around the struggle: 17 ♗xd5 ed 18 ♘e4 ♖f7 19 ♘c5 ♘f5 with a draw.

Also seen is 14 ♕d2 b6 15 h4 ♗b7 16 h5 ♘f5 17 ♗xf5 ef 18 ♗xg7 ♔xg7 19 ♖ad1 ♖c8 20 ♘e5?! ♕h4! (Kurass – Podgaets, USSR 1969) with a comfortable game for Black.

14...♔xg7 If White does not start the attack now, he will never start it.

Upon 15 ♗xd5 ♘xd5 16 ♘xd5 ♕xd5 17 ♖e5 ♕d6 18 ♖d1 f6 19 ♖c5 ♗d7 20 ♘d2 ♗c6 (Tal – Bagirov, Moscow 1967) a draw looks the most probable result – although Tal nevertheless won.

There was more interesting play in the game Tseshkovsky – Podgaets

(Alma Ata 1968): **15 ♕b3 ♘f6 16 ♘e5!?** (a pawn sacrifice for the initiative) **16...♕xd4 17 ♗f3 ♘f5 18 ♖ad1 ♕c5 19 ♕a4 a6! 20 ♕f4 h6 21 h4 ♖a7** with a double edged struggle.

q) **12 ♕d3** h7 is hanging and it makes sense to look at both defences – the traditional 12...g6 and the possibly even stronger 12...h6.

Not good is 12...♘g6?! – at once White has two ways to obtain an advantage:

13 ♗d2 b6?! 14 h4! ♗b7 15 h5 ♘gf4 16 ♕b1 ♕c7 17 ♗xh7+ ♔h8 18 ♗e4 with a healthy extra pawn (Kamsky – Epishin, Las Palmas 1994);

13 ♕b5!? (original but also very strong) 13...♘ge7 14 ♘e5 ♕d6 15 ♗d2 g6 16 ♗h6 ♗g7 17 ♗xg7 ♔xg7 18 ♖ac1 ♖d8 19 ♕b3 (Bologan – Salov, Engien-les-Bains 1999).

q1) **12...g6 13 ♗h6** Not terrible is 13 h4 ♗d7 14 ♘e5 ♗c6 15 ♗h6 ♖e8 16 h5 because of 16...♘f5! (Kveinis – Gahwehns, Bonn 1994).

13 ♘e5!? is met from time to time. The position after 13...♗d7 14 ♗h6 ♗g7 15 ♗xg7 ♔xg7 we looked at in detail when we spoke about 12 ♘e5. Now, however, we stop at 13...b6!?

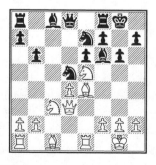

With the bishop on e4 the idea b7-b6 looks suspect. But if he does not succeed in refuting it (and meanwhile no one has succeeded), instead of the ponderous ♗c8-d7-c6 the bishop is developed, 'as it is supposed to', on b7.

In the game Kavalek – Hubner (Bugojno 1982) play continued 14 ♘xd5 ♘xd5 15 ♗h6 ♗g7 16 ♘c6 ♕d6 17 ♗xd5 ed 18 ♘e7+ ♔h8 19 ♕e3 ♗e6. The fianchetto did not happen, but this should not bother Black; the game is absolutely equal.

Stronger is 14 ♗h6 ♗g7 15 ♕h3!?

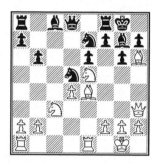

...with the idea on 15...♗b7?! to reply 16 ♗g5! From h3 the queen does not allow him to play f7-f6; Black is bound hand and foot.

In the game Hachian – Asrian (Erevan 1996) on 15 ♕h3 was played 15...f6?! 16 ♗xg7 ♔xg7 17 ♘d3 ♕d6, and after 18 ♖ac1!? (in the game White placed the queen's rook on d1) the picture for Black was miserable. The king is weakly defended, on the c and e-files the white rooks dominate, and the e6 square is on the point of collapse.

Here are some sample variations: 18...♗d7 19 ♗xd5 ♘xd5 20 ♘xd5 ♕xd5 (20...ed 21 ♕g3 ♕xg3 22 hg

♖f7 23 ♘f4 ♗f5 24 f3, and Black has a difficult endgame) 21 ♘f4 ♕xd4 (21...♕f5 22 ♖xe6!) 22 ♖ed1 ♕a4 (22...♖ac8 23 ♕g4!), and now

23 ♖xd7+! ♕xd7 24 ♖c7! winning.

So is the idea 13...b6!? not justified? No, it is too early to draw a conclusion. After 14 ♗h6 ♗g7 15 ♕h3!? it is necessary to try a very simple solution: 15...♗xh6!? 16 ♕xh6 ♗b7. In our view, Black has a fully defensible position. For example: 17 ♖ac1 (nothing is offered by 17 ♘xd5 ♗xd5 18 ♘f3 ♘f5 19 ♗xf5 ♗xf3, while the combination 17 ♗xd5 ♘xd5 18 ♘e4 f6 19 ♘xg6!? is good only for forcing a draw) 17...♘f5 18 ♗xf5 ef with equality.

13...♗g7 He can also preserve the dark-squared bishop: 13...♖e8, but the position after 14 ♖ad1 ♗d7 15 ♗xd5 ♘xd5 16 ♘xd5 ed 17 ♘e5 ♗e6 18 h3 ♖c8 19 ♖d2 ♖e7 20 ♕g3 ♖ec7 21 ♖de2 should be assessed in White's favour (Marin – Khaltin, Goteborg 2004).

14 ♗xg7 After 14 ♕d2 we want to draw your attention again to 14...b6!? It is surprising how few games have been played on this theme; and meanwhile this is the most logical move!

White can try to refute the fianchetto idea by 15 h4!? ♗b7 16 h5.

After 16...♘f5 17 ♗xg7 (17 ♗xf5 ef 18 ♗xg7 ♔xg7 returns us to the game Kurass – Podgaets) 17...♔xg7 18 ♘xd5 ♗xd5 19 ♗xd5 ♕xd5 20 ♖e5 ♕d8 21 d5 ed 22 ♖xd5 ♕f6 (Gipslis – Tavadian, Yurmala 1983) 23 ♖d1 and White has a minimal advantage.

Rather than putting up with the pawn on h5, it is better to take it: 16...gh!? It is not so easy to approach the black king. Apart from this, the g6 square beckons the knight. Here are some sample variations:

17 ♗xg7 ♔xg7 18 ♕g5+ ♘g6 19 ♕xh5 ♘f6;

17 ♕g5 ♘f5 18 ♗xg7 ♕xg5 19 ♘xg5 ♔xg7;

17 ♘e2 ♖b8! 18 ♘g3 ♘f6 19 ♗xb7 ♖xb7 20 ♗xg7 ♔xg7 21 ♕g5+ ♘g6 22 ♘xh5+ ♘xh5 23 ♕xh5 ♖d7! and Black has sufficient counterplay.

14...♔xg7 15 ♖ac1!? The position is very reminiscent of that which arose in one of the games of the candidates match for the world championship Smyslov – Ribli (London 1983). The difference lies in the fact that instead of the moves ♖f1-e1 and ♕d1-d3 in that game the moves ♘f3-e5 and a2-a3 were made.

Smyslov's plan (we looked at it above) is simple, but at the same time also very dangerous. White intends to capture twice on d5. No way does Black want to take with the pawn – how then he could he exploit the weakness of the isolani on d4? Besides this, upon the fixing of the pawn pair d4-d5, the centralised white knight on e5 will always be stronger than the light-squared bishop. Therefore more logical for Black is both times to take on d5 with a piece. But then (as happened in the above-mentioned game Smyslov – Ribli) the possibility appears of the rook getting in to c7!

15...b6 16 ♗xd5 ♘xd5 17 ♘xd5 ♕xd5 An important nuance! For Smyslov, as we recall, the pawn was already standing on a3 and he could place the rook on c7 without fear. Here, however, the move **18 ♖c7!** entails a pawn sacrifice. Over the board it is not easy to decide on such a sacrifice; this is why without exception every chessplayer on the 15th or 16th move plays a2-a3, losing precious time. However analysis

proves that after 18...♕xa2? 19 ♕c3! White wins in all variations:

19...♔g8 20 ♘e5 ♕d5 21 ♘g4! (this is stronger than 21 ♘c6 ♖e8 22 ♘e7+ ♖xe7 23 ♖xe7 ♗b7 24 f3 ♖c8) 21...♕g5 22 h3! with the threat of ♖e5;

19...♕d5 20 ♖e5 ♕d8 21 d5 ♔g8 (21...♕f6 22 de ♗xe6 23 ♖xe6!) 22 de fe 23 ♖xe6!

If it is not possible to take on a2, there remains **18...♗d7** But after **19 ♘e5** the game can in no way be considered equal.

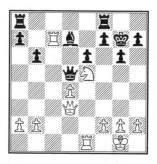

A difficult endgame without pawns awaits Black upon 19...♖fd8?! 20 ♕e3 ♗e8 21 ♕f4 ♕xd4 22 ♖xf7+! ♔xf7 23 ♕xf7+ ♔h8 (23...♔h6 24 ♕f6!) 24 ♕f6+ ♔g8 25 ♕xe6+ ♔g7 26 ♘c6 ♕f6 27 ♘xd8. Probably, he will not succeed in saving it.

Giving up the pawn at once is stronger – **19...♖ad8!? 20 ♖xa7 ♗b5**, placing the opponent in a dilemma: to cling on to the material to the end (21 ♕f3 ♕xf3 22 ♘xf3 ♖a8 23 ♖xa8 ♖xa8 24 a3 ♖c8) or to return it in exchange for a stable advantage in the endgame (21 ♕e3 ♕xd4 22 ♕xd4 ♖xd4 23 b3). We think that the character of the struggle in each case cannot suit Black.

q2) **12...h6!?** The plan with ♗h6 and ♖ac1 is now impossible and White has in prospect to think up something else.

13 ♘e5 The reconstruction ♕d3-e2, ♗d3-b1 and ♕e2-d3 looks ideal since Black cannot defend against mate by g7-g6 (the h6-pawn is hanging). But, tempo by tempo, a defence can be found: 13 ♕e2 ♗d7 (again it is worth turning our attention to 13...b6!?, for example 14 ♗d2 ♗b7 15 ♖ac1 ♘xc3 16 bc ♗xe4 17 ♕xe4 ♘f5 18 ♗f4 ♖c8 19 ♘e5 ♗g5 with equal chances, Becerra – Asrian, Linares 1999) 14 ♗b1 ♗c6 (inaccurate is 14...♘xc3 15 bc ♗c6: after 16 ♘e5! ♗xe5 17 ♕xe5 ♕d5 18 ♕g3 White, in the game Adams – Karpov, Monaco 1992, obtained the advantage of the two bishops) 15 ♕d3 ♘g6! (closing the dangerous diagonal) 16 a3 ♖e8 17 ♘e4 ♘df4 18 ♗xf4 ♘xf4 19 ♕d2 (we cannot see a continuation of the attack: 19 ♘xf6+ ♕xf6 20 ♕h7+ ♔f8 21 ♗e4 ♖ac8) 19...♘g6, and Black's position is rather more pleasant (Trabert – Murdzia, Hamburg 1995).

13...♘xc3 (we stopped at the continuation 13...♗d7 when we examined 12 ♘e5) **14 ♕xc3** Usually he will take with a pawn here, but in the present situation the endgame after 14 bc ♗xe5! 15 de ♕xd3 16 ♗xd3 ♗d7 17 ♗a3 ♖fe8 18 ♖ad1 ♗a4 19 ♖d2 ♖ac8 20 c4 b6 21 ♗d6 ♘f5 (S.-B. Hansen – L.-B. Hansen, Copenhagen 1996) does not promise White an advantage.

14...♘f5 Leading to interesting complications is 14...♕b6 15 ♗c2!? (once again intending to make way for the queen to go to d3) 15...♖d8 16 ♗e3.

One wrong advance – 16...♘d5?, and to all appearances the game already cannot be saved: 17 ♕d3 ♘xe3 18 fe ♗xe5 19 ♕h7+ ♔f8 20 de ♕xb2 21 ♖f1 ♕xe5 22 ♗g6 f5 23 e4. Black has two extra pawns but his king is hopelessly weak. For example: 23...♕f6 24 ef ♔e7 (24...e5 25 ♖ad1) 25 fe ♕d4+ 26 ♔h1 ♗xe6 27 ♗f7! ♖f8 (27...♗xf7 28 ♖ae1+ ♗e6 29 ♕g6 ♕c4 30 ♕xg7+ ♔d6 31 ♖c1) 28 ♗xe6 ♖xf1+ 29 ♖xf1 ♔xe6 30 ♕f5+ ♔d6 31 ♕b1!

In the game Dolmatov – Enklaar (Amsterdam 1979) Black played the stronger 16...♘f5. However White's pressure continued to increase: 17 ♖ad1 ♗d7 18 d5! ♕a6 (18...♘xe3 19 ♖xe3 ed does not solve the problem because of 20 ♕d3 ♗e6 21 ♖de1 ♔f8 22 ♘g6+! fg 23 ♖xe6 ♕xb2 24 ♕xg6 ♖ac8 25 ♗f5) 19 ♗xf5 ef 20 ♗d4 ♗e8 21 ♕f3! Dolmatov confidently led the game to victory with a decisive role being played by the passed d-pawn.

15 ♗e3 a5!? This move, thought up spontaneously by Karpov at the board (during his game against Topalov, Linares 1995), is apparently the strongest. The rook a8 starts to 'breathe' and besides this there is a concrete idea: to impose an exchange of queens on his opponent after a5-a4 and ♕d8-a5.

The move 15... ♘xe3 has had rich practice. In the world championship match Chiburdanidze – Ioseliani (Telavi 1988) was seen 16 fe ♖b8 17 ♖ad1 ♗d7 18 ♗b1 ♗e8 19 ♘g4 ♗g5 20 e4 h5!, and Black rid herself of difficulties.

After 16 ♕xe3 ♕b6 Black likewise equalised the game: 17 ♖ad1 ♖d8 18 b3 ♗d7 19 ♕f3 ♗b5! (Sher – L.-B. Hansen, Vejle 1994).

He can only fight for the advantage by 16 ♖xe3!? After 16...♕b6 17 ♖d1 ♖d8 arises a critical position.

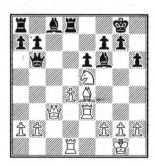

Black has a solid position without pawn weaknesses. It is clear that in protracted trench warfare his chances are at least not worse.

It is necessary for White to seek his fortune in direct attack. Three pieces, marshalled on the e-file, are ready for this, it remains to accommodate the queen. Therefore 18 ♗c2!? If the queen lands on h7, the deed will be done – 18...♗d7? 19 ♕d3!, and then: 19...♗e8 20 ♕h7+ ♔f8 21 d5! ♗xe5 22 ♖xe5 ♕xb2 23 ♖de1 or 19...♗c6 20 ♕h7+ ♔f8 21 ♗b3 ♕a5 22 ♘xf7! ♔xf7 23 ♗xe6+ ♔e7 24 d5!

It is best for Black to give up the two bishops at once (and the intention of playing for a win) and by exchanges and surviving an inferior endgame, try to draw – 18...♗xe5 19 ♖xe5 ♗d7. After 20 d5!? the following variations are possible:

20...ed? 21 ♕d3;

20...f6?! 21 ♖e3 ed 22 ♕d3 ♔f8 23 ♕h7 ♗e6 24 ♖de1 ♗g8 25 ♕h8 ♕c7 (or 25...♕d6 26 ♖g3 ♕c7 27 ♗h7 ♕f7 28 ♖ge3) 26 ♗f5;

20...♖ac8 21 ♕d3 g6 22 ♗b3 ♗b5 23 ♕f3 ♗c4 24 ♗xc4 ♖xc4 25 de ♖xd1+ 26 ♕xd1 fe 27 h3. Though it is quite agonising playing this endgame, the chances for a draw are not bad.

16 ♖ad1 In the stem game was played 16 ♖ac1 a4 17 ♖ed1. Karpov took on e3; later play turned towards 17...♕a5 18 ♕xa5 ♖xa5 19 ♗xf5 ♗xe5 20 ♗e4 ♗d6 21 d5 ed 22 ♗xd5 ♗e5 23 b4 ab 24 ab ♗e6 (Lesiege – Shipov, Moscow 2001). Instead of 17...♕a5 worth considering is 17...♖a5!? 18 ♘c4 ♖b5.

16...a4!? Also here he should not hurry to take the bishop: after 16...♘xe3 17 ♕xe3 (weaker is 17 fe ♖a6 18 ♖c1 ♖d6, Malaniuk – Adams, Hastings 1995) 17...♕b6 18 ♗c2! ♗xe5 19 de ♕xe3 20 ♖xe3 the endgame is defined in White's favour (Shchekachev – Galkin, Krasnodar 1996).

17 ♘g4 ♗g5 On 17...♘xe3 18 ♘xf6+ ♕xf6 19 fe ♕d8 20 ♖c1 ♖a5 21 ♖e2 b6 22 ♖ec2 once again no way can the position be called even (Shariyzdanov – Lygovoi, Toliatti 2003).

18 ♗xf5 ef 19 ♗xg5 hg It needs to be recognised that both sides have strayed quite a long way from the canons of struggle with an isolated pawn. In the game Molnar – Polak (Pula 2001) play continued 20 ♘e5 ♕a5? 21 ♕c4 ♗e6 22 d5 ♖ac8 23 b4!, but an improvement suggests itself: 20...♗e6! with equality.

Stronger is **20 ♘e3!?**

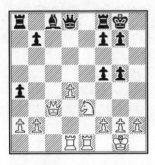

It might be pointed out that the black pawns have advanced too far, but variations do not confirm this. After **20...♖a6 21 ♕c5 ♖d6 22 ♘c4** (22 d5 ♖e8!) **22...♖d5 23 ♕a7 ♗e6 24 ♘e3 ♖a5 25 ♕xb7 f4 26 ♘c2 ♗d5 27 ♕e7 ♖b5** with mutual play.

r) **12 ♘e5** The main reply is rightly considered 12...♗d7, but first we look at the sidelines: 12...♗xe5, 12...♘f5, 12...♘c6 and 12...g6.

12...♗xe5 – this is the start of a great exchanging operation: 13 de ♘xc3 14 bc ♕xd1 15 ♖xd1. True, after 15...♘d5! chances for a draw are real, but why impoverish the

game like this? And whether Black can make a draw – is still a question. For example, in the game Mazura – Molina (San Paolo 1999) – he did not make it: 16 ♖d3 b5 17 ♖b1 a6 18 ♗a3 ♖e8 19 ♗d6 ♗b7? 20 c4! bc 21 ♖h3! Instead of 19...♗b7 stronger is 19...♗d7!? 20 ♗xd5 ed 21 ♖xd5 ♗e6 22 ♖d2 ♖ac8 23 ♗b4 f6! 24 ef ♖cd8 – such opposite coloured bishops, as a rule, do not win.

12...♘f5?! is considered dubious on the basis of an analysis by the Filipino grandmaster Eugenio Torre: 13 ♘g4! ♘xd4 14 ♗xd5 ed 15 ♘xf6+ ♕xf6 16 ♘xd5 ♕h4 17 ♗f4 In the game Novikov – Lugovoi (St.Petersburg 1995) Black did not actually take the pawn, limiting himself to 13...♘b6. After 14 ♘xf6+ ♕xf6 15 ♕g4 ♘c4 Lygovoi recommended 16 d5!? ♘cd6 17 de ♗xe6 18 ♘d5 ♕d8 19 ♗g5 with the initiative. In our opinion, the simplest way to an advantage lies in 14 ♗xf5!? (instead of 14 ♘xf6+) 14...ef 15 ♘xf6+ ♕xf6 16 d5.

12...♘c6!? Apart from anything else, this is still an invitation to peace negotiations: 13 ♘f3 ♘ce7 etc.

If he decides to play on, White usually chooses 13 ♕d3. After 13...g6?! 14 ♗h6 ♗g7 15 ♗xg7 ♔xg7 16 ♗xd5 ed 17 ♘xc6 bc 18 ♘a4 and Black stands noticeably worse (Sher – Asrian, Erevan 1996). There is more complicated play upon 14...♖e8 15 ♖ad1 ♗h8 (15...♘xe5 16 de ♗xe5 17 ♗xg6!) 16 ♕f3! (Ara Minasian – E. Danielian, Erevan 2000) but even here the chances are on White's side.

On 13 ♕d3 it is necessary to reply 13...h6!?, after which the play divides into two.

14 a3 has also been played:

14...♘de7 15 ♘xc6 ♘xc6 16 d5 ed 17 ♘xd5 ♗e6 18 ♘xf6+ ♕xf6 19 ♗e3 (Ljubojevic – Khalifman, Groningen 1993);

14...♗xe5 15 de ♘xe5 (Nijboer – van der Sterren, Hilversum 1989) 16 ♗h7+ ♔h8 17 ♖xe5 ♘xc3 18 bc f5 19 ♗xf5 ef 20 ♕xd8 ♖xd8 21 ♗e3 (analysis by Nijboer).

But the most interesting way has slipped away from practice: 14...♘xc3!? 15 ♘xc6 ♘e2+! 16 ♖xe2 bc 17 ♗xc6 ♕b6 18 ♕f3 (or 18 ♗xa8 ♗a6 19 ♕c2 ♗xe2 20 ♗e4 ♗a6) 18...♗a6 19 ♖e1 ♖ad8 20 d5 ed 21 ♗xd5 ♖fe8 with a bright and interesting game.

14 ♗xd5 is parried by the intermediate 14...♘b4! 15 ♕g3 ♗h4! After 16 ♕f3 he can start to 'dry up' the position: 16...ed 17 ♖e2 ♗e6 18 a3 ♘c6 19 ♘xc6 bc 20 ♘a4 with a minimal advantage for White (Smyslov – Ivanchuk, Moscow 1988). But it is also possible to play more entertainingly: 16...♘xd5 17 ♖e4!? f5 18 ♖xh4 (18 ♖e2!? ♗f6 19 ♗d2) 18...♕xh4 19 ♘g6 ♕xd4

(Mortensen – Jelling, Denmark 1989). True, if it turns out that the complications are in Black's favour, White can return to 17 ♘xd5 (instead of 17 ♖e4) 17...ed 18 ♘d3 ♕f6 19 ♕xf6 ♗xf6 20 ♗e3 ♗e6. The endgame is approximately even (Djurhuus – Asran, Erevan 1996).

12...g6 might prove to be premature. You see, now White does not need to spend time on 13 ♕d3; for him there is now a chance to get into a position known to be equal – but with an extra tempo!

After 13 ♗h6 ♗g7 14 ♗xg7 ♔xg7 we have quite an unpleasant idea for Black which we looked at in the game Smyslov – Ribli: 15 ♖c1!? b6 16 ♘xd5 ♘xd5 17 ♗xd5 ♕xd5 18 ♖c7!

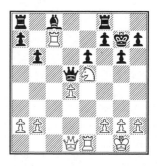

In the game Spraggett – Taylor (Ottawa 1984) Black could not cope with the arising problems and was quickly 'consumed': 18...♗b7 19 ♕g4 ♖ac8 20 ♖d7 ♕a5 21 ♖f1 ♗c6 22 ♖e7 ♔f6? 23 ♖xf7+! ♖xf7 24 ♕f4+ ♔e7 25 ♕xf7+ ♔d8 26 ♖c1. In fact everything is not so gloomy: after 22...♕d5!? 23 ♖xa7 ♗b7 24 ♘d3 ♔g8 25 ♘b4 ♕d6 26 ♖xb7 ♕xb4 it is still possible to put up stubborn resistance.

Apart from 14 ♗xg7 we stop and look in more detail at 14 ♕d2!? For a long time and on the basis of the game Liberzon – Podgaets (Alma Ata 1968) this move was not considered dangerous for Black. This is how the game went:

14...♘f6 (bad is 14...b6?! in view of 15 ♘g4! ♘f5 16 ♗xf5 ef 17 ♗xg7 ♔xg7 18 ♕h6+ ♔g8 19 ♘xd5 fg 20 ♘e7+ ♔h8, Grabics – Danielian, Hania 1994, 21 ♖e5! with the terrible threat of 22 ♖h5!, while on 21...♗f5 winning is 22 ♖ae1 ♕xd4 23 ♘d5!) 15 ♖ad1 ♘xe4 16 ♖xe4 b6! (16...♘f5?! 17 ♗xg7 ♔xg7 18 d5! Smyslov – Padevsky, Moscow 1963) 17 ♖h4 ♘f5 18 ♗xg7 ♔xg7 19 ♖h3 ♗b7 20 ♘e2 ♖c8 21 ♘g3 h5 22 ♘xf5+ ef and the opponents agreed a draw.

However later White found a way to strengthen his play: 16 ♘xe4!? Then he exchanged the dark-squared bishops and by means of ♘e5-g4 started a mating attack on the dark squares. How to defend?

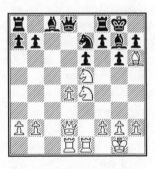

Only not by 16...♘d5 17 ♘g4 ♕e7. After 18 ♗xg7 ♔xg7 19 ♕h6+ ♔g8 20 ♘c3! (Winsnes – Astram, Sweden 1994) and White has essentially an extra piece in the attack – as the

bishop c8 with all the will in the world is not capable of covering the dark squares around his king.

Elena Danielian from Armenia twice defended this position. In her game against Monica Grabics (Medelin 1996) she chose 16...b6 and even won (in this way taking revenge for her defeat two years earlier – see above). But this has no relevance at all to the assessment of the present position since after 17 ♘g4! ♘f5 18 ♗xg7 ♔xg7 19 ♕c3! Black is facing defeat. Which, appropriately, is also confirmed by the game Hunt – Danelian (Zagan 1997), arriving by transposition of moves at the same position: 16...♘f5 17 ♗xg7 ♔xg7 18 ♘g4! b6 19 ♕c3! After 19...f6 20 ♘gxf6! ♖xf6 21 ♘xf6 ♔xf6 22 d5+ e5 23 ♕c6+ Black resigned.

Apparently the most stubborn defence is 16...♗xh6!? 17 ♕xh6 ♘f5 18 ♕d2 f6 19 ♘g4 ♔g7 20 ♘e3 ♘e7! 21 ♘c3 ♖f7. Somehow patching up the holes in his camp, Black prepares to repulse a new wave of attack.

It seems that although there are many moves, there is no worthy alternative to **12...♗d7**.

The following food for thought awaits Black after **13 ♕d3** The h7 pawn is hanging but 13...h6?! is not effective in view of 14 ♕g3 with the threats of ♗xh6 and ♘g4. Therefore it is necessary to choose between 13...♘g6 and 13...g6.

13...♘g6 has been played in surprisingly few games, though everything points to the fact that the move is no less strong than 'the people's favourite' – the advance of the g-pawn.

Exchanges do not promise White any advantage:

14 ♘xg6 hg 15 ♘xd5 ed 16 ♗xd5? ♕a5!, the same idea of double attack on d5 and e1 also works after 14 ♘xd5 ed 15 ♗xd5? ♕a5;

14 ♗xd5 ed 15 ♘xd5 ♗xe5 16 de ♗c6 or 15 ♘xg6 hg 16 ♘xd5 ♗c6. It is hard even to imagine that White can realise such an extra pawn.

In the game Ivanchuk – Karpov (Monaco 1992) White played 14 ♗d2 ♗c6 15 ♘xc6 bc 16 ♘a4. The simplest way to equality here is 16...♖b8! with the sample variations: 17 a3 (17 ♖ac1 ♘b4) 17...♘b6 18 ♘xb6 ♕xb6 19 ♗e3 ♖fd8 (on 19 ♗c3 would follow the same move) 20 ♖ed1 (20 d5 ♕c7) 20...♕b3 21 ♖ab1 ♕xd3 22 ♖xd3 ♘e7.

13...g6 14 ♗h6 Nothing is offered by 14 ♘g4 ♗g7 15 ♘h6+?! ♔h8 16 ♕f3 f5! 17 ♗c2 ♘c6, but interesting is 14 h4!?, and Black needs to play very accurately not to fall into a difficult situation: 14...♗c6 (after 14...♗xh4 15 ♕h3 ♗f6 16 ♘xd5 ♘xd5 17 ♗xd5 ♗xe5 18 ♗xb7 and White has the

advantage) 15 ♗g5 ♘f5!? 16 ♗xf6 ♘xf6 17 ♗xf5 (or 17 ♗xc6 bc 18 ♘xc6 ♕b6 19 ♕f3 ♔g7 with compensation) 17...ef 18 ♖ad1 ♘d5 19 ♕g3 f4! 20 ♕g4 h5 21 ♕f3 ♘xc3.

14...♗g7 15 ♗xg7 ♔xg7 The usual question: how to take on d5?

There are fewer arguments in favour of 16 ♘xd5 ed 17 ♗f3 ♗e6 18 ♕b3 ♕b6!? 19 ♕xb6 ab 20 a3 ♖fc8 21 ♖e2 ♘f5 22 ♖d2 ♖a4! 23 ♖ad1 b5! (we recall that twenty years before the game we cited, this plan was realised in the encounter Sveshnikov – Podgaets!) 24 g4 ♘d6 (Kharlov – Dzhandzhava, Moscow 1995).

It is obvious that in the situation with the fixed pawn pair d4-d5 White needs a knight far more than a bishop. Therefore **16 ♗xd5 ed** (worse is 16...♘xd5 17 ♘xd5 ed 18 ♕b3) **17 h3** We look briefly at the remaining moves:

17 ♕f3 ♗f5!? 18 ♖ad1 (if 18 g4, then 18...f6! 19 ♕g3 fe 20 ♕xe5+ ♔g8 21 gf ♘xf5 22 ♘xd5 ♖c8 with an unclear game) 18...f6 19 ♘d3 ♗xd3 20 ♖xd3 ♕d7 (Sturua – Burmakin, Biel 2000);

17 ♖e2 f6 18 ♘xd7 ♕xd7 19 ♖ae1 ♘c6 20 g3 ♖f7 (Topalov –

Vizhmanavin, Groningen 1993). Everywhere it's just a little more pleasant for White.

17...f6 18 ♘f3 Yet another important moment.

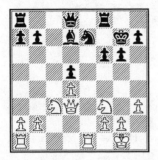

Black's position is worse, gloomily worse. He, so to speak, 'runs no risk' of winning. Reconciling himself to this, he needs to concentrate his efforts on neutralising White's pressure. How? Firstly, by developing the queen's rook to e8 and in this way gathering all his men into a unified force. Secondly, by improving the position of the knight

e7. The ideal place for it is on f4. If it all comes together as he thinks, then a draw becomes full reality.

18...♗c6! After 18...♖f7?! 19 ♖e2 ♖c8 20 ♖ae1 (Hracek – Dzhandzhava, Moscow 1994) Black did not manage to put right the coordination of his forces and lost accordingly.

19 ♖e2 It seems that more dangerous would be a build up of heavy pieces on the e-file: 19 ♖e6 ♕d7 20 ♖ae1 ♖ae8 21 ♕e2!? Black will not succeed in solving the problem of the pin tactically: the endgame after 21...♕xe6?! 22 ♕xe6 ♘f5 23 ♕xe8 ♖xe8 24 ♖xe8 ♗xe8 25 ♘xd5 ♗c6 26 ♘e3 is probably lost. But the quieter 21...♔f7! and then 22...♘c8 gives equal chances.

19...♕d7 20 b4 b6 21 b5 ♗b7 22 a4 g5! 23 ♖ae1 ♘g6, and the game ended in a draw (Kosten – Kuczinski, Saint Affrique 1995).

223

Index to Chapter Six

I 1 e4 c6 2 d4 d5 3 ed cd 4 c4 ♘f6
5 ♘c3 e6 6 ♘f3 ♗e7   141
I. 7 c5   141
7...0-0
  A. 8 b4   141
    1) 8...b6   142
    2) 8...♘e4   142
      a) 9 ♕c2   142
      b) 9 ♗b2   144
  B. 8 ♗g5   145
  8...b6 9 b4
    1) 9...a5   145
    2) 9...♘c6   146
    3) 9...♘e4   146
  C. 8 ♗f4   147
  8...b6 9 b4
    1) 9...bc   147
    2) 9...a5   147
    3) 9...♘e4   149
  D. 8 ♕c2   150
  E. 8 ♗d3   150
  8...b6 9 b4 a5 10 ♘a4
    1) 10...♘fd7   151
      a) 11 a3   151
      b) 11 b5   151
      c) 11 h4   151
      d) 11 ♕c2   152
      d1) 11...b5 152
      d2) 11...ab 153
      d3) 11...♘c6 153
    2) 10...♘bd7   154

    a) 11 c6   154
    b) 11 a3   154
    c) 11 ♗f4   154
    d) 11 ♕c2   155
II. 7 ♗g5   155
7...♘c6 8 c5 0-0 9 ♗b5 ♘e4
10 ♗xe7
  A. 10...♕xe7   158
    1) 11 0-0   158
    2) 11 ♖c1   158
    3) 11 ♕c2   159
  B. 10...♘xe7   159
  11 ♖c1 b6 12 c6
    1) 12...♘d6   160
    2) 12...♕d6   160
III. 7 cd   161
  A. 7...ed   161
    1) 8 ♗d3   161
    2) 8 ♗b5+   162
      a) 8...♘c6   162
      b) 8...♘bd7 163
      c) 8...♗d7   163
  B. 7...♘xd5   163
    1) 8 ♗b5+   164
    2) 8 ♗c4   164
  8...0-0 9 0-0 ♘c6 10 ♖e1
    a) 10...♘xc3   166
  11 bc b6 12 ♗d3 ♗b7
    a1) 13 ♕c2   166
    a2) 13 h4   167
    a21) 13...♗xh4   168

a22) 13...♕d5   169

a23) 13...♘a5   169

a24) 13...♗f6   169

a25) 13...♖c8   171

b) 10...a6   172

11 ♗b3 ♘xc3 12 bc b5

b1) 13 d5   174

b2) 13 h4   174

b3) 13 ♕d3   174

b4) 13 ♗c2   175

c) 10...♗f6   176

3) 8 ♗d3   176

8...0-0 9 0-0 ♘c6

a) 10 ♕e2   178

b) 10 a3   178

b1) 10...♘xc3   178

b2) 10...♗f6   180

b21) 11 ♗e4   180

x) 11...♕d6   180

y) 11...♘ce7   181

b22) 11 ♖e1   183

c) 10 ♖e1   184

c1) 10...b6   184

c2) 10...a6   185

c3) 10...♘xc3   185

c4) 10...♘cb4   186

c5) 10...♗d7   187

c6) 10...♕d6   187

c7) 10...♘f6   187

11 a3 b6

c71) 12 ♘e5   188

c72) 12 ♗g5   188

12...♗b7 13 ♗c2

x) 13...♘d5   189

y) 13...♖c8   192

c73) 12 ♗b1   193

c74) 12 ♗c2   194

x) 12...♗b7   194

y) 12...♗a6   199

c8) 10...♗f6   206

11 ♗e4

c81) 11...♕d6   206

x) 12 ♘b5   207

y) 12 ♘g5   207

z) 12 ♗g5   207

q) 12 h4   209

r) 12 ♕d3   209

w) 12 ♗c2   209

c82) 11...♘ce7   210

x) 12 h4   211

y) 12 ♕b3   212

z) 12 ♕c2   212

q) 12 ♕d3   214

q1) 12...g6   214

q2) 12...h6   217

r) 12 ♘e5   219

Appendix

Steiner System: 1 e4 c6 2 c4

At the end of the 20s – beginning of the 30s of the last century, the Hungarian player Lajos Steiner played some memorable games starting with the moves shown in the diagram postion. Inspired by his victories he published a series of analyses which endeavoured to prove that the move 2 c4 refuted the Caro-Kann defence.

It goes without saying that this is not so; upon correct defence Black should overcome all difficulties. However he should know precisely what problems are facing him and not in any way rely on general principles. Otherwise he will get into trouble.

It should be mentioned that the Steiner system not infrequently loses its independence and transposes to another opening variation. Thus after

2...e5 3 ♘f3 d6 4 d4 ♘d7 before us is an Indian (with the bishop on e7) or King's Indian (with the bishop on g7) defence. Upon 2...d5 3 ed cd 4 d4 arises the initial position of the Panov Attack. The moves 2...e6 3 d4 d5 4 ♘c3 de 5 ♘xe4 ♗b4+ 6 ♗d2 ♕xd4 lead us to the tabiya of the so called 'Slav Gambit'.

Let us go over to a review of the variations. After 1 e4 c6 2 c4 Black has three main possibilities: 2...e5 (I), 2...e6 (II), 2...d5 (III).

I
2...e5

In his turn, White has at his disposal three continuations: 3 ♘c3 (A), 3 d4 (B), and 3 ♘f3 (C).

A

3 ♘c3 A creation of the Latvian grandmaster Normunds Miezis. White is thinking about fianchettoing the light-squared bishop – which, quite frankly, is not a very energetic idea in the present position.

3...♗c5 (If, for time being, White declines to fight for the central squares, then Black himself will occupy them with pleasure) **4 g3 ♕f6**

Worth the most concentrated attention is the pawn sacrifice: 4...♞f6 5 ♗g2 0-0 6 ♘ge2 d5!?

In the game Miezis – Sasikiran (Djakarta 2001) White did not hit upon the necessary reaction to such daring and was soon forced to go over to defensive play: 7 ed cd 8 ♘xd5 ♘c6 9 0-0 ♗g4 10 h3 ♗h5 11 a3 ♘xd5 12 cd ♘d4 13 g4 ♗g6 14 d3 f5! 15 ♗e3 fg 16 hg ♛h4 etc. It looks like the treatment of Indian grandmaster Krishnan Sasikiran has every chance of becoming the main retort for Black in this variation.

5 ♛e2 d6 6 ♗g2 ♘e7 7 ♘f3 h6 Prophylaxis against the possible threat of ♗c1-g5. However there is also a flip side to this move...

8 d3 0-0 9 0-0 White acted in a cunning way in the game Miezis – Henley (Gausdal 2001): 9 h3!? a5 10 g4!? ♘g6 11 g5!, and it became clear that the move 7...h6 had become a useful lever for the pawn storm on the king's flank. There followed 11...hg 12 ♗xg5 ♛e6 13 h4! f5 14 0-0-0 fe 15 ♘xe4 ♘a6 16 h5! and the attack became irresistible: 16...♗g4 17 hg ♛xg2 18 ♘xe5! ♖xf2 19 ♖h8+!

9...♖e8 10 ♖b1 a5 11 ♘a4?! (a dubious manoeuvre, inundating Black with thoughts about the break b7-b5) **11...♘d7 12 b3 ♗a7 13 ♗b2 b5! 14 cb cb 15 ♘c3 ♗a6 16 ♘d1 ♘c5 17 ♘e3 b4 18 ♘c4 ♘c6 19 ♔h1**

This is how the encounter Miezis – Baljon (France 2000) went. It is obvious that with his last move White started to prepare f2-f4. Black should immediately commence active play on the queen's flank. For example: **19...a4!? 20 ba ♘xa4 21 ♘e3 ♘e7** (preventing the penetration of the knight to the d5 square) **22 ♛d2 ♘c5 23 ♘e1 ♛e6! 24 a3** (24 ♖a1 b3!) **24...♛a2!** After this strong move Black obtains the better endgame by force:

25 ♖a1 ♘b3! 26 ♖xa2 ♘xd2 27 ♖g1 b3 28 ♖a1 ♗d4! The blockade from the b2 square is removed, the white knight is forced to retreat, and Black can develop an initiative without hindrance:

29 ♘d1 d5! 30 ed ♖ad8 31 ♘c3 ♘xd5! (the sacrifice of the exchange is the shortest way to his objective) **32 ♗xd5 ♖xd5 33 ♘xd5 ♗xb2 34 ♖d1 ♗b7! 35 ♖xd2 ♗c1!** The b-pawn is untouchable; Black's position is easily winning.

Today the variation 3 ♘c3 ♗c5 4 g3 does not enjoy great popularity.

B

3 d4!? An idealistic move. Exploiting the fact that the c6 square is inaccessible to the knight, White immediately 'strains' the e5 and d4 points. He hopes (not without foundation), that Black will not have enough force to wrestle for these points, and the advantage in the centre will remain with White.

We look at the following moves: 3...ed, 3...♗b4+, 3...♘f6 and 3...d6.

1) **3...ed?!** (this seems the least strong of all four possibilities) **4 ♕xd4 ♕f6 5 ♗e3 ♘a6!?** After the exchange of queens there is no compensation for the weakness of the d-pawn in Black's camp.

6 ♘c3 ♗c5 7 ♕d2 ♗xe3 8 ♕xe3 d6 9 ♘f3 ♘e7 10 0-0-0 ♗g4 10...0-0 11 ♕d2 ♖d8 does not solve the problem in view of 12 e5! ♕e6 13 ed ♘f5 14 ♗d3!, and there is no way he can recover the d6 pawn: 14...♕xd6 15 g4; 14...♖xd6 15 ♖he1; 14...♘xd6 15 ♘g5 winning.

11 e5!? A positional sacrifice of a pawn. In return White obtains the e4 square for the knight and an enduring

initiative. The less forcing 11 ♗e2!? also does not look bad.

11...de 12 ♘e4 ♕f4 13 ♘d6+ ♔f8 14 ♕xf4 ef 15 ♗e2 ♘c5 16 ♖he1 ♗xf3?! Black gives up the important bishop in order to rule out the possibility of a jump of the white knight to e5 or g5. However the passivity of the black pieces remaining on the board is depressing.

More interesting is 16...♘g6!? 17 ♘g5, and then:

17...♗xe2?! 18 ♖xe2 f6 19 ♘gf7 ♖g8 20 b4, and the doubled rooks on the e-file are decisive: 20...♘a6 21 ♖de1 ♘c7 22 g3!

17...♘e5!? 18 ♔c2! (in this way he prevents the penetration of the knight to d3) 18...f6 19 ♗xg4 ♘xg4 20 ♘gf7 ♖g8 21 ♖d2 f3! 22 h3 ♘h6 23 ♘xh6 gh 24 g3 and probably White still wins.

17 ♗xf3

In the old game Becker – Beutum (Vienna 1931) there followed 17...h5?! and White missed the chance to conclude the struggle at once: 18 b4! ♘a6 19 ♘xb7 ♘xb4 20 ♖d7 ♘g8 21 ♘c5. Now 21...♘xa2+ is not possible in view of 22 ♔b2 ♘b4 23 ♖b7, indeed, generally speaking, ...nothing is possible.

Securing the outpost of the knight c5 would be more tenacious: **17...a5!** Although after **18 ♘e4 ♘xe4 19 ♖xe4 ♘g6 20 ♖d7** Black's position remains bad, possibilities of resistance do remain for him.

2) **3...♗b4+ 4 ♗d2 ♗xd2+ 5 ♕xd2 d6**

The main defect of this (moreover, also the previous) variation remains its passivity. It is easy for White to grab space, which in its turn brings him up against super-aggressive play.

6 ♘c3!? An unambiguous hint that before playing ♘g1-f3 White intends to send forward the f-pawn. On the other hand, 6 ♘f3 is not only lacking in ideas it is simply inaccurate: 6...♗g4! 7 ♗e2 ♗xf3! 8 ♗xf3 ♘f6 9 ♘c3 ♘bd7 10 ♖d1 0-0 11 0-0 ♖e8 12 b3 ♕a5 13 g3 ♖ad8 14 ♗g2 a6 15 ♖fe1 b5 gave Black play with fully equal rights in the game Imanaliev – Shabalov (Moscow 1994).

After 6 ♘c3 Black can choose between 6...♘f6 and 6...♕f6.

a) **6...♘f6** Dull is 6...♘d7?! 7 f4! ♘gf6 8 ♘f3 0-0 9 0-0-0 with a menacing initiative (Gulko – Maksimenko, Berne 1994).

7 f4 0-0 8 0-0-0!? More cautious is

8 ♘f3 with the following variations:

8...ef 9 ♕xf4 ♘h5 10 ♕d2 f5!? (in this lies the point of the exchange on f4) 11 e5 de 12 ♘xe5 ♕h4+ 13 ♕f2 ♕xf2+ 14 ♔xf2 ♘d7 15 ♘f3! The better pawn structure defines White's advantage;

8...ed 9 ♕xd4 c5 10 ♕d2 ♘c6 11 0-0-0 ♗g4 12 h3 ♗xf3 13 gf ♘d4 14 ♘b5!? By exchanging the opponent's only active piece, White establishes control over the whole board (Tal – Nei, Parnu 1971).

The given variations allow us to draw the conclusion that after 8 ♘f3 White's chances are superior. But the temptation to start an attack with opposite sides castling (indeed, even with a heavy superiority in the centre) is too great.

8...♕a5 9 ♘f3 ♘bd7

10 h3!? Intending to continue the offensive on the king's flank by g2-g4.

The other plan is to create a passed pawn in the centre: 10 fe de 11 d5. But it runs the risk of losing the initiative; apart from this he should not underestimate Black's counterattacking possibilities (b7-b5!). This is how the struggle turns out after 11...cd:

12 cd a6!? 13 ♔b1 b5 14 ♗d3 b4 15 ♘e2 ♖e8 (defending the e5 pawn and freeing the knight for active operations) 16 ♘g3 ♘c5 17 ♗c2 ♗d7 18 ♘h4 ♕b6 or

12 cd b5!? 13 ♘xb5 (on 13 cb Black, in the style of the Volga gambit, replies 13...a6!) 13...♕xa2 14 ♘c3 ♕b3 with an absolutely unclear game in both cases.

10...ed 11 ♘xd4 ♘c5 12 ♗d3 (T.Hansen – Bai, Gausdal 2000). Here Black missed the only chance to start a fight: **12...♗e6!? 13 g4 d5!** (upon a flank attack one should react with a counter-blow in the centre!) **14 cd** (or 14 ♗e2 ♘a4! 15 f5 ♘xc3 16 ♕xc3 ♕xc3+ 17 bc ♗d7) **14...cd 15 e5 ♘fe4!**

b) **6...♕f6!?** This was often played by the inexhaustibly inventive English grandmaster Anthony Miles.

Black is certainly not able to equalise but he can bring some diversity to the position. Indeed, he also saves himself against the attack after 7 0-0-0 ♕h6!? 8 ♘ge2 ♕xd2+ 9 ♖xd2 ♘f6 10 f3 ♘bd7 11 ♘g3 g6 12 ♗e2 ♘f8 13 d5 c5 14 h4 h5 15 a3 ♔e7 (Becerra – Miles, Havana 1997).

7 ♘ge2!? (now on ♕f6-h6 he always has f2-f4!) **7...♘e7 8 0-0-0**

0-0 9 f4 ♗g4

Prophylaxis – 10 ♔b1?! – here is not appropriate: 10...ef 11 h3 ♗h5 12 ♖e1 ♗xe2 13 ♗xe2 c5!, controlling the dark squares (West – Miles, Sydney 1991).

The offensive on the king's flank should continue: **10 f5!? ♘c8 11 de de 12 h3 ♗xe2 13 ♗xe2 ♘a6 14 g4!?** (Sax – Miles, Lugano 1989). Lest White is labouring under too many delusions, let us say: as a result Miles beat both West and Sax!

3) **3...♘f6!?** A move that is rejected as defective by many theoreticians on the basis of the game Tal – Garcia (Sochi 1986). However, in our opinion, in general this is the best reply to 3 d4.

After **4 ♘c3** Black has the right to choose between two moves, pinning the knight c3: 4...♗b4 and 4...♕a5.

a) 4...♗b4!? 5 de ♘xe4 6 ♕d4 ♕a5! A recommendation of Tal. Weak is 6...d5? in view of 7 cd ♕a5 8 ♕xe4 ♗xc3+ 9 ♔d1! as happened in the above mentioned game Tal – Garcia. Yet another blunder – 9...cd?, and after 10 ♕c2 one of the black bishops is inevitably lost. Soon Garcia resigned.

It was because of these trifles that the whole variation was buried!

7 ♘e2 ♘xc3 (it is interesting to test 7...♘c5!? 8 ♕d1 ♘a4!) **8 ♘xc3 0-0 9 ♗e2 ♖e8** (Black commences a siege of the e5 pawn) **10 ♗f4**

10...c5! 11 ♕d2 ♘c6 12 0-0 ♘xe5 13 ♖fe1 ♗xc3 14 bc ♕c7 15 ♖ad1 d6 Black's chances are superior and we do not know at what point White could have improved!

b) 4...♕a5!? If the move 4...♗b4!? has been poorly researched, then here this is generally not the case. Nevertheless we dare say that even after the queen move Black has every right to reckon on counterplay.

5 f3 ♗b4 6 ♘e2 ed 7 ♕xd4

7...d5! A blow on the most heavily defended square! However analysis shows that this is not only effective but also the only means of imposing his will on the opponent.

Insufficient for equality is 7...0-0 in view of 8 e5 ♘e8 9 ♗f4! White prevents the freeing advance d7-d6, while a break in the centre from the other side does not achieve its objective: 9...f6 10 0-0-0 ♗c5 11 ♕d2 fe 12 ♗xe5 d6 13 ♗g3 ♗b4 14 a3 ♗f5!? 15 ♘d4 ♗xc3 16 ♕xc3 ♕xc3+ 17 bc ♗g6 18 h4 h6 19 h5 ♗h7 20 c5! d5 21 c4! The endgame is obviously in White's favour.

In the game Ostermeyer – Meduna (Porz 1988) Black offered a pawn sacrifice: 7...d6 8 ♗f4 0-0!? But the fact of the matter is that the compensation for it does not look sufficient: 9 ♗xd6!? ♗xd6 10 ♕xd6 ♖d8 11 ♕a3 ♕xa3 12 ba ♘a6 13 ♘f4 ♘c5 14 ♖d1 ♖xd1+ 15 ♔xd1 etc.

Here also it turns out that there is no real alternative to 7...d5!

8 cd He can also decline the pawn – 8 ♗g5, but Black does not stop there: 8...de! Though his king's flank is subject to ruin, possession of the e5 square gives him counterchances. This is how events might further develop: 9 ♗xf6 gf 10 ♕xf6 0-0 11 fe ♘d7 12 ♕h4 ♘e5 13 0-0-0 (or 13 ♕g3+ ♚h8 14 ♘d4 f5!?, opening the e-file and including the bishop c8 in the game) 13...♘xc4 14 ♘d4 ♘e5 with very sharp play.

8...cd 9 ed 0-0 10 a3 ♗c5 11 ♕c4 ♕b6!? (striving to exploit the weakening of the a7-g1 diagonal) **12 ♘g3 ♗f2+ 13 ♚d1 ♘bd7 14 ♘ge4 ♘xe4 15 ♘xe4 ♖d8**

Is it not true that Black has achieved what he wanted? The white king is exposed, the development of his pieces delayed. In the sample variations 16 ♘xf2 ♕xf2 17 ♕c7 ♖e8 18 ♗d2 ♘b6 or 16 ♕c2 ♗d4 17 ♗c4 ♘f6, it is certainly senseless to look for an immediate win but the fact that it is Black who is directing the game is obvious.

Let us say this: the longer the variation 3...♘f6 remains in the shade, the... better it will be for Black!

4) **3...d6** The main continuation. Play in this variation in fact 'steers' towards a position that is characteristic of the 'Indian' but not the Caro-Kann scheme. Too vast to include here; and so where resemblance

transfers into full identity, our coverage has to stop.

White has a choice: 4 d5, 4 ♘c3 or 4 ♘f3 There is one other move, very 'simple': 4 de?!, but the endgame after 4...de 5 ♕xd8+ ♚xd8 can only be worse, for example: 6 f4 ♗b4+ 7 ♘c3 ♘f6 8 ♗d2 ♘bd7 9 fe ♘xe5 10 ♘f3 ♘fd7 11 a3 ♗d6 12 ♖d1 ♚e7 13 b4 ♖e8 (Frialde – Spraggett, Toronto 1996).

a) **4 d5?!** A premature move – the tension of the pawn pair d4-e5 is clearly in White's favour, and he should not break it too soon.

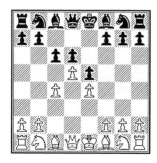

He can try to equalise by standard methods: 4... ♗e7 5 ♘c3 ♘f6 6 h3 a6 7 ♗d3 ♘bd7 8 ♘ge2 h5!? – firstly, to prevent g2-g4, and secondly, intending an operation to seize dark squares on the king's flank.

But he can play even more sharply: **4...f5!?** This is interesting even from the formal point of view – all eight half moves have been made by pawns. If, however, we are talking about essentials then White is in no position to maintain his centre.

5 ♗d3 fe 6 ♗xe4 ♘f6 7 ♘c3 ♘xe4 8 ♘xe4 ♕h4 (the early introduction of the queen is absolutely in order here) **9 ♕e2** (on 9 ♕d3 it is necessary to consider 9...♕g4!?) **9...cd 10 cd ♗f5** In the game Ciric – Burmakin (Berlin 1995) followed the more peaceful 11 ♘c3 ♘d7 12 ♘f3 ♕h5 13 ♘d4 ♕xe2+ 14 ♘dxe2 with an equal endgame.

More principled is **11 ♕b5+!? ♘d7 12 ♘g3**, and White wins a pawn. But after **12...♗c2!? 13 ♘f3 ♕a4 14 ♕xb7 ♖b8** Black has compensation.

Wherever the queen goes it will not find peace:

15 ♕c7 ♗d3!? (preventing castling) 16 b3 ♖xb3! 17 ♕c8+ ♔e7 18 ♗g5+ ♔f7 19 ab ♕xa1+ 20 ♔d2 ♕b2+ 21 ♔xd3 ♘c5+ 22 ♔e3 ♕c3+ with perpetual check, or

15 ♕c6 ♕b4+! (inferior is 15...♕xc6?! 16 dc ♘b6 17 ♗e3 ♖c8 18 ♖c1, and the endgame is in White's favour) 16 ♘d2 ♗a4 17 ♕c4 ♘c5!? 18 0-0 ♕b7! 19 ♖e1 ♗b5 20 ♕d4 ♘d3 21 ♖e3 ♖c8. The initiative fully belongs to Black.

b) **4 ♘c3** Quite a lot of games are played on this theme, but only a few of them remain on the track of the Caro-Kann defence. For example, 4...♕c7 5 ♘f3 ♘f6 6 ♗e2 ♗e7 7 0-0 ♘bd7 is a classical Indian defence (code A55). The same can be said

about the chain of moves 4...g6 5 ♘f3 ♗g7 – again an Indian, only the code has changed (this time it is A42).

4...♗e7 5 ♘f3 ♗g4 and 4...♘f6 5 f4 ♕a5 can be considered as relatively independent.

b1) **4...♗e7 5 ♘f3 ♗g4!?**

From the point of view of struggle for advantage, the endgame after 6 de?! ♗xf3 7 gf de 8 ♕xd8+ ♗xd8 is poor. Here the two bishops do not play any particular role; the main thing is the blockade on the dark squares.

All White's efforts to change the status quo lead to nothing: 9 f4!? ♘d7 10 ♖g1 ♗c7! 11 ♗h3 ♘gf6 12 ♖xg7 ef! (gaining the important e5 square) 13 ♖g5 ♘e5 14 ♔f1 ♘g6 15 ♖f5 ♘g8! 16 b3 ♘8e7 17 ♖h5 ♖d8 18 ♗a3 ♗e5 and Black stands better (Sax – Hort, Amsterdam 1983).

If it cannot be changed then it means that the d4 square needs to be held – **6 ♗e3**, but then the standard (again, however, purely 'Indian') exchanging operation snaps into action: **6...♗xf3! 7 ♕xf3 ♗g5!** It is to Black's advantage to remove from the board all (except the light-squared bishop) the opponent's minor pieces – then it will be quite an easy matter to bring about the blockade on the dark squares.

So as not to obtain a strategically hopeless game, White needs urgently to do something. For example, **8 ♕g3 ♗xc3 9 fc!? ♕f6 10 c5!**, wrecking Black's pawn chain and giving his light-squared bishop space on which to operate.

Unsatisfactory now is 10...dc because of 11 ♗c4! with the threat of ♖h1-f1. There remains **10...ed 11 ed dc**, but even then dreams of a blockade turn to dust:

12 ♗c4! ♘h6 (how else to defend the f7 square?) **13 0-0-0! ♘d7** (or 13...0-0 14 dc ♕e7 15 ♖d6 ♔h8 16 ♖hd1 with a great positional advantage) **14 ♖hf1 ♕g6 15 ♕c7 ♖d8 16 ♔b1** White draws ever close to victory and even **16...b5** does not help Black get out of the vice in view of **17 d5!**

b2) **4...♘f6!? 5 f4?!** (more reliable, it goes without saying, is 5 ♘f3, but then we once again move away from forcing Caro-Kann variations to the Indian labyrinth) **5...♕a5!** The correct order of moves. White is forced to defend the pawn with a not very attractive queen manoeuvre,

thereby losing tempi needed for the development of his pieces.

6 ♕d3 ♘a6 7 ♘f3 ed 8 ♕xd4 ♘c5 A double attack: the pawn on e4 and the fork on b3 are both hanging.

The natural defence is 9 ♘d2 but after 9...♗e7 10 ♗e2 0-0 11 0-0 ♗d8!? White is faced with a new wave of attack. The transfer of the enemy bishop to b6 is threatened; while the d6 pawn is untouchable: 12 ♕xd6? ♗c7! 13 ♕d4 ♘e6 14 ♕d3 ♘xf4 or 13 b4 ♕xb4 14 ♕xc7 ♕xc3 with a great advantage for Black.

The strongest chain of moves for both sides is 12 ♔h1 ♖e8 13 ♕xd6 ♗b6 14 e5 ♗f5! (theratening to trap the queen) 15 a3! ♖ad8 16 b4 ♖xd6 17 ba ♗xa5 18 ♘ce4!? ♘cxe4 19 ♘xe4 ♖dd8 20 ♘g3 ♗g4 – leads us to a position which we have to assess in Black's favour.

Possibly, in the game Prie – Anic (Cannes 1990), after wrestling with all these factors White decided to defend against the double attack in a different way: **9 ♖b1** And Black took his opponent at his word! After 9...♕b6?! 10 ♗d3 ♗e7 11 b4 ♘xd3+ 12 ♕xd3 ♘g4 13 ♖b2! f5 14 h3 ♘h6 15 e5 Prie pleasantly overcame his opening problems.

However on closer inspection it becomes clear that the defence is illusory and the pawn could be taken: **9...♘cxe4! 10 b4 ♕b6!** Thanks to this move Black not only saves the piece but also gains the advantage: **11 c5 ♕d8 12 ♘xe4 ♕e7 13 ♘fg5 d5 14 ♖b3 ♘xe4 15 ♖e3 f5 16 ♗e2 ♖g8! 17 0-0 g6** etc.

c) **4 ♘f3** (the most natural continuation) **4...♗g4** Yet again 4...♘d7 leads us to the Indian scheme with the code A55.

After 4...♗g4 begins the 'hanging' of the d4 pawn. There are three defences to choose from: 5 de, 5 d5 or 5 ♗e2.

c1) **5 de ♗xf3 6 gf** Also harmless is 6 ♕xf3 de 7 ♗e2 ♘f6 8 0-0 ♘bd7 9 ♘c3 ♕c7 10 ♕g3 ♘c5 with a particularly unpleasant transfer of the knight to d4 or f4.

6...de 7 ♕xd8+ ♔xd8 (nowhere in this endgame will Black risk getting the worst of it) **8 f4!?** (trying to 'wake up' his bishops) **8...♗b4+!?** The most concrete decision. The insipid 8...f6 is certainly weaker but even here White cannot count on much:

9 ♗h3 ♔c7 10 ♘c3 ♘a6! (intending to catch the important

dark-squared bishop on the e3 square) 11 ♗e3 ♖d8 12 ♔e2 ♗c5! 13 ♖ag1 g6 14 fe ♗xe3! (the catch is successfully completed) 15 ♔xe3 fe 16 ♖g5 ♖e8, and it is Black who is playing for a win (Seirawan – Nikolic, Tilburg 1990).

9 ♘c3!? ♗d6 10 fe fe 11 ♖g1 g6 12 ♗g5+ ♔c7 13 ♗h3 h6 14 ♗e3 g5 15 0-0-0 ♘f6 16 ♗f5 ♘bd7 (only not 16...♘a6? in view of 17 f4!, and White breaks through the dark square blockade, Kaidanov – Blocker, Washington 1994) 17 ♘a4! White has succeeded in preventing the exchange of the dark-squared bishops but as before there is apparently no way of developing an initiative.

9 ♘c3 The eccentric 9 ♔e2!? (in order to generally avoid exchanges) does not have the anticipated effect: 9...♘d7 10 ♖g1 ♘gf6! (enjoying an advantage in development, Black quite rightly sacrifices a pawn) 11 ♖xg7 ♔e7 12 f3 ♘h5 13 ♖g4 ♘xf4+ 14 ♗xf4 ef 15 ♖xf4 ♗d6 (and once again all the dark squares are under Black's control) 16 ♖h4 ♘e5 17 ♘c3 h5!? with more than sufficient compensation (Yagupov – Navarovsky, Budapest 1991).

9...♘f6 10 f3 ♘bd7 11 ♗e2 The alternative is 11 ♗d2 ef 12 ♗xf4 ♘h5 13 ♗d2 ♗d6 14 0-0-0 ♔c7 15 ♘e2 ♖he8 16 ♔c2 ♘e5! 17 ♘d4 ♖ad8 18 ♘f5 (or 18 f4 ♘g6 19 e5 ♗c5 20 ♘e2 f6!, undermining the e5 pawn) 18...♗f8 19 ♗e2 ♘g6! with an occupation of the f4 square.

11...♗d6!? Forcing White to

decide: either to close the position by 12 f5 – but then the light-squared bishop finally loses 'citizen's rights' – or to exchange in the centre and concede to a dark square blockade.

12 fe ♗xe5 13 0-0 On 13 ♗e3!? (Bunzmann – Brameyer, Germany 1993) the right reaction consisted of 13...♘h5!? **14 0-0-0 ♔c7** with an inevitable blockade of the f4 square.

13...g5! Black's conception remains unchanged for the whole course of the endgame: control of the dark squares and ideally – a complete dark square blockade.

So as not to allow a bind, White is forced to go for a break. But this simplification is favourable for Black and (in the first place) loses the most important defender of the dark squares – the bishop c1: **14 f4 gf 15 ♗xf4 ♖g8+ 16 ♔h1 ♔e7 17 ♗xe5 ♘xe5 18 ♖f5 ♘fd7 19 ♖af1 f6** (Nevednichy – Becerra, Erevan 1996). The Cuban grandmaster won this game, though upon accurate play White certainly has the right to reckon on a draw. But not more!

Practically all variations and versions of such an endgame – with exchanges on e5 and d8 – are harmless for Black.

c2) 5 d5!? In contrast to the approach to the problem seen in the previous variation – White closes the centre. It is worth adding that analogous to the variation 1 e4 c6 2 c4 e5 3 d4 d6 4 d5?! here the pawn advance is not appropriate: the inclusion of the moves 4 ♘f3 ♗g4 deprives Black of his most important resource f7-f5!

5...♗e7!? An idealistic move – above all Black wants to develop his dark-squared bishop.

The standard 5...♘f6 6 ♘c3 ♘bd7 7 h3 ♗xf3 8 ♕xf3 ♗e7 comes up against 9 h4!, and the light-squared bishop – the cinderella of this construction – suddenly bcomes a strong piece. In the game Vaulin – Savon (Warsaw 1992) followed: 9...0-0 10 g3! a5 11 ♗h3 ♘c5 12 0-0 cd 13 cd b5 (it seems that Black has found counterplay but this is no more than an optical illusion) 14 ♗e3! b4 15 ♗xc5! bc 16 ♗a3 cb 17 ♗xb2 ♘d7 and here White's advantage is consolidated by 18 ♖fc1 ♘c5 19 ♗a3 ♖b8 20 ♖c4.

6 ♘c3 ♗xf3!? (it was still not too late to return to usual play by 6...♘f6) **7 ♕xf3 ♗g5** (the dream has come true, but...) **8 ♕g3! ♗xc1 9 ♖xc1**

With the exchange of the dark-squared bishops Black is left with no bad pieces, but... none of them are in play! White's advantage in development (a minimum of three tempi) places a question mark against Black's strategical plan. Above all the break c4-c5! is threatened.

9...♕f6 (9...♔f8 10 c5!) **10 c5! dc 11 dc ♘xc6** He would like to play 11...bc, in order to prevent the knight going to d5, but after 12 ♘a4 ♘e7 13 ♘xc5 0-0 14 ♖d1! White's positional advantage is too great (Suba – Ceteras, Romania 1999).

12 ♘d5 ♕h6 13 ♖xc5 ♕d6 The other defence against the fork on c7 was the move 13...♖c8, but the simple combination 14 ♗b5 (the pawn on e5 is hanging) 14...♕d6 15 ♖xc6! bc 16 ♕xg7 cb 17 0-0 ♖c2 18 b4! gives this idea up for lost.

14 ♖b5 ♕h6 Threatening a check on c1. Black, of course, does not object to a repetition of moves: 15 ♖c5 ♕d6, but there are other plans for White...

15 ♗e2!

Neglect of development of his own pieces costs Black dear – he will not succeed in castling on the short side:

15...♖b8 16 ♘b4! ♘ge7 17 ♘xc6 ♘xc6 18 ♖xe5+! ♔f8 19 ♕a3+ ♔g8 20 ♖d5 ♕c1+ (also losing is 20...♖e8 because of 21 0-0 ♖xe4 22 ♕xa7!) 21 ♖d1 ♕f4 22 ♕g3 etc.

Does he want to castle long? Welcome to the suicide club: **15...♕c1+ 16 ♗d1 0-0-0** (nowhere to castle – also no way out: 16...♕c4? 17 ♖b4! ♕c5 18 ♖xb7 ♔f8 19 0-0) **17 0-0 ♕c4** After 17...♕h6? this sad short story ends in mate: 18 ♗g4+ ♔b8 19 ♖xb7+!

18 ♕xg7 ♕xb5 19 ♕xh8 ♕xb2 20 ♕xh7 ♕xa2 21 ♕xf7 ♔b8 22 ♕c7+ ♔a8 23 ♗g4 ♕a5 24 ♕g7, and White has an extra pawn in his pocket on the king's flank.

Of course this analysis needs to be carefully confirmed in practice but first impressions are that the idea of playing for an exchange of bishops – ♗f8-e7-g5 – might turn out badly.

c3) **5 ♗e2 ♘d7** Play, linked to an exchange of dark-squared bishops, already lacks its former optimism: 5...♗e7!? 6 0-0 ♗xf3 7 ♗xf3 ♗g5!? 8 ♗xg5 ♕xg5 9 ♕b3! ♕e7 10 ♖d1!

It is still a long way to the endgame, but with queens on the board the positional niceties fade into the background

The frontal attack c4-c5! is threatened, for example: 10...♘a6 11 c5! dc 12 d5! ♘f6 13 ♗e2!? ♖d8 14 d6!, and Black is closer than ever to his demise: 14...♖xd6 15 ♖xd6 ♕xd6 16 ♕xb7 ♘b4 17 ♘c3 0-0 18 ♖d1 ♕b8 19 ♕xb8 ♖xb8 20 ♖d2! with a technically winning endgame.

In the game Shchakachev – Varga (Lausanne 2001) Black, realising that he might be consumed without a great struggle, first of all tucked away his king: 10...♘h6 11 ♘c3 0-0. But this is hardly the way to equality. Here is a sample variation: 12 ♖d2 ♘a6 13 de! de 14 ♖ad1 ♘c5 15 ♕a3! (threatening 16 ♘a4) 15...♖fe8 16 b4 ♘e6 17 ♖d7 ♕f6 18 ♖xb7 ♘d4 19 ♘e2 and White has an unquestionable advantage.

6 ♘c3 There is no sense in 6 ♘g1!? ♗xe2 7 ♘xe2 ♘gf6 8 ♘bc3 ♗e7 9 0-0 0-0, and without the light-squared bishop he can boldly place his pawns on white squares: 10 f3!? a6 11 a4 a5 12 ♗e3 ♖e8 13 b3 ed 14 ♗xd4 ♗f8 15 ♕d2. In the game Mikhalchishin – Savchenko (Nova Gorica 1997) Black shed a pawn – 15...d5!? 16 cd cd 17 ed, after

which he missed the opportunity of obtaining compensation by 17...♘b6!? 18 ♗xf6 ♕xf6 19 ♔h1 ♖ad8.

6...♗e7 7 0-0 ♘gf6 The opportunity for the manoeuvre 7...♗xf3 8 ♗xf3 ♗g5 has already passed by. The more so that in the present situation there is the mirror reply – 9 ♗g4! ♗xc1 10 ♗xd7+ ♕xd7 11 ♖xc1 ♘f6 12 f4!, winning the struggle for the centre: 12...ed 13 ♕xd4 0-0 14 ♖cd1 ♖fd8 15 c5! dc 16 ♕xc5 ♕c7 17 ♖xd8+ ♕xd8 18 ♖d1 with advantage (Nunn – Groszpeter, Budapest 1978).

8 ♗e3 0-0 Before us is a tabiya, indeed, again from another opening – A53. But since there is an inconceivable number of games (with all possible move orders) passing through this position, we cannot leave it completely without attention.

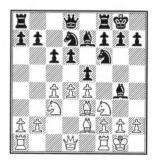

There are three methods of struggle for the advantage:

9 ♘d2!? ♗xe2 10 ♕xe2, and the way of the f-pawn is open: 10...ed 11 ♗xd4 ♖e8 12 f4!? ♘f8 13 ♖ad1 ♘6d7 14 ♘f3 ♗f6 15 ♔h1 ♕c7 16 ♕f2 ♘e6 17 ♗xf6 ♘xf6 (Bistric – Anic, Pula 1999) 18 ♘h4!? b6

19 ♘f5 ♘c5 20 e5!? de 21 ♕g3 g6 22 ♕h4!? with chances of attack;

9 d5 (consolidating his space advantage) 9...c5 10 ♘e1 ♗xe2 11 ♕xe2 ♘e8 12 g3!? (preparing the break f2-f4) 12...g6 13 ♗h6 ♘g7 14 ♘g2 ♗g5 15 ♗xg5 ♕xg5 16 f4! (Morozevich – Savchenko, Alushta 1993);

9 ♖c1!? (a cunning move: White waits...) 9...♖e8 But now follows with far greater effect 10 d5! The rook on e8 is doing nothing and it is some time before it returns to the place where it is needed.

10...c5 He must close the centre otherwise White's breakthrough will be even easier: 10...♗f8?! 11 b4 a5 12 dc! bc 13 b5! (Ivanchuk – Gallejo, Erevan 1996).

11 a3 ♖c8 12 ♘d2!? (here too this idea proves useful) 12...♗xe2 13 ♕xe2 ♖f8 14 b4 with advantage (Kharitonov – Savon, Moscow 1992).

The fact is that in the variations 1 e4 c6 2 c4 e5 3 d4 d6 4 ♘c3 or 4 ♘f3 a clear way to equality is not always apparent. But it must not be forgotten that he has a fine trump up his sleeve – 3...♘f6! Thus it is too early for White to rest on his laurels.

C

3 ♘f3! Namely this move (and not 3 d4) – is the most unpleasant for Black. He has five replies with various degrees of eccentricity: 3...d5, 3...f5, 3...♘f6, 3...♕c7 and 3...♕a5. The sixth, the most popular, is 3...d6, after which 4 d4 returns us to what we have already looked at.

1) 3...d5?! Giving up material, but for what is not clear: 4 cd cd 5 ♘xe5 de 6 ♗b5+ ♗d7 7 ♕b3 ♕e7 8 ♗xd7+ ♘xd7 9 ♕xb7 ♖b8 10 ♕xd7+ ♕xd7 11 ♘xd7 ♔xd7 (Florian – Zinn, Dresden 1959) 12 ♘c3 ♘f6 13 b3 ♗c5 14 ♗b2 with an easily winning endgame.

2) 3...f5?! a venture of pure water, but since it was devised by a grandmaster – the Swede Jonny Hector, then it needs to be taken seriously. Incidentally, we cannot imagine what is the strongest move here!

4 ♘xe5 is not just the strongest but also the only normal move: 4...♕f6 (defending against the threat of check on h5) 5 d4 d6 (5...fe?! 6 ♕g4!) 6 ♘f3 fe 7 ♘g5 d5 8 ♘c3 h6 9 ♘h3 ♕f7 (pointless is 9...♗xh3?! in view of 10 ♕h5+) 10 ♘f4 ♗d6 11 ♕h5!?

g5 12 ♕xf7+ ♔xf7 13 ♘h5 ♘e7 14 ♗e2 ♗e6 and it is quite possible to survive. True, in the game Jansa – Bobzin (Hamburg 1993) Black did not realise that he was threatened with the move 15 0-0 and went quickly downhill: 15...♘d7?! 16 f3! Certainly, the f-file needs to be boarded up before it is hit: 15...♘f5!? 16 cd cd 17 f3 e3! Possibly even here White has the advantage (18 ♗d3!?) but this still has to be proved.

4 ♗e2! – this is a clear solution. First he completes his development and then the pawn weaknesses will fall all by themselves – **4...fe 5 ♘xe5**, and then:

5...♘f6 6 0-0 ♗e7 7 ♘c3 d5? (this is quite bad but also after 7...0-0 8 ♘g4 ♖e8 9 ♕c2 Black is not be envied) 8 cd cd 9 ♗b5+ ♗d7 10 ♘xd7 ♘bxd7 11 ♘xd5! (Gofshtein – Hector, Manila 1992) or

5...♕h4 6 ♘c3 d6 7 ♗g4! ♘a6 8 ♗xc8 ♖xc8 9 ♘g4 ♘c5 10 0-0 ♘f6 11 ♘xf6+ gf 12 g3 ♖g8 13 ♖e1 f5 14 d3 and it is not clear how Black will manage to make a draw from this position (Sher – Hector, Vejle 1994).

3) **3...♘f6 4 ♘c3** We see some kind of wild blend of the Caro-Kann and Petroff defences upon 4 ♘xe5!? d6 5 ♘f3 ♘xe4. Moreover the path is quite untrodden and when the opportunity presents itself it can give White chances of success:

6 ♘c3!? (more interesting than 6 d4 d5 7 ♗d3 ♗b4+ 8 ♘bd2 ♗e6 9 0-0 ♘xd2 10 ♗xd2 ♗xd2 11 ♘xd2 0-0 with equality, Motwani – Speelman, Dubai 1986) 6...♘xc3 (also 6...♗f5?! does not solve his problems: 7 ♗d3

♘xc3 8 dc followed by long castling, Belyavsky – Tavadian, Yaroslav 1982) 7 dc ♗e7 8 ♗e2 ♘d7 9 0-0 0-0 10 ♗f4 ♘f6 11 ♕c2 d5 12 ♖ad1 ♕b6 13 h3 ♗d7 14 ♗e5 with some pressure (Kuporosov – Meduna, Lazne Bogdanec 1994).

4...♗b4 5 ♘xe5

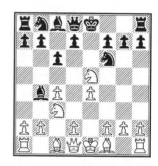

Should he immediately win back the pawn (5...♕e7) or wait a while (5...0-0)? This is the question.

a) **5...♕e7?!** (too conservative) 6 ♘d3! White's good fortune is that he finds a tempo to make this retreat. After 6 ♘f3, as shown long ago by the game van den Hoek – Euwe (Hague 1942), he did not reckon on the fact that 6...♘xe4 7 ♗e2 0-0 8 0-0 d6 9 ♕c2 ♘f6 10 d4 ♗g4 11 ♗g5 ♘bd7 12 ♖fe1 ♖fe8 led to a dull symmetrical position.

6...♘xe4 7 ♗e2!? The alternative is 7 ♕e2 with the better endgame or attack:

7...♘xc3 (endgame) 8 dc ♕xe2+ 9 ♗xe2 ♗e7 10 ♗f4! d6 11 0-0-0 ♗e6 12 ♘b4 (Votava – Meduna, Lazne Bogdanec 1995);

7...♗xc3 (attack) 8 dc 0-0 9 ♗f4 ♖e8 10 0-0-0 ♕f8 11 ♕c2 d6 12 f3 ♘f6 13 g4 ♘a6 (Tepla – Stefanova, Benasque 1997) 14 ♗g3!?

7...♗a5 (no use is 7...♗d6 – after 8 0-0 0-0 9 ♘xe4 ♕xe4 10 b3 ♗c7 11 ♗a3 ♖d8 12 ♖e1 White's advantage is in no need of explanation) **8 0-0 0-0 9 ♖e1 d6 10 ♗f3 ♘xc3 11 dc ♕f6 12 ♗e4 ♗b6 13 ♕h5**

An advantage in development, and the attack – all at once. In the meantime he threatens mate in one move, while on 13...h6 White had in store 14 g4!, and the pawn inexorably marches on. In the game Zaichik – Izeta (Spain 1991) Black defended in another way – **13...g6,** but after **14 ♗g5!** he did not last long.

b) **5...0-0!?** A pawn down, but in return a developed piece up!

6 ♗e2!? Possibly he should be satisfied with less – 6 ♘d3 ♗xc3 7 dc ♘xe4 8 ♗e2 d5 9 cd ♕xd5 10 0-0 ♗f5 11 ♗e3 ♕e6 12 ♖e1 ♘d7 13 ♗f1 ♕d5 14 ♘f4 ♕xd1 15 ♖axd1 ♘ef6 16 f3 pursuing the 'advantage of the two bishops' in the endgame (Tal – Mukhametov, Leningrad 1991).

6...d6 7 ♘d3 ♗xc3 8 dc ♘xe4 9 0-0 ♖e8 Lacking in prospects is 9...♘d7 10 ♖e1 ♕f6 11 f3 ♘ec5 12 ♘f2 a5 13 ♗e3 (Bareev – Volkov, Elista 1998). It seems, as distinct from the variation 5...♕e7, there is not really much in it...

10 f3 ♘f6 11 ♗g5

The opening has just about finished but there is apparently no ray of hope for Black. The game Vaganian – Nogeiras (Leningrad 1987) continued in this way: **11...♘bd7 12 ♘f2 ♕a5 13 ♗h4 d5 14 ♖e1 b6 15 cd ♘xd5 16 ♘e4 ♗a6 17 ♗xa6 ♕xa6 18 ♕d4 b5 19 a4!?** Again White is better.

4) 3...♕c7 Quite simply, without hassle, defending the e5 pawn. White can choose between 4 d4 and 4 ♘c3.

a) **4 d4 ♗b4+ 5 ♘bd2!?** 5 ♗d2 ♗xd2+ 6 ♕xd2 d6 7 ♘c3 ♘f6 8 ♗e2 0-0 9 0-0 looks more solid. In the game Bajovic – Meduna (Plovdiv 1982), after 9...♗g4 10 ♖fd1 ♘bd7 11 ♖ac1 a5 12 h3, Black mistakenly rejected the exchange.

12...♗h5? A tactical rather than a positional mistake. But White 'forgave' the opponent, not noticing

13 de! winning material: 13...de? 14 g4 ♗g6 15 g5 or 13...♘xe5 14 g4 ♗g6 15 ♕xd6 ♕xd6 16 ♖xd6.

He should have exchanged: 12...♗xf3 13 ♗xf3 ♖ad8, and there is nothing in particular for White.

5...ed 6 a3 ♗xd2+?! It is of course attractive to keep hold of the d4 pawn but concrete variations turn out in Black's favour. Therefore it was necessary to reconcile himself to 6...♗e7 7 ♘xd4 d6 8 ♘2f3 ♘f6 9 ♗d3 0-0 10 0-0 ♖e8 with an acceptable game.

7 ♕xd2 c5 8 ♕g5 ♘e7 (or 8...g6 9 ♗f4 d6 10 ♕g3!) **9 ♕xg7 ♖g8 10 ♕xh7 ♘bc6 11 ♘g5 ♘d8 12 h4!** A non-standard position requires a non-standard solution. In this way White includes the rook in the attack.

12...♕b6 13 ♖h3 d5 14 ♖f3 de 15 ♘xe4 f5

We are looking at the encounter Kosten – Szabolcsi (France 1997). All beauty in this game remained with the cadre. There could (and even should) follow **16 ♗g5 ♕e6 17 ♖e3!!** A study-like move on the theme of 'covering over': 17...de 18 ♘f6+. Also losing is **17...fe 18 ♖xe4 ♖g7!? 19 ♕h8+ ♕g8 20 ♕xg8+ ♖xg8**

21 ♖xe7+ ♔f8 22 ♖e5 Why is everything non-forced so beautiful?

b) **4 ♘c3 ♘f6** Not finding the logical idea 4...♗b4. Possibly because of 5 g3!? ♘f6 6 ♗g2 ♗xc3 7 bc ♘xe4 8 ♕e2 d5 9 ♗a3 ♗e6 10 0-0 ♘d7 11 cd cd 12 ♖fe1 ♘df6 13 ♖ab1. Black has an extra pawn, but joy – none: 13...0-0-0 14 ♘xe5! ♕xe5 15 d3 ♕c7 16 de ♘xe4 17 ♖ec1 ♘d6 18 ♗xd6 ♖xd6 19 c4! (A.Sokolov – Glek, Vilnius 1984).

5 d4!? White played the opening in an odd way in the game Franco – Abreu (Varadero 2000): 5 a3?! (preventing the development of the bishop on b4 but perhaps it is not worth bothering himself with this?) 5...♗c5 6 ♗d3?! (but this too is quite a strange move; why not 6 b4!?) 6...a5 7 0-0 d6 8 h3, and now...

8...g5! Exploiting the fact that White has tied his own hands, Black commences the attack. Serves him right! Instead of a2-a3 it is nearly always useful to play d2-d4...

5...♗b4 6 de ♘xe4 7 ♕d4!? ♕a5 8 ♕xe4 ♗xc3+ Yet another fresh position. General words and criteria do not apply here; it is necessary to consider all variations deeply and skilfully.

9 ♗d2 Worthy of attention is 9 ♘d2!?; at least this move cannot be refuted at once: 9...♗b4 10 a3! (but not 10 ♗d3?! in view of 10...♘a6! 11 ♗c2 ♘c5 12 ♕e2 ♘e6, and Black adroitly transfers the knight from b8 to e6) 10...♗e7 (now 10...♘a6 is parried by 11 ♖b1! ♗e7 12 b4) 11 ♖b1! (none the less!) 11...♕c7 12 b4 d6 13 ♗b2 0-0 14 ♗d3 g6 15 ed ♗xd6 16 ♕e2 ♘d7 17 c5, and White has all the play.

9...♗xd2+ 10 ♘xd2 ♘a6 11 a3 (preparing to castle long) **11...0-0 12 0-0-0 d5!?** (without this pawn sacrifice it is difficult for Black to finish his development) **13 ed ♗f5**

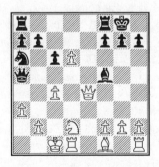

In the game Kharlov – Shabanov (Kuibyshev 1990) White carelessly played 14 ♘b3?! There and then the queen became 'enraged' (or in diplomatic language, became a 'desperado'): 14...♕xa3! 15 ba ♗xe4 16 ♖d4 ♗f5 17 c5 ♘b8 18 ♗c4 ♘d7 19 ♖e1 b5! The position is full of life.

But meanwhile even dropping Black into a pit was very possible: **14 ♕e3! ♖ad8 15 ♘b3 ♕a4 16 c5! ♖fe8 17 ♕c3 ♕f4+ 18 ♘d2 ♘b8 19 ♗c4 b6 20 g3!** Driving away the enemy queen from its central position, White seizes the e-file and breaks through to the 7th rank: **20...♕h6 21 ♖he1 bc 22 ♖e7! ♖f8 23 f4 ♕xd6 24 ♖xa7** with advantage.

5) **3...♕a5!?** Originality increases from move to move: Black wants to slow down as much as possible the advance d2-d4.

4 ♘c3 There was a fresh treatment of this position by Joel Lautier: 4 ♗e2 ♘f6 5 0-0!? ♘xe4 6 ♖e1 d6 7 d4 ♘f6 8 ♗d2 ♕c7 9 de de 10 ♘xe5! ♗e7 11 ♗f4 ♕b6 12 ♕c2 0-0 13 ♘c3 ♗e6 14 ♖ad1 ♘bd7 15 ♘f3! White has won back the pawn and his pieces occupy significantly better squares (Lautier – Kuczynski, Polanica Zdroj 1991).

4...♘f6 White's next move is very important.

It is clear that Black is thinking of playing ♗f8-b4. This idea can be prevented (5 a3 or 5 d3 ♗b4 6 ♗d2) or ignored: 5 g3 or 5 ♗e2.

5 a3 looks nothing special because of 5...♗c5 and dubious is 6 ♘xe5?! ♗xf2+! 7 ♔xf2 ♕xe5 8 d3 d5 with the better prospects for Black. While after 6 ♗e2 d6 7 0-0 ♕c7 8 ♖b1 ♗g4 9 b4 ♗b6 10 d3 ♗xf3!? 11 ♗xf3 ♘bd7 12 ♘e2 0-0 13 ♗b2 ♖fe8 14 ♕c2 c5!? 15 g3 ♘f8 16 ♗g2 ♘e6 Black comes out of the opening with a fully worthwhile position (Kharlov – Volkov, Samara 2000).

5 d3!? was tried in the game Ivanchuk – Dominguez (Erevan 2001). Black, perceiving that on 5...♗b4 follows 6 ♗d2, decides to play with dash: 5...d5?! But, just like Lautier, Ivanchuk could have exploited the advanced position of the black queen for a very rapid development of his forces: 6 cd cd 7 ♘xe5 ♗b4 8 ♗d2! de 9 ♘c4! ♕c5 10 a3 ♗xc3 11 ♗xc3 ed 12 ♗xd3 0-0 13 0-0 with a weighty advantage.

The plan 5 g3!? is reminiscent of what Miezis did in the variation 1 e4 c6 2 c4 e5 3 ♘c3 ♗c5 4 g3?! (There we criticised this plan, but here the black queen is not very useful in the struggle on the king's flank). In the game Balashov – Volkov (Elista 2000) White obtained a promising position: 5...♗b4 6 ♕c2 0-0 7 ♗g2 d6 8 0-0 ♘bd7 9 d3 ♗xc3 10 bc a6 11 ♘h4 b5 12 ♘f5 ♕c7 13 ♕d2! (a highly unpleasant move – threatening a queen thrust to g5) 13...♔h8 14 d4 (14 f4!?) 14...bc 15 de de 16 ♕d6.

5 ♗e2 (for the present this remains the most popular, although 5 d3!? looks at the very least no worse)

5...♗b4 6 ♕c2!? A flexible continuation. In defending the e4 pawn, White intends an assault on the queen's flank by means of a2-a3 and b2-b4. However in the event of an exchange on c3, White has the possibility of recapturing with the d-pawn followed by doubling his heavy pieces on the open central file. After 6 0-0 0-0 7 d3 Black has more levers for counterplay:

7...d5?! (apparently premature) 8 cd (now Black has to give up the bishop and the factor of the advantage of the two bishops becomes significant; not so clear is 8 ed cd 9 ♘xe5, Korchnoi – Gurevich, Barcelona 1992, 9...d4!?) 8...♗xc3 9 bc cd 10 ♘xe5 de 11 ♘c4 ♕c7 (11...♕xc3? loses the exchange: 12 ♗b2 ♕b4 13 ♗a3) 12 de ♘xe4 13 ♗d3 ♗e6 14 ♗xe4 ♗xc4 15 ♖e1 ♘a6 16 ♗e3 (Cholovic – Volkov, Ohrid 2001);

Devoid of ideas is 7...♖e8 8 ♗d2 ♗f8 9 d4 d6 10 b4! ♕c7 11 d5 ♘bd7 12 ♖e1 ♗e7 13 ♗f1 c5 14 a3 b6 (Tsermiadianos – Miles, Agios Nikolaos 1997) 15 ♘h4!? g6 16 g3 with a space advantage;

7...♗xc3! (best and meeting the requirements of the position, you see

White cannot take with the d-pawn) 8 bc d6 9 ♕c2 ♖e8 10 h3 ♘bd7 11 ♘h2 d5 12 cd cd 13 ed ♘xd5 14 ♗d2 ♘7f6 15 ♖ab1 ♕c7 with comfortable play (Castilio – Ravi, Linares 2000).

6...0-0 7 0-0 ♖e8 8 a3 One way or another Black has to retreat. He must either concede space (8...♗f8) or allow the formation of a weak d-pawn in his camp (8...♗xc3 9 dc).

In the game Lastin – Volkov (Perm 1997) equality proved to be close at hand: 8...♗xc3 9 dc d6 10 ♗g5 ♘bd7 11 ♖ad1 ♕c7 12 ♘e1 h6 13 ♗e3 ♘f8 14 g3 ♗h3 15 ♘g2 ♖ad8 16 f3 b6 17 ♖d2 d5!, but White's play does not make the best impression.

8...♗f8 (conceding space). White has a choice: which pawn should he advance?

9 b4!? White intends to attack on the broadest possible front. But he has to take into account that the position of the pawn on b4 allows Black to attack it later with by a7-a5.

More circumspect is 9 d4 d6 10 h3 ♘bd7 11 ♗e3 a6 12 de ♘xe5 13 ♘d4! (with an advantage in space, it is unfavourable to exchange pieces; apart from this, White will 'charge forward' with f2-f4!) 13...♕c7

14 ♖ac1 b6 15 f4 ♘g6 16 g4!? ♗b7 17 ♘f5 c5 18 ♗f3 with a strong initiative (Ivanchuk – Miles, Biel 1989).

9...♕c7 (not falling into the trap, even if it is quite unpretentious: 9...♗xb4? 10 ab! ♕xa1 11 ♘a2 a5 12 b5, and the queen is lost) **10 ♗b2 a5! 11 c5 d6 12 ♘a4 ab 13 ab ♘bd7 14 ♖fc1 b5!** White, it seems, is beginning to wonder whether 9 b4 has turned out to be a minus for him. But pawns cannot be moved backwards... If now 15 cb, then after 15...♘xb6 16 d4 ♘xa4 17 ♖xa4 ♖xa4 18 ♕xa4 ♗d7 19 ♕c2 ♕b8 the weakness on b4 will not allow White a quiet life.

15 cd ♕xd6 16 ♘c5 ♖xa1 17 ♗xa1 ♘xc5 18 bc ♕c7 19 h3 Thus continued the game Erikalov – Sitnikov (Smolensk 2000). Black did not test the attacking potential of his forces and quite wrongly so.

After **19...♘h5! 20 d4 ed 21 ♘xd4?!** (stronger is 21 ♗xd4, though even here, Black's position is not worse in view of the weakness on c5: 21...♘f4 22 ♗f1 ♕e7 etc.) the rook is included in the attack with decisive effect: **21...♘f4 22 ♗f3 ♖e5! 23 ♘b3 ♖g5 24 ♔h1**

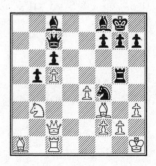

**24...&xh3! 25 gh &c8 26 &g4
&xg4! 27 hg &xg4 28 f3 &xf3+
29 &h2 &e2** winning.

A beautiful variation, but it has no
bearing on the assessment of the
system 1 e4 c6 2 c4 e5. The system is
dubious. Has Black any objection to
going into Indian channels? Alright,
but why go via the Caro-Kann
defence?! The combination of an
early c7-c6 and e7-e5 leads to a
struggle in which Black loses the
central squares d4 and e5 without a
fight: 3 &f3! d6 4 d4! And his
extravagant and intricate moves do
not change this assessment at all.

II
2...e6

Giving Black a solid, albeit
somewhat passive position. In reply
White can choose between 3 &f3,
3 &c3 and 3 d4.

A

3 &f3!? An old, respectable move.
Today it is rarely employed though it
is not so easy for Black to equalise
the game.
3...d5 4 ed ed 5 cd cd 6 &b5+
Possible then:
6...&d7 7 &xd7+ &xd7 8 &e5!?
&c7 9 0-0 &d6 10 d4 &e7 11 &c3
0-0 12 &f4 with a minimal 'plus'
(Botvinnik – Flohr, Leningrad 1933)
or
6...&c6 7 &e2+ &e7 8 &e5 &d7
9 &xc6 bc 10 0-0

10...&d8!? (renewing the threat of
f7-f6 after which, as before, would
follow a check on h5) **11 b3!?** (White
is alert, now on 11...f6 he has
12 &a3!) **11...&e6 12 &b2 f6 13 &f3
&d6 14 &xd7 &xd7 15 &c3 &h6
16 &a4 &f5 17 &c3** Inventive play
by both opponents has led to a
position in which White's chances
are nevertheless superior (Gulko –
Shabalov, Berne 1992).

B

3 &c3 d5 4 cd ed 5 ed cd In this
variation (as also the previous one)
everything lies in fine points invisible
to the naked eye. Should he give an
immediate check on b5 or wait a
while? And after the check – should
he first develop the queen to a4 or the
knight to f3 and then to e5? The order
of moves in this sort of variation has
decisive significance.
1) **6 &b5+ &c6 7 &a4 &d6?** An
imperceptible inaccuracy – now the
position already cannot be saved. The
only correct way is 7...&e7 8 &f3 a6
9 0-0 &e6, as played in the game
Giorgadze – Oll (Tbilisi 1983). There
followed 10 &xc6+ &xc6 11 &d4

♕d7 12 ♘xe6 fe 13 ♕g4 0-0-0 14 d3 ♗d6, and everything is in order for Black.

8 ♘f3 ♘f6 9 0-0 ♗e7 10 ♘e5 ♗d7 11 d4 ♕b4 12 ♘xd7 ♔xd7 13 ♕c2 ♖ad8 14 ♗f4 ♗d6

We have reached a critical moment in the game Tartakower – Cohn (Carlsbad 1911). White did not notice the simple combination: **15 ♕f5+! ♔c7 16 ♕xf6! gf 17 ♘xd5+ ♔b8 18 ♘xb4 ♗xf4 19 ♘xc6+ bc 20 ♗xc6 ♖xd4 21 g3** with a technically winning endgame.

2) **6 ♘f3 ♘f6 7 ♗b5+ ♗d7 8 ♕b3 ♗xb5 9 ♕xb5+ ♕d7 10 ♘e5 ♕xb5 11 ♘xb5 ♘a6** The opponents have reached this endgame by force, but how should it be assessed? Practical players say that Black has every right to reckon on a draw. But he has to conduct the defence with the utmost discipline.

The encounter Olafsson – Shabalov (San Martin 1993) developed in the following way: **12 d4** (worth considering is 12 d3!?, denying the black knight the e4 square, for example, 12...♗b4+ 13 ♔d1 0-0 14 ♗g5 with a slight advantage)

12...♗b4+ 13 ♔e2 0-0 14 ♗e3 ♘e4 15 ♖hc1 ♘d6 16 a4

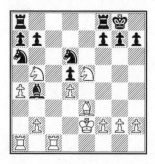

Here he should play **16...♘f5!?** with the idea that after **17 ♘c7 ♘xc7 18 ♖xc7 ♖ab8! 19 ♘d7** Black has the resource **19...♖fc8!** White's initiative gradually comes to naught: **20 ♖ac1 ♖xc7 21 ♖xc7 ♗d6 22 ♖c1 ♖e8** etc. However if 19 ♖d7 (instead of 19 ♘d7), then 19... f6 20 ♘d3 ♗d6 with an equal game.

C

3 d4 d5 4 e5 Weaker is 4 cd ed 5 e5 in view of 5...♘a6! It turns out that on 6 ♗xa6 follows 6...♕a5+, Black transfers the knight to e6 with counterplay: 6 ♘c3 ♘c7 7 ♘ge2 ♘e7 8 ♘f4 ♘f5 9 ♗e3 ♘e6 10 ♘xe6 ♗xe6 11 ♗d3 ♘xe3 12 fe ♕h4+ 13 g3 ♕g5 14 ♕d2 h5 (Tal – Bisguier, Bled 1961).

On 4 ♘c3 the struggle goes over to the channels of the Slav defence (code D31) – both in the case of 4...♗b4 5 e5, and 4...de 5 ♘xe4 ♗b4+ 6 ♗d2 ♕xd4 (Slav gambit).

After 4 e5 Black's choice is not easy.

Going for the advance – 4...c5?! – is hardly a good idea, since White has the possibility of favourably simplifying the position: 5 cd ♕xd5 6 ♘c3! ♕xd4 7 ♕xd4 cd 8 ♘b5 ♘a6 9 ♘f3 ♗c5 10 a3! The endgame is extremely difficult for Black, for example: 10...♘h6 11 ♗xh6 gh 12 ♗e2 ♔e7 13 0-0 ♗d7 14 ♘fxd4 ♖ac8 15 ♖fd1 ♗xd4 16 ♘xd4 ♘b8 17 f4 (Kaidanov – Zamora, New York 1997).

The attempt to modify the idea – 4...dc 5 ♗xc4 c5?! is also not good: 6 d5! a6 (Stohl – Shabalov, Werfen 1990) 7 d6! ♘c6 8 ♘f3 f6 9 ♗f4 with the better prospects for White.

In all probability, Black should not get excited and immediately provoke a crisis. He should calmly complete his development and then and there try to break out of the vice.

In precisely this way – cooly and logically – Black played in the game Vaganian – Dolmatov (Vilnius 1980): **4...♘e7 5 ♘f3 b6! 6 ♘c3 ♗a6!** (provoking White's next move, after which the position of the knight c3 is weakened) **7 b3 ♘f5 8 ♗e2 ♗b4 9 ♗b2**, and here and now – **9...c5!?**

Black's development is no worse than his opponent's, indeed, concrete variations reveal no defects in his position. For example, **10 0-0 ♘c6 11 cd ♗xc3 12 ♗xc3 ♗xe2 13 ♕xe2 ♕xd5 14 dc bc 15 ♖fd1 ♘fd4 16 ♗xd4 ♘xd4!? 17 ♘xd4 cd 18 ♖ac1 0-0** with an equal endgame.

The system with 2...e6 has never become popular, even more so a main line. It is too heavy-going for this. The system is for people with strong nerves, not inclined towards showy effect. Such people arrive, sit down, work long and patiently at the board and as a result calmly make a draw with Black.

Is this such a bad thing?

III
2...d5!?

A critical continuation for the assessment of the whole Steiner system. Black shows his preparedness to sacrifice a pawn, albeit with various modifcations.

3 ed It makes sense to restrict Black's possibilities by 3 cd, since the pawn sacrifice 3...♘f6?! 4 dc ♘xc6 is dubious in this position: 5 d3 e5 6 ♗e2 ♕b6 7 ♘f3 ♗c5 8 0-0 ♘g4 9 ♕e1 ♗d7 10 ♘bd2 ♕c7 11 ♘b3

♗b6 12 ♕c3 0-0 13 h3 ♘f6 14 ♗e3. The activity of Black's pieces is variable but White's extra pawn – constant (Mestel – Ruxton Plymouth 1989).

After 3 ed Black can continue sharp play to take over the initiative – 3...♘f6 (A), but he can also change his mind, returning to the channels of normal, 'correct' play: 3...cd (B).

A

3...♘f6!? In this position the sacrifice has more basis. White has two independent paths: 4 ♕a4 and 4 dc. The third continuation – 4 d4 – leads to the Panov Attack.

1) 4 ♕a4!? And here he cannot avoid a fork in the road.

It is not easy to rid himself of the pin on the a4-e8 diagonal. However practice has shown that the appearance of a piece on d7 brings disharmony to the black ranks. For example, 4...♕d7 5 dc ♘xc6 6 ♘f3 e5 7 d3, and then:

7...e4!? 8 de ♘xe4 9 ♗e3 ♘c5 10 ♗xc5 ♗xc5 11 ♗e2 0-0 12 ♘c3 ♗b4 13 ♕c2 ♖e8 14 0-0 ♗xc3 (Black exploits the possibility to spoil the opponent's pawn structure, however White obtains play on the b-

file, while the doubled pawns control the central squares) 15 bc ♕g4 16 ♗d3 ♕h5 17 ♖ab1 with advantage (Vaulin – Zurek, Pardubice 1994);

7...♗c5 8 ♗e2 0-0 9 ♘c3 ♕f5 10 0-0 ♗d7 11 ♕c2 ♖ad8 12 a3 ♖fe8 13 ♘e4 ♘xe4 14 de ♕g6 15 ♗e3 and Black's initiative is coming to an end (Chernyshov – Afek, Pardubice 1998).

4...e6!? 5 de ♗c5!? Correct! The beginning of a gambit – he cannot stop halfway. The more so that quite frankly the risk is not great. For example, 6 ef+ ♔xf7 7 ♘e2 ♘g4 – f2 is hanging and White is catastrophically behind in development. Black pulls up his heavy pieces on the e and f-files – and it's the end.

In the game Hubner – Luther (Saarbrucken 2002) White hurried to give all the material back, but still it did not safeguard him against a crushing defeat:

6 ♘f3 ♘g4! 7 d4 ♗xd4 8 ♘xd4 ♕xd4 9 ♕c2 ♘a6 10 ♘a3 (10 h3?! ♘b4 11 ♕e2 ♘e5) **10...♗xe6 11 h3 ♘b4 12 ♕d2 ♕e4+ 13 ♗e2 ♕xg2 14 ♖f1 ♘h2 15 ♕xb4 0-0-0 16 ♘b5 cb 17 ♗f4,** and finally – an attractive combination: **17...♕xf1+! 18 ♗xf1**

♘f3+ 19 ♔e2 ♘d4+ 20 ♔d2 ♘c6+ etc.

2) **4 dc ♘xc6 5 ♘f3?!** One of those cases where the most popular move is at the same time the weakest.

The normal path – 5 d3 e5 6 ♗e2! (but no way 6 ♘f3?, why – becomes clear later) 6...♗f5 7 ♘f3 ♕d7 8 0-0 0-0-0 9 ♕a4 ♗xd3 10 ♗xd3 ♕xd3 11 ♗e3 (Selezniev – Bogoljubow, Triberg 1917), and here 11...♘g4! 12 ♗xa7 e4 13 ♘g5 ♕d6 unleashing a very powerful attack, for example: 14 g3 ♕g6 15 h4 ♗e7 16 ♘h3 ♗xh4!

But the most interesting idea in this position is to try to do without the development of the knight to f3: 5 ♘c3!? e5 6 d3 ♗c5 7 ♗e3 ♗xe3?! (he probably should not improve the opponent's pawn structure) 8 fe ♕b6 9 ♕d2 ♗e6

In the game Korchnoi – Gat (Zurich 1988) White did not continue his policy to the end, eventually playing 10 ♘f3?! After 10...♖d8 11 ♕c1 ♘g4 12 ♘d1 Black missed a forced win: 12...e4! 13 de ♖xd1+! 14 ♕xd1 ♕xb2 15 ♗e2 ♕c3+ 16 ♘d2 ♘xe3.

He should secure himself against the break e5-e4, by playing 10 e4! and only later develop the knight.

5...e5 6 d3 e4! In this lies the whole business! As distinct from the variation 5 d3 e5 6 ♗e2, here White has no bishop on e2. Therefore the king is forced to set off on a long (and probably hopeless) journey.

7 de ♕xd1+ 8 ♔xd1 ♘xe4 9 ♗e3 ♗f5 10 ♘h4 0-0-0+ 11 ♔c1 ♗e6

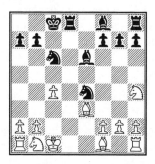

Despite the extra pawn, White should be thinking about saving himself. However there does not seem to be any way out:

12 ♘d2 ♘xd2 13 ♗xd2 ♗c5 with a future doubling of rooks on the d-file;

12 ♘f3 ♗c5 13 ♗xc5 ♘xc5 14 ♘c3 ♘b4 (striving to get to the weak d3 square) 15 ♘e1 ♗f5 (among other things, threatening mate in two moves: 16...♘xa2+! and 17...♘b3 mate) 16 b3 ♖he8 17 ♗e2 ♖xe2! 18 ♘xe2 ♘bd3+ 19 ♘xd3 ♘xd3+ 20 ♔d2 ♘xf2+ 21 ♔e3 ♘xh1 22 ♖xh1 ♖d3+ etc.

In the game Chandler – Adams (Hastings 1989) White tried to repair his position with the help of **12 ♘c3**, but after **12...♘xc3 13 bc ♔b8!? 14 ♘f3 ♘a5** anyone would take Black's side.

B

3...cd 4 cd ♕xd5 5 ♘c3 ♕d8 In this branch Black does not sacrifice anything and in general plays quietly.

6 d4 ♘f6 7 ♘f3 e6 8 ♗d3 (8 ♗c4!? leads to a position from the Queen's Gambit Accepted, well known since the time of the Zukertort – Steinitz world championship match of 1886) **8...♗e7**

This position can be reached from the Panov Attack, Queen's Gambit, Nimzo-Indian defence, the 2 c3 variation against the Sicilian defence and many other opening schemes.

How can White develop his forces? After covering the b4 square against a knight fork, he can set up a battery on the b1-h7 diagonal with his queen on d3 and bishop on c2 (or b1). Black cannot withstand such pressure and will be forced to weaken the pawn cover of his king. The white rooks will occupy the central files, the dark-squared bishop – the g5 square, the knight will be established on e5. Such is the disposition.

How does White intend to decide the game in his favour? There are two basic ideas. Either to carry out the break d4-d5 (but only when it is actually effective otherwise the break provokes mass exchanges and a quick draw), or include his pieces in a mating attack. In the last case there are not infrequently sacrifices (most often – the knight on f7).

When the opponent has an isolated d-pawn the basic principle of defence is this: with the manoeuvre ♘f6-d5 or ♘c6-b4-d5 Black should blockade the d4 pawn and try to simplify the position as much as possible. Together with this, the 'bad' light-squared bishop should be fianchettoed (♗c8-b7 or ♗c8-d7-c6).

First and foremost White has to decide what will be his next move: 9 ♗g5 or 9 0-0. One would think what is the difference? The difference is enormous.

Upon **9 ♗g5!?** Black easily carries out the unloading manoeuvre ♘f6-d5 – providing he finds the right order of moves. But if he does not find it then he will succumb to a devastating attack.

a) **9...0-0?** (a superficial move) **10 ♗c2! ♘c6 11 a3! b6 12 ♕d3 g6 13 h4! a5 14 h5 ♗a6**

15 ♕d2?! After 15 ♕e3! (placing in his sights the e6 square) Black cannot save himself.

15...♘xh5? 16 ♖xh5! gh, and the very brilliant 17 ♗f6!! ♗xf6 18 ♕h6 with an unavoidable mate;

15...♘g4 16 ♕e4 ♗xg5 17 ♕xg4 ♗f6 (there is also no saving himself on the more stubborn 17...h6 18 ♖d1 f5 19 ♕g3) 18 hg hg 19 ♗xg6! fg

20 ♕xg6+ ♗g7 21 ♘g5 ♖f6 22 ♖h8+!, again with mate;

15...♘d5 16 ♘xd5 ed 17 hg hg (or 17...♗xg5 18 ♘xg5 hg 19 ♗xg6!) 18 ♗xg6! fg (declining the sacrifice does not mean he can withstand the attack: 18...♖e8 19 ♗h7+ ♔g7 20 ♗xe7 ♕xe7 21 ♘e5! ♕f6 22 ♖h5) 19 ♕e6+ ♖f7 20 ♕xg6+ ♖g7 21 ♕e6+ ♖f7 22 ♖h7 with an uncomplicated win.

We are following the game Vadasz – Sapis (Budapest 1977), given in many opening books. Practically all the so called commentators, 'rush past' the key moment of this encounter. They only mention that after 15 ♕d2 ♕c7 16 hg fg (in no way better is 16...hg? because of 17 ♗f4 ♕d8 18 ♗e5) 17 ♗b3 ♘d8 18 ♕e3 ♗c4 19 ♗xc4 ♕xc4 20 ♘e5 White gained an easy victory. The whole of White's play, beginning with 10 ♗c2, is acknowledged as exemplary.

However 15 ♕d2?! is essentially inaccurate, after which White might have denied himself a deserved victory. Concretely: what to do after **15...♘xh5!?**

Analogous to the variation 15 ♕e3 ♘xh5, also here 16 ♖xh5!? suggests

itself. But then, like a cold shower, follows 16...f6! This is the difference between having the queen on e3 and d2: the e6 square is not in his sights! He cannot completely correct the position – 17 ♕e3 gh 18 ♕xe6+ ♔h8 19 ♕xc6 fg 20 ♕h6 ♖f7 21 ♘e5 ♖g7. The outcome of the struggle remains unclear. Many commentators mention the move 15...♘xh5!, but indicate that it is refuted by 16 g4 ♗xg5 17 ♘xg5 ♘f6 18 ♘xh7. In fact this is a false trail: instead of 17...♘f6 stronger is 17...♘xd4! 18 ♗d1 (18 ♗e4 ♘b3) 18...♗b7 19 ♖h3 f6 20 ♘xh7 ♔xh7 21 gh g5!, and it is Black who is playing for a win.

Strongest is **16 ♗xe7!? ♘xe7 17 g4** ♘f6 (weak is 17...♗b7? 18 ♖xh5!) **18 ♕h6 ♔h8 19 ♘g5 ♕xd4** (on 19...♘eg8 Black gets mated: 20 ♕xh7+!) **20 ♘xh7** Though even here by transferring play to the endgame – **20...♘xg4 21 ♕h4 ♕xf2+!** – Black retains chances of a draw.

However these variations, undoubtedly worthy of attention, are interesting only as corrections in an opening manual. For the theory of the given variation (9...0-0?) there is something more important: after 10 ♗c2! ♘c6 11 a3! b6 12 ♕d3 g6 13 h4! a5 14 h5 ♗a6 15 ♕e3! White develops an irresistible attack.

b) **9...♘c6!** The right reaction. There is no sense at all in Black hurrying with castling.

10 0-0 In the event of 10 a3, a negative side to the early development of the bishop on g5 comes to light – by means of

10...♘d5! Black can make favourable exchanges: 11 ♗xe7 ♘cxe7 12 ♗b5+ ♗d7 13 ♗xd7+ ♕xd7 14 ♘e5 ♘xc3! 15 bc ♕d5.

10...0-0 11 ♖c1 (with the idea of moving the bishop to b1)

11...b6!? Not hurrying to reveal his plan regarding which knight will blockade the d4 pawn. It is more usual to see Black trying to solve this problem at once.

11...♘d5 12 h4!? (Zakharov – Malakhov, Kolontaevo 1997) 12...h6 13 ♘xd5 ed 14 ♗xe7 ♕xe7, and he would prefer the h-pawn to be on h2;

11...♘b4 12 ♗b1 b6 13 a3 ♘bd5 14 ♕d3 g6 (the opponents place their pieces 'according to the book') 15 ♗h6 ♖e8 16 ♘e5 ♗b7 17 ♘e4 ♘xe4 18 ♕xe4 (Yubishiev – Lovkov, St.Petersburg 2001) 18...♗f6, and the whole struggle still lies ahead.

12 ♖e1 It is necessary to know how to neutralise the pressure on the c-file – 12 ♗xf6!? ♗xf6 13 ♘e4 ♗b7 14 ♘xf6+ ♕xf6 15 ♗e4 ♖ac8 16 ♖c3!? The right reaction consists of 16...♕f4! 17 ♖e1 (nothing is offered by 17 ♕b1 because of 17...f5 18 ♗xc6 ♖xc6) 17...h6! 18 ♕a4 ♕d6 19 ♖ec1. It seems that White has

reinforced his position to the utmost but tactics will come to Black's aid.

19...♘xd4! 20 ♗xb7 ♘e2+ 21 ♔h1 ♖xc3! (on 21 ♔f1 would follow the same move) 22 ♖xc3 ♘xc3 23 bc ♖d8. In this position the most probable result is a draw.

12...♗b7 13 ♗b1 The traditional plan is to play a2-a3, in order to prevent the knight fork, and develop the queen on d3, provoking a weakening of the opponent's king's flank.

13...♖c8 14 a3 g6 15 ♕d3 ♖e8 (over-protecting the bishop on e7 and preparing the unloading manoeuvre ♘f6-d5) **16 ♗a2 ♘d5!**

It should be recognised that it is Black who has won the strategical battle. All vulnerable squares are covered and a favourable simplification for him is inevitable. In the game Onischuk – Rogers (Djakarta 1997) play continued **17 ♗xd5** (nothing is offered by 17 h4 ♘xc3 18 bc ♘a5 or 17 ♗d2 ♘xc3 18 ♗xc3 ♗f6) **17...♗xg5 18 ♘xg5 ♕xg5 19 ♗f3 ♖ed8 20 ♕e3 ♕xe3 21 fe ♘a5** with an equal endgame.

The move 9 ♗g5 nevertheless helps Black put right his defence – giving him a flywheel for exchanges after ♘f6-d5.

2) **9 0-0 ♘c6! 10 a3 0-0** In view of the fact that the d4 pawn is hanging, White is forced to adjust his plan. The deployment of the bishop on g5 is called off; the bishop goes to e3. The rooks are placed not on e1 and d1, but on d1 and c1. The queen goes to e2, while the light-squared bishop – to a2, in order to control the d5 square and at the first convenient opportunity to assist in the carrying out of d4-d5.

11 ♗e3 b6 12 ♕e2 ♗b7 13 ♖fd1 ♕b8!? Freeing the d8 square for the rook and threatening a timely ♘f6-g4. Also worth considering is the more natural 13...♖c8.

14 h3 ♖d8 15 ♖ac1 ♖d7 16 ♗b1 ♕d8 17 ♗a2 ♖c8 (Black completes the regrouping of his forces and prepares to renew the pressure on the d4 pawn) **18 ♖c2!?** A flexible move, leaving the opponent in ignorance. First White doubles on the c-file, then concentrates his heavy pieces on the adjacent files, thereby 'speeding up' the break d4-d5.

18...♘a5 (Black prevents the pawn break, but at the high price of losing control of the e5 square) **19 ♘e5** (looking in real earnest at the f7

square...) **19...♖dc7 20 ♖dc1** While here is the first concrete threat: 21 b4! ♘c6 22 ♘b5 winning the exchange.

20...♘e4?! Black quite naturally tries to simplify the position but overlooks a tactical blow by the opponent. However it is not clear what one might suggest instead:

In the event of 20...♘d5?! White obtains a great advantage by 21 ♘xd5 ♗xd5 22 ♖xc7 ♖xc7 23 ♖xc7 ♕xc7 24 ♗xd5 ed 25 ♕f3!;

Likewise unsatisfactory is 20...a6? (parrying the threat of 21 b4! and 22 ♘b5) in view of 21 d5! ♘xd5 22 ♘xf7! ♔xf7 23 ♗xb6! winning.

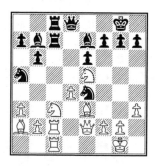

21 ♘xf7! It goes without saying that the sacrifice bears a purely intuitive character; it is not really possible to calculate its consequences in practical play.

21...♔xf7 22 ♕g4! (an extremely unpleasant resource for Black) **22...♕d7** (22...♗d5 does not save him because of 23 ♘xd5! ♖xc2 24 ♖xc2 ♖xc2 25 ♕xe4 ♖xb2 26 ♘f4 ♖xa2 27 ♕xe6+ ♔e8 28 ♕xa2 and White is already attacking with extra material) **23 ♘xe4!!** In this move lies the point of the tactical operation begun on the 21st move. Even a rook down White

254

continues to play positionally, improving the positions of his pieces.

23...♖xc2 24 ♖xc2 ♖xc2 25 ♕f5+! ♔e8 (25...♗f6? loses because of 26 ♗xe6+! ♕xe6 27 ♘g5+) **26 ♗xe6 ♕a4 27 ♘d6+!** Exploiting the invulnerability of the knight, White transfers it to a more active position.

27...♔d8 (27...♗xd6 28 ♕f7+ ♔d8 29 ♗g5+) **28 ♘f7+ ♔e8 29 ♘e5!**

Threatening 30 ♗d7+ winning the queen. In the game Podgaets – Zhuravlev (Leningrad 1971) Black tried to defend himself by **29...♗c6**, but after **30 d5!** the pawn is included in the attack with decisive effect: **30...♗b5 31 ♕f7+ ♔d8 32 d6!** After a few moves Black resigned.

Black also had another possibility at his disposal – 29...♔d8, but even this would not have saved him: 30 ♗d7!, and then:

30...♕b3 31 ♘f7+ ♕xf7 (31...♔c7 32 ♗f4+) 32 ♕xf7 ♔xd7 33 ♕f5+ and 34 ♕xc2 or

30...♗c8 31 ♘f7+ ♔c7 32 ♗xc8 g5 (otherwise 33 ♗f4+) 33 ♗a6! ♘b7 34 ♕e4!

The Steiner system even today is found in the repertoire of many of the world's leading players. Certainly it cannot be said that they play it absolutely seriously but on the other hand it is also hard to call it an over-indulgence.

Such a system is good as a one-off tournament weapon. For example, you have a foreboding (or just simply know), that your opponent, on 1 e4 c6 2 c4, invariably replies 2...e5. But you only need to know this – that the Indian scheme will work perfectly for you. Or on the other hand – your opponent has an inclination for 2...d5 3 ed cd 4 cd ♕xd5 5 ♘c3 ♕d8, and you like to play positions with an isolated pawn on d4. It is clear that you will not find your next 'Black' opponent unaware that you play the Steiner system – but it doesn't matter. Pack it away... until the next tournament!

If, however, you are playing Black, then the Steiner system requires one thing from you: knowledge! The last thing to do is to sit and think at the board, how are you going to react to 1 e4 c6 2 c4!? No, you should be aware beforehand: how you intend to repulse the offensive, what type of position you are prepared to go in for. We hope that the variations presented in this book will help you make a conscious choice.

And then no way will the Steiner be terrible for you.

Index to the Steiner System

1 e4 c6 2 c4	226
I. 2...e5	226
A. 3 ♘c3	226
B. 3 d4	228
1) 3...ed	228
2) 3...♗b4+	229
4 ♗d2 ♗xd2+ 5 ♕xd2 d6 6 ♘c3	
a) 6...♘f6	229
b) 6...♕f6	230
3) 3...♘f6	230
4 ♘c3	
a) 4...♗b4	231
b) 4...♕a5	231
4) 3...d6	232
a) 4 d5	232
b) 4 ♘c3	233
b1) 4...♗e7	233
b2) 4...♘f6	234
c) 4 ♘f3	235
4...♗g4	
c1) 5 de	235
c2) 5 d5	236
c3) 5 ♗e2	237
C. 3 ♘f3	239
1) 3...d5	239
2) 3...f5	239
3) 3...♘f6	240

4 ♘c3 ♗b4 5 ♘xe5	
a) 5...♕e7	240
b) 5...0-0	241
4) 3...♕c7	241
a) 4 d4	241
b) 4 ♘c3	242
5) 3...♕a5	243
II. 2...e6	246
A. 3 ♘f3	246
B. 3 ♘c3	246
3...d5 4 cd ed 5 ed cd	
1) 6 ♗b5+	246
2) 6 ♘f3	247
C. 3 d4	247
III. 2...d5	248
3 ed	
A. 3...♘f6	249
1) 4 ♕a4	249
2) 4 dc	250
B. 3...cd	250
4 cd ♕xd5 5 ♘c3 ♕d8 6 d4 ♘f6	
7 ♘f3 e6 8 ♗d3 ♗e7	
1) 9 ♗g5	251
a) 9...0-0	251
b) 9...♘c6	252
2) 9 0-0	254

Illustrative Games

No.1
M. ADAMS –
R. PONOMAREV
Sofia 2005

**1 e4 c6 2 c4 d5 3 ed cd 4 cd ♘f6
5 ♘c3 ♘xd5 6 ♘f3 ♘c6 7 d4 ♗g4
8 ♕b3 ♗xf3 9 gf e6** The variation
9...♘b6 has been ousted from
grandmaster practice. Forever? We
don't know, but already for a few
years no one has been keen to risk
playing the position after 10 d5! ♘d4
11 ♗b5+! (page 24).
10 ♕xb7 ♘xd4 11 ♗b5+ ♘xb5

12 ♕c6+ The main expert on the
present system for Black –
grandmaster Alexei Dreev – managed
not only to equalise but also to beat
White in this supposedly "dull

technical endgame". Here is a recent
example: 12 ♕xb5+ ♕d7 13 ♕xd7+
♔xd7 14 ♘xd5 ed 15 ♗e3 ♗b4+
16 ♔e2 a5 (in the theoretical section
we were inclined towards the move
16...♖hc8 and the game Rozentalis –
Bologan – page 27) 17 ♖hd1 ♔e6
18 ♖ac1 ♖hc8 19 ♔d3 f6 20 b3 ♗d6
21 h3 g5 22 ♗d2 ♗b4 23 ♗e3 ♗a3
24 ♖xc8 ♖xc8 25 ♗b6 ♗b4 26 a3
♖c6 27 ♗d8 ♗xa3 28 ♗xa5 ♗c5
29 b4 ♗xf2 30 b5 ♖c4 (Bartel –
Dreev, Internet 2004). Objectively
the position is unclear (Black has an
extra pawn, White has a dangerous
passed pawn), subjectively... Dreev
won!

**12...♔e7 13 ♕xb5 ♕d7 14 ♘xd5+
♕xd5 15 ♕xd5** The alternative is the
intermediate check 15 ♗g5+ f6, and
only now 16 ♕xd5 ed 17 ♗e3. In the
encounter Onischuk – Bologan
(Poikovsky 2005) Black was easily
able to defend himself and in the
variation which was previously
considered dangerous: 17...♔e6
18 ♖g1!? (for the idea of this move –
see page 33). Here Bologan played:
18...g6 19 0-0-0 ♗b4 20 ♖d3 ♖ac8+!
21 ♔b1 ♗c5! (the main defensive
resource is to exchange bishops)

22 ♖e1 ♗xe3 23 fe ♖c5, and a draw was agreed.

15...ed

16 ♗e3 An important novelty in the variation 16 ♗f4 ♔f6 17 0-0-0 was introduced by Alexei Dreev. Actually, he improved on his own game against Onischuk (page 30). There 17...♖d8 was played but it turned out that it was not necessary to defend the d5 pawn! After 17...♗c5!? 18 ♖xd5 ♗xf2 19 ♔b1 ♖he8 20 a4 ♖e2 21 ♖c1 ♖ae8 and Black has no difficulties (Sulskis – Dreev, Tallinn 2004).

16...♔e6 17 0-0-0 ♗b4 18 ♖d3 Also this position in included in theory. How it is included, we repeat, is also the main idea of the defence: to strive as much as possible to exchange the bishop e3. On page 30 is the game Franco – Dominguez: 18...♖hd8 19 a3 ♖ac8+! 20 ♔b1 ♗c5! In the present game Ponomarev demonstrates the same idea only a move earlier:

18...♖hc8+! 19 ♔b1 ♗c5! (what improvement had Adams thought up?) **20 ♖c1 ♗b6 21 ♖g1 ♗xe3 22 ♖xe3+ ♔f6** It seems none at all. White's position is in no way better and the English grandmaster quite

reasonably forced a draw.

23 ♖g4 ♖c7 24 ♖f4+ ♔g6 25 ♖g4+ ♔f6 26 ♖f4+ ♔g6 27 ♖g4+ Drawn. As we see, justifying the conclusion on page 34: "it is only possible to reckon seriously on an endgame victory after 9...e6 if the opponent is significantly lower rated.".

No.2
A. GRISCHUK – E. BAREEV
Moscow 2004

1 e4 c6 2 d4 d5 3 ed cd 4 c4 ♘f6 5 ♘c3 ♘c6 6 ♗g5 dc There is a total overestimation of the value of the present variation. The move 7 d5, the main line for over half a century, has faded into the background. For a clue, as we have already mentioned, we should look into 7...♘a5!? 8 b4 cb 9 ab ♗d7! 10 b4 ♖c8! (page 42).

In return it is improbable that the theory of the move **7 ♗xc4!?** will grow at a fast tempo. In reply Evgeny Bareev chose the most principled continuation but, as will be seen from the sequel, it is not quite ready to enter into the debate.

7...♕xd4 8 ♕xd4 ♘xd4 9 0-0-0 e5 10 f4! ♗g4 11 ♘f3 ♘xf3 12 gf ♗xf3 13 fe ♗xh1 14 ef

Here ends the analysis of B. Kantzler (page 37). The evaluation – White's initiative outweighs the sacrificed material.

14...♖c8 Improbable, but true: this natural move loses by force!

15 ♖e1+ "It is important to exclude the possibility of castling by Black". A. Grischuk.

15...♔d7   16   ♖d1+!   ♗d6 Alexander Grischuk presents variations to prove a win for White after 16...♔e8 17 ♗d3!:

17...♗d5 18 ♔b1 h6 19 ♘xd5 hg 20 ♗b5+ ♔d8 21 ♘e7+ ♔c7 22 ♖c1+ ♔b6 23 ♖xc8 ♔xb5 24 ♖xf8! ♖xf8 25 fg or

17...♗f3 18 ♖e1+ ♔d7 19 ♗f5+ ♔c7 20 ♖e3 ♗h1 21 ♗f4+ ♗d6 22 ♖e7+ ♔c6 23 ♗d7+ ♔c5 24 ♗e3+ ♔c4 25 ♔c2 ♗xe7 26 fe ♗c6 27 a3!!

17 ♗e2! gf 18 ♗xf6 ♗g2 19 ♗e5 ♔e6 20 ♗xd6 ♖hd8 21 ♗g3 ♖xd1+ 22 ♔xd1 a6 23 ♔d2 Black's position is very difficult and after the next move – hopeless:

23...♔f5? 24 ♗d3+ ♔g4 25 ♘d1! ♔g5 Not possible is 25...h5 because of 26 ♘e3+ ♔f3 (26...♔h3 27 ♗f5 mate) 27 ♗e2+ ♔e4 28 ♘xg2. With the fall of the h-pawn no hope

remains for Black. As the self-critical Grischuk himeself acknowledged, he did not conduct the technical part of the game faultlessly – but all the same it was good enough not to allow Black a single moment to hope for a draw.

The funeral of a variation? Not a bit! At the start of 2005 in the prestigious tournament at Wijk aan Zee was played the game Mamedyarov – Smits. Instead of 14...♖c8? Black produced an improvement – 14...h6! And though Mamedyrov played 'à la Grischuk', by depriving Black of castling – 15 ♖e1+ ♔d7 16 ♖d1+ ♔e8, after 17 ♗h4 ♖c8 18 ♗e2 g5! 19 ♗g3 ♗e4 20 ♗g4 ♖xc3+ 21 bc ♗a3+ 22 ♔d2 h5 chances were mutual. The game was actually won by Smits.

An improvement, but now obviously for White, should be sought in the region of 18 ♗e2. The Petersburg grandmaster Sergei Ivanov suggests instead of this 18 ♖e1+ ♔d7 19 ♗xf7 ♖xc3+ 20 bc g5 21 ♗g3 ♗a3+ 22 ♔c2 ♗f3 23 ♗e6+ ♔c6 24 f7 with advantage. There is no end to refining the analysis...

No.3

**V. IVANCHUK –
P. HARIKRISHNA**
Tripoli 2004

1 c4 c6 2 e4 d5 3 ed cd 4 d4 ♘f6 5 ♘c3 ♘c6 6 ♗g5 dc 7 ♗xc4 e6 As we have already mentioned (page 38), this solid move will gain widespread practice if and when the

assessment of the complications after 7...♕xd4 finally proves to be Black's favour.

8 ♘f3 ♗e7 9 0-0 0-0 10 ♖c1 a6 11 ♗d3 ♗d7 12 ♖e1 ♖c8 Not unlike the usual tabiya with the 'isolani', but no one could have forseen the storm...

13 h4!? The most delicate moment! On page 39 was presented the game Ivanchuk – Dreev: 13 a3 ♘d5 14 h4!? ♘xc3 15 bc h6 16 ♗xe7 ♘xe7, and Black succeeded in defending himself. In what sense does Ivanchuk's novelty improve upon his own game? It turns out that if Black goes along the same path as Dreev – 13...♘d5, then he will lose at once and very beautifully! Here is the main variation: 14 ♘xd5! ♗xg5 (14...ed 15 ♖xc6! ♗xg5 16 ♖xc8) 15 ♗xh7+! ♔xh7 16 ♘xg5+ ♔h6 (16...♔g8 17 ♕h5) 17 ♕d2! ♔g6 (17...♕a5 18 ♘xf7+ ♔g6 19 ♘e5+ ♔h7 20 ♕xa5 ♘xa5 21 ♘xd7) 18 ♘f4+ ♔h6 (18...♔f6 19 ♘e4+ ♔e7 20 ♘d5+! ed 21 ♕g5+) 19 ♘gxe6! fe 20 ♘xe6+ and 21 ♘xd8.

A brilliant idea! However, the Indian grandmaster Harikrishna unravelled it and rendered it harmless. After **13...♘b4!** for a long

time the game transferred to quiet positional channels.

14 ♗b1 ♗c6 15 ♘e5 g6 16 ♕b3 ♘bd5 (possibly Black was playing it safe by rejecting 16...♕xd4) **17 ♘xc6 bc 18 ♘a4 ♘d7 19 ♕g3 ♗xg5 20 hg ♕a5 21 b3 ♖fd8 22 ♗e4 ♕d2 23 ♖ed1 ♕b4** The key moment in the game. Taking on a2 is dangerous – it might lose the queen. But to take... is necessary! After 23...♕xa2 24 ♖a1 ♕e2 25 ♗d3 ♕h5 26 ♗xa6 ♖b8 the outcome of the struggle is unclear. Now, however, White's advantage increases with each move.

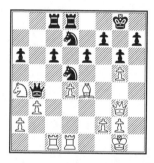

24 ♗xd5! cd 25 ♖c7! ♖xc7 26 ♕xc7 ♕b8 27 ♖c1 ♕a8 28 ♖c6 ♘f8 29 ♘c5 e5 30 ♖f6 ed 31 ♕xf7+ ♔h8 32 ♖xa6 ♕b8 33 ♖a7 ♕e5 34 ♘d3! Black resigned.

No.4

L. ARONIAN – M. CARLSEN
Tripoli 2004

1 c4 c6 2 e4 d5 3 ed cd 4 d4 ♘f6 5 ♘c3 g6 6 ♕b3 ♗g7 7 cd 0-0 8 ♗e2 ♘bd7 Let us deepen (see pages 88-89) our knowledge of the position after 8...♘a6 9 ♗f3 ♕b6 10 ♕xb6 ab 11 ♘ge2 ♘b4 12 0-0 ♖d8 13 d6 ♖xd6 14 ♗f4 ♖d7 15 ♖fd1 ♘fd5!

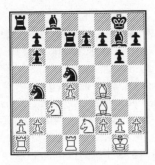

It is surprising but the main expert in the present system Vladimir Burmakin played it inaccurately! After 16 ♘xd5 ♘xd5 17 ♗e5 he did not remove the knight from exchange, preferring the routine 17...♖d8?! There followed 18 ♗xd5! ♖xd5 19 ♘c3 ♖d8 20 ♗xg7 ♔xg7 21 d5! We looked in detail at this idea on page 89. White has a noticeable advantage and Burmakin did not manage to shake this assessment: 21...♗d7 22 ♖d4 ♖dc8 23 f3 h5 24 a3 ♔f8 25 ♖ad1 ♖c5 26 ♖b4 b5 27 ♔f2 etc. (Umbach – Burmakin, Zurich 2004).

Our recommendation also proved correct in the variation 16 ♗g3 ♘xc3 17 bc ♘c6. We pointed out that after 18 ♘f4 ♖a5 19 h4, Black, without wasting time, should immediately counterattack in the centre: 19...e5! In the encounter Popovic – Zelcic (Bosnjaci 2005) White wanted to fight for the advantage himself: 18 ♖db1!? The reaction of the Croatian grandmaster Robert Zelcic was predictable and... absolutely correct: 18...e5! After 19 ♗xc6 bc 20 ♗xe5 ♗xe5 21 de ♖d2 22 ♘g3 ♖dxa2 23 ♖xa2 ♖xa2 24 h3 b5 already White must redouble his efforts in order not to lose.

9 ♗f3 ♘b6 10 a4!? A new idea! White forces an advance of the a-pawn in return, but why?

10...a5 11 ♘ge2 ♗f5

This position is well known to us (see pages 84-85) but without the inclusion of the moves 10 a4 a5. Let us try to work out what are the pluses and minus in the position for White.

The plus is obvious: the resource ♛d8-d7, at one time the main line, in the present position is not possible – the knight is hanging on b6. There is also an obvious defect: in a number of variations the knight is transferred to b4, from where it can no longer be driven away with the move a2-a3. But on the whole... the concrete variations are not so different from those that we looked at on pages 84-85. Here are the key lines:

12 0-0 ♗d3! 13 d6 ed 14 ♗xb7 ♖b8 15 ♗f3 ♘bd5;

12 ♘f4 g5! 13 ♘fe2 g4 14 ♘g3 ♗g6 15 ♗e2 ♘bxd5;

12 d6!? ed 13 ♗xb7 ♖b8 14 ♗f3 ♘bd5 15 ♛d1 ♘b4.

12 ♛d1 But this is already a surprise! By rejecting the shadowing of the knight b6, White also rejects any claim to an opening advantage. Apparently the Armenian grandmaster had missed something in his home laboratory...

12...♘bxd5 13 0-0 ♕d7 14 ♘g3 ♗e6 15 ♘ge4 ♘xe4 16 ♘xe4 b6 The development of forces is practically complete. The black pieces are arranged harmoniously and in prospect is a siege of the d4 pawn.

17 ♘g5 ♖ad8 18 ♘xe6 ♕xe6 19 ♖e1 ♕d6 20 ♗g5 ♗f6 21 ♕d2 ♗xg5 22 ♕xg5 ♘b4 23 ♖ad1 ♘c2 24 ♖e4 ♕f6 25 ♕xf6 ef 26 g4 ♖d6 27 ♖d2 ♘b4 28 ♖e7 ♖fd8 29 ♖b7 ♖xd4 30 ♖xd4 ♖xd4 31 ♖xb6 ♘d3 32 b3 ♘f4 33 h4 Already a draw could be agreed here by repetition of moves: 33 ♖b5 ♖d3 34 ♗g2 ♘e2+ 35 ♔f1 ♘f4 36 ♔g1 etc.

33...♔g7 34 ♖b5 ♖d3 35 ♗e4 ♖c3 36 ♖xa5 White finally accepts the inevitable. He could prolong the game by means of 36 f3, but after 36...h5 Black's chances would at least be no worse.

36...♖xb3 37 ♖b5 ♖a3 38 a5 ♘e2+ 39 ♔g2 ♘c3 40 ♖b4 ♘xe4 41 ♖xe4 ♖xa5, and after a few moves the opponents agreed a draw. Obviously a moral victory for the talented Norwegian teenager – you see, he was facing one of the strongest grandmasters in the world!

No.5
R. RUCK – A. HORVATH
Austria 2005

1 e4 c6 2 d4 d5 3 ed cd 4 c4 ♘f6 5 ♘c3 e6 6 ♘f3 In the variation 6 a3 dc 7 ♗xc4 ♗e7 8 ♘f3 0-0 9 0-0 Yudasin's idea 9...♗d7!? 10 ♕e2 ♗c6 11 ♖d1 ♗d5 (page 92) was tested in a game between... two computer programs! After 12 ♘xd5 ♘xd5 13 ♗d3 ♘d7 White played a novelty: 14 ♘e5 (we recall that Topalov against Yudasin played 14 ♕e4 – page 93). The game continued: 14...♖c8 15 ♕f3 f5 16 ♗f4 ♘xf4 17 ♕xf4 ♘xe5 18 ♕xe5 ♖c6 19 ♗c4! (19...♖xc4 20 ♕xe6+ and 21 ♕xc4). White obtained some initiative but Black managed to defend himself ('IsiChess' – 'The Baron', Leiden 2004).

6...♘c6 7 c5 ♗e7 8 ♗b5 0-0 9 0-0 ♘e4 10 ♖e1 On page 99 we recommended 10 ♕c2 – and continue to support our recommendation. Why spoil one's own pawn structure?

10...♘xc3! 11 bc ♗d7 12 ♗f4 b6! 13 cb ab

14 ♖e3!? Not quite new but in any event not a redundant plan.

Obviously White is playing for mate!

14...♖a3 15 ♗xc6 ♗xc6 16 ♘e5 ♗e8 17 ♕g4 ♗f6 18 ♖g3 ♕a8! Time and again Black defends very accurately. It seems that 19 ♗h6 is winning but the attack can be beaten off in all variations: 19...♖xa2 20 ♖f1 (or 20 ♖xa2 ♕xa2 21 h4 ♕b1+ 22 ♔h2 ♕f5) 20...♖a1 21 ♗xg7 ♖xf1+ 22 ♔xf1 ♕a1+ 23 ♔e2 ♕b2+ 24 ♔e1 ♕c1+ 25 ♔e2 ♗b5+ 26 c4 ♗xc4+ 27 ♘xc4 ♕xc4+ 28 ♔e1 h5! etc.

19 ♕e2 ♕a6 20 ♖d2 Also now, when White's plan appears to be a failure, two weak moves in a row follow.

20...♕a7?! 21 ♗h6 ♔h8? After 21...♕e7 Black would still have nothing to fear (22 ♗xg7? ♗xg7 23 ♕h6 f6). But grandmaster Adam Horvath gives his opponent a chance to produce a brilliant (but not complicated) combination:

22 ♗xg7+! Black's mistake is all the more surprising in that White has another less forcing way to victory: 22 ♘g4 ♗e7 23 ♗xg7+ ♔xg7 24 ♕h6+ ♔h8 25 ♘f6 ♗xf6 26 ♕xf8 mate.

22...♗xg7 23 ♖xg7! ♔xg7 24 ♕g5+ ♔h8 25 ♕f6+ ♔g8 26 ♘g4

h6 27 ♘xh6+ ♔h7 28 ♘g4 Black resigned. Grandmaster Robert Ruck conducted this game aggressively – but he hardly managed to shake the conclusions of theory.

No.6
M. ADAMS – G. KALLAI
France 2004

1 e4 c6 2 d4 d5 3 ed cd 4 c4 ♘f6 5 ♘c3 e6 6 ♘f3 ♗b4 7 cd ♘xd5 8 ♕c2 ♘c6 We briefly touch upon the side-lines.

About the dangers of the immediate 8...0-0?! – because of 9 ♗d3! – we have spoken in detail on page 115. Here is a fresh example on this theme: 8...♘f6 10 0-0 ♘c6 11 a3 ♗e7 12 ♗e3 a6? (Black is already balancing on the edge of a precipice, and in this predicament loses time – an inadmissible luxury) 13 ♖ad1 ♕c7 14 ♖fe1 ♗d7

After 15 d5! there and then Black's position falls apart: 15...♘a5 (also bad is 15...ed 16 ♘xd5! ♘xd5 17 ♗xh7+ ♔h8 18 ♖xd5) 16 ♗g5 ♗d6 17 ♗xf6 gf 18 ♘e4 ♔g7 (or 18...♕xc2 19 ♘xf6+! ♔g7 20 ♘h5+ ♔h6 21 ♗xc2 ♔xh5 22 de ♗xe6 23 ♖xd6) 19 ♘xd6 Black resigned

(A.Sokolov – M.Fischer, Lenk 2005).

In the variation 8...♘d7 9 ♗d3 ♘7f6 10 0-0 ♗d7 11 ♘xd5 ♘xd5 12 ♘e5 ♗d6 13 ♗e4, a serious improvement for Black was demonstrated in the game Kharlov – Bachin (Dagomis 2004): 13...♕c7! In the theoretical section (page 116) we were inclined towards the game Benjamin – Seirawan, where after 13...♖c8 14 ♕b3 ♗c6 15 ♕g3 White held the initiative for a long time. What is the point of 13...♕c7 ? It all comes down to the fact that the manoeuvre 14 ♕b3 ♗c6 15 ♕g3 is now simply impossible in view of 15...f6! Kharlov has to exchange queens, but the endgame after 14 ♕xc7 ♗xc7 can easily be held by Black.

9 ♗e2 0-0 10 0-0 ♗e7 Another popular direction is 10...♖e8 11 ♖d1 ♗f8 12 ♕e4 ♗d7. Formerly 13 ♗g5 (page 128) was played here without any particular thought but in the world championship Michael Adams did without this move: 13 ♗d3!? The game continued 13...f5 14 ♕e2 ♗d6 15 ♗c4 ♘xc3 16 bc ♘a5 17 ♗d3 ♗c6 18 ♖b1 ♕c7 19 c4!? (a promising pawn sacrifice) 19...♗xf3 20 ♕xf3 ♘c6 21 ♗e3 ♗xh2+ 22 ♔f1 ♗d6 23 c5! ♗f8 24 d5! White has already seized the initiative and did not let it out of his hands until the end of the game (Adams – Asrian, Tripoli 2004).

11 ♖d1 ♗f6 The move 11...♗d7?!, rejected as defective by theory, was encountered in the game Adams – Bologan (Internet 2004). It was not rejected because two pawns are hanging after 12 ♘xd5! ed 13 ♕b3! As shown on page 124, after 13...♗e8 the pawn is 'not worth' taking: 14 ♕xb7 ♖b8 15 ♕a6 ♘b4 16 ♕xa7 ♖a8 17 ♕b7 ♗c6. But here after 14 ♘e5! Black is not to be envied – he has a passive position without the slightest hint of counterplay. Bologan chose 13...♗c8, but after 14 ♗f4 ♘a5 15 ♕c3 ♘c6 16 ♘e5! he was still squeezed in a vice from which he could not escape: 16...♘xe5 17 de ♗e6 18 ♗f3 ♕d7 19 ♗e3 ♖fc8 20 ♕d3 etc.

12 ♘e4 Previously Adams preferred to attack in another way: 12 ♕e4 ♘ce7 13 ♗d3 g6 14 ♗h6 ♖e8 15 h4 (about this – see page 125). But for the present game he had prepared a new idea...

12...♗e7?! And Black immediately becomes unnerved! Why on 'a level playing field' does he give the opponent two tempi? He should choose between 12...♘ce7 and 12...h6.

13 ♗c4 ♗d7 14 ♘eg5 ♘f6 15 ♘e5 The first threat appears (16 ♘exf7!? ♖xf7 17 ♘xe6). However Black's position is quite solid. It is even hard to imagine that the struggle in this game will last only two more moves!

15...♘b4 16 ♕e2 (a new threat is on the agenda: 17 ♘xd7 ♕xd7 18 ♘xe6!) **16...♖c8?** Rather than place the rook on c8, it would be better for Black in general not to move at all! But if we want to be serious, then the threat to the f7 and e6 squares can be repulsed by both 16...♘bd5 and, if the worst comes to the worst, also by 16...♗e8.

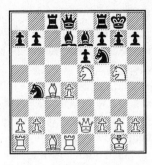

17 ♘exf7! And it becomes clear that in the variation 17...♖xf7 18 ♗xe6 ♗xe6 19 ♕xe6 ♕f8 20 ♘xf7 ♕xf7 the unfortunate rook comes under fire: 21 ♕xc8+. The mistake so demoralised Black that he... immediately resigned. But meanwhile 20...♖c6! (instead of 20...♕xf7) still allows White to put up stubborn resistance.

No.7

D. SCHNEIDER –

M. KUIOVICH

Dallas 2004

1 e4 c6 2 d4 d5 3 ed cd 4 c4 ♘f6 5 ♘c3 e6 6 ♘f3 ♗b4 7 cd ♘xd5 8 ♕c2 ♘c6 9 ♗d3 ♗a5!? 10 a3 ♘xc3!? 11 bc ♘xd4 12 ♘xd4 ♕xd4 The Gambit variation – one of the most interesting places in the Panov Attack.

13 ♗b5+ ♗d7 Nor does the theoretical discussion end upon the line 13...♔e7 14 0-0. Thus, in the game Blauert – Pascal (Budapest 2004) Black took the pawn, which we wrote was 'poisoned' (page 120): 14...♕xc3?! However what was Black thinking about this time? It turns out... nothing! After 15 ♕e4 ♖d8 16 ♕h4+ ♔f8 17 ♕xh7 it becomes clear that he cannot play 17...♕xa1 in view of 18 ♕h8+ ♔e7 19 ♗g5+ ♕f6 20 ♕xg7! Black waits one move – 17...♕e5, but 18 a4! (threatening the standard inclusion for these positions of the bishop on a3) forces him to reconcile himself to the inevitable: 18...♕xa1 19 ♕h8+ ♔e7 20 ♗g5+ ♕f6 21 ♕xg7! and soon White won.

In the game N.Kosinsteva – J.Houska (Dresden 2004) Black went along the main road: 14...♕e5 15 a4 ♗b6. And rightly so – because the novelty 16 ♖d1!? (we looked at only 16 ♗a3+ – page 120) proved harmless: 16...♗c5 17 g3 ♕f5 18 ♗d3 ♕h5 19 ♗e4 ♖e8 20 c4 ♔f8. Black has scarcely completed her development – but when all the pieces have entered play she will have chances of realising the extra pawn.

14 0-0 ♕d5 15 c4 ♕f5 16 ♗xd7+ ♔xd7 17 ♕b2 It goes without saying that more natural is 17 ♕b3. Nadezhda Kosintseva demonstrated in this variation yet another novelty in a game against Leila Dzhavachishvili at the Olympiad in Calvia (2004). After 17...b6 she played 18 ♗b2!? (for 18 ♖d1+ ♔e7

19 a4 – see page 122). And again the novelty did not produce the desired effect. There followed 18...♔e7 19 ♕g3 ♖hd8 20 ♖ad1 ♗d2 21 a4 ♗f4 22 ♕xg7 ♗xh2+! 23 ♔xh2 ♕h5+ 24 ♔g3 ♖xd1 25 ♖xd1 ♕xd1, and the activity of the remaining white pieces was at best sufficient for a draw.

The retreat of the white queen to b2 looks artificial but there is at least one advantage: it is less studied!

17...b6 18 a4

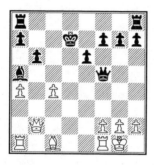

18...f6?! After the present game it is necessary to finally place this continuation in the archives. Black has the right to choose between 18...♖ad8, 18...♖hd8 and 18...♔e7, for which detailed information is on pages 122-123.

19 ♖d1+ ♔c6 20 c5 ♖ad8 21 ♗e3 In the theoretical section we referred to the game Al. Karpov – Ovechkin, in which was played 21 ♕b5+ ♔c7 22 ♗e3 ♔b8 23 ♕c6 ♕h5 24 ♖d6 etc. But apparently White's position is so good that he has more than one way to win.

21...♕e4 Also losing is 21...♖d5 22 ♕b5+ ♔c7 23 ♕a6! (Ravi – Ramesh, Calcutta 2002), now however the position is ripe for a combination:

22 ♕b5+ ♔c7 23 cb+ ab 24 ♖ac1+ ♔b7 25 ♗xb6! ♗xb6 26 a5! ♔a8 27 ab ♔b8 28 ♖xd8+ ♖xd8 29 ♕c5! Black resigned.

The Gambit variation is not completely bad for Black. He has the right to play it, but... only if he has sufficient knowledge. If, however, he does not, then punishment for his lack of application will be quick, and a rout – complete!

No.8
I.SOLOMYNOVICH – Z. ZELIC
Neum 2005

Illustrative games is a section in which we turn to the experience of established grandmasters. But for the present game we have decided to make an exception. Igor Solomynovich, representing Germany, does not have a high rank (he is 'only' a master), but he conducted this encounter in inspired fashion. And, to the point, he overturned our presentation of the opening variation which previously seemed of high calibre for Black.

1 e4 c6 2 d4 d5 3 ed cd 4 c4 ♘f6 5 ♘c3 e6 6 ♘f3 ♗e7 7 cd ♘xd5 8 ♗c4 0-0 9 0-0 ♘c6 10 ♖e1 We recall (see pages 165-166), that accepting the pawn sacrifice – 10 ♗xd5?! ed 11 ♕b3 ♗g4 12 ♕xb7 – effectively means signing a peace agreement. This was shown yet again by the game Bachin – Galkin (Dagomis 2004): 12...♘b4 13 ♗f4 (bearing down on the b8 square, but... not for long) 13...♗xf3 14 gf ♗d6! 15 ♗g3 a6 16 a3 ♖b8 17 ♕a7 ♖a8 18 ♕b7 ♖b8 19 ♕a7 Draw.

10...♘xc3 (more reliable is 10...♗f6 and then ♘ce7) **11 bc b6 12 ♗d3 ♗b7 13 h4! ♗f6** It is dangerous to take on h4 – 13...♗xh4 14 ♘xh4 ♕xh4 15 ♖e3; but perhaps after this game the only narrow path for Black remains the variation 13...♖c8 14 ♘g5 ♗xg5 15 ♗xg5 ♕d5 16 ♕g4 f5 17 ♕g3 ♘a5.

14 ♘g5 g6 15 ♕g4 h5 (15...♘e7 16 h5!) **16 ♕g3 ♘e7** (16...♕d7 17 ♘e4 ♗g7 18 ♗g5 ♘e7 19 ♕d6!) **17 ♗a3 ♕d7** (17...♖c8 18 ♘xe6! fe 19 ♖xe6). It is not by accident that we 'run' so quickly through a game accompanied by variations. Firstly, it was expounded in a detailed way in the theoretical section (pages 170-171). And, secondly, the most interesting part is only just about to begin!

18 ♖ad1! Over the course of many years the basis for this variation was considered the game Banas – Ostenstad (it was given on page 171): 18 ♘e4 ♗xe4 19 ♗xe4 ♖ac8 20 ♖e3 ♖fe8 21 ♕f4 ♗g7 with a comfortable game for Black. However, what is it that changes with the entry into the battle of the queen's rook?

18...♖fe8

19 d5!! A great deal and possibly even everything! White advances his central pawn into a fourfold attack. The variations given below prove that Igor Solomynovich's idea is very beautiful and... absolutely correct:

19...ed 20 ♘xf7! ♔xf7 21 ♖xe7+! ♖xe7 22 ♕xg6+ with an immediate win;

19...♗xd5 20 c4 ♗c6 21 ♗xg6;

19...♕xd5 20 ♗e4 (there is no need for 20 ♗xg6 ♘xg6 21 ♖xd5 ♗xd5) 20...♕xa2 21 ♖a1 ♕c4 22 ♗xb7;

19...♘xd5 20 c4 ♘c3 21 ♗xg6 ♘xd1 22 ♗xf7+ ♔h8 23 ♗xh5 ♖g8 (23...♘c3 24 ♘f7+ ♔h7 25 ♕g6 mate) 24 ♖xd1, developing a mating attack with equal material on the board.

However, if there is somewhere that Black can count on survival, it should be found precisely in the variation 19...♘xd5 20 c4 ♘c3 21 ♗xg6. Only instead of 21...♘xd1 it is necessary to decide on 21...♕xd1!? or even 21...♘e2+!? This line remains unclear. However after the move made by Black **19...e5** Solomonynovich completed the picture with two or three energetic brush strokes:

20 ♘e4! ♗g7 21 ♘d6 ♖f8 22 ♘xb7 ♕xb7 23 d6 ♘c6 24 ♗c4 ♖ad8 25 ♗d5! (rightly rejecting 25 ♕xg6 ♘a5 26 ♗d5 ♕xd5 27 ♕xg7+ ♔xg7 28 ♖xd5 ♘c4) **25...♕a6 26 c4 ♘d4 27 d7! ♖xd7 28 ♗xf8 ♔xf8 29 ♖xd4!** And without waiting for 29...ed 30 ♕b8+, Black resigned. Brilliant work!

But... it is hard nowadays to think up something genuinely new. It turns out that even at the beginning of 2004 in Cappelle la Grande was played a game Timofeev – Eliet, in which Black instead of 18...♖fe8 played 18...♖ac8, and White replied...

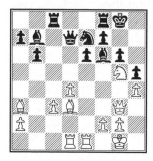

...yes, you guessed it: 19 d5!! The idea of the Russian grandmaster is even cleaner; the black rook remains on f8, and as a consequence the knight cannot take on d5. There followed 19...ed 20 ♕f4 ♔g7 21 ♗b5 ♗c6 22 ♘e4 ♕f5 23 ♕xf5 ♘xf5 24 ♗xf8+ ♖xf8 25 ♘xf6 ♗xb5 26 ♘xh5+!, and Black resigned. A second rout in what it seemed was a reliable variation! It looks like the idea 13...♗f6 will have to placed in the archives...

No.9
A. SHARIYAZDANOV – V. PETYKHOV
Dagomis 2004

1 e4 c6 2 d4 d5 3 ed cd 4 c4 ♘f6 5 ♘c3 e6 6 ♘f3 ♗e7 7 cd ♘xd5 8 ♗d3 0-0 9 0-0 ♘c6 10 ♖e1 ♘cb4?! A second rate move (more details on this – on page 186), but with its own 'spirit'. The combinational storm is now irresistible!

11 ♗b1 ♘f6 12 ♘e5 ♗d7 13 ♗g5 ♖c8 We stop at the position after 13...♗c6 14 ♖e3 g6. In the game Podgaets – Novak (a discussion of this is found on page 186) was played 15 ♖h3, while here in the encounter Szabados – Muller (Zurich 1962) White played otherwise: 15 ♗h6 ♖e8 16 ♖g3 and after 16...♘bd5 an excellent opportunity presented itself to carry out a mating combination. Yes, but how will he take on g6, with the knight or the bishop?

"What essentially is the difference, I have to take twice on g6 anyway" – Eugenio Szabados probably thought and he continued 17 ♘xg6?! hg 18 ♗xg6 (reckoning only on 18...fg 19 ♕d3 mating). There followed the unforeseen 18...♗d6! Still it was good that he found a perpetual check: 19 ♗xf7+ ♔xf7 20 ♖g7+ ♔f8 21 ♘xd5 ♗xd5 22 ♕c2 (the consequences of 'winning' the queen 22 ♖d7+ ♔g8 23 ♖xd8 ♖axd8 24 ♗g5 ♔f7 are completely unclear) 22...♗e4! 23 ♖g3+ ♔f7 24 ♖g7+ ♔f8 25 ♖g3+ etc. While here, in the event of the correct order of moves 17 ♗xg6! hg 18 ♘xg6!, White would have, after 18...♗d6, a worthy reply:

19 ♘e5+ ('discovered check' and at the same time 'covering over'!) 19...♔h7 20 ♘xf7 ♗xg3 (20...♕e7 21 ♖g7 mate) 21 ♕d3+ ♔g8 22 ♕g6 mate.

Why are we discussing in such detail this old and forgotten game? Because in 2004 grandmaster Andrei Shariyzhdanov had to solve the same problem as master Eugenio Szabados had to – in 1962!

14 ♖e3 g6 15 ♖g3 ♗c6 16 ♗h6 ♖e8 17 a3 ♘bd5

18 ♗xg6! And Shariyzhdanov coped excellently with the task. It is superfluous to recall that in the event of 18 ♘xg6?! hg 19 ♗xg6 White again has to look for a draw – 19...♗d6! It is very surprising that this mistake... is also the same as an old example from practice! 20 ♗xf7+ ♔xf7 21 ♖g7+ ♔f8 22 ♘xd5 ♗xd5 23 ♕d3 ♗e4 24 ♖g3+ ♔f7 25 ♖g7+, draw (Filip – Pogats, Budapest 1961).

18...hg 19 ♘xg6 fg (repetition – is the mother of teaching and that is why once again we point out the mate after 19...♗d6: 20 ♘e5+ ♔h7 21 ♘xf7 ♗xg3 – 21...♕e7 22 ♖g7 mate – 22 ♕d3+ ♔g8 23 ♕g6 mate) **20 ♕d3!** It was still not too late to make a mistake: 20 ♖xg6+? ♔h7 21 ♕d3 ♘xc3 22 ♖g7+ ♔h8! (22...♔xh6 23 ♕g6 mate) 23 bc ♖g8 24 ♕g6 ♗e4 25 ♕f7 ♕f8. However after the correct 20 ♕d3! Black would be left with nothing else than immediate surrender.

No.10

V. POTKIN – A. GALKIN

Dagomis 2004

1 e4 c6 2 d4 d5 3 ed cd 4 c4 ♘f6 5 ♘c3 e6 6 ♘f3 ♗e7 7 cd ♘xd5 8 ♗d3 ♘c6 9 0-0 0-0 10 ♖e1 ♘f6 11 a3 b6 12 ♗g5 Another path continues to enjoy popularity – 12 ♗c2 ♗b7 (more concrete is 12...♗a6; in order to avoid this move White again chooses 12 ♗g5 – with the aim of 'waiting' until the bishop develops to b7) 13 ♕d3. In the game Sedina – I.Vasilevich from the European women's championship (Kishinev 2005) Black fell into a well-known trap: 13...♖c8? 14 d5! ed 15 ♗g5 g6 (no better is 15...♘e4 16 ♘xe4 de 17 ♕xe4 g6 18 ♗h6 ♖e8 19 ♖ad1 ♕c7 20 ♗b3) 16 ♖xe7! ♘xe7 (16...♕xe7 17 ♘xd5 ♘xd5 18 ♗xe7 ♘cxe7 19 ♗b3) 17 ♗xf6 and in the end she lost – on page 194 we forewarned that there could be nothing else.

But in the game Srivachiranot – Tan Lian An (Singapore 2004) the opponents decided to test a long theoretical variation 13...g6 14 ♗h6 ♖e8 15 ♖ad1 ♖c8 16 ♗b3 ♘a5 17 ♗a2 ♘d5 18 ♘e4 ♘f6 19 ♘eg5 ♗d5.

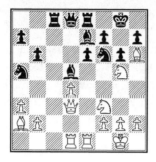
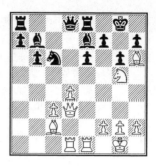

On page 199 we presented a game that was important for the assessment of the whole system with 10...♘f6 and 12...♗b7, Lechtivara – Gheorghiu, in which White sacrificed a piece: 20 ♘xf7!? ♚xf7 21 ♘e5+ ♚g8 22 ♘xg6, but after 22...♗d6! was not able to obtain compensation sufficient even for a draw.

In Singapore we were able to find an improvement: 20 ♗xd5!? ♘xd5, and only now 21 ♘xf7!? ♚xf7 22 ♘e5+ ♚g8 23 ♘xg6. The idea is clear: on 23...♗d6 follows 24 ♖e4! (there is no bishop on d5, guarding the e4 square).

But White had not reckoned on something. And namely: 23...♗g5! (as occurred in the game), and once again the attack was not worth the sacrificed piece: 24 ♘e7+ ♕xe7 25 ♕g3 ♚h8 26 ♗xg5 ♕g7 27 ♕h4 ♖g8 28 ♖e5 ♖cf8 etc.

12...♗b7 13 ♗c2 ♘d5 14 ♕d3 g6 15 ♗h6 ♖e8 16 ♖ad1 (the alternative is 16 ♗a4) **16...♘xc3!? 17 bc ♗xa3 18 ♘g5 ♗e7** This move has a decent reputation but we continue to insist on the fearless 18...♘a5!? (see page 191).

19 ♘xf7!? A novelty – or perhaps it is more correct to say that a bomb has exploded close to the black king! After this game the theory of the variation (inclined towards variations of the type 19 ♕g3 ♕d6 20 ♕h3 ♗xg5 21 ♗xg5 f5!) has to be completely rewritten.

19...♚xf7 20 ♖xe6! Threatening 21 ♖xg6! mating, while taking the rook is impossible – once again because of mate: 20...♚xe6 21 ♕h3+ ♚f6 22 ♗b3! ♗f8 23 ♕h4+ ♚f5 24 ♕f4 mate or 20...♘b4 21 cb ♚xe6 22 ♕h3+ ♚f6 23 ♗b3 ♗d5 24 ♖e1! ♗xb3 25 ♕f3 mate.

20...♗f6 21 ♖xe8 ♚xe8 22 ♕c4 ♕d6 23 ♗a4 The first of a series of unforced moves. It is possible, as grandmaster Potkin showed, that in the variation 23 ♖e1+ ♚d7 (23...♚d8 24 ♖e6) 24 ♗a4 ♖e8 25 ♖xe8 ♚xe8 26 d5 White's advantage is not big enough. But he wants more...

23...♚d8 24 ♖e1 ♘e7 25 ♖e6 ♕d5 But here it is is difficult to understand the rejection of 25...♕a3. The threat is 26...♗d5, while on 26 ♖xf6 ♕a1+ 27 ♕f1 ♕xa4 Black is close to a drawing haven.

26 ♕xd5+ ♘xd5 27 ♖d6+ White is still playing for a win... Objectively it is worthwhile for him to switch over to a struggle for a draw (in the sample variation 27 c4 ♗e7 – 27...♘c3? 28 ♖e8+ ♔c7 29 ♗f4+ – 28 cd ♗xd5). However the game also finished this way – in a draw after **27...♔c7 28 ♖d7+ ♔c8 29 c4 ♘c3 30 ♖f7 ♘xa4 31 ♖xf6 ♗e4 32 ♖f7 a5 33 ♗f4 ♘c3 34 ♗e5 b5 35 f3 ♗f5 36 ♖f8+ ♔b7 37 ♖f7+** But it must be said that White achieved this result with quite a large slice of luck.

However that may be, the idea 19 ♘xf7!? ♔xf7 20 ♖xe6! is very strong and probably wins. The wait to confirm this hypothesis, we think, will not be very long...

No.11
B. MACIEJA – L. DOMINGUEZ
Bermuda 2005

1 e4 c6 2 c4 d5 3 cd cd 4 ed In the theoretical section (pages 250-251) we paid attention to the capture on d5 with the queen. Now however we try to systematise grandmaster experience from 2004-2005 in the most popular development – **4...♘f6**
5 ♕a4+!? Black has a simpler task in the event of 5 ♗b5+. Here is an example from a recent Olympiad: 5...♘bd7 6 ♘c3 a6 7 ♗e2 b5 8 d4 b4 9 ♘a4 ♘xd5 10 ♗f3 ♗b7 11 ♘e2 e6 12 0-0 ♗d6 13 ♘g3 ♕h4 14 ♖e1 0-0, and already White can do little more than think about how not to lose (Delgado – Dreev, Calvia 2004).

5...♘bd7 6 ♘c3 g6 7 ♘f3 ♗g7 8 ♗c4 0-0 9 d3 a6 Georgian grandmasters treat this position in their own way. They do not advance the a and b-pawns, preferring free piece development: 9...♘b6 10 ♕b3 ♗g4. Here are just two examples:

11 ♘e5 ♕c7 12 ♘xg4 ♘xg4 13 h3 ♕e5+ 14 ♘e2 ♘f6 15 ♗f4 ♕f5 16 g4 ♕d7 17 ♘c3 h5 18 f3 ♖ad8 19 ♗b5 ♕c8 (Jones – Izoria, Warsaw 2005) or

11 ♘g5!? (a modern idea; we shall return to it again) 11...♖c8 12 ♗e3 h6 13 ♘ge4 ♘xe4 14 ♘xe4 ♘xc4 15 dc ♕a5+ 16 ♘d2 e6 17 de ♗xe6 18 0-0 ♖fd8 19 ♖fd1 b6 (Gagunashvili – Kacheishvili, Dubai 2005), in both cases with full rights for Black.

10 ♕a3 b6 Also here, possible is 10...♘b6. After 11 ♕b3 the difference from the variation just looked at lies in the fact that the black pawn is on a6 and not on a7.

The game Naer – Erenburg (Ashdod 2004) developed in an extraordinarily interesting way: 11...♗f5 12 0-0 ♕c7 13 ♗g5 ♘xc4 14 dc ♗d3 (Black obviously thought that he had outcalculated his opponent, but far from it...) 15 d6! It is not good to take the pawn: 15...ed 16 ♗xf6 ♗xf1 (16...♗xf6 17 ♘d5) 17 ♘d5 ♕xc4 18 ♖xf1 ♕xb3 19 ab ♗xf6 20 ♘xf6+ etc. There is also no relief in 15...♕xc4 16 de ♖fe8 17 ♖fe1 ♕xb3 18 ab ♗f5 (with the aim of closing the e-file to the e6 square), and White had a pleasant choice between 19 ♗xf6 ♗xf6 20 ♘d5 ♗xb2 21 ♖a2 ♗e6 22 ♘c7 and the surprising 19 ♘b5!? ab 20 ♖xa8 ♖xa8 21 ♗xf6 ♖e8 22 ♗xg7 ♔xg7 23 ♘d4.

However in the game followed 15...♕xd6 16 ♖fd1! ♖ac8 17 ♗xf6 ♗xf6 18 ♘e4 ♗xe4 19 ♖xd6 ed 20 ♖d1. To realise such an extra queen is very difficult but it goes without saying that chances of victory lie only with White.

11 0-0 ♗b7 12 ♖e1 ♖e8 The most 'hot-headed' in today's tabiya of the Steiner System.

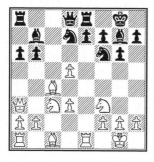

13 ♘g5!? It is precisely this idea that revives interest in the position. Taking in his sights the f7 square, White intends to go for favourable complications with the advance of the d-pawn. Formerly the lifeless 13 ♗g5 was played, and Black equalised without difficulty: 13...b5 14 ♗b3 ♘b6 etc.

13...b5 The most popular, but hardly the strongest continuation. Perhaps theoretical investigations will sweep to the side of one of the two following continuations:

13...h6 14 ♘ge4 ♘e5 15 ♗f4 ♘h5 16 ♗xe5 ♗xe5 17 ♖ad1 ♕c7 18 g3 ♖ad8 19 ♗b3 ♘f6 20 d4 ♗d6 21 ♘xd6 ♕xd6 22 ♕xd6 ♖xd6 23 ♖e5 ♘g4 24 ♖e4 ♘f6 25 ♖e5

♘g4 with a draw by repetition of moves (Radjabov – Azmaiparashvili, Dos Hermanas 2005);

13...♖c8 14 d6 e6 15 ♗f4 b5 16 ♗b3 ♘c5 17 ♖ad1 ♘h5 18 ♗e3 ♘xb3 19 ab f5 20 ♘h3 ♕d7 21 f3 ♗f8 22 ♗c5 ♖cd8 23 d4 ♗xd6 and Black is in charge of the whole game (Kadziolka – Erenburg, Warsaw 2005).

14 ♗b3 ♘b6 Black played enterprisingly in the game Naer – Mittelman (Ashdod 2004): 14...h6 15 ♘ge4 ♘xe4 16 de ♘e5 17 ♖d1 ♕c7 18 d6 ed 19 ♕xd6 ♕xd6 20 ♖xd6 ♖ac8 21 ♗b6 ♗xe4! 22 ♘xe4 ♘c4. Accepting the piece sacrifice – 23 ♗xc4 ♖xc4 24 f3 – is pointless in view of 24...♖cxe4! 25 fe ♗d4+ 26 ♔f1 ♗xb6. In reply White... himself sacrifices: 23 ♗xh6! ♘xb6 24 ♘d6 ♗xh6 25 ♗xf7+ ♔f8 26 ♗xe8, possibly achieving some advantage.

15 d6 e6 16 ♘ge4 ♘xe4 Two rounds later the Cuban grandmaster Lenier Dominguez tried to improve on his own play: 16...♘bd7 17 ♘xf6+ ♘xf6 18 ♕b4 ♗c6 19 ♗g5 h6 20 ♗h4 g5 21 ♗g3 ♕b6 22 ♘e4 ♘h5 23 ♖ac1 ♘xg3 24 ♘xg3 ♖ed8. But after 25 h4 ♗e8 26 hg hg 27 ♕g4! he again suffered defeat (Harikrishna – Dominguez, Bermuda 2005).

17 ♘xe4 ♗xe4 18 de ♗e5 19 ♖d1! The forcing stage of the game is at an end. White has two bishops and a far advanced passed pawn in the centre; Black can reckon only on a blockade. Obviously White's chances are superior.

19...♕h4 20 g3 (it goes without saying that the variation 20 f4 ♗xf4 21 g3 ♗xg3 22 hg ♕xg3+ cannot suit White) **20...♕xe4 21 ♗e3 ♘d7 22 ♖d2 ♖ed8 23 ♖ad1 ♘f6** An incomprehensible decision. Black voluntarily removes the blockade from the d7 square, allowing the enemy queen to e7 – in whose name? 23...♖dc8 looks simpler and more natural.

24 d7! ♕b7 A loss of tempo, but also in the event of 24...♕c6 25 ♕e7 White's attack can hardly be stopped. You see, there is the deadly threat of 26 ♖d6! ♗xd6 27 ♕xf6 ♗f8 28 ♗d4 or 27...♗c5 28 ♖c1.

25 ♕e7 ♕c6 26 ♗g5 As before, 26 ♖d6! looks strong (and if 26...♕f3, then he has the choice of 27 ♖xa6! or 27 ♗xe6!). But White finds another, no less convincing way to victory.

26...♕f3 Allowing a simple tail-piece. However in any event there was no salvation, for example, 26...♔g7 27 ♖e2 (but not 27 f4 ♕b6+ 28 ♔g2 ♘g8) 27...♘e4 (27...♘g8 28 ♕xd8!) 28 ♖xe4! ♕xe4 29 ♗xe6 ♕f3 30 ♖d3!

27 ♗xe6! ♔h8 (losing are both 27...fe 28 ♕xe6+ ♔g7 29 ♕xe5, and

27...♘e4 28 ♗d5 ♘xg5 29 ♕xg5 ♗f6 30 ♗xf3 ♗xg5 31 ♗xa8 ♗xd2 32 ♖xd2) **28 ♖d3** Black resigned.

No.12
ZHANG ZHONG –
Al. KHARITONOV
Moscow 2004

1 e4 c6 2 c4 d5 3 cd cd 4 ed ♘f6 5 ♘c3 ♘xd5 Simplest. Although also quite possible is 5...g6 6 ♗c4 ♗g7 7 ♘ge2 0-0, putting off the capture of the d5 pawn 'until later'. After 8 0-0 the following games are interesting:

8...b6 9 d3 ♗b7 10 ♕b3 ♘a6 11 ♗g5 h6 12 ♗xf6 ♗xf6 13 ♘e4 ♗g7 14 ♖fe1 ♔h7 15 ♖ad1 ♘c7 16 ♘f4 ♗e5 17 ♘h3 ♗d4 18 ♘d2 ♘xd5 (Martos – Burmakin, Linares 2005) and

8...♘bd7 9 ♘f4 g5 10 ♘fe2 ♘b6 11 d3 h6 12 ♕b3 ♗f5 13 ♗e3 ♗g6 14 a4 ♘g4 15 h3 ♘e5 16 ♖fd1 ♖c8 (Zhang Zhong – Volkov, Internet 2004). In both cases Black quite quickly grabbed the initiative.

6 ♘f3 ♘c6 7 ♗b5 e6 8 0-0 ♗e7 9 d4 0-0 10 ♖e1 This rook is also placed on d1 – without particular effect. For example, 10 ♕e2 ♗d7 11 ♖d1 ♖c8 12 ♗d2 ♖e8 13 ♗d3 ♘cb4 14 ♗b1 ♘f6 15 ♘e5 ♗c6 16 a3 ♘bd5 (Damljanovic – Dreev, Alboks 2005).

The position after 10 ♖e1 is quite popular – but it is hard to understand the reason for this popularity. In the final account it all comes down to the isolated pawn type of position (which we looked at in detail in the theoretical section of the Panov

Attack), but with one reservation: White, having spent time on moves with the light-squared bishop (♗f1-b5-d3), cannot lay claim to an advantage!

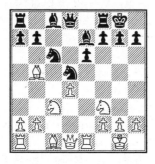

10...♗d7 Also played here is 10...♕d6 11 a3 ♖d8 – the character of the struggle in each case remaining constant. Black successfully directs his play against the isolated pawn. For example: 12 ♗d3 ♘f6 13 ♗e3 b6 14 ♕e2 ♗b7 15 ♖ad1 h6 16 ♗b1 ♗f8 (Miezis – Dreev, Reykjavik 2004).

The only defect of 10...♗d7 in comparison with 10...♕d6 is the fact that now White can if he wants simplify the game: 11 ♘xd5 ed. A draw is practically inevitable – but the Chinese grandmaster, as will be seen from the future play, was not in the least bit in the mood for a draw...

11 ♗d3 ♘f6 12 a3 ♖c8 13 ♗c2 In the old encounter Gligoric – Pomar (Nice 1974) White won quickly and beautifully: 13 ♗b1 ♖e8 14 ♕d3 g6 15 ♗a2 a6 16 ♗h6 ♕a5 17 d5! ed 18 ♘xd5 ♗f5 19 ♖xe7! ♖xe7 (the queen is untouchable: 19...♗xd3 20 ♘xf6+ ♔h8 21 ♗g7+! ♔xg7 22 ♖xf7+ ♔h6 23 ♖xh7 mate) 20 ♘xf6+ etc. But the Moscow junior

Aleksander Kharitonov, in order not to waste time for nothing, thought of an economical and very functional way of arranging his pieces. The queen goes to a5, the king's rook – to d8, at the same time allowing the bishop to e8. And the pressure on the d4 pawn becomes very perceptible.

13...♕a5!? 14 ♗g5 ♖fd8 15 ♕d3 g6 16 h4 ♗e8! 17 ♖ad1 ♕b6 18 ♗b1 ♖d7 (frightened of ending up with his queen on a1 – 18...♕xb2 19 ♘a4 ♕a1) **19 ♕e2**

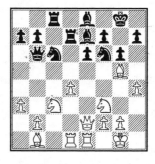

19...♘xd4!? Certainly Black can build up the pressure – 19...♖cd8 or 19...♕d8; but commendably Kharitonov wants to bring clarity to the position – albeit at the cost of the queen!

20 ♘xd4 ♖xd4 21 ♗e3 ♖xd1!? The alternative is 21...♗c5 22 ♗xd4 ♗xd4, again with full compensation for the sacrificed material.

22 ♗xb6 ♖xe1+ 23 ♕xe1 ab How to assess the present position? In return for the queen Black has a rook, bishop and pawn – which just about represents material equality. Plus the two bishops, in an open position, which are waiting for a cause to show themselves.

Possibly White should have shown more caution and started peace negotiations But Zhang Zhong continues to look for a non-existent win:

24 &a2 &d8 25 b4 &c6 26 &b3 b5 27 &e2 &d4 28 &xb5 &e4 29 &f1 &xh4 30 &c4 &e4 31 &e2 &f6! Discovering a vulnerable link in the pawn cover of the enemy king – the f2 pawn. With the same objective, also worth considering is 31...&d8.

32 &e3 &g5 33 &b6 &g3! (by now Black will not agree to a draw) **34 fg &xc4 35 &d6 &c2 36 &c7** A tragic loss of time. Despite the apparent danger he should play 36 &xb7 &xg2+ 37 &f1 &c2 38 &c5, and Black does not succeed in creating mating threats. Now, however, in a single moment White's position caves in:

36...&e3+ 37 &h2 &xg2+ 38 &h3 &f2 39 &d8+ Already here 39 &xb7 is too late: 39...&g2+ 40 &g4 (40 &h2 &xb7+) 40...&f1! 41 &c8+ &g7 42 &c3+ f6 43 &xe3 h5+ 44 &h4 &h1 mate.

39...&g7 40 &e8+ &xe8 41 &xe8

h5 **42 &b5 g5 43 g4 hg+ 44 &g3 f5**

A beautiful position! White can hope only for perpetual check, but the opportunity never arises. Gaining a respite after a series of checks, Black pushes on his pawns. Then this procedure is repeated again and again – until White acknowledges defeat...

45 &d7+ &f6 46 &d8+ &e5 47 &c7+ &d4 48 &b6+ &d3 49 &xe6 &f3+ 50 &g2 f4 (pawn push!) **51 &b3+ &d4 52 &b2+ &d5 53 &b3+ &d6 54 &d3+ &c7 55 &c4+ &b8 56 &b5 &f2+ 57 &h1 g3** (second push!) **58 &e5+ &c8 59 &e8+ &c7 60 &e7+ &b6 61 &d8+ &b5 62 &d5+ &a4 63 &d1+ &xa3 64 &a1+ &a2** White resigned.

Index to Games

(numbers refer to pages)

1	M.Adams – R.Ponomarev	257
2	A.Grischuk – E.Bareev	258
3	V.Ivanchuk – P.Harikrishna	259
4	L.Aronian – M.Carlsen	260
5	R.Ruck – A.Horvath	262
6	M.Adams – G.Kallai	263
7	D.Schneider – M.Kuiovich	265
8	I.Solomynovich – Z.Zelic	266
9	A. Sharyazdanov – V. Petykhov	268
10	V.Potkin – A.Galkin	269
11	B.Macieja – L.Dominguez	271
12	Zhang Zhong – Al. Kharitonov	273